THIRD EDITION

The Practice of Family Therapy

KEY ELEMENTS ACROSS MODELS

SUZANNE MIDORI HANNA
Loma Linda University

JOSEPH H. BRO
University of Louisville

THOMSON

BROOKS/COLE

Australia Canada Mexico Singapore Spain
United Kingdom United States

KH

THOMSON

BROOKS/COLE

Executive Editor: Lisa Gebo
Acquisitions Editor: Julie Martinez
Assistant Editor: Shelley Gesicki
Editorial Assistant: Amy Lam
Technology Project Manager: Barry Connolly
Marketing Manager: Caroline Concilla
Marketing Assistant: Mary Ho
Advertising Project Manager: Tami Strang

Project Manager,
Editorial Production: Katy German
Print/Media Buyer: Jessica Reed
Permissions Editor: Joohee Lee
Production Service: Carlisle Publishers Services
Copy Editor: Judy Duguid
Cover Designer: Andy Norris
Printer: Webcom

For more information about
our products, contact us at:
**Thomson Learning Academic
Resource Center
1-800-423-0563**

For permission to use material from this text, contact us by: **Phone:** 1-800-730-2214
Fax: 1-800-730-2215
Web: http://www.thomsonrights.com

Library of Congress Control Number:
2003103446
ISBN 0-534-52251-3

Brooks/Cole—Thomson Learning
10 Davis Drive
Belmont, CA 94002
USA

Asia
Thomson Learning
5 Shenton Way #01-01
UIC Building
Singapore 068808

Australia/New Zealand
Thomson Learning
102 Dodds Street
Southbank, Victoria 3006
Australia

Canada
Nelson
1120 Birchmount Road
Toronto, Ontario M1K 5G4
Canada

Europe/Middle East/Africa
Thomson Learning
High Holborn House
50/51 Bedford Row
London WC1R 4LR
United Kingdom

Latin America
Thomson Learning
Seneca, 53
Colonia Polanco
11560 Mexico D.F.
Mexico

Spain/Portugal
Paraninfo
Calle/Magallanes, 25
28015 Madrid, Spain

12/30/04

In memory of Frank Bockus, 1932–2002, for his intelligence, inspiration, compassion, wisdom, unconquerable spirit and . . . the twinkle in his eye!

Contents

Chapter 3

Integration of Theory: Common Themes   *58*

Chapter 6

The Initial Interview: A Template for General Tasks in Family Therapy   131

Chapter 7

Relational Assessments: Exploring Client Experience   161

Chapter 8

Beginning and Maintaining Relational Change   196

Part Three

THE FUTURE OF FAMILY THERAPY: EVALUATIONS, RESEARCH, AND COLLABORATION   223

Chapter 9

Evaluations and Research in Family Therapy   227

Chapter 10
Family Therapy Collaborations   250

Appendix A
Ethical Considerations   279

Appendix B
Films of Interest to Students of Family Therapy   291

Appendix C
Global Assessment of Relational Functioning (GARF)   293

Appendix D
Evaluations for Supervision   297

Preface

In the third edition of this book, we are keenly aware that students who are learning about marriage and family therapy are often exposed to many different sources of information simultaneously. They might learn one thing from an academic course and another from their clinical supervisor. They might attend the workshop of a favorite presenter, but have no one available to help them incorporate their learning into a therapy session. For beginning family therapists, the challenge is how to integrate a broad array of information and develop a framework for practice that works for them and their clients.

This book provides practical guidance that acknowledges the breadth of our field while helping the student of family therapy to integrate common elements of practice from first- and second-generation approaches to family therapy. It can be used as a text in an entry-level course or as a guide for students and supervisors in a practicum. It has also been used by busy clinicians who just want some new ideas for troubleshooting that are easy to implement. If they are trained in one or two models of family therapy, this helps them to fine-tune and integrate other models into their standard practice. We summarize 12 different models of family therapy and suggest a plan for getting started by walking the reader through systemic/relational aspects of clinical process from referral to termination. We make the assumption that beginning students often want suggestions as to what to say or where to start. Each chapter contains many sample questions, dialogues and corresponding commentaries. The end product is a mosaic created from our critical analysis in which we suggest how the strengths from different approaches can be used for different stages in the therapeutic process, for different cases, and for different settings.

NEW MATERIAL IN THE THIRD EDITION

Since our second edition, we have witnessed many exciting developments in the profession and practice of marriage and family therapy. Thus, two new chapters include information on evidence-based models of family therapy and applications of the common elements to cases in school-based work, medical family therapy and interdisciplinary collaboration. As an example of interdisciplinary work, we use family art therapy. We also provide expanded coverage of post-modern models and some new information on the importance of attachment in human development. We have also consolidated sections on joining and strength-based work into an entire chapter on the therapeutic relationship. For instructors and supervisors, we have provided new materials in our appendices, including an Ethics At-Risk test for students to take as a self-assessment, the Global Assessment of Relational Functioning (GARF) for use in treatment planning, a list of films for teaching and learning about family process and examples of therapist evaluation scales that can be used to assess clinical skills in students and trainees.

OUR CLINICAL APPROACH

Our general approach to the practice of family therapy conceptualizes problems as embedded in multisystemic interpersonal process over time. Thus, we emphasize the importance of inter- and intra-personal dynamics woven into presenting problems and we illustrate how to track historical and day-to-day sequences of interaction related to problem formation. Our theory of change is strength-based and client centered, drawing from those approaches that maximize the therapeutic alliance and that realistically address the nature and severity of a problem. We also think a trend is developing within the field that places equal emphasis upon modern and post-modern approaches. Thus, you will find solution-focused suggestions for developing a genogram and narrative approaches to taking a family's history. Behavior management plans for children are used alongside family art therapy interventions. Models of family therapy aside, students in various settings are usually required to provide a treatment plan and manage the practical aspects of each case. For these aspects, we make suggestions and compare different viewpoints for organizing clinical work. As in the second edition, we consider the pragmatic elements of each session to be negotiating structure, exploring client experience, addressing relationships and developing a shared direction.

ORGANIZATION OF THE BOOK

We have divided the book into three sections that move gradually through the past, present and future of family therapy practice. Each section has an introduction that gives the reader an idea of the main direction for that section. Within each section, the chapters cover material sequentially, starting with a given point in time and moving forward. We use the metaphors of travel, driving a car and even eating cake to focus upon multidimensional processes that make up the creativity and spirit of adventure in our field. Each chapter has tables to summarize key points and figures to illustrate our interventions. A summary at the end of each chapter pulls together the main themes and desired outcomes. Appendices are arranged in the order they are mentioned in the book.

Part One: From Theory to Practice

This section includes four chapters that cover 12 models of family therapy practice, locating them within the evolution of our field. In Chapter 1, we take the reader on a journey into the past by walking through samples of family therapy history in the making. There are "snapshots" of six first-generation approaches as they might have applied to a single case. The models covered are structural, M.R.I., strategic, intergenerational, experiential and behavioral. For each one, we describe theory, goals, role of the therapist, the focus of assessment and interventions. By the end of this chapter, readers have been guided through the history of family therapy up to 1970 with a table summarizing these early approaches and a chart that shows some overlapping similarities.

In Chapter 2, we summarize the impact of social and philosophical trends upon first and second generation models. These trends are listed in chronological order as they emerged in the culture of family therapists and they include a focus upon feminism, transitions (formerly referred to as life cycle), culture, race and attachment theory. We then review four post-modern approaches: Milan, solution focused, collaborative language systems and narrative. Sample questions are provided for each of these. A summary of the trend in evidence-based approaches introduces beginners to the strengths of research. We make two approaches more accessible to clinicians, cognitive-behavioral family therapy and multisystemic therapy for adolescents. By providing sample questions and guidelines from these models, we give clinicians a view of research as art (e.g., how they are applied in therapy), not just science.

Chapter 3 examines common themes of family process most pertinent to a given situation. In some cases these themes come from models of family therapy in Chapter 1 and in other cases, they come from the trends reviewed in Chapter 2. We suggest that these common theoretical themes that can be addressed in family therapy through the liberal use of questions that explore gender, race, culture, intergenerational relationships, family structure, transitions and individual experience. Each section provides a list of questions that the family therapist can use to maintain a sense of direction while conducting an assessment. Suggestions are made regarding how each area might be most useful. Proceeding from macro factors such as gender and race to micro factors such as individual phenomenology, the chapter also helps the student of family therapy to see the value of exploring content on a multidimensional continuum. New to this chapter is a section on attachment, with some questions clinicians can ask to explore a person's development in this area.

Chapter 4 emphasizes the therapeutic relationship as a basic building block in a process that is multilayered and requires personal growth in the developing therapist. This chapter combines revised material from our second edition on therapist attitudes and adds information gleaned from research on engagement in the therapeutic process and common factors related to psychotherapy outcomes.

Part Two: Organizing Treatment

This section contains four chapters that cover therapeutic process from referral through change. We address each stage by summarizing aspects of various models that address the issues for that stage, making suggestions to the beginning practitioner. As examples, compared to other approaches, the Milan team places more emphasis upon the referral process; in the first interview, solution focused therapists assess whether the client is a customer or a visitor. These ideas each have special utility during different stages of the process. We provide guidelines for therapists that give them a place to start without eliminating other possibilities.

Chapter 5 covers referral and intake, making suggestions for a multisystemic awareness to help beginners prepare to see a client for the first time. We make the point that these considerations may vary according to setting, and logistics may require that these initial considerations become part of the first interview. This chapter also includes our answers to questions that clinicians often ask as they anticipate the challenge of real life situations such as suspected substance abuse, suicide risks, violence, and family secrets.

Chapter 6 is an in-depth examination of the first interview, walking the reader through a step-by-step process using our four tasks of family therapy process. This chapter is a comprehensive view of many important elements that can form a troubleshooting checklist for the first stage of therapy. We note that these issues reach far beyond the first interview and that often, the checklist might be covered across the first few sessions as the therapeutic relationship develops. For example, treatment planning may begin in the first session, but usually goes through revisions as the process unfolds. This chapter covers initial interviews in practical ways that direct the student to provide leadership in the therapy process. We emphasize exploration, negotiation, and collaboration as important aspects. Defining the problem in interactional terms underscores the relational aspects of this work. The agreement between therapist and client is given particular attention as the foundation for further cooperation. This information constitutes a way of organizing the beginning stage of treatment; administrative and relational processes that promote clarity in the early stages of the therapeutic process are itemized. The major points in Chapters 5 and 6 are summarized in a series of boxes, which serve as a guide to help entry-level clinicians stay on task.

Chapter 7 is devoted to an in-depth assessment process for exploring client experience that highlights common family therapy concepts and practices. We explore levels of communication, different types of genograms and how time lines can incorporate first- and second-generation models of family therapy. This chapter helps students with pragmatic skills that gather multidimensional information. While some might associate genograms and circular questions with a specific family approach, this chapter clarifies how these techniques can be used to accommodate multiple views of the problem. In the same manner, tracking interactional sequences is described in a way that generalizes across models, and tracking longitudinal sequences introduces a way of integrating historical information into narratives that are both systemic and interactional. We have added more figures and case material to illustrate how information is organized graphically when diagramming during a session. This chapter also contains new material on how assessment information can be conceptualized for the purpose of treatment planning.

In Chapter 8 we acquaint readers to some common interventions in family therapy that will give them a toolbox for beginning and maintaining the change process. There is a combination of in-session and out-of-session interventions that represent the broad spectrum of our field. This chapter breaks down complex skills into behaviors that can be easily learned. The chapter can also be used as a supervisory resource by matching the therapist's therapeutic intent with several skills designed to accomplish that intent (e.g., changes in beliefs, behaviors, or both). Some skills relate to facilitating cognitive change and others to facilitating behavioral change. Taken together, these sections provide a foundation for integrating the most common interventions in the field. For each intervention, we provide step-by-step instructions and guidelines for how to implement these interventions. The chapter summary underscores the therapeutic alliance as a crucial process that underlies all interventions.

Part Three: The Future of Family Therapy

We use this section to address the future in three ways. First, to provide an understanding of how termination in clinical work is a process of preparing a family for the future. Second, to teach how evaluations and research are becoming an indispensable part of the present and future of family therapy. Third, to illustrate new cutting-edge applications of family therapy that are taking off in different places as another step of innovation in our field. We also challenge family therapists to see into the future and to be flexible in adapting to changes in thinking that are being driven by many different sectors of the societies in which we live.

Chapter 9 is aimed at helping family therapists understand how evaluation can be an integral part of treatment. We provide material in terms of process and outcomes. A section on evaluations for termination or follow-up offers practical guidelines by which the clinician can help clients continue the process of change into the future and mobilize their resources. In the final section, we discuss the possibility of integrating clinical practice with clinical research by introducing the concept of research as systematic inquiry. Evaluation provides a context for learning from client feedback, which is essential if the beginning clinician is to advance to intermediate-level practice.

Chapter 10 covers new material on types of collaborations that are becoming a growing part of our field. Sections on school-based work and medical family therapy build upon basic principles of collaboration that are illustrated through case material. We provide sample outlines to use in school consultations. The traditional concept of mind-body is expanded to include mind-body-spirit and relationships in medical work. A project that combines family therapy and art therapy illustrates how professionals with different traditions can work together toward common goals. We think this chapter is unique in its emphasis upon developmentally appropriate practice with children, a concept that we have borrowed from our colleagues in early childhood education and one that is usually foreign to the mainstream family therapist. In addition, we have provided guidelines for beginners on how to foster successful teamwork in their communities and how to develop projects with other professionals.

INSTRUCTORS AND SUPERVISORS

The Instructor's Manual contains a conceptual overview of each chapter, points of interest to guide the learning process, learning objectives for each chapter, discussion and examination questions for personal growth and evaluation, and quizzes to assess recognition and comprehension of information. It is available on the Web and via e-mail from your local sales representative. For instructors and supervisors, if you find that a favorite part of your personal clinical approach is missing from the book, let us know and we'll be happy to share additional materials on our Brooks/Cole website: *http://helpingprofs.wadsworth.com.*

ACKNOWLEDGMENTS

We are truly indebted to our editors and their staff for talented guidance during the production of this edition—Shelley Gesicki for her encouragement and organization of the review process and Janet Kiefer for her skillful management as all the pieces fell into place. We thank the following reviewers for their helpful suggestions: David M. Kleist, Idaho State University; Marlene Kuskie, University of Nebraska at Kearney; M. Janelle Disney, McNeese State University; Gary Paquin, University of Cincinnati; James A. Barnes, Pennsylvania State

University Altoona; Viola Sutherland, College of Saint Elizabeth; Mary Helen Hayden, Florida International University; and Renato L. Nero, Houston Baptist University.

We also thank important others who have been invaluable and generous with their time and talents. Roberta Reid, a graduate assistant at Loma Linda University, made this project possible with her level head and excellent technical skills. Zephon Lister also provided valuable research assistance and insight. Dr. Dale Bertram and his students at Louisville Bible College provided helpful feedback from the reader's point of view. Colleagues at Loma Linda University have been stimulating and supportive problem-solvers who mobilized creativity in many ways.

Finally, we pay tribute to our students, past and present, characterized by "two timid white girls," as their client first called them. They had courage to win her over, skill to help her through troubled times and patience with us as supervisors. Their knack for balancing complexity is a model of resilience for their clients and of professionalism for their peers and instructors. They have our deepest respect and admiration as we pass the baton to another generation of marriage and family therapists.

FROM THEORY TO PRACTICE: FAMILY THERAPY AS A MOVEMENT ACROSS TIME

Welcome! You are about to embark upon an exciting journey—one that will take you to many parts of the world and one that starts in the past, comes into the present and goes forward to glimpse the future of the practice we know as marriage and family therapy. Although our name sounds as though we only work with marriages and families, it is really a name that we use to honor the past and our roots. We work with many types of individuals, couples and families who bring to us a variety of additional problems including chronic mental illness, the effects of trauma, grief and loss issues, child development issues, school problems, job problems, and even health problems. We hope to provide beginning family therapists with a guide to the practice of our profession.

We begin our journey with a review of our roots and some samples of how the practice of family therapy developed from a rich blend of professionals who dared to "think outside the box"and to build bold conceptual bridges across disciplines. These were not all mental health practitioners. Thus, there is an interesting mix of concepts that inspired the practice of family therapy. We think this is the foundation of our uniqueness as a profession. We often use the term, *systemic thinking,* and we often have other professionals reply that they use *systems theory,* too. On this point, we share some common thinking with other professions such as organizational development, social work, and philosophy. However, our professional history and culture has also made us different from others because we took the far-reaching ideas of general systems theory, added mathematical theory, cybernetics, communication theory, strategies from Ericksonian hypnosis, and the laws of biology that govern all natural systems in the world. In Part One, we explain these concepts. Family therapists took theories about relationships and added innovative, successful theories about how to help people grow, change and solve their problems. This combination is what makes our profession an adventuresome undertaking as a helping profession. Although our goal is simple, our design is as complex as the courageous and interesting people who we help. Thus, understanding the theory and the practice of family therapy is challenging. However, in this book, we will help beginners break the process into smaller parts. In Part One, we will take you into the past of family therapy, on a journey through some unique highlights that have influenced our field. To be sure, there is more to it than what we have space to present! However, it helps therapists to understand how our profession came to be so diverse and why creativity is an important value we share. As we move through time, the remainder of Part One reviews some of our current practices and describes the common elements that unite us as a group of professionals. These common elements will help therapists find a place to start. If your journey is similar to ours, we think you will find many rewarding experiences ahead as you learn the practice of family therapy.

FAMILY THERAPY

A Journey Through Diversity and Integration

The history of marital and family therapy has always been one of professional diversity. The early interests of clergy, physicians, and child-welfare advocates led researchers across the United States to study communication and behavior related to schizophrenia and the family. The collaboration among these groups led to an exchange of publications and joint presentations at major national conferences. As these parallel efforts evolved across the United States, the practice of these groups produced a paradigmatic shift in thinking: Rather than view problems within the individual, therapists began to see problems from a relational perspective. As understanding about human development increased, family therapists invited traditional psychotherapists to view individual symptoms within an interpersonal context. This *interpersonal context* ranged from the impact of verbal and nonverbal communication in any relationship to the evolution of emotional process within three generations of a family.

Today, the field of family therapy is characterized by numerous approaches, all claiming this common heritage. However, when we teach marital and family therapy to beginning practitioners, they often become overwhelmed. After learning about each model, they inevitably ask, "So, where do I start?" The intent of this book is to find a common ground from which to begin practicing family therapy. In this chapter, we will help this process by briefly reviewing significant history that has shaped the practice of family therapy. Then, we will examine six pioneering approaches that use these basic concepts. Finally, we will illustrate how these models apply to a sample case. In Chapter 2, we will show

how the history of family therapy practice led to the development of current integrative models for practice. We use the term *integrative* rather than *eclectic* because integrative relates to making connections between parts (Grunebaum, 1988). This suggests that there should be a cohesive framework that connects various practice ideas together. After the introduction to these pioneering and integrative approaches, we will take the beginning family therapist through the steps necessary to find a starting point and begin practice.

A JOURNEY THROUGH TIME: CONCEPTUAL ROOTS

To begin our study of the practice of family therapy, we will provide a review of the concepts embedded in our theoretical roots. Below is a brief historical journey through a few of our pioneering concepts. After showing how these concepts evolved, we will illustrate how they came to be used in the early practice of family therapy. From 1900 to 1970, we see that many traditional mental health professionals began thinking "outside the box," expanding beyond the concepts of Freud to more relational and interpersonal perspectives. Early practitioners in the field represented a wide range of professional training and a wide range of mental health settings. These leading figures brought to the developing profession of family therapy the courage to critique prevailing practices of their day and a willingness to experiment with new methods.

With respect to the early models these leaders proposed, each has elements that are unique to the person as well as to the setting within which they worked. Take a step back in time and imagine the various contexts and populations that stimulated this new thinking about relationships and interactions. At the same time, keep in mind how revolutionary these events were, given the world around them. Psychoanalysis was the primary mode of treatment for mental, emotional, and relational problems, and these mavericks stood apart from the prevailing medical establishment.

1911. Alfred Adler, MD, departs from Freud and the Vienna Psychoanalytic Society to develop a more holistic approach to understanding human nature. He believes that all behavior is an interaction and that the goal of psychotherapy is to encourage more "social interest" in the individual. *Social interest* is the awareness individuals have of their relational world, the desire to belong and to make a contribution to it.

1919. Milton Erickson, a 17-year-old Wisconsin farm boy, is stricken with polio and told he will never walk again. Within a year, from his own power of mental concentration and creativity, he is walking on crutches and is well enough to work at a sit-down job while he attends college. In spite of being tone-deaf, color blind, and dyslexic, he succeeds at the University of Wisconsin and attends a hypnosis demonstration by Clark L. Hull. Impressed with the connection between his own recovery from polio and the process of hypnosis as he learned about it, he begins practicing hypnosis on classmates, friends, and anyone else who will allow him to work with them (Haley, 1967). Erickson becomes a psychiatrist in 1929 and begins a legendary academic and practice career working with psychotic and severely mentally ill patients long before the age of psychiatric medications. This career brings him to the attention of Gregory Bateson, Jay Haley, and hundreds of others who use his philosophy and techniques to start the practice of family therapy. He teaches others how the *power of close observation* could inform the helping relationship and discern opportunities to help people overcome their *learned limitations.* Committed to the power of an individual's personal resources, he often said, "I create a new theory for each person" (Rosen, 1988).

1948. Norbert Wiener coins the term *cybernetics,* referring to the science of communication and human control systems such as physiological nervous systems or complex electrical systems. Engineers use cybernetics to make guided missiles and to explore space. The anthropologists Gregory Bateson and Margaret Mead (once married) begin to apply cybernetic concepts to social systems. Bateson becomes involved in a number of projects studying patterns in human communication, hypnosis, psychotherapy, and psychiatry.

1949. Ludwig von Bertalanffy, a theoretical biologist, gives his first paper about *general systems theory* as a methodology that is valid for all sciences. By 1960, he is writing on general systems theory and behavioral sciences, influencing many of the pioneers of the family therapy movement. He applies biological concepts of *systems as organisms* of interrelated parts, where each part is distinguished by its *boundaries* and all systems have higher and lower levels (*suprasystems* and *subsystems*). From a global sense of responsibility to the cellular exploration of cancer, Bertalanffy explores the characteristics of systems in all realms of life, noting patterns of interaction, information exchange, and degree of openness between neighboring levels of activity (*open vs. closed systems*).

1949. John Bowlby, MD, concludes that too much of psychoanalysis favors the work of Freud. He organizes his interpersonal research efforts at Tavistock Clinic in England. His lifelong work leads to *attachment theory*, which addresses family interactions and the emotional development of children and adults. In a paper, "The Study and Reduction of Group Tension in the Family," he reports his success from including parents of an adolescent boy in the treatment session.

1949. Emily Mudd, PhD, begins original research, "Marriage Counseling as an Aid to Good Mental Health," funded by the U.S. Public Health Service. The title of her pioneering project characterizes a growing interest in the quality of marital relationships and the connection between parental relationships and the health of all family members. This theme provides a strong rationale for much of marital therapy today. She devotes much of her career to marital therapy, sex education, and sex therapy and is the founding director of the Marriage Council of Philadelphia (now renamed the Penn Council for Relationships), a leading influence in the development of marriage counseling as a profession.

1951. John Ruesch and Gregory Bateson publish *The Social Matrix of Psychiatry,* a book on the role of feedback and information in communication theory. Their work suggests that all communication has *report* (content) and *command* (process) levels: The report level is the *verbal* information transmitted; the command level is the *nonverbal* way in which the sender defines the relationship. In time, Bateson becomes a major theoretical influence in family therapy, leading a team of researchers who eventually become the Mental Research Institute (M.R.I.) in Palo Alto, California. Bateson's early collaborations with Don Jackson lead to many significant contributions such as the *double-bind theory of schizophrenia* (Bateson, Jackson, Haley, & Weakland, 1956). Today, a number of contemporary models of family therapy practice continue to relate their process to his applications of cybernetics, communication, and ecology. His seminal work, *Steps to an Ecology of Mind* (1972), is an application of cybernetic theory to understanding mental process. In particular, he introduces the pioneers of family therapy to ideas about interactional process, one of which is known as *feedback loops* that are aimed at stability or change in a system. He explains how therapists can use these feedback loops to call attention to *exceptions* in problem behaviors. Bateson (1979) goes on to suggest that change comes about from "information that makes a difference." He suggests that information about comparisons and changes is information that makes a difference in the system.

1953. Jay Haley, a graduate assistant of Gregory Bateson, attends a hypnosis workshop given by Milton Erickson. This begins a long and important relationship, first characterized by periodic visits in which Haley and another graduate assistant, John Weakland, would audiotape interviews with Erickson about hypnosis. Eventually, Haley begins to teach physicians and practice hypnosis with their referrals. These activities become part of the work at M.R.I., and as Haley sees changes in these clients, he also notices how these changes affect their families (Simon, 1992). Haley goes on to publish many books about Milton Erickson and his work, illustrating the application of his interventions to family therapy.

1954. Murray Bowen, MD, leaves the Menninger Clinic and begins a project for the National Institute of Mental Health (NIMH) with Lyman Wynne in which families and their schizophrenic children live in a research inpatient unit. Considered a central figure in the field, Bowen develops the set of concepts taken from biological systems called *family systems theory* that contributes to decades of therapists exploring their own families of origin. One of these concepts, *differentiation of self,* is the process by which adult children develop a balance of independence (autonomy) and connection with their families of origin and with other important social–emotional systems. This concept comes from Bowen's analysis of *family emotional process,* the balance of emotional reactivity (anxiety) and rationality that each family exhibits during times of change or stability. Through Bowen's work, therapists today often explore beliefs, values, and interactions that influence the emotional growth and maturity of family members.

1957. Ivan Boszormenyi-Nagy (the last syllable is pronounced Nahzsh), MD, begins a family therapy project at East Pennsylvania Psychiatric Institute that includes intensive psychotherapy of hospitalized psychotics. Emphasis is on inclusion of the entire family, communication, and behavior patterns. However, he finds that general systems theory ignores issues related to personal issues of entitlement and injustices (*fairness*) in family life. He evolves a model called *contextual family therapy* that defines a person's context as *relational ethics,* or the dynamic and complex balance of fairness, trust, and loyalty between people. The concept of the *parentified child* is developed in this model, referring to children who have assumed so much responsibility for parental functions that they no longer trust that fairness will prevail. As this model develops, practitioners also recognize that issues of fairness and justice extend beyond the intergenerational family to society. They acknowledge the "societal background of ripped-off, overburdened, abandoned nuclear families" (Boszormenyi-Nagy & Ulrich, 1981, p. 161).

1958. Nathan Ackerman, MD, sometimes referred to as the grandfather of family therapy, publishes *The Psychodynamics of Family Life.* This is the first book describing the diagnosis and treatment of family relationships and bridging the gap between intrapsychic and interpersonal theories. Ackerman is a child psychiatrist, and his interest in the welfare of children takes him into homes and stirs his interest in seeing the entire family. He notices a "live type of history" emerging as families review the history of the problem. As these historical disclosures are related to present emotional experience, he considers this "the 'live past,' not the 'dead past' of family life" (Ackerman, 1981, p. 319). For him, the main tasks of the therapist are *reeducation* of the family, *reorganization* of family communication, and facilitation of growth through an exploration of the *emotional experience* of the family.

1958. Lyman Wynne, MD, also involved in the NIMH initiative to study families and schizophrenia, develops a theory of pseudomutuality related to families of persons with schizophrenia. *Pseudomutuality* refers to a family's tendency to avoid open conflict or negative emotion, instead preferring to maintain a pleasant appearance in which individual differences, though present, are not acknowledged. Wynne goes on to refine his work, helping the profession to develop conceptual models that integrate family development, health and illness (Wynne, 1984; Shields & Wynne, 1997).

1959. Don Jackson, MD, a psychiatrist, organizes the M.R.I. and applies the physiological concept of homeostasis to the family. As used in family therapy, *homeostasis* is the family's tendency toward stability through maintaining consistent patterns of thought, emotion, and interaction over time. Although the concept was originally thought of as a social force within the family that re-sisted change, later applications suggest that any family or social system has two balancing dimensions, one of maintaining *stability* during the threat of change and one of flexibility (*adaptability*) in the wake of change, whether it is normal, developmental, or a time of crisis. The M.R.I. incorporates the work of the Bateson team and the work of Erickson, Haley, Weakland, and others into cre-ative theory and practice projects that continue to have a compelling influence on the practice of family therapy and psychotherapy. Another important con-cept that was addressed at M.R.I. was that of *circular causality*, which refers to the way in which any behavior is understood by seeing it as part of a cycle of in-teraction, rather than as an isolated entity.

1960. Salvador Minuchin, MD, a psychiatrist, begins a project at the Wiltwyck School in New York to study the inner-city families of delinquent boys. He and colleagues develop a structural approach to family therapy that relates patterns of delinquency to the degree of disorganization in the family (Minuchin, Montalvo, Guerney, Rosman, & Schumer, 1967). Minuchin takes concepts from general systems theory and applies them to family organization. *Hierarchy* is the pattern of leadership and power manifest in the family. *Bound-aries* are imaginary lines that describe who is included in an interpersonal event (i.e., who interacts with whom, for what purpose, and how often). They also de-note the closeness of relationship on a continuum (i.e., too close, balanced, or too disengaged). *Power* is the "relative influence of each family member on the outcome of an activity" (Aponte, 1976b, p. 434). *Alignment* is the level of agree-ment or disagreement between members or subsystems in the family.

1964. Virginia Satir, MSW, a social worker, publishes the first edition of *Conjoint Family Therapy*, a pioneering work in family therapy that highlights her beliefs about human beings as evolving and capable of growth, change, and intimacy with each other. As a founding member of M.R.I. and one of the few women recognized as making pioneering contributions to family therapy, she becomes a leading figure in the human growth movement. After leaving her childhood in rural Wisconsin, she began her professional life as a teacher and then was drawn to the profession of social work through her keen interest and concern for the disenfranchised. By the late 1950s, she was associated with M.R.I and became "a kind of living legend as family therapy's most celebrated recruiter and goodwill ambassador . . . perhaps the most imitated family ther-apist of her time" (Simon, 1981, p. 168). She emphasized the development of positive *self-esteem* through self-acceptance and family relationships that fos-tered the *individuality* of each member.

1967. Paul Watzlawick, Janet Beavin, and Don Jackson publish *Prag-matics of Communication: A Study of Interactional Patterns, Pathologies and Paradoxes*, a seminal work on communication theory that builds upon work from the Bateson projects at M.R.I. They describe all behavior as a type of communi-cation and categorize specific interactions as either *symmetrical* (egalitarian) or *complementary* (opposite in some way). In 1974, Watzlawick, Weakland, and Fisch publish *Change: Principles of Problem Formation and Problem Resolution,* an integration of mathematics, cybernetics, and communication applied to relational and mental health problems. They emphasize an analysis of the client's *attempted solutions* as a way of assessing which interactions were unsuccessful. This work ushers in a type of family therapy known as brief family therapy.

1967. Jay Haley is offered a position at the Philadelphia Child Guidance Clinic by Salvador Minuchin. He joins Minuchin and Braulio Montalvo in developing a family counseling and training institute. For 10 years, the three men drive in a car pool back and forth from work, developing their shared ideas about families and family therapy (Simon, 1992).

1971. Gerald Patterson publishes the first edition of *Families: Applications of Social Learning Theory to Family Life.* In 1975, he publishes *A Social Learning Approach to Family Intervention.* Both these works show the effective and positive contributions of *parent training* and *behavior modification* upon family relationships. The influence of social learning theory spawns a number of prominent family therapists who bring research training from their degrees in psychology, closely study minute details of *interactional sequences* in family life, and use their findings to develop intervention strategies for child problems and marital distress.

From this array of developments and others, the field of family therapy emerged in the twentieth century. The organized efforts of those early pioneers brought a variety of family therapy practices and backgrounds. From anthropology, mathematics, communications, cybernetics, and hypnosis, the ancestors of present-day family therapy combined the knowledge of their original mental health discipline (psychiatry, psychology, social work) with these additional knowledge bases. Their synthesis occurred as members of these interdisciplinary networks conversed and debated across the country. Gradually, experimentation gave way to models of intervention that developed around the practices of these charismatic innovators. The development of family therapy in the United States is paralleled with developments in European countries, especially England, Germany, Belgium, and Italy. As we will see in Chapter 2, many of these influences play a significant role in the worldwide growth of the field from 1970 to 2000. However, first, we will illustrate how these ground-breaking concepts influenced practice of the first family therapists.

THE EVOLUTION OF FAMILY THERAPY PRACTICE: A SNAPSHOT OF EARLY PRACTICES

By 1970, various groups were organized into counseling centers, training institutes, and research groups. We will review a sample of these and their unique contributions to family therapy practice. *M.R.I.* approaches, through the work of Watzlawick, Weakland, and Fisch came to be known as brief, pragmatic, and interactional. *Experiential* approaches, through the examples of Virginia Satir and Carl Whitaker, came to be known for their attention to human growth and development. *Structural* and *strategic* approaches, from the mentoring of Minuchin, Haley, and Montalvo, came to be known as directive and engaging therapy that focused explicitly on relationships surrounding the presenting problem. *Intergenerational* family therapists, led by Bowen and Boszormenyi-Nagy, targeted the *family of origin* (birth or childhood family) and those developmental experiences related to a given problem. *Behavioral* approaches were started from the work of Gerald Patterson and others who developed systematic, research-based, problem-focused interventions.

By reviewing these general approaches and identifying their unique contributions, beginning family therapists will have an introduction to assessment and treatment skills they may ultimately integrate into their practice. To illustrate the primary contributions between the various approaches, a case will be examined through different perspectives, illustrating how a family therapist from each approach might assess the problem and develop a treatment plan.

Paul Nelson, 14, was admitted to a residential group home for adolescent males when his truancy and behavior problems became such that his parents could no longer keep him at home. A caseworker was assigned through juvenile court, and Paul was placed in a local facility where parents were involved in parent education and family therapy. The adolescents had a structured school experience and could earn weekend visits home through good behavior.

Paul's parents Roy, 45, and Lilly, 42, were a white, working-class couple who had three children, Ed, Janet, and Paul. Ed, 18, had dropped out of high school 2 years before and was working at a local gas station. His girlfriend, Roxanne, 17, was pregnant. Ed was living at home, trying to save enough money to support this forthcoming child. At the time of treatment, Ed was uncertain whether he would marry Roxanne, although they were currently seeing each other on a regular basis. Janet, 17, was in her senior year of high school. She was an A student and enjoyed such school activities as cheerleading and chorus. She hoped to finish high school and go on to college. Paul had been held back in the seventh grade because of absences and was in the eighth grade at the time of his placement. (see Figure 1.1)

Structural Family Therapy

Therapists using this approach observe the interactions and activities of family members to determine the organization or structure of the family. Symptoms

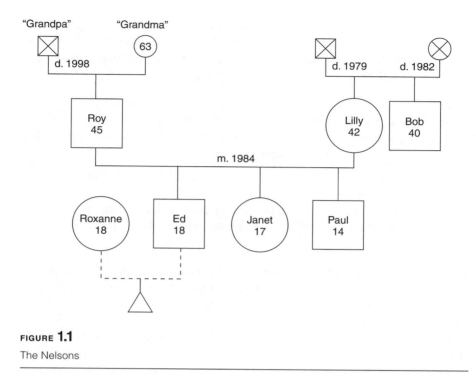

FIGURE **1.1**

The Nelsons

are regarded as a consequence of organizational difficulties. According to Minuchin, this organization must evolve to meet the developmental tasks for each stage of the family life cycle. The concepts of hierarchy, boundaries, subsystems, and coalitions are invoked in describing family structure.

Theory   Within families, *hierarchy* is often expressed by the pecking order, by shared perceptions of who is the boss, and by interactional patterns that indicate who gets the last word. The *parental subsystem* is supposed to provide leadership for growth and development of the child or sibling subsystem. In turn, children are influenced by leadership style and interpersonal patterns of parents. Relationships are defined by the level of closeness within them, such as *enmeshed* (too close), *disengaged* (too distant), or balanced. The corresponding type of interpersonal boundary in a given relationship would be labeled as *diffuse, rigid,* or *permeable.* Sometimes parents develop complementary roles with their children (that is, one close, one distant). When this happens, the parental hierarchy is thought to lack balance.

A *cross-generational coalition* can occur when one parent joins in a coalition with one or more children against the other parent. Such a coalition is often indicated if the therapist notes critical discussions about a parent who is absent, if one parent confides in a child about marital discord, or if one parent openly sides with a child against the other parent. In structural terms, parent–child coalitions are thought of as a violation of the boundary between the parental and sibling subsystems since it changes the role of the child from one of dependent to one of confidant or emotional peer.

Goals   Structural goals are based on hypotheses formulated from interactional sequences in the family (Aponte & Van Deusen, 1981). These goals are often specified in the form of altered transactional patterns or sequences of behavior related to the problem. Common goals are:

Strengthen the marital subsystem to improve parental functioning.
Help detached parents become closer to their children.
Help overinvolved parents develop some distance with their children.
Become more balanced (flexible boundaries) in personal roles and less rigid
    or chaotic.

Role of the therapist   Minuchin, as he developed his model of structural family therapy, characterized his role as that of a director, actively moving in and out of involvement with the family during a treatment session. As a director, Minuchin would guide interaction between members in a session, develop rapport with hesitant members, or assign tasks for the family to perform in the session. While the directives given to the family are diverse, the clinician plays a specific role in this model: the role of a pragmatic stage manager who enacts old and new dramas that help the family members reorganize their relational difficulties.

In the session with the Nelsons, the structural therapist joins the family by discussing Roy's and Lilly's work. Paul is asked about his hobbies and what musical groups he prefers. The therapist comments on their ability to have fun and work hard as strengths in the family. As patterns become evident, the therapist comments on these (i.e., "It sounds like Janet has become Mom's sounding board and Paul is at a standoff with Dad"). Through these reflections, hypotheses are formulated out loud.

Assessment   The family therapist must ask: How is the family organized? In this particular social context or culture, does the family sufficiently meet the needs of all its individual members? To answer these questions, therapists using this model determine who interacts with whom, for what purpose, and how often. While gathering this information, they also observe whether family relationships appeared close, distant, chaotic, or authoritarian. For example, when an adolescent is truant from school, the following questions would be key to gathering information from the family:

Who would be first to find out? What would be his or her reaction?
Who would be told next? What would be his or her reaction?
What would the youth do in response to the reactions?
How would other family members get involved?
Who sits by whom during the initial session?
Could their placement in the session be symbolic of how relationships are
    conducted at home?

---

*The therapist asks the above questions and discovers that when Mrs.
Nelson is called by the school, she responds by leaving work and
confronting Paul. When Paul refuses to interact with her and withdraws
to his room, she reports to Mr. Nelson about the situation. Mr. Nelson
confronts Paul about his behavior and threatens him with punishment
if his behavior does not improve. When Janet becomes aware of the
problem, she spends time with Paul, encouraging him to behave better.
She has also become Lilly's sounding board, providing a listening ear as
her mother worries out loud. The therapist asks Paul about his
relationship with each member of the family. Of his parents, he spends the
most time with Lilly and is uncomfortable with Roy. Of his siblings, he is
closest to Janet and feels some disgust that Ed has gotten himself into
"trouble." Roy and Lilly are asked about the time they spend together.
Because they work different shifts, they have very little time together until
the weekend. Recently, Roy has been asked to work overtime at the
meatpacking plant, as a result of layoffs and employee reductions.*

*The structural family therapist hypothesizes from this information that
the marital subsystem has become distant as a result of the family's
economic situation. In addition, Lilly seems to be overinvolved with Janet
and Paul in contrasting ways. By confiding in Janet, she has elevated Janet
from the status of child to that of peer. By engaging in repetitive
interactions with Paul, she is equally enmeshed with him, but in a way that
produces opposition rather than peer status. Because Paul has been
persistent in his misbehavior, he has rendered the parental subsystem
ineffective at this time, obtaining a level of power that is inappropriate.*

Intervention   The structural therapist relies heavily on in-session interventions to produce initial behavioral changes. These changes are thought to stimulate cognitive and perceptual changes as well. By involving the hierarchy, the
structural therapist hopes to help the family reorganize itself so that the parental
subsystem is strengthened with appropriate boundaries. In a family therapy session, the goal at the beginning of the session is to join with the family to become
a comfortable part of the family system. *Joining* requires the therapist to build

rapport by being personable and responsive to family members. Colapinto (1991) suggests that the role of the structural family therapist is that of producer, stage director, protagonist, and narrator. Further, he suggests the model requires "a respectful curiosity about diverse forms of family experience and strengths . . . a preference for concrete behavioral changes over talk about changed feelings . . . a willingness to direct . . . a tolerance for intensity in human transactions, and the courage to raise intensity when necessary" (p. 436).

The therapist becomes directive, asking the family to participate in specifically designed enactments. For example, Paul and Roy are asked to sit together and discuss a family activity. The therapist nudges them to be direct and honest with each other. Lilly is asked to explore her own reaction to the suggestion that Roy become more involved in addressing Paul's behavior. When she tries to interrupt the discussion between Roy and Paul, the therapist interrupts her interruption and directs Roy and Paul to continue. Suggestions are made regarding ways that Roy and Lilly can alter their roles. The therapist shares personal stories that demonstrate an empathy with the family's struggle. As Roy's isolation becomes more evident, the therapist works to strengthen the therapeutic bond with him, pointing out his strengths and acknowledging his good intentions. As the session concludes, the family is asked to bring the other two siblings next time. Eventually, the therapist discovers that Roy's mother is also very involved with Paul and persuades the family to include her in sessions as well.

Mental Research Institute

Brief family therapists believe that symptoms in the family are messages about some aspect of the family system. This concept comes directly from communication theory. These therapists are also influenced by the work of Milton Erickson, who was pioneering hypnotic and paradoxical techniques that emphasized the uniqueness of the symptom and the importance of behavioral directives. This blend of communication, cybernetics, and Ericksonian influences results in a pragmatic approach to therapy that avoids any personal conflict with the client.

Theory   Because behaviors often communicate meaning on more than one level, the symptom can contain an explicit message (I have a stomachache) as well as an implicit message (I want more affection). This is an example of the *report* and *command* levels of communication. Since these therapists view *all behavior as communication*, a symptom is a communicative act between two or more members that symbolizes some problem within the interpersonal network (Watzlawick, Weakland, & Fisch, 1974). Thus, any behavior can potentially be an attempted solution to some unidentified problem (I want my divorced parents to reconcile). In addition, family members' attempts to address problem behavior may become a vicious cycle in which *the solution becomes a problem* (p. 31).

Goals   Brief therapists have one main goal: to resolve the presenting problem. However, their theory of problem formation leads to intermediate goals such as:

- Disrupt patterns of interaction that are vicious cycles maintaining the problem.
- Motivate clients to change attempted solutions.

Role of the therapist   Therapists at M.R.I. see themselves as consultants to clients. They are active and directive, but they do not seek an emotionally based bond with the client. Since all therapeutic behavior is supposed to be relevant to solving the presenting problem, there are times when the therapist chooses to be passive or to focus upon clients' emotions. This is for purely pragmatic purposes.

Assessment   They suggest a four-step procedure for solving any problem, therapeutic or nontherapeutic:

1. Obtain a clear description of the problem in behavioral and interactional terms.
2. Investigate the attempted solutions and their results.
3. Develop a clear description of the concrete change desired.
4. Formulate and implement a plan to produce the change (Watzlawick, Weakland, & Fisch, 1974, p. 110).

Thus, all presenting problems are immediately cast in interactional terms. In developing a treatment strategy, therapists at M.R.I. explore what solutions have been tried to resolve the problem (Weakland, Fisch, Watzlawick, & Bodin, 1974). Often the attempt to solve the problem has worsened the original situation.

In exploring the Nelsons' attempts at solving the problem of Paul's behavior, the therapist discovers that their primary solutions have been verbal (nagging, criticizing, and threatening), and Paul's responses have been nonverbal; furthermore, none of these attempted solutions has been successful. These would be considered first-order attempts at change, rather than second-order solutions that change the nature of the relationship. In first-order change, the method changes slightly, but the category of the method stays the same (negative interaction). Second-order

change *would require Lilly and Roy to identify options they could*
implement in order to be more action-oriented and less verbal and negative
(change in category leading to a more constructive relationship).

Intervention   M.R.I. models assume that change takes place through
client response to *in-session directives* and *out-of-session tasks*. This model
gave birth to the use of *paradoxical interventions*, in which "giving up" on
solving the problem in the old way would pave the way for a new and better
solution to emerge. Similarly, M.R.I. introduced the technique of *reframing*
into the repertoire of family therapists as a way of providing an interactional
conceptualization of the problem. These therapists defined reframing as a
reconceptualization of some context that keeps the clients from exercising
other options in solving their problem. These practitioners attempted to re-
construct their clients' view of the problem in a way that would produce new
options. Therefore, they would generate multiple meanings for various problem behaviors. They found that when they could help their clients assign a
new meaning to an old problem, new attitudes brought forth new options for
problem solving.

After getting a definition of the problem, brief family therapists explore
what solutions have been tried to resolve the problem (Weakland, Fisch,
Watzlawick, & Bodin, 1974). Often the family's attempt to solve the
problem actually has worsened the original situation. To withhold
privileges or other pleasures generally would be considered a more action-
oriented option, provided the parents can accomplish that with a minimum
of argument or discussion. In addition, since Paul may be aligned with
Lilly, a second-order plan might also incorporate a shift in the relationship,
by having Lilly administer the consequences while Roy rewards Paul's
good behavior.

Strategic Family Therapy

Many new students of family therapy are unaware that Haley took the uncon-
ventional ideas from M.R.I. and Milton Erickson and influenced Minuchin's
evolving model on the east coast. Likewise, Minuchin influenced Haley with
his applications of structure and function. With each refinement came different perspectives about the role and responsibility of the therapist. Haley's
unique integration of these influences resulted in a model that conceptualized
the family in terms of organization but emphasized an unwavering focus upon
the presenting problem. For Haley, all therapeutic interactions should relate
directly to the presenting problem. Otherwise, they are irrelevant (Simon,

1992). Strategic family therapists emphasize a particular approach or strategy for each presenting problem.

Theory   Symptoms often occur when a family is stuck at a particular stage in the family life cycle; that is, while Paul Nelson's behavior may be a metaphor for conflictual interactions between his parents, his behavior may also be saying something about the family's adaptation to a new stage in the life cycle (the launching stage). In this way, the symptom is often an attempted solution to some other problem that goes unacknowledged or unnoticed by others in the system. Such metaphorical messages help the therapist to conceptualize the relationship between symptoms and interactional patterns within the family. By targeting specific interactions that occur during the session, the therapist works on the premise that small initial changes will lead to greater changes over time (Weakland et al., 1974).

The strategic family therapist would assume that Paul's behavior is a metaphor or nonverbal message about something else going on in the family. It might be related to the distance between his parents, challenges with Ed in entering the launching stage of the family life cycle, or some other aspect of the family's well-being that has not yet come to light. As strategic therapists explore opinions and interactions within the family, they will be searching for possible clues to clarify the message of the symptom.

Goals   Like structural therapists, strategic family therapy defines the therapeutic goal as interactional change within the family system. Haley often targets the hierarchy as the primary focus of change.

Role of the therapist   The therapist is expected to assume a leadership role, leading the family through four stages in the first session (social, problem definition, interaction, and goal setting). Strategic family therapists are also supposed both to direct various family members to discuss certain topics and to potentially suggest changes in interaction during the discussion. They are to avoid looking for underlying causes or pathology. Instead, as the therapist helps the family to interact differently in the session, it is important to attribute positive motives to clients (Stanton, 1981, p. 376). Problem behaviors are relabeled to have more positive meaning.

A positive label for Lilly's interference is caring, and Paul's anger is relabeled as desired attention. The new labels aim to provide family members with a new way of thinking about the problem, so that it can be resolved. Further interaction with the therapist might generate a list of attempted solutions other than caring that Roy and Lilly have employed, so that they can begin to see what has worked to their benefit and what has not.

Assessment   Like structural family therapists, strategic therapists are also chiefly interested in how family members interact with each other: Assessment and intervention are based on observations of interactional sequences:

Do family members speak for each other?
When a child speaks, does Mom or Dad interrupt him or her?
Do parents agree about how to solve the problem?
Is the symptom a metaphor for something else in this family?
How is the symptom maintained by the system, and how does the system
     maintain the symptom?
What system function could these symptoms serve?

The therapist attempts to understand the sequence of interactions surrounding the presenting problem. By determining the sequence of interaction, the therapist gains information useful in developing an intervention to alleviate the problem. While structural and strategic approaches emphasize the interactional sequence, each treats it somewhat differently. Strategic family therapists are more symptom-focused, and structural therapists may take time to explore the quality of relationships in general, not merely how they relate to the presenting problem (Stanton, 1981). For instance, strategic therapists focus on dysfunctional sequences of interaction that contribute to the problem. Structuralists center their attention on how family members interact to carry out specific functions within each subsystem (marital, parental, and sibling). For both models, the emphasis on interactional change corresponds to a focus on behavioral change.

The therapist is thinking about the sequence of interactions surrounding the presenting problem. Lilly is the first to speak. Roy remains silent. Both Roy and Paul wait to be spoken to by the therapist. When the therapist asks Roy to describe what happens when Paul gets stubborn, Roy outlines the usual sequence of interactions: his arrival from work, Lilly's complaints about Paul's truancy, Roy's questions to Paul about why he is behaving this way, and Paul's silence. At that point, in exasperation, Roy tells Paul that if he keeps up with his behavior, he will never amount to much of anything. With this, finally, Paul retreats to his room and begins to listen to his collection of heavy metal music.

Intervention   Madanes (1981) states that the *directive* is to strategic therapy "what interpretation is to psychoanalysis." Directives can be direct or indirect, depending on the receptivity of the family and skill level of the therapist. Indirect interventions include paradoxical prescriptions and the creation of rituals. Some guidelines for these strategic interventions will be reviewed in later chapters. The interruption of current behavior patterns is thought to be the most important starting point of change. This entry point allows family members to experience the new and strange with the help of the therapist. With that experience comes the increased likelihood that the family will view new possibilities for themselves and extend their experimental behaviors outside of the session. Positive labels and an analysis of solutions strengthen this momentum by stimulating changes in thinking.

The strategic therapist must decide what type of task to assign for the week. Sometimes, strategic therapists use straightforward tasks, on the assumption that clients will comply with the suggestions. At other times, strategic therapists use paradoxical directives, on the assumption that clients are ambivalent about change, even though they are in distress from the problem. Families with a schizophrenic member or an addict and those in which one or more members are characterized by personality disorder generally have difficulty completing straightforward tasks (Stanton, 1981). These families are very effective in getting the therapist to work hard for improvement while they resist his or her efforts (Haley, 1976).

The therapist directs Roy and Lilly to discuss the problem, to see if they can talk about it in the presence of Paul. When Paul interferes, the therapist identifies a problem area and directs Lilly to ignore his comment and return to her discussion with Roy. The therapist is careful not to be central to this interaction. As Roy and Lilly interact, family structure and hierarchy begin to emerge. As noted in the structural example, Lilly is overinvolved with Paul, whereas Roy is underinvolved. When the therapist asks Roy and Paul to talk without interference from Lilly, the directive has both diagnostic and therapeutic value.

Since the therapist is new to the Nelson family, a straightforward task is assigned. This serves the purpose of assessing the family's ability to comply with direct suggestion and providing direction for changes in their interactional sequences. Since Paul is currently in residential treatment, some of the family's typical interactions are already disrupted. Therefore, the therapist assigns Roy to be in charge of the weekly telephone call to Paul and suggests that he ask Paul about his future ambitions. What would he like to be when he grows up? Whom does he consider to be his heroes? If he had a million dollars, how would he spend it? The therapist suggests that Roy keep his opinions and advice to himself, so that he can focus entirely on understanding and recording what Paul says. Once Roy returns and reports on his efforts with the task, the therapist can decide whether more straightforward tasks are in order or whether to shift focus toward more indirect and paradoxical tasks.

Intergenerational Family Therapy

Several pioneers share an attention to family dynamics across several generations and a history in psychodynamic theory. They conceptualize families and their problems in terms of psychological dynamics passed from generation to generation. They see the past as operating in the present and have evolved theories that help them chart a therapeutic course across time. Here, we will feature only a few of the many concepts from the work of Murray Bowen and Ivan Boszormenyi-Nagy. While each developed various ideas that are unique to their separate approaches, together they represent the primary roots of most intergenerational therapy practiced today.

Theory   Unlike structural and strategic therapists, the practitioners of this model consider information about past relationships to be a meaningful springboard from which to design interventions in the present (*live past*). Intergenerational therapists would assume that parenting and marital patterns have been influenced by experiences in each parent's family of origin. As parents pass on their level of differentiation to children, relationships are often fused (too close and too emotionally reactive). This model of family therapy would assume that each member of the family acts impulsively out of emotion or tradition and is unaware of how the power of reason could generate improved relational patterns. This imbalance of emotionality over rationality is referred to as a *lack of differentiation.* The fact that the family members engage in repetitive interactions that bring about the same unsatisfactory results is an indication of the intense anxiety that motivates their behavior. In addition, this anxiety leads to a process of *triangulation,* in which one person enlists the support of another person against a third party in the family. This model suggests that when family members can discern the difference between the anxiety of their current behavior and the logic of alternative solutions, they can develop more healthy relationships in the future.

Bowenians would assert that both Roy and Lilly respond out of emotion rather than rationality when addressing Paul's behavior. They would reason that Paul and his siblings are mirrors of a transmitted family process (family projection process) rooted in the historical evolution of previous generations. Paul's behavior would be thought of as coming from some gut-level instinct that manifests the same level of differentiation as his parents'.

Boszormenyi-Nagy (1987) might assume that each person in the family is motivated, in part, by a subjective sense of fairness that can only be understood from his or her unique development (relational ethics). This ledger system provides a framework by which the family therapist discovers each person's subjective justification for his or her current behavior (Boszormenyi-Nagy & Krasner, 1986).

Paul's motivation for skipping school could come from an unspoken sense of entitlement based on some contribution that he perceives himself to be making to the family. For example, having seen his brother drop out of school at age 16 (a perceived privilege), Paul may think he is entitled to the same privilege in return for the loyalty he manifests to his mother against his father. Understandably, Roy and Lilly may also be motivated by a sense of justice that comes from their experience in their own families (We were expected to obey our parents unconditionally, and we are entitled to the same obedience from our children). Paul's behavior would be thought of as coming from some gut-level instinct that manifests the same level of differentiation as his parents'.

Goals   From an intergenerational perspective, the goals for this family could include:

- Teach Roy and Lilly how to differentiate and detriangulate.
- Help the entire family to recover more fully from intergenerational losses.
- Rebalance the family ledger system to improve their sense of trust and fairness.
- Utilize family strengths to restore trustworthiness.
- Restore age-appropriate roles and power.

Role of the therapist   The therapist remains central to the process. Bowen usually worked with individuals or couples, gathering family information and coaching them into new behaviors. He (1978) was noted for his work in coaching clients toward a more rational perspective vis-à-vis their family of origin. Instead of remaining passive, he took an active, involved role in facilitating change. For example, he would encourage Lilly to avoid taking sides with Paul when he complains about Roy. He would also encourage Lilly to avoid complaining about Roy to Paul.

Boszormenyi-Nagy usually worked with the entire family, learning about the family members' sense of loyalty and fairness with each other. He encouraged *multidirected partiality*, which is the art of consecutively siding with each member in order to develop trust and fairness in relationships (Bernal & Flores-Ortiz, 1991). If anger is expressed over current conflicts, the therapist does not take sides but seeks understanding of each point of view, allowing each member to confirm or correct the therapist's understanding. As each side of the conflict is clarified, the therapist asks questions intended to diffuse emotional reactivity and to help each member listen to the other. Throughout the session, the therapist engages in continuous self-monitoring, in order to manage personal anxiety that might allow triangulation to occur.

Assessment   Bowen's intergenerational approach was characterized by information gathering about the nuclear family, each spouse's family of origin, and the relationship of nodal events over time to the development of the symptom in question. To facilitate this, a family map called a *genogram* is constructed. This diagram identifies each member of the three-generational extended family, noting dates of births, deaths, marriages, and divorces. Intergenerational family therapists frequently inquire about deaths and losses experienced in the family. The occurrence of such events is often linked with the subsequent development of symptoms in the family (Petker, 1982). When viewing the problem as part of a sequence of family events, some families will be seen as going through emotional shock waves, from which they may not have recovered fully (Bowen, 1978). With this family story in place, the therapist would coach the client in developing a strategy that could be executed over time, outside of sessions.

The historical development of the Nelsons illustrates how a lack of differentiation can be passed down through the generations and also how it can be exacerbated through traumatic life events. It emerges that Paul's behavior did not become problematic until the sixth grade, approximately one year after Grandpa's death. This was also the year that Lilly went to work. During the early parts of the interview, Roy and Lilly describe the first years of their marriage as very happy. Lilly's parents died when she was young, and she was happy to be adopted into Roy's family.

The therapist discovers that Roy's mother lives in their neighborhood and has been widowed for 5 years. As family members begin discussing the loss of Grandpa, Paul becomes animated and talkative for the first time. He relates his memories of Grandpa, giving particular emphasis to the sadness that he can still vividly remember feeling on the day of the funeral. Other family members also describe the family vacations that Grandpa organized and the great void his death left in the family. Since his death, there have been no family vacations. The year after his death, Lilly went to work outside the home for the first time. Paul was 10 at the time.

The Nelsons can be seen as having not recovered fully from Grandpa's death. The void in the family was not filled by anyone else taking on the planning of family vacations. For Paul, the void may have widened when Lilly went to work and Janet graduated from elementary school, leaving him to attend his school alone for the first time.

Intervention   The first session with the Nelsons includes all members of the household. For this model of practice, no purpose is served by asking family members to interact with each other. Instead, family therapists ask questions about the history of the symptom, paying specific attention to significant life events in the chronology of the family. This is how the therapist discovers the *nodal event* of Grandpa's death. However, the therapist begins by asking about the parents' courtship and marriage and then traces significant life-cycle transitions from that time to the present.

When the family becomes emotional during the discussion about Grandpa, the therapist asks each person for his or her reflections and memories; the therapist models differentiated (calm) behavior that is empathic but not emotionally reactive to the levels of emotion expressed in the responses. When Paul begins to accuse his parents of being unfair, the therapist is most interested in having Paul express his thoughts and feelings, not in discovering all areas of the parents' perceived unfairness. Since Paul is actually talking to the therapist, he is able to develop some emotional distance about the problem instead of engaging in the same repetitive interactions with his parents. Roy and Lilly are given the opportunity to listen to Paul with some distance instead of having to respond to him in direct interaction. In this manner, the process provides opportunities for the therapist to help family members differentiate, and the actual content of their discussions is of lesser importance.

As this session comes to a close, the therapist has received an overview of the Nelson family history, of the family members' emotional evolution with each other, and of the significant events that may have influenced their current lack of differentiation. In Bowenian therapy, this overview might actually be accomplished in several sessions. Eventually, family members will be given assignments such as gathering more family history, writing letters (to the living or the dead) that will be reviewed with the therapist, visiting relatives, or visiting the cemetery. With the Nelsons, the therapist decides to ask them to plan a hypothetical family vacation since they have not had a vacation in 5 years. Now that Paul is in a residential facility, the weekly telephone call to his family can be used in vacation planning, so that his views will also be represented. Paul is also asked to write a letter to his Grandpa. In subsequent sessions, reviews of the assignments provide useful information to help detriangle relationships and help the family discuss unresolved issues; the therapist coaches family members with their assignments, so that emotional reactivity decreases as each issue is addressed.

Experiential Family Therapy

Although Virginia Satir and Carl Whitaker are both described as experiential in their approach to family therapy, they evolved from different traditions. Satir came out of the communcation tradition at M.R.I. and later aligned closely with the human potential movement. Whitaker came from a psychiatric background in which he worked with families of schizophrenics. However, these pioneers share an investment in "spontaneity, creativity and risk-taking . . . a commitment to freedom, individuality and personal fulfillment" (Nichols & Schwartz, 2001, p. 175). Both believed that when the therapist is open and spontaneous, family members will learn to behave in the same way.

Theory   Experiential family therapists focus on subjective needs of the individual in the family and facilitate family interactions that address the *individuality* and *self-esteem* of each member. These clinicians believe that all individuals have the right to be themselves; however, family and social needs may often suppress the individuality and self-expression by which a person becomes fully understood and known in the family (*intimacy*). As parents are the architects of the family (Satir, 1972), it is incumbent on them to provide sufficient structure and nurturance so that the individuality of each child can be fostered. However, parents often manifest their low self-esteem through embarrassment, helplessness, criticism, or hostility that they feel regarding their children's struggles. With empathy and support from the therapist, the parents come to accept their own emotional experience, thereby becoming more intimate and caring. As *self-awareness* increases, the quality of communication improves, fostering self-esteem and growth in family members. By fostering *self-acceptance*, the experiential family therapist helps parents to become who they want to be. They can learn to forgive themselves for not being perfect parents or marital partners. As they do this, they can also risk more intimate self-expression with each other. As they learn to tolerate intimacy (and the accompanying risk of conflict), their acceptance of themselves and each other generalizes to their children. Interactions become opportunities for family members to be heard and understood, rather than contests to control or judge.

Goals   Whitaker (1983) considers the goals of family therapy to be an increased sense of competency and self-worth. Symptoms are considered an attempt toward growth. Whitakar and Keith (1981) suggested that the two-dimensional goal of experiental family therapy was to increase each member's sense of inclusion in the family and to increase the freedom to differentiate. This can be accomplished through:

- Increasing anxiety to develop greater family unity.
- Teaching families how to play in order to foster greater acceptance and creativity.

Satir (1972) emphasized personal growth through the following steps:

- Increase honest communication so that family members can express their feelings about self and others.
- Use exploration and negotiation to reach decisions instead of coercion.
- Increase acceptance of each person's uniqueness.

Role of the therapist   The therapist's *use of self* is an important role in this model. These therapists are described by Piercy and Sprenkle (1986) as those who "participate actively and personally in therapy sessions; they do not attempt to hide behind a therapeutic mask. . . . If the therapist expects the family to have the courage to be real, the therapist must also demonstrate that courage" (p. 53). By *modeling* good communication, the therapist helps the family tolerate honest emotional expression. At the same time, the therapist demonstrates self-acceptance through having the courage to admit mistakes and fallibility. In addition to modeling and teaching, the therapist facilitates the family's process during the session so that effective communication can occur. This may include increasing self-disclosure or changing the direction of communication flow within the family.

Satir describes a therapist as a resource person and a model of congruent communication. The therapist helps family members to clarify and alter their values so they can communicate openly with one another. The therapist teaches family members how to observe discrepancies between the intent and impact of their messages. The therapist becomes a standard by which family members can evaluate themselves and the effectiveness of the communication.

Meeting each family member, the therapist makes a gesture or expression that personalizes the therapeutic experience and helps each family member to feel accepted. As introductions proceed, the therapist looks for opportunities to demonstrate frankness and candor, commenting on some aspect of each person that normally might be ignored in typical communication.

Assessment   Whitaker explored the family on many dimensions, including behavioral, interpersonal, and intrapsychic. Information was gathered informally on the entire family, on subsystems within each generation, and on any triads, collusions, and individual dynamics (Whitaker & Keith, 1981).

Satir was interested in *locating pain* in the family and exploring what would be needed to resolve it. Coming from her days at M.R.I., she introduced a number of activities into the assessment (Bodin, 1981). She would direct the family to *plan something together*. This would be directed by having different dyads, triads, and the entire family each develop a plan. By observing different combinations of family members, she could observe how each subsystem functioned, in this order: the entire family, all except father, all except mother, children only, mother and daughters, mother and sons, father and sons, father and daughters, husband and wife.

In another assessment section, entitled "Similarity and Differences," questions similar to these would be asked, rotating to all family members:

Which of your children is most like you?
Which of your children is most like your spouse?
Are you more like your mother or father?
If you are more like your mother (or father), how are you also like the other?

If you are more like your mother (or father), how are you also different from
    her or him?
How are you alike and different from your spouse? (Bodin, 1981)

---

*In asking these questions of the Nelsons, the therapist discovers that Ed
does not see himself like either parent. He dropped out of school with his
parents' permission. He felt discouraged about his school performance
and did not want the continued humiliation of failure. He was never a
behavior problem at school or at home. However, as the family discussed
ways in which they tried to help Ed with his studies, it emerged that
both Lilly and Roy thought Ed was like them because they had no
understanding of the math techniques being taught at the high school
and they felt intimidated and helpless in the process. However, they
would usually become angry and embarrassed when he received his
report card, telling him he should ask his teachers for more help. When
Ed announced that he wanted permission to drop out of school, Roy had
few words to say and Lilly was relieved.*

Intervention   Experiential family therapists refrain from emphasizing specific therapeutic techniques; however, their use of questions, empathic responses, clarification, and directives facilitates effective communication in the
family. Through more honest communication, family members learn to solve
their own problems. The therapist trusts that the family members will find a
creative solution to their problem within the therapeutic relationship. Experiential family therapists often encourage increased self-disclosure or influence
the direction of communication flow within the family.

---

*If Carl Whitaker were meeting with the Nelsons, he would focus first on
Roy, in order to address the alienation that keeps him from being a more
nurturing father. He might also become argumentative with Paul, to
encourage the honest expression of the anger that conceals his pain (Napier
& Whitaker, 1978). If Virginia Satir were meeting with the Nelsons, she
might start by asking Paul to help her construct a live sculpture of his
family, by placing family members in physical locations that represent the
degree of emotional distance present within the family. As the sculpture is
constructed, she would use the resulting scene as a catalyst for honest
communication about relationships in the family.*

Satir would emphasize nurturance, whereas Whitaker makes liberal use of
confrontation and modeling with frankness. Satir (1972) directs family members to follow three rules for effective communication:

1. Family members should speak in the first person and express what they think and feel (the therapist might ask, "I want to know how you feel about that").
2. Family members are asked to take responsibility for their feelings ("Tell me how you feel when he ignores you").
3. Family members are required to level with each other ("Tell your son what you want him to do when he gets home")

Such directives shift the responsibility for communication as well as the content.

Children are asked, "How do you know when your Dad is feeling good toward you? What does he do to show his love?" Parents are asked, "What are the ways you prefer to show your love to your children?" As family members squirm at such uncharacteristic openness, the therapist models respect for their fears and discomfort. "I know this discussion might be hard for you. It takes courage to come together in honesty."

The therapist develops rapport with the family through empathy, questions, and directives. "You don't have to do everything at once. We can take one small step at a time." The therapist also models genuineness by disclosing fears, embarrassments, fantasies, and foibles. "People often think I'm crazy. Sometimes I wish everyone could like me, but I know that's not always possible, so I have to have the courage to make mistakes and forgive myself for making them." In so doing, experiential family therapists trust the universality of human experience to help family members identify with them and see the potential for themselves. "Roy, if you could forgive yourself for your own mistakes, what would you say differently to Ed?"

As therapy continues, the Nelsons find some opportunity for emotional experience and interaction with each other, through the therapist's directives and various techniques borrowed from Gestalt psychotherapy. Central to this process is the therapist's ability to model the confrontation of difficult issues with courage and humanity.

Behavioral Family Therapy

This approach started from the work of Gerald Patterson, a psychologist, whose background in research led to designing programs that would yield quantifiable results. As he began to consider the cost-effectiveness of the treatment of children, he paid increased attention to employing the child's parents as agents of change. He combined social learning theory with systems theory to address child behavior problems. As he began to help parents with the behavior of their children, he also observed and noted the interactional patterns of other family members (Patterson, 1971). Research began to shift from investigating the child's inappropriate behavior to studying patterns of interaction between family members (i.e., how two family members influence each other in ways that maintain the behavior).

Theory   The behavioral approach has traditionally focused on the behavior of individuals and the events in the social environment that trigger their behavior (*antecedents*) and that shape and maintain their behavior. The *consequences* of behaviors (what follows) are considered goals and reinforcements to them. The social learning approach views family dysfunction as the result of infrequent *positive reinforcement* between family members (i.e., not enough rewards for positive behavior). Thus, positive behavior is consistent when it is rewarded accordingly. Often an *aversive stimulus*, or punishment, is used by one family member to control the behavior of another. Social learning theory views family conflict as the use of aversive control rather than the use of positive reinforcement. The eventual outcome is a low rate of positive reinforcers exchanged over an extended period of time.

Goals   The early models of behavioral parent training were aimed at increasing the prosocial behavior of children. In their simple form, behavioral goals are (1) to increase positive behaviors and (2) to decrease negative behaviors. Usually, positive behaviors that replace negative behaviors are the ideal target for change. For example, if a child is aggressive during dinner, the first goal would be to increase the contrasting behavior (i.e., passive or agreeable) with positive reinforcement. If this approach alone is not successful, a related goal would be to add some type of negative reinforcement (e.g., silence) instead of the previous response (e.g., attention).

Role of the therapist   Behavior therapists often take an educational stance. A great deal of early work consisted of parent training manuals that were used to help parents bring about desired behaviors in their children.

Assessment   Initial assessments seek to *identify the problem* in behavioral terms through gathering a history of the problem and examples of the behavior in question. Next, the problem situation is described through a *functional analysis* of sequential interactions that occur before and after the problem behavior. Often, parents are taught to observe and record these events in the natural environment. Events that precede the behavior (antecedents) are thought to trigger or provide stimulus for the behavior. By noting what happens immediately after a behavior (consequences), the therapist hypothesizes that these responses are the reinforcement for the behavior. In addition, the practitioner must assess potential positive reinforcements. It is important to remember that careful, accurate, and objective observations form the basis for an effective functional analysis.

When the behavior occurs, what happens right before and right after?

What triggers the behavior?

What reinforces the behavior?

What desired behavior could replace the misbehavior?

What are potential reinforcements for the new behavior? What are the child's likes and dislikes? Priorities? Values? Interests?

What is the parent's capacity to provide reinforcement?

Before skipping school, Paul reports getting up in the morning and wishing that he didn't have to face his teacher, Mr. Rawls. He is self-conscious about being held back a year in school, and he's jealous that Ed doesn't have to get up that early. When he goes in the school door, he feels a heaviness in his chest. Out of his mother's view, he walks down the hall and out the other door. He walks through the neighborhood and sometimes goes to the gas station where Ed works.

The remaining sequence of these events appears in the earlier section on structural family therapy. Although the questions are similar, note the antecedent information that comes from a functional assessment. The therapist can hypothesize that Paul's interactions with his teachers serve as an aversive stimulus, signaled by the heaviness in his chest. This may be a phobic reaction (fear). His visits to the gas station may serve as positive reinforcement. After school, his mother's reaction may be a negative reinforcement and his sister's attention may be a positive reinforcement.

Intervention   Typically, treatment would involve parent training in which both parents were instructed to systematically intervene using social learning principles (e.g., modeling, time-out, and extinction) to eliminate the problem. A "cost–benefit" analysis is conducted to develop a treatment plan that will increase the costs of the undesirable behavior and increase the benefits of desired behavior. Common techniques that are used in behavioral family therapy include:

Time-out, in which children are removed from reinforcing persons or objects.

Positive reinforcement, in which parents increase their natural reward system for desired behavior.

Token systems, in which special rewards, contracts, or gifts are negotiated for the desired behavior.

Modeling, in which the therapist demonstrates reinforcing or nonreinforcing behavior with children.

After making an assessment, the behavioral family therapist explores Paul's relationships with his teachers and what experiences his parents report with the school. Similar to Ed's predicament, Roy and Lilly were hesitant to ask for additional help from the school. In addressing the specific situation with Paul and Mr. Rawls, the therapist obtains a specific account of each minute-by-minute interaction in behavioral terms. Mr. Rawls gives an English assignment. Paul works on the essay at school but doesn't finish it. He leaves it at school that afternoon. The next day, Paul turns in his paper, incomplete. Mr. Rawls grades the paper and returns it with an "F." After class, Mr. Rawls calls Paul to his desk and asks him about the unfinished paper. Paul, afraid to admit he forgot to take the paper home, replies, "I just couldn't think of anything else to say." Mr. Rawls tells Paul that if he doesn't start completing his work, he will fail the class. Paul's chest tightens. He doesn't tell his parents because he doesn't want their reaction to his problem. After that, he begins skipping class.

From a behavioral view, the goal would be to explore how Paul could be reinforced for finishing his work. Could parents and teachers discuss his assignments, so that parents could help and reward Paul for work he completes at home? Could Mr. Rawls explore some of Paul's interests so the assignment would be more meaningful and reinforcing? Regarding consequences of Paul's behavior, the therapist reviews with his parents various strategies for decreasing the reinforcements that may come after school. Removing privileges, increasing help with school assignments, and providing rewards for completing the assignments are discussed. The family and therapist decide what strategies are appropriate for the situation. Once they implement the plan, it is evaluated regularly to monitor results and make refinements as needed.

FROM EARLY PRACTICES TO INTEGRATION: "THE BEST IN US ALWAYS LEARNS FROM THE BEST IN OTHERS"

The models presented in this chapter have discussed the Nelson family using many different perspectives. Table 1.1 summarizes key aspects of the pioneering models. We think these are the characteristics that have withstood the test of time. While each model provides somewhat different concepts and language, we think *the therapist's ability to integrate the family's reality with a given theoretical reality may really be at the heart of successful family therapy.* As the field of family therapy has developed over the past several decades, the movement toward distinct schools of thought has given way to integration of these major modes of thinking. While early pioneers spoke of their particular

TABLE 1.1

EARLY MODELS OF FAMILY THERAPY

	Theory	Goals	Role	Assessment	Intervention
Structural	Hierarchy Subsystems Proximity Boundaries Coalitions	Effective leadership of parents Balanced relationships	Director Stage manager Narrator	Quality of leadership Interactional sequences related to health and wellness Coalitions	Joining Enactments In-session interactions
M.R.I.	Levels of communication Behavior as communication Solutions as problems	Successful solutions Disrupt vicious cycles	Consultant	Behavioral descriptions Attempted solutions Description of the desired change	Out-of-session tasks Paradoxical interventions Reframing
Strategic	Adaptation to life stages Symptoms as metaphors Small changes lead to greater changes	Effective leadership of parents Successful solutions	Leader Director	Quality of leadership Interactional sequences related to problem-solving	Out-of-session tasks Direct and indirect directives

(Continued)

TABLE 1.1 **EARLY MODELS OF FAMILY THERAPY (CONTINUED)**

	Theory	Goals	Role	Assessment	Intervention
Intergenerational	Level of differentiation	Differentiation	Coach	Genogram	Address nodal events
	Past affecting the present	Detriangulation	Multi-directed partiality	Family ledger (perceptions of trust and fairness)	Trace transitions over time
	Triangulation	Resolving losses		Triangles	Decrease emotional reactivity
	Relational ethics	Restore trust and fairness		Emotional process	Encourage adult to adult relationships
					Credit each member's contribution
Experiential	Individuality	Acceptance	Use of self	Nurturing behavior	Directives toward clear communication
	Self-esteem	Creativity	Modeling	Conflict	Empathic responses
	Intimacy	Interpersonal competence	Self disclosure	Location of pain	Nurturance
	Self-awareness	Family unity	Directing flow of communication		Confrontation
		Healing			
Behavioral	Antecedents of behavior	Pro-social behavior	Educator	Behavioral descriptions	Parent training
	Consequences of behavior		Coach	History of the problem	Cost-benefit analysis
	Reinforcements			Functional analysis	Time-out
	Aversive stimuli				Token systems
					Modeling

approach as a certain type of truth, current thinking has led toward greater emphasis upon the family's unique reality (truth) and a flexible inclusion of contrasting points of view. Representative of such integration is Minuchin's (1987) reflection on the factors influencing his own practice:

> Recently, I was working with a family with three adult children whose mother committed suicide 20 years ago. I surprised myself by asking them to watch family movies and to mourn the mother's death. I thought Norman Paul might be proud of me. Another day I was seeing a family with an anorectic child. I found myself remembering some of the writings of Hilde Bruch. I didn't know she was one of my voices, but so it seems. Naturally pulling many voices together usefully demands an organizing frame. Briefly, the business of family therapy is change. Within this framework the possibilities are many and varied, as are the voices that speak to me. Within the possibilities open to us, the best in us always learns from the best of others. I am pleased to acknowledge that when I say to a man, When did you divorce your wife and marry your office?, it is Carl [Whitaker]'s voice speaking. He might not recognize it in my accent, but it is there, as are all the others. (pp. 13–14)

Here, we see Minuchin shifting from his own tradition when the family's context requires a different lens. We can only imagine that if his early career had brought him in contact with hundreds of mid-life families whose mothers had died tragically, he would have pioneered a therapy different from his structural approach. On the other hand, we might also imagine, in the latter case, that his personal style, insight, and daring would still be inspiring to us today.

Another early example of integration comes from Stanton (1981), who coined the term *structural–strategic* and then applied that model with Todd in their groundbreaking work on drug addiction (Stanton & Todd, 1982). This term is now used frequently to describe those who attend to structural themes while using strategic interventions. In an additional move toward integration, Stanton (1992) developed the use of a "Why now?" question, integrating it into his structural–strategic approach. This question incorporates elements of family history into the process that might be overlooked by a more present-focused orientation. Other models of practice were developed by those who made further innovations on the basis of their own experience. These integrative models combine the best elements from early approaches and also account for gender, race, culture, life-cycle issues, and individual experience.

SUMMARY

From the beginning of the twentieth century, worldwide changes in thinking led to the development and refinement of mental health practice. Those changes continue today. In the United States, practitioners listened to innovative thinkers at home and abroad, developing a more holistic and interpersonal

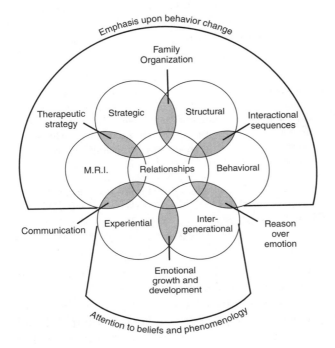

FIGURE **1.2**

Common factors across early models

approach to understanding human problems and to resolving them. This led to the development of family therapy, first as early practice and research, then as diverse approaches with different populations. Now, as the institutionalized profession of marriage and family therapy, it is regulated (licensed) and practiced in most of the United States and many other parts of the world. Many family therapists learn one predominant model and then integrate other approaches according to client needs and treatment settings. We think the models in this chapter represent those most often used as a starting point.

We can also see that family therapy has an early history of integration. The pioneers made their own transformations and changes along the way. The models presented in this chapter and summarized in Table 1.1 are the basis of our integrative approach for beginning practitioners. In Figure 1.2, we illustrate the commonalities that we believe existed, even in the early years. The old phrase "All roads lead to Rome" suggests that there are some general outcomes that can be achieved in a variety of ways. In the world of families and relationships, this is especially true. We think the therapist is as much on a journey of discovery as the client and must be open to shifting directions as new information comes forth. With this goal in mind, we invite the beginning practitioner to adopt a spirit of discovery and see what happened to the practice of family therapy as the twentieth century came to an end.

THE JOURNEY CONTINUES

Second-Generation Trends in Family Therapy

Social and Theoretical Movements

Post-Modern Models of Practice

Evidence-Based Practice

Summary

The evolution of marriage and family therapy took pioneering approaches and added additional dimensions that moved family therapy practice from more technical to more human terms. We started with strategy and evolved toward reflection and questioning. After the establishment of early practice models, the field, as an open system, was influenced by social movements that acknowledged the importance of gender, culture, and race. As these dialogues developed across the United States in general, established family therapists opened to these new ways of viewing people and their problems. Some family therapists, like Minuchin (himself, a Russian-Jewish immigrant raised in Argentina), had always worked with disadvantaged families. However, many second-generation family therapists were from the middle class. Thus, the voices of those marginalized within American culture (women, people of color) and those from the outside (Europe, South America, and Australia) were heard as different and innovative. These influences made the study of family therapy more inclusive and personal. Tied to this developmental trend was a growing interest in how life transitions related to common presenting problems.

At the same time, constructivism and social construction theory were gaining more attention in the field. These schools of thought are part of the *post-modern* era in the history of philosphy. This era is known as one that challenges traditional thought and questions authority. The result was a continued integration of pioneering concepts with greater sensitivity to the resources of diverse people evolving in their relationships. Attention turned from an emphasis upon behavior change alone to the beliefs and values that influenced a family's interaction patterns. This transition included changes in our thinking about the therapist's role as a better listener and collaborator. Present-day adaptations emphasize clients' personal wisdom and the egalitarian side of therapy (i.e., collaborative, narrative).

Finally, other developments came from research (i.e., multisystemic, cognitive–behavioral) and applications of relational and family-focused work in a number of different settings. The most recent developments include greater attention to the role of family therapists in nontraditional (non-mental health) settings such as schools, courts, and primary health care settings. We think this is a sign of growing maturity for our field. These integrative models are a bridge between the past and future of family therapy. They represent the cutting edge and demonstrate the utility of family therapy practice across many populations and settings.

Our review of historical trends in Chapter 1 suggested the order in which thinking began to change in the area of mental health. However, the evolution of the family therapy field after 1970 cannot be captured as easily, step-by-step. Since a number of trends were developing at once, we prefer to think of development in the field as layered, like a cake with different flavors that merge together over time (see Figure 2.1). Foundational layers consist of more inclusive and insightful social movements. Between these layers is a filling, rich with thoughts about the philosophy and practices of family therapy and with results of important research projects. The icing on the cake is made from specific models of family therapy that illustrate the colorful creativity of these trends (sounds delicious, doesn't it?). Since food is needed to survive every long journey, the integrative models practiced today will be reviewed in light of these blended flavors.

SOCIAL AND THEORETICAL MOVEMENTS

Feminist Theory

In 1978, Rachel Hare-Mustin publishes a pioneering article in *Family Process,* "A Feminist Approach to Family Therapy." Her critique of the field and thoughtful suggestions for a more gender-sensitive approach to family therapy began decades of reflection upon how to understand a problem as it relates to *societal practices such as sexism.* Other reviews and critiques followed, including those of the Women's Project in Family Therapy, a group of feminist colleagues who added their voices of support for *changes in hierarchical practices* in our therapy and in our professional organizations (Simon, 1992). At the most general level, the *feminist movement* in family therapy suggested that all families are influenced by patterns of socialization that lead to rules and roles governing family process

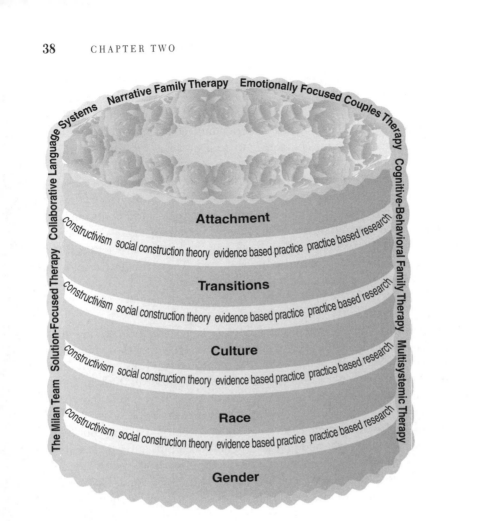

Narrative Family Therapy Emotionally Focused Couples Therapy

Systems

Collaborative Language

Solution-Focused Therapy

The Milan Team

Cognitive-Behavioral Family Therapy

Multisystemic Therapy

Attachment

Constructivism social construction theory evidence based practice practice based research

Transitions

Constructivism social construction theory evidence based practice practice based research

Culture

Constructivism social construction theory evidence based practice practice based research

Race

Constructivism social construction theory evidence based practice practice based research

Gender

FIGURE 2.1

Second-generation trends in family therapy

(power). Gender-related roles and rules are the most fundamental of these patterns. Goldner (1988) argued that gender should not be a special topic in family therapy, but is "at the center of family theory" (p. 17). Because *gender influences structure* in the family, it should be a fundamental element in family assessment.

Transitions

In 1980, Betty Carter and Monica McGoldrick publish the first edition of *The Family Life Cycle: A Framework for Family Therapy.* This book began a trend toward looking at the family as an evolving unit that progressed through many transitions, some as *normative stages* and others as *nonnormative, life-changing events.* These *nodal events* became focal points in family therapy as family therapists discovered that many presenting problems began during some nodal event in the family's history. Understanding the relationship between these events and the presenting problem gave new meaning to clients and family therapists alike. Carter and McGoldrick began their integration by building upon their own training in Bowen theory and adding a *multigenerational approach to family development.* As their work evolved, they added an emphasis upon aspects of culture and gender that interacted with stages of development in the family.

Culture

In 1982, McGoldrick, Pearce, and Giordano become the first family therapists to review ethnicity in a broad way. Their book *Ethnicity and Family Therapy* surveys diverse ethnic groups in terms of their history, values, and other distinguishing *cultural characteristics.* It explores the process of family therapy for each group, with particular attention to ways in which therapy could be respectful of *cultural norms and values.* Often a family's cultural heritage had been overlooked as an *important resource and strength* that may be at the center of the family's ability to overcome its current difficulties. *Social class and background* was also considered a critical factor in how therapists were drawing conclusions about the family. Spiegel in McGoldrick, Pearce, & Giordano (1982) summarized some typical therapeutic values:

> Middle-class therapists, no matter what their ethnic origins, have been socialized in terms of mainstream values. The therapist will be future oriented, expecting clients to be motivated and to keep appointments punctually. He or she will also expect families to be willing to work on therapeutic tasks (Doing), over reasonable periods of time (Future), with the prospect of change before them (Mastery-over-Nature). All this is to be done while taking a pragmatic view of moral issues (Neutral), and at the very least the therapist will expect to help clients to distance themselves from any overwhelming moral burden or intense feelings of shame. And clients will be expected to separate themselves from enmeshment in the family structure and to develop increased autonomy (Individual). (p. 46)

Culture-sensitive family therapy has continued as an important topic in family therapy theory and practice today. Charles Waldegrave (1990), a family therapist in New Zealand, has developed a therapy of social justice, or "Just Therapy" to *include the native culture* of Maori and other Pacific Island people into the therapeutic process. Harry Aponte (1994) has highlighted issues of *spirituality* for family therapists in working with low-income and disadvantaged families.

Race

In 1989, Nancy Boyd-Franklin published *Black Families in Therapy: A Multisystem Approach* that called attention to the differential *issues of race* for African American families. While many practitioners believe that culture and race are similar, Boyd-Franklin began a trend of family therapists speaking out about the important differences. Summarizing the fundamental premises of her book, she lists the first five as these:

1. There is a great deal of *cultural diversity among Black families* that is often overlooked or misunderstood.
2. Black Afro-American culture represents a *distinct ethnic and racial experience* that is unique for a number of reasons, including: history; the African legacy; the experience of slavery, racism, and discrimination; and the victim system.
3. The illusion of *color blindness* or the myth *needs to be challenged* are both misguided and counterproductive.
4. There are *many myths about Black families* in the social science literature that have painted a pejorative, deficit picture of Black family functioning.
5. There is a need to clarify and *understand the strengths of Black families*, which can serve as a foundation for therapeutic work. (p. 5) [emphasis added]

Adding to Boyd-Franklin's work, Hardy and Laszloffy (1995) punctuate the need for White therapists to learn that trust building with people of color comes from seeing and acknowledging that racial differences exist in a relationship, rather than trying to be color blind (minimizing differences). They believe that positive relationships develop from the common ground of acknowledging and discussing differences.

Attachment

Although John Bowlby's work in England influenced a number of British and American family therapists, his work was not widely embraced during the early years of family therapy practice. Perhaps because American society was caught up in social changes dominated by life-saving medical practices and time-saving technology, early family therapists were fascinated by problem development rather than human development. However, as divorce, trauma, and violence rates persist, an awareness of the complexity of human development has also steadily increased in the field. Thus, family therapists are revisiting early interpersonal theories of development and finding important keys to therapeutic turning points.

In 1998, Susan M. Johnson, a Canadian family therapist, published an article, "Listening to the Music: Emotion as a Natural Part of Systems Theory." This title would almost seem to state the obvious were it not for the fact that many early approaches to family therapy ignored emotion altogether (see Figure 1.1 for a reminder). As part of a growing awakening to the power of emotion (as opposed to thoughts or behavior) in relationships, Johnson's work brings together all the best that family therapy has to offer: sound interpersonal theory that explains complex problems, congruent interventions tied to theory, and research regarding therapeutic process and outcomes.

Johnson and her colleague, Les Greenberg, began watching videotapes of their work, analyzing therapeutic process at the times when clients seemed to have insights or breakthroughs that led to significant changes in their relationships. Their analysis led to research projects in which their techniques were compared with other models of couple therapy. These results led to the formal development of emotionally focused couples therapy (EFT), a manualized treatment program that applies Bowlby's (1969) theory of *attachment, separation,* and *loss* (Greenberg & Johnson, 1988). In this model, secure interpersonal attachments are considered a primary human motivation. These are addressed in EFT. The main tasks in EFT are *accessing emotional experience* and *changing interpersonal patterns.* This is accomplished through a series of steps in which (1) problematic cycles and related emotional states are identified, (2) the cycle is viewed as the enemy instead of either partner, (3) emotional experiences are explored in depth, and (4) new communication patterns are reinforced. The authors have paid special attention to repairing *attachment injuries,* those turning points in a relationship when a given partner has felt emotionally abandoned by the other (Johnson, Makinen, & Millikin, 2001). These turning points may be times of transition or crisis, when one partner had a particular need for support from the other and the other was unavailable. Miscarriages, illnesses, accidents, joblessness, and deaths are examples of times when some attachment injuries have occurred. We think this conceptualization is what makes EFT so successful in cases of trauma and couple distress. The important contribution of this work is the attention to emotional impasses and to the power of emotion in the process of attachment that directs the therapist in developing effective interventions.

These trends in thinking about human development have added depth and understanding to a field that was already rich in creativity and innovation. Accordingly, they have influenced family therapists to integrate these added dimensions into their work. The result has been a continual analysis of therapeutic process and a persistent willingness to ask ourselves some critical questions, namely, What do we know? How do we know what we think we know? As we will see in the following section, the maturing of the field has come from asking and answering these questions in a variety of ways. Through philosophical explorations into *epistemology* (the study of knowledge) and an increasing emphasis upon clinical research, family therapists continue to challenge traditional thinking about mental health treatment and expand their applications into non-mental health settings.

Post-Modern Models of Practice

During the 1970s, the heavy influence of the M.R.I. led to continued analysis of mental health practices, including those that were developing within the field. Under the broad umbrella of constructivism, family therapists began to question the limits of their early models and propose alternative views of the therapeutic process. *Constructivists* believe that *a given situation can be interpreted in many different ways.* For example, they would argue that traditional approaches to family therapy represent many different ways of viewing the same case (as in Chapter 1). The question of which view is most correct becomes irrelevant. Instead, they would ask which view is most helpful to the family. They would also suggest that the family's view of the problem may be the most important to consider since it may be restraining the family from discovering more effective solutions. They emphasize Bateson's idea that, if brought forth, information that provides a contrast to the family's dominant mode of thinking is information that moves the family toward the change process. Thus, as Goolishian and Anderson (1992) point out, individuals are thought of as a "storehouse of maps and lenses" (p. 11). Constructivists try to capitalize on this human capacity for change by shifting attention to alternative ways of thinking.

With increasing frequency, family therapists assumed that any problem could be seen through multiple lenses. Practitioners began to look not only at the *possibility* of alternative perspectives but at the *interactional process that leads to adopting new perspectives.* Looking beyond constructivism, *social constructionists* consider a person's view to be the product of conversations, dialogues, and interactions. What meaning a person makes of a situation comes through social process, not an isolated internal process (Goolishian & Anderson, 1992). This view of the therapeutic process places more emphasis upon developing *collaborative dialogues with and among* clients, rather than searching for a given reality that is assumed to be flawed. *Language*, from this perspective, is highlighted as a critical element in therapy because a choice of words has influence over what attitudes are formed. Thus, social constructionists often encourage the use of words based in human experience (i.e., stories, conversations, etc.) and in the language of the clients (i.e., metaphors from their relationships, work, neighborhood, hobbies, etc.) in order to downplay the influence of the therapist.

The evolution of early models from constructivism to social constructionism is associated with a trend in thought called *postmodernism.* Present in other disciplines and professions, postmodernism challenged traditional epistemologies about how family therapists should think about problems, people, and their role in the therapeutic process. Today, a number of social constructionists refer to the narrative trend as a way to describe their work (i.e., narrative family therapy). However, we believe there is confusion in this term, with no one "model" emerging with a specified set of principles and interventions. Instead, we have chosen to describe a sample of integrative models that use social constructionist ideas in creative and successful ways. We consider the work of the *Milan team* and those that practice *solution-focused work* to be examples of constructivist thinking. They see the role of therapist as one that *actively intervenes and strategizes to construct a new reality* with the family. The social constructionist work of Harlene Anderson adopts a more *reflective*, collaborative stance and even questions whether the therapist should be an agent of change or, instead, a promoter of dialogue. In our opinion, Michael White's work is a blend of both perspectives as he develops specific and *concrete interventions* through a *collaborative dialogue* that includes the *language of the family.*

The Milan Team

In 1967, Mara Selvini Palazzoli organizes the Milan Center for Family Studies. Selvini Palazzoli is joined by Luigi Boscolo, Giuliana Prata, and Gianfranco Cecchin. This group develops a systemic approach for treating the families of anorectic, encopretic, and emotionally disturbed children that was informed by work at M.R.I. They combine the directives of brief and strategic therapists with the reflection of Bateson's ideas on communication and knowledge systems. Their book *Paradox and Counterparadox* (Selvini Palazzoli, Boscolo, Cecchin, & Prata, 1978) provides a comprehensive description of their early therapy which ushers in an emphasis upon changing *meaning* and *beliefs,* not behaviors alone. Their work had a dramatic influence on the field.

In their early strategic work, the Milan team pursued research and practice in Haley's area of cross-generational coalitions. They developed the *invariant prescription,* which is a standard directive given to every family. The directive instructs the parents to continue coming to therapy secretly without their children knowing. Their early research suggested that when parents did this successfully, symptoms in the children remitted. However, if the secret was broken, symptoms would recur (Selvini Palazzoli, Cirillo, Selvini, & Sorrentino, 1989).

Through the systematic use of questions, they had a direct and indirect impact upon family dynamics. Termed *circular questions,* these explored family interactions, the history of the problem, and emotional issues still influencing the family. *Circular* was used as a synonym for *systemic,* assuming circular causality related to the problem. Circular questions start with *present concerns,* shift to an interest in the *relevant past,* and evolve toward *future transitions.* The questions are of four types: *problem definition, sequence of interaction, comparison/classification,* and *intervention* (see Table 2.1). The intent of such questions can range from the exploratory to the provocative. When the intent is *exploratory,* the Milan team emphasizes the usefulness of questions that draw comparisons, whether between people, between points in

TABLE 2.1	CIRCULAR QUESTIONS		
Present	**Past**	**Future**

Problem Definition

What is the problem in the family now? In addition, what other concerns does the family have now?	Has it always been this way? When have things been different? Why do you think things changed?	What will happen if things don't change?

Sequences

What happens when it (the presenting problem) happens? Who does what? What happens next? Who else has a reaction to the problem?	Who first noticed the problem? What was happening in the family at that time? How did you try to solve the problem?	What would happen if (a family member) did _____ instead of _____? What would each person do?

Comparisons

Who agrees and disagrees about the problem? Who is in the most pain in the family? Then who (rank order)?	Who else was different back then? Who was close to whom? Compared to (a family member), what do you remember back then?	If (the problem) improves, who will be the most/least relieved? How would each person adjust to the changes?

Intervention

From whom did your son learn to be so persistent and caring (positive connotation)? How would you like to teach your son about being independent? What do you think your parents need to learn to improve their relationship?	When did you first think that your father needed your support in dealing with your mother? What led you to conclude that he needed your help?	How will your parents get along without you? What would you need in order to adjust to the change of allowing your parents to settle their own disagreements?

time, or between definitions of the problem. This direction relates the problem to current interactions and significant events in the family history. When questions are provocative, they are used as an indirect intervention to make some implicit family dynamic explicit and verbalized.

Once patterns, comparisons, and relevant history are identified, the therapists look for opportunities to provide a *positive connotation* for problematic behaviors. This is a positive explanation of why a family member's behavior may be useful for self or others in the family. Going beyond the strategic idea of positive labeling, these clinicians used positive connotation to elucidate how and why family members may be covertly cooperating with the problem (Boscolo, Cecchin, Hoffman, & Penn, 1987). For example, if a son seems to be taking the side of one parent over another, the therapists may describe the child as "sympathetic and soft-hearted; one who is very sensitive to father's feelings." They may suggest that the son wants his father to be happy and can't stand to see him uncomfortable. At the same time, the father would be described as one who had taught his son about the virtue of loyalty, and they would suggest that perhaps the son should continue standing up for the father, in case the father would see him as disloyal if he did not.

Once positive connotations are identified, they are used as a rationale for the *paradoxical* argument to *go slow* for fear of the stress from too much change too quickly (i.e., we don't want father to feel abandoned by his son). In addition to this in-session intervention that targets changes in thinking, the Milan team might also create a *ritual* for the family (see Chapter 8 for a description) or prescribe other interactions that might help the family reorganize its behavior so as to accommodate developmental transitions. For example, in the same case of father and son, a ritual might be developed that helped the son to express his loyalty in other ways. Father and son might decide upon some activity that would become a substitute for the previous pattern.

The Milan team remains open to multiple interpretations of any problem. As the team members analyzed and changed their work, they decided to "approach the family in a far less arrogant, far more collaborative spirit" (Selvini Palazzoli et al., 1989, p. 250). Confrontation gave way to normalization in which they would empathize with family dilemmas and suggest that "it could have happened to anyone in the same circumstances, including me" (Selvini Palazzoli et al., 1989, p. 250). They considered indirect interventions to be the most appropriate for difficult cases because they are more respectful of the client's reality and minimize resistance to change. Paradoxes indirectly legitimize client ambivalence toward change and provide an atmosphere that is accepting and respectful of these client dilemmas. As a result of their influence, family therapists developed an increasing emphasis on the use of questions as a way to be "curious, yet hopeful" (Fleuridas, Nelson, & Rosenthal, 1986; Penn, 1982; Tomm, 1984).

Solution-Focused Therapy

Solution-focused therapy is often practiced in individual psychotherapy. However, many family therapists have integrated solution-focused strategies into their relational work. This branch of Milton Erickson's work describes therapy as changing "the viewing" or "the doing" related to a problem (O'Hanlon & Weiner-Davis, 1989). Following Erickson's early ideas that people have learned limitations that can be bypassed, these models recognize the therapist's role in assisting a family to identify its *resources,* to build on *what is working,* and to manage its problems. The therapist accomplishes this through the liberal use of questions as interventions. This is representative of a trend toward competency-based treatment, in which strengths and successes are systematically investigated and highlighted as a central element in the treatment process. Similar to structural family therapy and the Milan team, these investigations often take the form of tracking interactions between family members or significant others (Lankton, 1988; O'Hanlon, 1982).

In this model, therapists do not see problems as signs of failure, but rather as an inevitable part of family development. The relationship between the therapist and the family becomes less hierarchical and moves closer to a collaborative problem-solving relationship. In this model, a collaborative stance is thought to help clients adopt a more hopeful attitude about solving their problem. In fact, when a solution-focused therapist assesses clients' motivation, the clients are considered either *"visitors or customers"* (Berg & Gallagher, 1991). A visitor is often someone who does not see the presenting problem as a problem or who has become defensive when discussing the problem, particularly when there is a previous history with public agencies from whom he or she has felt criticism. A customer is a person who wants some change to occur and believes therapy may be a means to that end. However, this model also assumes that client motivation can be mobilized through client–therapist interaction and that visitors can become customers through careful interviewing (Lipchik, 1987). Consider the sequence and its analysis in Table 2.2. Because solution-focused therapists do not adopt a position of pathology, client perceptions about helping professionals often begin to change in solution-focused interactions. This does not mean that therapists normalize violent or abusive behavior. Rather, the practitioner *acknowledges the family's point of view* and addresses problem behavior within the context of the family's perceptions. The therapist wants to know what a child does when a parent behaves in a certain way and what happens to the child's behavior if the parent behaves in an unexpected way. Problem-free interaction sequences are elicited, and these exceptions become the basis for future solutions. Thereafter, assignments, tasks, or questions are designed to maintain and highlight positive changes that are already occurring.

TABLE 2.2	SAMPLE SOLUTION-FOCUSED SEQUENCE

Therapist Questions	Explanation
So, you'd like to get your probation officer off your back. Should I list that as one of your goals?	This type of interviewing includes accepting (not necessarily agreeing with) the clients' view of the problem and using their language.
What will convince your probation officer that you're really a changed person? What will you have to do to make that happen? What exactly will you have to do or say?	Once the family's goals are accepted and listed, each goal is recast in specific behavioral descriptions of what will be different. Clients begin to think in action-oriented terms. Thus, goals become action-oriented.
What is life like for you when the probation officer isn't on your back? What are you doing when that happens? How do you get that to happen?	As this hopeful and collaborative pattern continues, behavior change occurs from a discussion of behaviors related to exceptions, or times when the problem is not occurring. This highlights client strengths and downplays the authority of the therapist.
On a scale from 1 to 10, with 10 being the best, where would you say you are with respect to getting your probation officer off your back?	Scaling questions help the client focus on a situation as part of a continuum.
What do you have to do to move from a 3 to a 4?	Exploring the problem in terms of small steps of progress makes goals reachable.

We believe the popularity of solution-focused approaches has come from at least three directions. First, therapists recognize the benefits of a positive approach that breaks from the pathologizing traditions of mainstream mental health practice. Second, managed care companies find the notion attractive that common problems can be resolved in only a few sessions. Third, students have found the step-by-step instructions of solution-focused workshops to be easy to learn. However, as solution-focused work has become popular, there has been a trend toward expanding solution-focused practice to include attention to emotion (Kiser, Piercy, & Lipchik, 1993), not just behavior alone. In addition, beginning practitioners are cautioned to consider the client's world view, not just about the problem—but also about therapy. Specifically, in working with victims of trauma, a traditional solution-focused approach may be premature if they need an opportunity to review and retell their story of trauma as part of the healing process. It is best to explore directly with the client what pace and timing would be best for their situation. Are they ready to move from the time of trauma to a time of healing? Do they need more time in one stage over another? A helpful suggestion comes from Berg and Gallagher (1991): "Discover what matters to the client the most" (p. 97).

Harlene Anderson: Collaborative Language Systems

Frustrated by the concept of intervention taken from cybernetics, Harlene Anderson developed (with the late Harry Goolishian) an approach to therapy they call *collaborative language systems.* They see the early models of family therapy based upon constructivism as being too focused on the *doing* of therapy *to* a client rather than *being with* a client in a helpful way. They consider the emphasis on technique and outcome to hinder the caring quality of their relationship and hence to reduce the opportunities for change. These clinicians generally emphasize elements of social construction theory that would define therapy as a helpful conversation. Similar to solution-focused approaches, these approaches use language that will keep the therapist from the role of "expert." However, they place more emphasis upon learning with the client in a dialogue of understanding, rather than pursuing a certain outcome.

Anderson (1991) suggests that her approach is rooted in hermeneutics, the methodology of interpretation. On this basis, she distinguishes her approach from those called narrative (Anderson, 1999). Thus, it is thought that conversations can inspire multiple interpretations (constructivism). As these interpretations become a dialogue that is modeled and encouraged by the therapist, communication leads to shared or new understanding (social constructionism). The intent is to facilitate a process that leads to a sense of discovery for those included in the dialogue. A session related to family problems might be punctuated by the questions in Table 2.3.

As participants talk and share their perspectives, they change *with* each other through these thoughtful, questioning conversations. As they change with each other, the original problem "dis-solves" and the need for a facilitator of conversations disappears. The issue of who should be talking with whom would be addressed in a flexible and inclusive way, allowing the final direction to emerge from the participants who are present. Listening and mutual understanding would be given as much value as speaking. There would be care taken not to imply that anyone is the "cause" of the problem. Instead, all would be valued for the unique perspective they contribute.

Michael White: Narrative Family Therapy

As one who has continued the constructivist tradition in family therapy, Michael White has also integrated processes that illustrate social construction thinking. He evolved from structural–strategic approaches to a Batesonian emphasis upon the beliefs that may limit families from pursuing new solutions to their problems. He has been successful in integrating the search for competencies with an analysis of interactional cycles and assignments that instill hope in his clients. Although his therapeutic process is quite different from that of the Milan team, he is also successful at helping families find a face-saving way out of their present difficul-

| TABLE 2.3 | SAMPLE SEQUENCE COLLABORATIVE LANGUAGE SYSTEMS |

Therapist Questions	Explanation
Who are the people with whom you talk most about the problem? Who is the most concerned?	The consultant identifies the problem-defining system.
How many of these might come and participate in a discussion? The problem sounds serious enough that it might be helpful to have as many ideas as possible.	The consultant seeks to convene a meeting. If others are not available, their presence is invoked by asking one person to volunteer to listen to the discussion as if the person were one of the others in the system.
I'd like to start with each person listing what he or she considers to be the dilemmas or problems related to the situation.	In a meeting with the problem-defining system, the therapist reflects each family member's comments. The therapist remains open to all perspectives so as to help the family members provide full meaning to their experience. Therapeutic opinions or ideas are offered tentatively and respectively.
I see that some of you think ____ is one of the main issues. I'm curious about your ideas regarding a perfect solution. If it was possible, what might it be?	The therapist may collaborate with the family to generate solutions if the family wishes. Through modeling and "modesty," Anderson (1991) would seek to create an environment where family members can talk with each other in a sustained way.
In addition to these ideas, what might be some other possible solutions?	The conversational process would also include speculation and curiosity about any given train of thought, seeking others' opinions and expanding the number of possible views about any one idea.

ties. In an early article (White, 1983), he indicates how important it is to minimize those interactions in which family members might become defensive. Thus, he accepts multiple views of the problem (constructivism) and sees his role as one who is responsible for leading the family into hopeful and life-changing conversations about their lives (social construction).

In describing their work, Epston and White (1992) emphasize that they do not want to name their work or have it thought of as a school of family therapy. Instead, they expect to explore and change their work on a regular basis—hence, what they might write one year could drastically change the next. This is in keeping with the value they place on a "spirit of adventure" (p. 89) and how that spirit keeps their work vibrant and rewarding. However, White was the first to introduce narrative ideas to the field of family therapy and has continued as a leader in the narrative trend in family therapy. We applaud his spirit of adventure and believe that this spirit is what keeps the profession of marriage and family therapy stimulating and creative. We encourage beginning practitioners to adopt this same spirit to keep their work inspiring and successful.

White most commonly addresses themes of oppression and liberation. This distinguishes his approach from other models covered in this chapter. In working with families, he assumes that the dominant view held by much of the mental health system has led to the depersonalization of his clients. He also assumes that the family is feeling oppressed by the influence of their problems. By using social justice theory regarding oppression and liberation, White helps families to notice their own expert knowledge, that is, to notice those times when the problem did not interfere with their lives. He uses a process described by Bateson (1972) that looks for small exceptions to their negative experiences. This increased awareness of successes is thought to help the family develop a new life story of victory, competence, and leadership.

Although his focus upon exceptions sounds similar to solution-focused therapy, White emphasizes the importance of oppression and characterizes the problem as some influence outside the family. Similar to EFT, a cycle or pattern is often labeled as the culprit. This might be "a truant lifestyle" or "a tradition of bickering," or it might be a make-believe character that children can understand, such as a monster or a tiger. This process, called *externalization,* is one of White's distinctive contributions to family therapy.

A session with Michael White consists of a progression through various sets of questions (see Table 2.4). White adapts easily to the family's subculture. He would carefully note in writing their words and their language, incorporating them into his analysis and into their story of liberation. As therapy proceeds, they would be invited to think about their lives and problems as an old story that they are rewriting together. He is the audience, director, and editor of the emerging work of art. Family members are the authors and principal characters in the production. His use of literary metaphors (i.e., a good story has a plot, characters, drama, intrigue, etc.) reframes family problems by placing the problem in an alternative knowledge base (Epston & White, 1992). His use of rituals, games, and assignments has led to such creative therapeutic goals as "monster taming" (childhood fears), "beating sneaky poo" (encopresis), and "going from vicious to virtuous cycles" (marital conflict). He prefers thinking of solutions in these terms rather than adopting the dominant language of traditional mental health practice. The goal is to liberate the family from the oppression of the problem and from that of larger systems that stereotype and label them.

White uses sessions as a time for the family to report on their successes, similar to solution-focused models. When difficulties occur, they would be compared to situations that were even worse, in order to help the family members maintain their sense of momentum. For example, if family members remain persistently discouraged about their lack of progress, a sequence might be similar to that in Table 2.5.

TABLE 2.4	SAMPLE NARRATIVE SEQUENCE

Therapist Questions	Explanation
How does the problem influence or defeat the family?	Similar to structural, strategic, and Milan, White carefully tracks interactional sequences and learns how each person reacts and behaves related to the problem. Attention is on specific behaviors. What do the family members do? The family therapist must be able to visualize how people act and what people say when they are overcome by the problem and when they are overcoming the problem.
What are the times when things go well, when you are challenging the problem? Is it possible that coming here today is a challenge to the problem?	White would spend much time elaborating upon these few experiences as examples of the family's expert knowledge of how they have influenced and controlled the problem. If someone fails to recognize exceptions, White would use his own observations to begin creating a picture of competence and cooperation.
Would you prefer to be someone who is being held hostage by a truant lifestyle or someone who has battled the influences of a truant lifestyle and won?	White provides a benevolent confrontation with present destructive cycles while pointing toward a hopeful future.

White's approach is known for the way it addresses societal oppression, empowers discouraged families, and diminishes isolation with the use of their language, values, experience, and natural support system. He provides a counterpoint to existing cultural practices that label and categorize those who need help. Although a social constructionist, he is very active in sessions and leads through his suggestive and interventive questions. His artistry lies in his balance between leading and following what a family brings to the experience.

The Milan team, solution-focused approaches, Harlene Anderson, and Michael White are some examples of how postmodern thinking influenced the philosophy and practice of family therapy. At the same time, other family therapists were asking similar questions (What do we know? How do we know what we think we know?), but answering them from explorations in empirical research rather than from explorations in philosophy. This development, known as *evidence-based practice,* has influenced a number of integrative models that use foundational family therapy practices with pragmatic enhancements that have led to successes in settings outside of mental health such as schools, health care facilities, and social service agencies.

TABLE 2.5	NARRATIVE FOCUS UPON STRENGTHS	

Therapist Questions	Explanation
How did you manage to lecture him for only 10 minutes instead of the usual 45 minutes, like in the old days?	Questions focus on how they were able to stop the old pattern so quickly and what they thought made the difference.
Even though you're feeling discouraged, I'm curious about how you were able to develop such insight about the old patterns.	Noticing that "the glass is half full" punctuates even the smallest bit of progress.
How did you decide to face this situation so directly?	Exploring and extending the progress.
What difference do you think it will make in your future if you are able to continue this type of awareness?	Highlighting the influence that small steps can have over time by exploring clients' beliefs about their own progress.
What would it say about you as parents if you are able to continue exercising this type of awareness?	Anchoring the new story in the future and in a person's own thoughts and language about self and others.
Who would most appreciate this story of progress and liberation?	After the family feels a sense of progress, a celebration, ritual, or meeting is planned to anchor the new story within the social network of the family by inviting others to witness and become part of the new story.

EVIDENCE-BASED PRACTICE

Evidence-based practice is a trend that began with evidence-based medicine (EBM) during the 1990s and influenced many health and mental health professions. It developed from studying the practice patterns of physicians and how they made their decisions in patient care. Studies showed that many difficult decisions were made based on the advice of colleagues or from outdated textbooks because the information explosion during the twentieth century made research reports in scientific journals difficult to organize. The aim of EBM is to help doctors access research reports electronically so they can integrate *clinical judgment, patient values,* and *research evidence* into *sound decision making.* For example, if Mrs. Adams has asthma and has side effects from one medication, the clinician may turn to EBM databases to review various medications and their utility, given that she is elderly. Then, in consultation with the patient about her personal priorities (i.e., a choice between one side effect vs. another), a decision is made. Since then, other professions have adopted an interest in the principles of EBM and how they might improve their decision making.

In marriage and family therapy, the interest in EBM has grown out of an increasing interest in medical family therapy. As more family therapists work *with and for* physicians in health care settings, the need to speak "many languages" becomes evident. It may seem ironic, but we think it is predictable that family therapy would begin as a revolution against the medical establishment and come full circle with an interest in the latest medical innovations. From our knowledge of systems, healthy adaptations often begin as polarities (e.g., adolescent rebellion) and evolve into a respect for difference that values what each side has to offer the other (differentiation). In this circle, we bring our history of interactional paradigms and pragmatic successes; medicine brings its history of rigorous research and technological advances.

In 1995, the *Journal of Marital and Family Therapy* published a special issue as a monograph, *The Effectiveness of Marital and Family Therapy.* This was a comprehensive review of *outcome research* in the field. It reviewed decades of family therapy research for a variety of therapeutic problems, highlighting the most favorable results and calling for continued research to develop the knowledge base in our field. In 2002, a sequel was published that provides a progress report on successfully researched models of practice. In Chapter 9, we will review some of the findings from these research reports and demonstrate how they can be of use to the beginning clinician.

Evidence-based practice in family therapy most often comes from specific approaches that are developed for a given research project. Sometimes the approach is easy to implement by mainstream practitioners, and sometimes it remains a successful report with scientific merit but without a following to implement it in real-world settings. Still at other times, separate elements from a given approach are taken and applied to improve clinical outcomes. For example, the successful work of Anderson, Reiss, and Hogarty (1986) with schizophrenia predated the labeling of social constructionist approaches as such. However, their model adopted a collaborative, nonblaming, sympathetic approach with family members that helped them develop successful patterns of coping. As one of the many family *psychoeducational approaches* to the management of schizophrenia, this model, while rarely practiced in its entirety, influenced a host of family therapists toward a *collaborative, sympathetic stance* with those affected by mental illness. Thus, research in family therapy has produced entire models of therapy where detailed instructions are given for replication and individual components of models that can be integrated informally into one's own work. Two examples highlighted here are cognitive–behavioral family therapy and multisystemic therapy.

Cognitive–Behavioral Family Therapy

In the second generation of practice, family therapists built upon Gerald Patterson's (1971) early work and applied behavioral principles to couples therapy, delinquency, schizophrenia, and bipolar disorder (Barton & Alexander, 1981; Falloon, 1991; Jacobson, 1991; Miklowitz & Goldstein, 1997). In this section, we will focus primarily on the evolutionary trends within these approaches that expanded traditional behavioral family therapy into *cognitive–behavioral family therapy,* or CBFT (Weiss, 1984). This integration exemplifies a number of approaches to family therapy during the 1990s that are research-based and problem-focused and that address multiple levels of the change process.

To cognitive–behavioral therapists, a person's internal process affects behavior (e.g., unspoken self-talk influences what one does). Unrealistic expectations of another (spouse, child) often produces undesirable behavior (e.g., anger, criticism). These behaviors may be viewed as a response to the expectations and not necessarily to the behavior of others. In such cases, the spouse or parent may need to develop more realistic expectations to adjust to the situation. Cognitive–behavioral therapists often use self-report inventories to assess the effects of these cognitions on a couple's relationship. For example, one spouse may think the other is trying to control him or her, and this may lead to arguments over who controls the finances or who should clean the house. Thus, it may not be the area of disagreement (finances, cleaning the house) that is the problem, but, rather, the underlying thought (the intent to control) may be the major issue. CBFT has demonstrated its effectiveness in improving couple relationships. Baucom, Sayers, and Sher (1990) found cognitive restructuring produces meaningful changes in the way that couples view their relationship and improves marital adjustment. It appears that when spouses alter their cognitions as well as their behavior, positive change in the relationship is more likely.

In 1996, behavioral family therapists Neil Jacobson and Andrew Christensen published their book, *Integrative Couple Therapy,* in which they integrate cognitive dimensions (e.g., thoughts, expectation, images, etc.) that influence behavior. They expanded their model after examining their research and finding that only 50 percent of couples were improving from traditional behavioral couples therapy. Of particular interest was how thoughts and attitudes serve to both trigger and maintain behavior. As a model for close relationships (e.g., heterosexual, gay and lesbian, married or common law), it addresses the issue of *acceptance* in working with couples. This model of family therapy attempts to balance traditional behavioral methods for change with an equivalent emphasis on the acceptance of elements that cannot be changed (e.g., developmental histories, traditions, values). A sequence using this model might follow these steps:

1. Define the primary conflict: Look for themes such as closeness/distance, responsibility, etc.
2. Describe the negative interaction pattern: Obtain a clear picture of behavioral sequences.

3. Decrease blaming and increase vulnerability: Teach communication skills that use "I" statements to communicate fears, inadequacies, uncertainties (i.e., "I'm afraid she'll leave me").
4. Address other beliefs about significant others: Explore beliefs about why certain situations occur in the family, how family life should be, and what is needed to improve relationships.
5. Teach support and empathy for each partner: Assign reading and provide practice time in sessions.
6. Use behavioral contracting: Assign partners to make a list of what the other can do to please them. Ask each partner to choose items from the list to begin positive cycles. Assess the couple's ability to solve problems and spend time in pleasurable activities.

CBFT shares commonalities with the Milan, structural, and strategic approaches. First, these approaches share a functional view of problem behaviors and interactional sequences. This means problems are seen as serving some function within the family and as being maintained by family members' behavior. Next, CBFT focuses on the present interaction of family members rather than on past history. It also employs cognitive restructuring (reframing) and assigns tasks to facilitate behavior change at home. Finally, in increasing vulnerability, Jacobson and Christensen's model includes elements similar to Susan Johnson's emotionally focused couples therapy and Virginia Satir's approach to intimacy, self-acceptance, and communication.

Multisystemic Therapy

During the 1980s, various approaches emerged that deliberately included therapist interventions aimed at family–school, family–church, family–peer group, and family–agency relationships. Boyd-Franklin (1989) found that successful therapy for an African American family would often involve a "multisystem" approach. Her approach has expanded to address the role of the family therapist in nontraditional therapeutic settings such as schools, medical facilities, and churches (Boyd-Franklin & Bry, 2000). As part of this trend, Henggeler, Schoenwald, Borduin, Rowland & Cunningham (1998), through extensive research projects with juvenile crime and substance abuse, developed a multisystemic (MST) approach to child and adolescent problems. The model was derived from social–ecological, structural, strategic, and cognitive–behavioral theories (Bronfenbrenner, 1979; Haley, 1976; Kendall & Braswell, 1993, Minuchin, 1974). This home-based approach positions the therapist to significantly reduce crime and substance abuse.

The outcome results of MST have been impressive. In a review of multiple studies, it was found that 70–98 percent of inner-city families were successfully engaged and completed the desired 4-month treatment protocol (Cunningham & Henggeler, 1999). Success was the same for Caucasian and families of color. The authors suggest that their success comes from paying

TABLE 2.6

MST Principles	Elaboration
1. The primary purpose of assessment is to understand the fit between the identified problems and their broader systemic context.	How does the problem make sense? What interactions between the child, family, peers, school, and neighborhood will explain the problem in a nonblaming way?
2. Therapeutic contacts emphasize the positive and use systemic strengths as levers for change.	Home-based contacts build trust, credibility, and a positive relationship upon which to develop goals and assignments.
3. Interventions are designed to promote responsible behavior and decrease irresponsible behavior among family members.	Therapists work positively and strategically to help parents increase or change parental supervision and to develop consequences for positive and negative behaviors of the youth.
4. Interventions are present-focused and action-oriented, targeting specific and well-defined problems.	Overarching goals are the family's long-term hopes for the child. Intermediate goals are day-to-day progress described in behavioral terms.
5. Interventions target sequences of behavior within and between multiple systems that maintain identified problems.	Interactional sequences within and between multiple systems are addressed in a hands-on way by the therapist's intensive involvement.
6. Interventions are developmentally appropriate and fit the developmental needs of the youth.	The needs of parents and children alike are considerations for tailoring tasks and goals that are realistic for each family's situation.
7. Interventions are designed to require daily or weekly effort by family members.	Intermediate goals are broken down into small, immediate tasks such as assigning chores, giving rewards, or having a meeting about consequences for incomplete chores.
8. Intervention effectiveness is evaluated continuously from multiple perspectives, with providers assuming accountability for overcoming barriers to successful outcomes.	Given the focus of interventions, their effectiveness can be assessed in a few weeks. The therapist monitors this standard and uses immediate feedback to make midcourse corrections.
9. Interventions are designed to promote treatment generalization and long-term maintenance of therapeutic change by empowering caregivers to address family members' needs across multiple systemic contexts.	MST emphasizes the skill development needed for success in the family's social ecology. Skills include assessing future challenges and adapting to forthcoming developmental changes as youth and parents mature.

specific attention to the barriers of engagement and to implementing the nine principles of MST. When certain treatment principles are learned, therapists can be systematic and consistent while still tailoring treatment to the family's culture. Emerging from multiple projects with children and adolescents, the nine treatment principles of MST are shown in Table 2.6 with our elaborations.

The therapeutic process begins by linking the *goals* of the larger system with the individualized goals of the family or guardian system that is caring for the adolescent. For example, the court system has one goal (e.g., prevent reoccurrence of crime, increase school attendance, etc.), and the family generally has other goals (i.e., "get the system out of our life," "make him mind," "get money to turn on the phone," etc.). These divergent goals are brought under a general umbrella (e.g., help Jake succeed) that will enable each stakeholder to be part of the same plan. Then, intensive time is spent building *trust and credibility* with the family (Cunningham & Henggeler, 1999). Next, goals of the family are broken down into *behavioral* goals that are related to *strengths* of the family. Therapists are trained to be goal- and action-oriented. In addition, weekly supervision by the therapist is aimed at individualizing the process for each family using the concept of "fit" (Schoenwald, Henggeler, Brondino, & Rowland, 2000).

MST is an excellent example of integration, as it uses structural–strategic family therapy, ecological social work, culturally sensitive practice, and systematic data gathering for practice improvement. It also has commonalities with the other models presented in this chapter, such as a focus upon behavioral sequences, concrete tasks, and respect for the uniqueness of each family. The emphasis upon strengths and the engagement process is compatible with Michael White's approach and with solution-focused notions of inviting the client to move from visitor to customer through careful interactions that respect the client's worldview. Although the model does not cite social constructionism as one of its influences, we think the nine principles of MST put into practice are excellent examples of this trend in family therapy.

SUMMARY

As the twentieth century ended, the field of marriage and family therapy changed over time in response to societal changes, creative practitioners, health care trends, and ongoing research. Trends in human development theories led to greater sensitivity to gender, culture, and race. Trends in philosophy were led by the influence of social constructionism. These developments led to less technical and more personable interactions in family therapy practice. They also led to an increase in research that produced evidence-based clinical models. Today, the pioneering models are rarely practiced in their original form. Instead, integrative models such as those highlighted in this chapter incorporated the best and most relevant aspects of those approaches and wove them into coherent frameworks. While each attempt at integration led to continued diversity in the field, we believe there are common themes in theory and practice that can guide the beginning practitioner. In Chapters 3 and 4, we will review these common themes. Then, we will help readers organize the treatment process to put these themes into practice.

INTEGRATION OF THEORY

Common Themes

As shown in Chapters 1 and 2, family therapy has many conceptual models that guide the practitioner, but this diversity can often be overwhelming for the beginner. The structural therapist might assess the boundaries, coalitions, and hierarchy of a family (Minuchin & Fishman, 1981). The intergenerational therapist might focus on family beliefs, conflicts, and losses transferred from one generation to another (Framo, 1981; Paul & Paul, 1975). The Milan team might search for different points of view related to a symptomatic impasse in family interactions (Selvini Palazzoli et al., 1978). While theoretical models offer practitioners a way to organize their thinking, trainees must often incorporate concepts and techniques from various schools. This can be confusing—different theoretical models use different terms to describe similar concepts. For example, Bowen's concept of differentiation is similar to Minuchin's concept of boundary. Likewise, certain techniques have proved useful in a number of schools of family therapy. For example, several approaches (structural, strategic, experiential, and contemporary) clarify communication, direct enactments, and describe the symptom (Nichols & Schwartz, 1991).

These overlapping concepts can be confusing, but the pursuit of conceptual purity has pitfalls of its own. We think the adoption of a rigid theoretical framework may limit a family therapist's effectiveness; there may be a tendency to distort observations so as to conform to theoretical precepts. For example, if practitioners are interested in assessing structural boundaries, they may only attend to specific interactions (e.g., when family members talk for each other). Practitioners who utilize this approach can easily organize their observations, but they may miss some important information merely because it does not fit within that framework (e.g., an important issue raised even though members are talking for each other). To use an old cliché, a person with a hammer starts to think everything is a nail.

In a review of family therapy approaches applied to later-life families, Hanna and Hargrave (1997) found most early models of family therapy to be lacking in their pure form:

> Structural Family Therapy tends to ignore longitudinal changes over time with a family, thus ignoring historical factors that play heavily into the development of legacies. Bowenian Family Therapy does not offer enough pragmatic thinking to intervene in crises brought on by chronic illness. Behavioral Family Therapy does not have a framework for addressing the phenomenology of losses experienced by elders. Experiential Family Therapy may be too direct for some families who prefer to cope with changing family roles in silent, persevering ways. (p. 27)

While this critique is given in light of the needs of later-life families, we have seen similar shortcomings appear with minority families, court-ordered cases, and families who are not "therapy-wise." Given that the early approaches came from clinicians socialized according to certain norms in the culture of psychotherapy, it is not difficult to understand how those first approaches became the foundation, but not the entire structure, of the family therapy movement.

The majority of practicing family therapists do not draw from a single theory or school of techniques (Quinn & Davidson, 1984). Even therapists who have been trained in a single theory eventually incorporate other theories and techniques (Todd & Selekman, 1991a). Therapists integrate their own blend of methodologies based on training, personality, and the population of families they are serving. Thus, we think of integrative practice as that which moves away from separate family therapy theories toward a systematic combination of models. Broderick and Schrader (1981) write:

> Although there are still strong networks of therapists loyal to one or another pioneer, particularly in the areas of family therapy and sex therapy, the enormous majority of marriage and family and sex therapists today are trained in secular settings. That is, in programs that impartially have them read a wide range of current textbooks rather than those representing only one view. Perhaps, the university or agency will invite Haley or Bowen or Satir or Stuart or Masters for a special workshop, and for a period of weeks everyone is a convert to that philosophy. These men and women are charismatic and articulate, but after a series of such appearances, learning from such specialized workshops tends to become integrated into the therapist's own views. (p. 34)

The integration spoken of here comes from reviewing the range of thinking available in the field and combining these perspectives into a useful method of practice. Each of the early approaches provides an assessment of family functioning in relationship to problems (theory). These models also make suggestions about what is considered appropriate therapeutic functioning (practice). In addition, later contributions to the field have added ideas about gender, race, and culture missing from earlier models. Thus, we begin this process of integration by identifying major themes that provide ways of thinking about relationships, interactions, and problems.

These themes can be organized along a continuum that proceeds from larger to smaller spheres of observation. These differences are sometimes referred to as macroviews versus microviews of family process. The macroview includes broad social factors that affect interpersonal process such as the influence of gender, race, and culture. As the view narrows slightly, intergenerational and extended family relationships become additional influences on the problem. In the immediate relationship, it is possible to look at relational transitions and structural interactions. Finally, individuals can be studied as systems in their own right—as a combination of thoughts, feelings, behaviors, and intentions, and in tandem with their psychodynamics, as a collection of biological subsystems that operate at all times. Like a camera with a zoom lens, the family therapist must maintain a flexible viewpoint to make an assessment from different angles and about multiple levels of process. Sometimes the problem must be viewed from a macrolevel of observation. At other times the microlevel reveals important information. In addition, the problem-solving system may comprise formal family relationships, friendships, or other important associates that may be resources in problem solving. The following discussion focuses on common conceptual themes and when it might be useful to explore them.

GENDER

At the most general level, all families are influenced by patterns of socialization that lead to rules and roles governing family process. Gender-related roles and rules are the most fundamental of these patterns. Goldner (1988) argued that gender is not a special topic in family therapy but is "at the center of family theory" (p. 17). Because gender influences structure in the family, it should be a fundamental element in family assessment.

In a pioneering article on the subject, Hare-Mustin (1978) offered suggestions for implementing gender-sensitive family therapy:

> My purpose in what follows is not to analyze family therapy techniques, per se, but rather to consider certain areas of intervention in which a feminist orientation is important. These areas are: the contract, shifting tasks in the family, communication, generational boundaries, relabeling deviance, modeling, ownership and privacy, and the therapeutic alliance with different family members. (p. 185)

To begin assessment, the following questions pose hypotheses that address each area:

Tasks. Could role inflexibility regarding tasks be related to the problem?

Communication. Are communication styles disempowering to the females in the family?

Boundaries. Have generational coalitions developed as a result of disempowerment in the marriage?

Relabeling. Can disempowering stereotypes ("nag," "passive–aggressive") be relabeled to account for the context of powerlessness?

Modeling. Can the female therapist model more egalitarian relationships with males in the family, and can male therapists affirm female strength within the family?

Privacy. What are family rules around females' personal development and autonomy outside the family?

Alliance. What will each family member need from the therapist in order to feel understood and accepted?

As family therapy proceeds from the initial interview to the assessment process, these questions can be considered by the therapist as the definition of the problem is explored in greater depth. Then, during the assessment process, it may be useful to explore the individual family members' point of view regarding gender development and the way they arrived at their current position. An initial set of questions posed to clients might be:

1. What are some of the differences between how you each grew up as a female or male in our society?
2. How does your family address the differences between females and males in our society?
3. Are there certain traditions in your family that are more closely related to either women or men?
4. How do you feel about these traditions and practices?
5. Are there any ways you think these ideas and traditions might be related to _____ (the presenting problem)?

Such a line of questioning acknowledges gender differences in a neutral, exploratory way. While the ultimate goal may be to correct gender imbalances, beginning with neutral questions allows families to describe themselves without feeling any pressure to change. As exploration continues, family therapists can decide which issues might be targeted for change later in the process.

Some clinicians provide suggestions for therapeutic dialogue that combines assessment and intervention. For example:

1. "What best explains your not wanting to tell me too much: that I am white, female or highly educated?" (Goldner, 1988, p. 29)

2. "Should you accommodate to prescriptions for men's greed and expediency or defy these prescriptions and insist that wisdom influences your decisions?" (White, 1986, p. 15)
3. "Would you prefer a life where you are a slave to tradition, or would you prefer a life where you are free to develop new views of people and relationships?" (White, 1990)

While these questions are generally employed after extensive groundwork to establish a relationship and develop empathy, they illustrate the creative use of questions that not only assess readiness for change but motivate families to consider change.

How to Focus on Gender

General questions about gender differences should be incorporated into all assessments. Each person's experience should be heard. In cases of marital conflict, gender differences are often the core issue and should be identified. For example, Jacobson, Holtzworth-Monroe, and Schmaling (1989) found that women often complain more than men about their current relationship. Indeed, women often desire greater involvement and closeness from their husbands, whereas husbands prefer to maintain the status quo and create greater autonomy and separateness for themselves. Moreover, women are more likely to seek therapy and push for an egalitarian relationship, whereas men are less likely to seek therapy and are inclined to maintain traditional gender roles.

When any family member exhibits extreme masculinity or femininity, this can become an opportunity to explore issues of gender socialization. Although therapists always have subjective views from their own socialization, it is possible to engage clients in discussions about their subjective gender experiences while acknowledging one's own biases. Such modeling on the part of the practitioner can provide a new environment from which a person may explore unacknowledged influences. In discussing gender issues with men who manifest extreme masculinity, Frank Pittman (1991) notes that a therapist must remember three things:

1. A hypermasculine display indicates the man is frightened of his own inadequacy. The show of hypermasculinity is an effort to scare off whoever is coming to measure his shortcomings.
2. Men who suffer from hypermasculinity cannot tolerate female anger; they will wet their pants and run away, or do something hypermasculine, as if they think every angry woman is their mother come back to take their puberty away.
3. Hypermasculinity is armor, just a protective coating, a shell—like mussels, or clams, or lobster, or shrimp. Just beneath the shell the meat may be sweet. It's there you'll find the beautiful, vulnerable boy. (p. 23)

Hypermasculinity often contributes to domestic violence and child abuse. In such cases, it is critical that both survivors' and perpetrators' beliefs and traditions about gender be explored in detail. Current trends in the treatment of abuse suggest a focus on both perceptual and behavioral change. Exploring beliefs and attitudes about gender differences is an important step toward identifying which beliefs and behaviors are ultimately targeted for change.

Implications for Treatment

The client's understanding of how gender relates to the presenting problem should dictate whether the therapist addresses gender directly or indirectly. When families are not ready to address gender differences directly, the practitioner should refrain from confrontation and address the issues in more indirect ways. For example, child and adolescent problems may be an opportunity to explore the impact of gender on developing children, thus introducing parents more indirectly to their own limitations.

Sheinberg and Penn (1991) list four categories of gender questions:

1. The first category examines the "norm" the man or woman aspires to and the relational consequences of changing it . . .
2. These questions can be followed by hypothetical questions: ideas about the relational consequences of changing these norms . . .
3. Questions that identify norms to which the couple's parents aspired: how those affected both the couple and their parents . . .
4. Once the family considers different possibilities of gender behaviors, future questions address the potential for establishing new norms as well as altering how the problem continues. (pp. 36–37)

Marital partners may be highly sensitive to discussions regarding gender if they feel criticized. For example, men may be sensitive to the label "chauvinistic" and women may be sensitive to the label "just a housewife" when a therapist begins to explore issues of sex-role stereotypes. Practitioners should maintain a curious but hopeful position as they explore and identify patterns of thought and behavior related to gender differences. A lack of readiness on the part of families to discuss gender directly suggests the need for a more thorough assessment of the family's experience before choosing an intervention strategy. Then, the therapist can develop indirect ways of addressing imbalances.

RACE AND CULTURE

While gender is undoubtedly the first element that distinguishes human beings from each other, race and culture must rank second. Although race is similar to gender in that both are biologically determined, it is considered with culture in this discussion because of its influence on social and family groups. However, it is important to note that race is not synonymous with culture. For example, many cultural groups experience a sense of difference from other groups but do not experience racial oppression.

Family therapists who have reviewed ethnicity in a broad way include Mc-Goldrick and Giordano (1996), who have surveyed diverse ethnic groups in terms of history, values, and other distinguishing cultural characteristics:

> Italians rely primarily on the family and turn to an outsider only as a last resort. Black Americans have long mistrusted the help they can receive from traditional institutions except the church. . . . Puerto Ricans and Chinese may somatize when under stress and seek medical rather than mental health services. . . . Likewise, Iranians may view medication and vitamins as a necessary part of treating symptoms. (p. 2)

In addition, these authors explored the process of family therapy for each group, with particular attention to ways in which therapy could be respectful of cultural norms and values. Often, a family's cultural heritage is overlooked as an important resource and strength that may be at the center of the family's ability to overcome its current difficulties.

Thus, ethnicity—a sense of shared identity that has developed over many generations—can be a critical variable in understanding client families and mobilizing their strengths. If clinicians are not aware of differing worldviews and values, they are apt to be critical rather than complimentary of differences exhibited by families out of the mainstream.

In addition to acknowledging differences between cultural groups, it is also important to avoid stereotyping. The practitioner's intent should be to strike a balance between understanding the common ground of general patterns and clarifying distinctions and variations within the larger group. Boyd-Franklin provides valuable help in this area with African American families. Noting that there are often negative stereotypes that generate a fear of Black men or that suggest most African Americans actually have issues of poverty, not issues of race, she encourages White therapists to engage in "soul searching" in order to avoid conveying an unconscious belief that thwarts authenticity with the client. To move beyond the common challenges White therapists face in working with African Americans, she suggests certain guidelines in learning about the uniqueness of the client. Table 3.1 shows her guidelines with our suggestions for how to implement them. When family therapists serve minority families, they can prepare by referring to Boyd-Franklin (1989), and McGoldrick and Giordano (1996) for helpful specifics related to many minority groups in the United States.

The questions in Box 3.1 may be used to develop an assessment process that accounts for the effects of culture. Whatever questions the practitioner chooses, it is important to acknowledge and respect cultural differences between the family and therapist. Then, families can be invited to teach therapists about the significant parts of their cultural identity. As clinicians pursue this type of assessment, their role is similar to the anthropologist who lives with the

TABLE 3.1	SUGGESTIONS FOR WHITE THERAPISTS

Guideline	Therapist Statement
Allow the family to express feelings of anger, rejection, mistrust, etc.	I've often found that families in your situation have some good reasons for feeling angry, upset, and frustrated. Does this fit your experience?
Raise the issue of race.	I don't always know the best way to bridge the gap between White and Black, but I'd like to know if you have any advice for me.
Invite the family to share their experience of being Black.	When I begin working with a family, I like to start by sharing about how I've dealt with issues of race. Then, I wonder if you could share some of your experiences.
Do not expect family members to "air their dirty laundry."	I'll let you be the judge of how much information is necessary to share. I'm comfortable working with what you think is most important.

people and understands them while being a participant in their culture. Such a role is in contrast to the physician or scientist who analyzes, categorizes, and treats people from a distance.

A critique of the social service system by Minuchin (1984) illustrates that cultural conflicts can often be central to the definition of a problem. In reviewing selected court cases from British social services, he describes the plight of Mrs. Obutu, a Ghanian mother rearing her family in London. After her daughter, Sylvia, was arrested for shoplifting, Mrs. Obutu was summoned to the police station and was observed beating her daughter with a stick. Court proceedings determined that Sylvia should not return to the family home. After the mother's poignant objections, Minuchin (1984) provides this commentary:

> The magistrates return, looking upset. Not because Mrs. Obutu roared in pain; in their many years on the bench, pain has become a frequent witness in the chamber and they have learned how to deal with it. . . . No, they are upset because their sympathies are with Mrs. Obutu. They understood, because all of them are parents, that Mrs. Obutu is a Ghanian mother trying her best with her English daughter. Cultural gaps are familiar to them. But they were caught in their own legal structure. Nobody protected Mrs.Obutu from giving evidence against herself. Nobody defended her because nobody represented Mrs. Obutu. And certainly it didn't occur to anybody to have Mrs. Obutu and Sylvia talk to each other in the court to put in evidence for the magistrates the conflicting sets of loyalties, affection, care, frustration, and rage that characterized their relationship. Just as in all families. (p. 130)

3.1   *Questions for the Assessment of Racial and Cultural Factors*

1. How does your racial/cultural/religious heritage make your family different from other families you know?
2. Compared to other families in your cultural group, how is your family different?
3. What are the values that your family identifies as being important parts of your heritage?
4. At this particular time in your (family's) development, are there issues related to your cultural heritage that are being questioned by anyone? What and by whom?
5. What is the hardest part about being a minority in this culture?
6. When you think of living in America versus the country of your heritage, what are the main differences?
7. What lesson have you learned about your people? About other peoples?
8. What have you learned about disloyalty?
9. What are people in your family really down on?
10. What might an outsider not understand about your racial/cultural/religious background?

How to Focus on Race and Culture

As the preceding example illustrates, cases that involve families of an immigrant or minority culture invariably have cultural issues to which the clinician should attend. With these families, the focus on culture is an important part of the joining process. As clinicians invite families to teach them about their culture, the opportunity to join emerges in a context that is familiar and comfortable for the family. In this way, the family becomes the expert and the therapist becomes the learner.

If the joining process does not evolve into a comfortable collaboration, family therapists are encouraged to invite a native consultant to the sessions. This individual can provide support for the family and clarify the cultural differences between therapist and family (Waldegrave, 1990). This consultant might be a bilingual extended family member, a professional from the native culture, or anyone else of the family's choice who could serve as a bridge between cultures. Such an effort on the part of the practitioner nonverbally communicates an acknowledgment of differences, a respect for his or her limitations, and a desire to tailor the therapeutic process to the family's unique circumstances.

With respect to families who appear mainstream, it is recommended that family therapists still ask one or two basic questions about culture, race, or religion because many subcultures in the Western Hemisphere are not set apart by physical or biological characteristics. For example, military families form a subculture in the United States characterized by certain patterns of mobility and a degree of patriotism not found in many nonmilitary families. In addition, certain religious groups have histories of persecution that may leave members with a heightened sense of alienation from the dominant culture. While on the surface such families might appear to be White, middle class, and Protestant, questions about the effects of military life or religion could alert the therapist to the family's uniqueness and relevant cultural differences.

Implications for Treatment

As mentioned earlier, therapist inquiry into culture facilitates the joining process. When specific personalities clash or the clinician is having difficulty, attention to culture can overcome difficulties that might arise at the microlevel of the therapeutic relationship. This is because an inquiry into the world of the family moves the therapist away from a hierarchical position (Do what I want you to do) and into a collaborative position (Teach me what is important for me to know about you). This exploration shifts practitioners into a macrolevel of experience, and the new information broadens their perspective about the interpersonal impasse.

Therapists such as White (1990) use gender and culture as concepts to define the problem so that the family can be helped to externalize blame and minimize shame while assuming more responsibility for solving the internal experience. These practitioners come to understand interpersonal dynamics through the lens of socialized cultural practices.

In addition, as therapists learn details of the client's culture, then rituals, tasks, directives, and their rationale can be couched in language and practices that are comforting and empowering. Very often, seemingly mainstream clients feel alienated from some part of their world because of the problem that brings them into therapy. This alienation may be addressed as a cultural problem to acknowledge the family's pain and isolation. As treatment proceeds, the family therapist can assist the family members in feeling more connected to their world by a process known as *normalizing* (helping them see their similarities with others). One way of accomplishing this task is to explore intergenerational patterns.

INTERGENERATIONAL RELATIONSHIPS

Not only is the family the usual vehicle for socialization within a given culture, but it also evolves more specific traditions, roles, rewards, and obligations that bind family members together. Each family's history shapes unique patterns of belief and interaction analogous to cultural practice. These patterns often take the form of nonverbal rules (what people should do) that shape attitudes, communication, and intimacy.

Many family therapists have recognized previous generations as a major influence on family life in the present. Bowen (1978) conceptualized multigenerational transmission as the process by which dysfunctional patterns of coping are passed from one generation to the next. Boszormenyi-Nagy and Spark (1973) focused on loyalties or transgenerational obligations, suggesting that these were represented by symptoms in various family members. Ferreira (1963) discussed the significance of family myths, those beliefs that go unchallenged within the family and enable members to maintain a certain image of themselves. Other family therapists applied object–relations theory to family life, theorizing that we unconsciously attempt to change intimate relationships on the basis of those in our past either by making them familiar or by making them fit our fantasies of idealized relationships that would compensate for past rejection or abandonment (Framo, 1976; Jacobson, 1984; Sager, 1981).

Trends in intergenerational family therapy include a wide range of issues. Williamson (1981) focuses on how an individual can develop a sense of personal authority within the family of origin. Kramer (1985) resolves generational conflicts through an emphasis on acceptance of differences rather than approval or agreement on the issues. Boszormenyi-Nagy and Spark (1973) assist family members to explore their invisible loyalty or debts and to find appropriate tasks by which to balance the ledger of indebtedness to the previous generation. Anderson and Bagarozzi (1989) explore family and personal myths on the grounds that they give meaning to the past, define the present, and provide direction for the future. These developments represent attempts at integration that work to resolve historical conflicts in multigenerational families.

In assessing intergenerational dynamics, the therapist might ask questions regarding past family issues, current extended family relationships, and future hopes and expectations for these relationships:

1. What stories from your own life would best describe your development in your family of origin?
2. What stories from your family's history still influence the thinking of family members?
3. Which family members have strong feelings about this situation?
4. Are there family members who have tried to help you with this situation?
5. Does this situation seem similar to any other situation that you recall in your family of origin?
6. Have other family members had experience in resolving a similar situation for themselves?

7. With which extended family members do you feel most comfortable? Least comfortable?
8. What are the emotional debts in the family?
9. What are the issues of loyalty?
10. What past experiences trigger current problems?

For interviewing couples, Wamboldt and Wolin (1989) developed a structured interview that incorporates questions such as:

1. How did you meet?
2. What is the state of your relationship now?
3. What are some of the important challenges that the two of you have made it through?
4. What are some of the most important similarities and differences between you and your family members?
5. What do you most want to conserve from your family background?
6. What do you most want to change from your family background?
7. Given the family you grew up in, is there a reason that your partner is a particularly good or meaningful choice? Is your partner ever too much that way? What is that like?
8. What do your parents think about your relationship? How do they react?
9. Is there anything I haven't asked that you think is important?

How to Focus on Intergenerational Relationships

Unattached adults who are not in significant relationships can benefit from intergenerational exploration because the intensity of family-of-origin relationships has not been diminished by relationships in a family of procreation. For clients whose goal in therapy is to understand some aspect of their lives, an intergenerational assessment often lays a foundation for later discussions of self-understanding. Additionally, adults who would normally seek individual counseling for the healing of traumatic childhood experiences can benefit from an intergenerational perspective, which encourages reflection on past experience as a springboard for future change.

Frequently, clients seek family counseling for a marital or child-rearing difficulty. In these cases, questions about present extended family relationships may alert the therapist to historical family issues that may be restraining the change process in some way. For example, the therapist might assume that the family member has an internalized critical voice that keeps saying, "I am incapable of changing this problem or my perception of the problem." In addition, problems related to aging and the elderly must often be put in the context of relationships that have evolved through the generations to assist adult children in making necessary transitions with their parents.

Implications for Treatment

Erickson and Rossi (1979) suggest that change can be brought about in individuals by facilitating "an inner resynthesis of past experience." Analogously, it is also possible for families to change their views and behavior toward each other by identifying restraining myths, exploring unconscious patterns of communication, and detaching from their current experience to develop a broader and more hopeful perspective with positive possibilities.

Durrant (1988) illustrates such a case in which intergenerational messages are identified for a female client and used as an externalized influence over which she was helped to triumph. Because the intergenerational process was used as the definition of the problem, blame was not personalized to any one person, but was assigned to tradition. In this way, motivation for change is facilitated, and clients do not need to feel disloyal to parents. Even in cases of painful abuse, an intergenerational perspective can often help families and individuals explore the historical issues without becoming weighed down with unproductive introspection. Because intergenerational therapy maintains a focus that is interpersonal, clients can be helped to focus on interactions rather than internal pain alone and to discover important insights while also claiming the necessary strength to heal. By addressing stories, myths, rules, and roles from their family of origin, clients can also gain a sense of moving through time, just as the generations of their family have evolved. This opportunity for a sense of temporal movement can be enhanced by reflecting on family transitions that may have influenced the development of intergenerational dynamics.

TRANSITIONS AND DEVELOPMENT

The critical timing of traditional *nodal events,* or transitional periods for each stage of life, was first undertaken by Evelyn Duvall (1977). She conceptualized the family as passing through eight stages, with developmental tasks for each stage. While there are many variations to Duvall's eight stages, all emphasize nodal events: entering and leaving the family, birth, parenthood, children leaving home, retirement, and death (Carter & McGoldrick, 1989b). Hiebert, Gillespie, and Stahmann (1993) have paid particular attention to stages of marital relationship and the interactional and psychological nuances that occur during each of the important nodal events.

Nodal events often require a reorganization of rules and roles for the family to remain functional. This reorganization can be thought of as a set of developmental tasks for each stage. Box 3.2 outlines assessment questions that can be used to understand family functioning at each stage of life. For some cases, questions from the current stage are all that is needed. For other cases, a complete review, with a sampling of questions from each stage, may be required to fully understand the family's experience.

3.2   *Questions for Developmental Interviews*

I.   Stage One: Forming Relationships
     When did you meet? What year?
     Who introduced you to each other?
     Who initiated further dates?
     Were you dating other people at the time?
     When did this relationship become exclusive?
     What did you like about each other?
     What did you discover? How were you different from each
     other?
     What didn't you like?
     How did your families react to each of you during dating?
     When did each of you say on the inside, "You're for me"?
     When did each of you say to one other, "You're for me"?
     When did you get engaged? How did that happen?
     Did the relationship change after the engagement?
     How did you determine the wedding date?
     How did you determine who was to attend the wedding?
     Were you sexually involved prior to marriage? Were you able to
     talk about sex?
     Did you have any serious disagreements before marriage? How
     did each of you know the other was angry?

II. Stage Two: Commitment
     How did the wedding go? What were your expectations?
     How did the honeymoon go? What were your expectations?
     When did the first difference of opinion come about?
     What kind of social life did the two of you have at the beginning
     of this relationship? Who initiated it?
     How were decisions arrived at in regard to what you would do?
     Who were your friends? His, hers, both?
     How did the two of you decide to handle your money? Who
     decided that?
     Did anybody have veto power?
     How much could each of you spend without asking the other?
     When did the two of you begin your sexual relationship? Did you
     discuss it before it happened?
     How did you each experience the first time?
     Who initiates it now?
     How did each side of the family feel about the marriage?

Questions for Developmental Interviews (continued)

What were early relationships like between each of your families?
How were disagreements handled between in-laws in the early years?
How did you each define happiness?

III. Stage Three: Parenting, Values, Goals
How did the two of you decide whether to have children?
Did you talk about contraception and family planning?
What were your different attitudes and ideas about it?
How did your husband react to the pregnancy?
How did your wife react to the pregnancy?
How did the pregnancy go? How was the delivery?
What kind of changes took place after the child was born?
Did you notice any differences developing between you after the birth of the child? How did you resolve these?
What attitudes from your families of origin have influenced your child-rearing relationships?
What percentage of your time is spent taking care of your marriage as opposed to taking care of your children?
Who do the children turn to for support? If they want something fixed? If they want to play?

IV. Stage Four: Adolescence
Who do the children think is stricter, more lenient, moodier, and so on?
How do Mom and Dad feel about school? Friends? Other issues?
What privileges do your teenagers have now that they did not have when they were younger?
How do you think your parents will handle it when your younger sister wants to date?
Will that be different from when you wanted to date?

V. Stage Five: Launching Children
How did your parents help you leave home?
What is the difference between how you left home and how your children are leaving home?
Will your parents get along better, worse, or the same with each other once you have left home?
Who, between your Mom and Dad, will miss the children the most?
Did you confide in one or more of the children if you were having difficulties with each other?

Questions for Developmental Interviews (continued)

What effect did the children's leaving home have on your marriage?

Have either of you thought about goals for yourselves after the children leave home?

What type of support do you need from each other to adjust to the children being away?

Are there any unresolved issues between you that can be traced back to an earlier stage of development?

Have you discussed this time as an opportunity to resolve those issues?

VI. Stage Six: Legacies

As you see your child moving on with a new marriage, what would you like your child to do differently than you did?

If your parents are still alive, are there any issues you would like to discuss with them?

When you look back over your life, what aspects have you enjoyed most? What has given you the most happiness?

About what aspects do you feel the most regret?

What was the one thing you wanted but did not get from the children?

Have there been any changes in the way you and your children relate since they have become adults?

How does your family deal with the effects of illness and advanced age?

How do you maintain a zest for life as you get older?

Have you discussed issues such as death, living wills, and life supports with your children and each other?

Do you have a plan for resolving conflicting feelings over any of the foregoing?

SOURCE: ADAPTED FROM HIEBERT, GILLESPIE, AND STAHMANN, 1993.

All couples have the task of solidifying their commitment and placing friends and family of origin second to their relationship. When this task is not negotiated successfully, in-law conflicts may be chronic. In the next stage, many families may renegotiate rules and relationships to allow for the entry of children. Parenting roles may be established, and the relationship with the extended family may be redefined to include parenting and grandparenting. For couples without children, this stage may involve the establishment of shared values, interests, or goals that provide a sense of unity and identity for both partners. If children were desired, this stage may also be a time to resolve grief in order to create alternative stages of growth and development.

The adolescent stage begins when the first child enters puberty. The primary task during this stage involves increased autonomy for adolescents in the household. Parents must continually alter their relationships and rules to allow the adolescent to move in and out of the family system. At the same time, the parents are facing midlife decisions and emotions. The ways in which critical tasks of communication and boundary negotiation have been resolved in previous stages affect the resolution of challenges in this stage.

To the degree that previous developmental tasks have been mastered, the family can move into the launching stage. At this stage, the parents and the adolescent are ideally in a position to attain greater independence from one another. Parents must develop adult relationships with their children and renegotiate their marital relationship without children. Stress occurs when parents are alone for the first time in many years and must renegotiate their time, new careers, and other issues.

If couples do not have children, stages four and five may still involve interpersonal tasks related to structure, discipline, dependency, and autonomy. However, these tasks may surface in a variety of situations such as work, friendships, and the development of personal identities and competence through family and community relationships.

The later-life family must deal with its declining health. Family members must reassess their life structures and explore new ways of living. At this stage, they may have to deal with the loss of a parent or spouse or the loss of vitality and with fears concerning senility and death—both their own and others'. These developments affect all members of the family.

The divorced or remarried family goes through additional stages of development. Box 3.3 contains interview questions for divorced and remarried families. Like other stages of family process, the stages of divorce and remarriage include developmental issues that can guide the clinician and family toward the most beneficial adjustment. It may be more difficult for divorced and remarried families to complete developmental tasks than it is for the original nuclear family. Remarried families may have role models for parenthood but lack such models for single parenthood or stepparenthood. While society focuses on the joys of family living through advertising and television, divorced and remarried families have difficulty adjusting to this pattern. Moreover, at the time of remarriage, spouses must deal with many of the issues unresolved in the previous marriage.

In addition to the traditional transitions and tasks that have been conceptualized for White middle-class families, each family and individual also has a particular developmental path that evolves from the different settings where development occurs (Falicov, 1988). Nodal events such as untimely deaths, chronic illnesses, or other unusual circumstances may affect the course of life and the completion of various stage-related tasks. In addition, many other types

3.3   *Interview Questions*

Questions for Divorced Family Development Interviews

Have you accepted your inability to continue this relationship?

How do you and your ex-spouse deal with the issue of custody? Visitation? Finances?

What do your parents think about the divorce?

What do you miss from your old family?

How are things different for you now?

What do you like about your new life? What don't you like about it?

Do you ever wish you were back together?

Have you developed any new relationships? Activities?

What kind of relationship do you have with your ex-spouse?

How did you tell your children about the divorce?

What have you learned about yourself in this process?

What kinds of problems are your children having?

How are you responding to those problems?

Questions for Remarried Family Development Interviews

When did your last marriage end?

Do you think you had enough time to finish your first marriage?

What kind of communication do you have with your ex-spouse?

How are each of your children getting along?

How do each of them feel about your marriage?

How often do they see their mother/father?

How do your children get along with your spouse?

What do you do to help them get along with your spouse?

Which of your children has had the most difficulty with the new marriage?

How do your children get along with their stepbrothers? Stepsisters?

Do your children accept your spouse?

How do you expect your spouse to relate to your children?

Who is mostly in charge of the children?

What kind of help do you get from your spouse for your parenting role?

Are each of you responsible for disciplining your own children?

of transitions may occur for unmarried adults, gay and lesbian couples, adoptive families, and family groups from nonmajority cultures.

The level of stress is much greater for families today than for those of past generations. The increasing divorce rate, the women's movement, and sexual and technological revolutions have had a profound impact on family development.

The vast amount of change produced by these events puts a great deal of stress on families today. Job loss or divorce often precipitates a crisis that sends the family to therapy. However, if therapy focuses only on the symptom or the interactional patterns at the time of crisis, the therapist may be missing information from a macroview that will help normalize the current difficulties, thus making them easier to overcome.

To trace a family's or individual's development over time, the family therapist must understand traditional and alternative patterns of evolution. Carter and McGoldrick (1989b) do this by enlarging upon Duvall's work and discussing stages of divorce adjustment and remarriage. Howard (1978) researched related and nonrelated family groups. In her work, she surveyed individuals from all walks of life about what makes a "good" family. The consensus was that high satisfaction was related to the following aspects of family life. In diverse and nonrelated family groups, these aspects can be considered as developmental tasks that lead to relational satisfaction over time. The respondents to Howard's survey suggested that satisfying family groups:

1. have a chief—someone around whom others cluster.
2. have a switchboard operator—someone who cannot help but keep track of others.
3. are hospitable.
4. deal squarely with directness.
5. prize their rituals.
6. are affectionate.
7. have a sense of place.
8. find a way to be involved with children.
9. honor their elders.

Landau-Stanton (1986) uses a practice known as *transitional mapping* to pinpoint the impact of social and cultural changes that may be transforming a family. Such issues as migration, changes due to illness or death, and shifts from rural to urban society have important effects on the family. They begin as an event, such as a geographic relocation, but evolve as a gradual process of adaptation and change. Families can track their process in retrospect and begin to capture the complexity that contributes to their dilemmas (see Chapter 7).

In mapping transitions, the practitioner becomes aware of sequences and processes that evolve. The result is a perspective that identifies family and individual problems according to their developmental place in time:

1. What stage of relationship are the family and individual members in now? What other major life transitions have they lived through? What is the next stage?
2. How did things come to be the way they are now?
3. Has the problem always been this way? When did it change?
4. When were things better than now? When were they worse?

5. Does the family view their current life situation as part of a temporary stage or part of a permanent problem?
6. Does the family therapist have a view of the problem that uses time as a dimension of hope or as an indictment of despair?
7. Does the use of parental control fit the developmental needs of the individual?
8. Does consideration of differences allow developmentally appropriate growth?
9. Are there signs that tasks of previous stages have not been successfully accomplished?
10. Is each person in the family attaining his or her needs in a fashion that helps the parents maintain control?

When to Focus on Transitions and Development

Many family therapy theorists focus on developmental issues in some way (Haley, 1980; Hoffman, 1983; Minuchin, 1974; Selvini Palazzoli et al., 1978). Most commonly, client populations with children, adolescents, and elders are best served by focusing on these issues because common life transitions can be easily implicated as part of the problem. In addition, individuals and nontraditional family groups can benefit from an assessment that helps them identify and label their unique developmental progression, giving them a sense of movement through time, which helps create a positive context for targeted changes.

Implications for Treatment

The advantage of a developmental perspective is that it offers the family therapist increased options for defining the problem. Rather than seeing a problem as a permanent condition, the therapist is able to view behavior and symptoms as a response to a unique transition in the person's life (Haley, 1980). If a couple's marital conflict became serious after the birth of their first child, that developmental stage can be explored for circumstances that might have prevented the couple from developing problem-solving strategies. These developmental circumstances (e.g., isolation, poverty, or in-law interference) can be labeled as the problem, and the couple can then be invited to join together to overcome this problem rather than blaming each other and remaining adversaries (White & Epston, 1991).

When a person or a family does not proceed through traditional stages, the problem brought into therapy can be thought of as an opportunity for clients to pioneer a new societal pattern or as an opportunity for the therapist and the clients to collect information from their unique experience to share with others. In a developmental interview, the family therapist might ask participants to talk about what they perceive as the major stages of their life thus far and, more specifically, to reflect on perceptions of self and others and also the challenges and abilities that characterized each stage. By focusing on developmental milestones in family and individual history, the family therapist can conduct an assessment that invites the process of change to begin with affirmations of strength and resilience.

As the therapist assesses the developmental process, information begins to emerge about the interactional process between family members—that is, the microprocess that accounts for small, specific behavioral sequences in families, such as who started the fight or who stole the last cookie from the jar.

Interactional process within the family is generally assessed as an indicator of family structure.

FAMILY STRUCTURE

The study of family structure is primarily concerned with interactions within the family that determine its organization. According to Minuchin, this organization must be modified to meet the developmental tasks for each stage of the family life cycle. He used the concepts of hierarchy, boundaries, subsystems, and coalitions in describing family structure. The family organism, like other social organizations, functions through an internal organization of subsystems (couple, parental, and sibling). When the functioning of subsystems breaks down, the family is unable to provide support and autonomy to meet the developmental needs of individual members.

In addition to Minuchin's pioneering concepts related to structure, other family therapists have refined these ideas. Breunlin, Schwartz, and Mac Kune-Karrer (1992) refer to family organization, with related concepts of leadership, balance, and harmony. Their work illustrates the trend we noted in Chapter 1, that of marital and family therapy moving toward concepts that are more human and less mechanistic. As this trend continues, it provides greater clarity for those who are learning to think systemically. Well-functioning systems have some form of leadership. Effective leaders use their influence judiciously in person-to-person interactions. As influence is exercised, members of the system have their needs addressed in tandem with the needs of the group. The intended outcome of these interactions is harmony. Questions to assess leadership, balance, and harmony include:

1. How much time do you spend with each other? Whom does each family member spend the most time with and what things do they do together?
2. How do you decide what gets accomplished within the family?
   What is the process of decision making, and who is involved?
3. Who is close to whom? Who are most alike and most dissimilar in the family?
4. How are the mother and father different from each other?
5. How is each sibling different from the others?

6. Who agrees and disagrees with stated views about the problem?
7. How do you decide the rules for your children?
8. Who seems to be most upset by this problem?
9. What are some things you have tried to do to solve this problem?
10. Which of these seem helpful to you? How are they helpful?

The therapist assesses family interaction by observing various kinds of behavior. Useful nonverbal clues include tone of voice, facial expression, or eye contact with other family members. It is important to take careful note of who speaks for whom and when. The therapist may also probe other family members to assess their view of the family problem. Using these data, the therapist formulates hypotheses about the family problem and the underlying organization of the system.

The Importance of Family Structure

It is a basic practice in family therapy to assess the pattern of leadership in each family and to develop a collaborative relationship with the family members who have the greatest ability to influence family life. Thus, a structural assessment is recommended for all cases because treatment is maximized when it is aligned with the family's primary leaders. In addition, information about balance in relationships is important to assess specific interactions in the family and determine who is actually involved in problematic sequences.

Implications for Treatment

While structural assessment is most closely associated with the clinical work of Minuchin, Haley's strategic therapy also makes use of structural concepts in defining child and adolescent problems. Structural–strategic forms of family therapy routinely emphasize the goal of strengthening the parental subsystem and addressing parent–child coalitions. These goals are often pursued by tracking interactional sequences in detail and intervening in these to change a targeted relationship. In addition, the Milan team and other practitioners have developed circular questions designed to elicit information about family structure and family politics: Who is close to whom? How did the family come to their conclusions about the problem? Whose opinion has the most influence? What purpose might the symptom be serving? What is the exact sequence of events when the problem is occurring? As these questions are answered, the therapist can describe the structure of the family and note, in particular, how family interactions are influenced by the personal dynamics of each family member.

INDIVIDUAL EXPERIENCE

Despite the tendency in the field of family therapy to de-emphasize the analysis of intrapsychic dimensions within the individual, many approaches provide very helpful information related to how a family therapist would address individual concerns. In fact, even approaches that may overtly discourage attention to psychodynamics eventually reveal that they have not totally thrown the baby out with the bathwater. For example, although Watzlawick has long been an advocate of analyzing failed solutions, rather than analyzing people (in the traditional psychoanalytic sense), he suggests that in finding solutions, "the tactic chosen has to be translated into the person's own 'language'; that is, it must be presented to him in a form which utilizes his own way of conceptualizing 'reality' " (Watzlawick, Weakland, & Fisch, 1974, p. 113).

Thus, without a framework facilitating empathy for each person's position, the family therapist is likely unable to successfully elicit trust and cooperation from the significant parties involved. The following review illustrates the variety of views related to understanding individuals from a systems perspective.

Attachment   With the growing interest in emotionally focused couples therapy, Bowlby's (1969) theories of attachment, separation, and loss have been revisited by an increasing number of family therapists. *Attachment* is considered an inborn process that promotes the survival of infants by prompting them to seek closeness and communication with caregivers. When attachment is secure, parental responses are emotionally sensitive to the child's nonverbal (and later, verbal) communications. To the extent that these interactions are soothing, the child develops a safe haven, referred to as a *secure base.* Adults continue attachment by seeking out connection with others during times of stress or anxiety. This tendency toward connection versus isolation is categorized as secure, avoidant, ambivalent, or disorganized attachment styles in children. These are related to various parenting styles. Siegel (1999) has described the type of questions that are used in the assessment of attachment. Examples of such questions are these:

1. What was the person's early relationship with parents like?
2. What was the experience of being separated, upset, threatened, or fearful?
3. What was the impact of any loss upon the person and family?
4. How did the person's relationship with parents change over time?
5. How have these factors shaped the person's adult development and parenting practices?

Self-Esteem and Self-Awareness   Experiential family therapy focuses primarily on individual growth. As an extension of this emphasis, experiential theorists have conceptualized self-esteem as the result of interpersonal processes. Virginia Satir (1972) was particularly interested in teaching others about the impact of family functioning on individual self-esteem. Satir was noted for therapeutic interventions in which she adopted a nurturing role with clients while coaching them toward more honest, open, and accepting communication with each other. In a statement that she called "My Declaration of Self-Esteem," Satir (1972) envisions the potential of every person to become an aware, self-responsible, growth-oriented person.

Satir also influenced other personal growth theorists who were interested in interactional models based on self-awareness and communication. One model of communication skills integrates the study of interpersonal interaction with humanistic psychology and family studies (Miller, Nunnally, Wackman, & Miller, 1988). Known as the couples communication program, this approach begins with five basic elements of self-awareness that can be taught to a student or family member to enhance the self-awareness and communication skills needed for personal satisfaction in relationships. These elements, as a set of interacting parts, are known as the *awareness wheel.* In family therapy, they can guide the practitioner toward an understanding of individual experience as it relates to significant relationships.

1. *Senses* Information from the five senses is the initial link between the individual and the outside world. Sensory information is present at the beginning of all human life and continues to the end as part of an interactional cycle.

    Sensory data are regarded as factual; carefully assessed, they yield a limited but verifiable truth. For example, if a wife hears her husband's voice raised, this is an objective fact distinguishable from her subjective response, which may be the thought, "He's angry." Only her husband can really verify what his emotion is at that moment, even though family members commonly consider their subjective information to be fact.

2. *Thoughts* This category includes interpretations, assumptions, opinions, beliefs, and the conclusions that an individual makes in response to sensory information. Often the result of history and experience, thoughts become a frame of reference that influences a person's actions, feelings, and intentions.

    In addition, assumptions are distinguished from objective facts in that they are constructed by the person in response to sensory data. If a wife says, "I think you're angry," the statement legitimately communicates a fact about what she is thinking and distinguishes her thought process from what her husband's emotion might really be. In addition, self-esteem in individual family members is often related to their beliefs or thoughts about themselves as well as what they perceive to be the beliefs of others about themselves.

3. *Feelings* This category encompasses the physiological and behavioral responses associated with feeling a certain emotion. Common feelings include sadness, anger, happiness, fear, shame, and hurt. However, there are hundreds of words in the English language that label an even wider range of emotional states. Self-awareness entails individuals' ability to label their emotions, whether pleasant or unpleasant, and to accept them as part of being human.

    Self-esteem involves an acceptance of emotions as important information about the self and an ability to act responsibly on those feelings. When individuals are not able to tolerate their fears or anxieties, they develop controlling or addictive behavior intended to numb unpleasant emotional states.

4. *Intentions* These are personal and general goals, hidden and open desires, short-term and long-term needs, motivations, dreams, and hopes. They can involve both the self and others and are related to an individual's thoughts and feelings as they evolve. Behavior is viewed as always having a purpose; thus, intentions provide a personal context for actions. For example, when family members wish to please others as much as possible, they may develop behavior patterns that consistently accommodate others and do not assert on behalf of self. In other cases, intentions may underlie symptomatic behavior that serves a function in the family, as in the case where a child's problem interrupts parental conflict. While the intention in young children may not be conscious, adolescent and adult family members are often able to identify their systemic intention when the therapist asks, "How might this problem actually be preventing something worse from happening in the family?"

5. *Actions* These are behaviors that can be communicated with verbs. We suggest that an individual can increase self-awareness by becoming aware of actions. Sitting, smiling, talking, shifting eye contact, listening, shouting, initiating, waiting, breathing, and walking are examples of actions that are related to the individual's feelings, intentions, thoughts, and senses. When the clinician begins to track interactional sequences, it is helpful to focus on actions because family members often move quickly to their subjective experience before weighing the facts related to another's actions:

> THERAPIST: Tell me exactly what happened.
> CLIENT: He was trying to get me to do his homework for him. [a statement of assumption—thoughts]
> THERAPIST: No, I mean what was he actually doing when you had that thought?
> CLIENT: Well, I guess he was sitting on the couch, watching TV.

[sensory data—"I saw him sitting"]

> THERAPIST: What else was he doing that made you think he was trying to get you to do his homework for him? [asking for more sensory data to inform assumptions]
> CLIENT: He doesn't have to do anything else! He knows that if he hasn't already started working on his homework before I get home, then I will do it when I come in! [statement of assumption—thoughts]
> THERAPIST: Now, how do you think he knows that?
> CLIENT: He knows because I've told him time and time again that I want his homework done before I get home so I won't have to worry about it. [action and feeling statement—I tell him because I will worry.]

THERAPIST: So, aside from what your son may think, you have a desire that you put into action when you walk through the door. Is that right?

CLIENT: Yes, I want to know if he's done his homework, and if he hasn't, I want him to get busy right then. [statement of intention]

THERAPIST: Is this pretty predictable behavior for you? I mean, does it happen nearly every night?

CLIENT: Well, lately, yes, because he's been getting so bad. [statement of perception—senses]

THERAPIST: Well, we might want to start by seeing if we can help you to become more "unpredictable" in your son's eyes! Sometimes, surprising behaviors help kids change their minds about things.

Taken together, the five elements of self-awareness represent the individual as a system of interrelated parts. These parts interact with each other to form an individual's contribution to a relationship, regardless of whether the relationship is with self or others. Interactional patterns consist of sequences that use all five elements:

Actions: Wife is fixing dinner in the kitchen.

Senses: She notices her husband coming up the driveway.

Thoughts: I wonder if he's still thinking about the argument we had this morning.

Intentions: I hope he isn't still mad at me.

Feelings: I'm afraid he won't be happy.

Actions: Husband comes in the door. He is frowning.

Feelings: He is tired and embarrassed about a traffic ticket just issued to him on the way home.

Intentions: He wants to save face; he wants his wife to think well of him.

Senses: Wife sees his frown.

Actions: She asks, "Are you still mad about this morning?"

Thoughts: He thinks, "She's criticizing me and belittling my feelings."

Actions: Husband says, "Why do you always think you can read my mind?"

By paying attention to all five dimensions of experience, the clinician is able to track a sequence while also understanding the individual's experience as it evolves in the interaction. Then, as the therapist helps the couple clarify and accept both their own and their partner's emotions, they are able to increase intimacy by understanding each other's intentions and emotions—especially their particular sensitivities. If each person had begun his or her part of the interaction with a statement of intent (e.g., "I want you to be happy" or "I want your approval") or with a statement of feelings (e.g., "I'm afraid" or "I'm embarrassed"), the interaction might have taken a different turn. When family members feel most vulnerable, their intent is to protect themselves from anticipated psychological or emotional hurt.

The five dimensions of the awareness wheel are also useful with social construction models that focus on communication and personal belief systems. These new theoretical frameworks have been greatly influenced by theorists such as Jean Piaget (1952), George Kelly (1963), and Kenneth Gergen (1985, 1994). They posit that personal belief systems (thoughts) are an evolving set of meanings that continue to emerge from interactions (actions) between people. However, unlike traditional psychologists, who view the individual as a reactive being, the social constructionist asserts that personal meaning (beliefs) derives from the individual's perception (feelings and intentions) of what occurs in interactions with others (Mahoney, 1991). For example, if a young unattached man characterizes himself as "weak" and "independent," this may be because he has neglected those aspects of his life that are incongruent with his self-image of helplessness. The individual may have ignored times when he was able to overcome his helplessness (exceptions). Likewise, through his interactions with the members of his family, he may allow them to describe him as helpless, which likely influences the way they interact with each other. In this case, personal narratives become an internalized set of conversations ("I must depend on others for help") that are consistent with our behavior (acting in ways that elicit help from others). Thus, for social constructionists, the meaning that family members attribute to an event determines their behavior.

Related to this view, the influence of Milton Erickson has brought a new understanding of the unconscious. For Erickson, the unconscious was an untapped reservoir of positive resources, not a complex stockpile of repressed anguish (Erickson & Rossi, 1979). As he put his own belief system into operation, he was able to help his patients begin to use their perceived deficits as strengths and assets. Some of his techniques relevant to the practice of family therapy are reviewed later in this book. Although the terms were not widely used in family therapy literature until the later 1980s, we think Erickson was a constructivist and a social constructionist. Evidence of his similarities with these orientations can be seen in the way he views the formation of individual or family problems:

> Patients have problems because of learned limitations. They are caught in mental sets, frames of reference, and belief systems that do not permit them to explore and utilize their own abilities to best advantage. Human beings are still in the process of learning to use their potentials. The therapeutic transaction ideally creates a new phenomenal world in which patients can explore their potentials, freed to some extent from their learned limitations. . . . As the therapist explores the patient's world and facilitates rapport, it is almost inevitable that new frames of reference and belief systems are created. This usually happens whenever people meet and interact closely. (Erickson & Rossi, 1979, p. 2)

Thus, Erickson considered the importance of the belief system of the patient and the meaning attributed to the ongoing flow of the person's life to be a critical factor in problem formation. He then paid particular attention to the dialogues he shared as a part of problem resolution.

An intergenerational approach that addresses personal beliefs in a slightly different way is the contextual family therapy of Ivan Boszormenyi-Nagy (Boszormenyi-Nagy & Krasner, 1986). In this approach, exploring a person's beliefs about the give-and-take in relationships helps the clinician understand how an individual experiences fairness and equity within the family. These family therapists suggest that human beings carry a subjective family ledger consisting of personal beliefs about how much they have contributed to family members and how much they are entitled to receive in return. According to Boszormenyi-Nagy and Krasner (1986), this concept of relational ethics is based on the premise that there is an innate sense of justice or fairness that exists within people. This approach suggests that dysfunction occurs within families when relational imbalances lead to a lack of trustworthiness or the development of "destructive entitlements" that involve individual symptoms (actions) developed in response to beliefs (thoughts) about unfairness within the family.

When to Focus on Individual Experience

Although many family therapy models address behavioral change before perceptual change, cases that do not respond to behavioral interventions most likely need a greater focus on personal dynamics that may be restraining behavioral change. Therefore, cases where behavioral interventions are not successful can benefit from a shift to an exploration of personal dynamics (self-esteem, self-awareness, personal beliefs, or feelings of entitlement). In addition, when the joining process seems stalemated or the practitioner begins to notice subtle power struggles with clients, it is very important to step back from the normal operating procedure and explore personal dynamics to understand and affirm clients' beliefs about their process and about the process between therapist and clients.

Too often, clinicians forget to focus on their own personal dynamics. How is their work related to their sense of self-esteem? Are they aware of their own hidden agendas that may be incongruent with what clients have stated as their priorities? Do clinicians have certain beliefs that may lead them to harbor critical or condescending views of their clients? Is their sense of entitlement such that they pursue unrealistic goals for their clients in family therapy? A focus on individual elements on both sides of the therapy experience often helps the clinician develop goals and expectations that match the developmental level of the family.

It is also appropriate to focus on individual dynamics when the client goal is more process-oriented than problem-oriented (e.g., "I need help getting over the death of my daughter"). When the client goal is related more to coping, growth, or adjustment to some transition, focusing on individual dynamics also fits better with client expectations of the therapy experience.

Implications for Treatment

While many models of family therapy have de-emphasized traditional Freudian views of individual psychodynamics, all models use some newer understanding of personal dynamics. Whether it is the structural therapist joining with the family, the strategic therapist looking for a directive that the client will accept, or the intergenerational therapist who seeks to help family members with unfinished business, the ability to understand personal dynamics is a clinical imperative in the practice of family therapy.

Falloon (1991) takes a strong position by suggesting that the individual goals of every family member should be targets for treatment:

> At times, these goals may be highly personal and inappropriate for intergenerational problem solving. For example, the resolution of sexual difficulties between parents, obsessive–compulsive rumination, or prophylactic drug therapy for schizophrenia. Such problems may be addressed in an individual or a marital context, where this seems most appropriate. (p. 79)

There seems to be increasing evidence that individually oriented strategies work best within a systemic framework. This is particularly so when the presenting problem involves major mental disorders, such as phobia, severe depression, or schizophrenia (Falloon, 1991).

Returning to the continuum of macroconcepts and microconcepts of family process, an emphasis on microdynamics facilitates therapeutic effectiveness as a complement to all other levels of assessment. By starting with a larger view of life and evolving to an exploration of personal dynamics, family therapists are able to fluctuate between macropositions that minimize personal shame and blame and micropositions that liberate clients to think of themselves and their relationships in new ways.

SUMMARY

Each conceptual theme presented here can be thought of as a different reality or lens from which to view families who seek treatment. Each lens has its own set of issues and questions that range from larger societal views of human problems to smaller dissections of personal and interpersonal process. The beginning family therapist can learn flexibility by using different lenses to view panoramas or get to the heart of the matter, depending on the clients' needs and the type of problem. Taken individually, each level provides a sense of direction that is informed by theories of family functioning and social process. Sluzki (1992), drawing from narrative ideas, makes these observations about how any given model becomes a catalyst for effective family therapy:

> In order for new stories . . . to consolidate themselves in the therapeutic conversation, they must evolve from and yet contain elements of the old, "familiar" sto-

ries. The transformed stories are usually a recombination of the components of the old story to which new elements—characters, plot, logic, moral order—have been introduced either by the therapist, by the patient, or by the family. . . . (p. 220)

The next chapter explores common themes of practice that have developed in the field. In contrast to theories about families, practice themes center on theories of change as they relate to therapeutic process and those factors related to positive therapeutic outcomes. We believe that family therapists often continue their tradition of innovation by adding other modes of thinking quite apart from family theories. With the same spirit of discovery that led us through innovation, integration, and consolidation, we will now look at common themes of practice that have led marriage and family therapists to the forefront of creative and inspiring successes in their work.

INTEGRATION OF PRACTICE

Common Themes

The Therapeutic Relationship
The Self of the Therapist
Summary

Historically, family therapists focused on the interactional context related to the problem. Practitioners who emphasized the role of the family considered the goal to be the treatment of mental illnesses such as schizophrenia. For those therapists, the goal of therapy was relationship change, and the treatment of choice was the involvement of family members with the symptomatic person. This placed the therapist in a traditional doctor–patient relationship but with a more active, directive role than typified traditional psychoanalysis, which encouraged the therapist to remain aloof and detached. As we have shown in Chapters 1 and 2, family therapists continued to change the way in which they thought about the therapeutic relationship. Increasingly, they considered each encounter as an opportunity to develop egalitarian, collaborative working relationships in which the parties brought their individual expertise to bear upon the task at hand—that of solving problems. From this perspective, families are considered experts on their experience, with special understanding about the complexity that comes from life's dilemmas. They teach practitioners about their culture and worldview. They know best what fits for them. Therapists are considered experts on the process of change and the type of process that might fit the family, given its unique circumstances. Together, they evolve a relationship, each dependent upon the contribution of the other for desired outcomes to occur.

Thus, the practice of family therapy has evolved from doctor–patient, to therapist–client, and now consultant–consultee. Early and integrative models of family therapy have a collection of elements that teach therapists to develop a *positive and productive relationship* with all clients, no matter how challenging they may be. Research has also continuously shown that the therapeutic relationship is one of the most critical factors in the effectiveness of outpatient psychotherapy (Hubble, Duncan, & Miller, 1999; Pinsof & Catherall, 1986). As a key factor that is given priority in all models of family therapy, the beginning practitioner must consider the development of this relationship as a top priority. In order to develop an authentic therapeutic relationship, practitioners must pay attention to their beliefs, values, worldviews, and coping styles. These personal attributes are often referred to as the *self of the therapist*. When these clash with any client, the chances of being helpful are limited. In this chapter we will review how marriage and family therapists have influenced the nature of the therapeutic relationship and the development of the self of the therapist. These elements form a bridge between the personal and professional sides of our practice.

THE THERAPEUTIC RELATIONSHIP

In an interesting study conducted at an agency emphasizing solution-focused brief therapy, researchers found that the espoused model had little to do with clients' reported experience (Metcalf, Thomas, Duncan, Miller, & Hubble, 1996). Miller, Duncan, and Hubble (1997) describe their final results:

> . . . while therapists tended to attribute therapeutic success to the use of solution-focused techniques (e.g., specialized interviewing techniques, miracle quesions), the clients consistently reported a strong therapeutic relationship as *the* critical factor in treatment outcome (e.g., therapist acceptance, non-possessive warmth, positive regard, affirmation, and self-disclosure). (p. 85)

Thus, we think the therapeutic relationship should be emphasized as a critical factor that organizes integration. As beginning family therapists analyze their process with clients, they should continually ask, How will my position contribute to a positive relationship *from the client's point of view?* We think all models of family therapy address the therapeutic bond with some universal methods. These are (1) joining, (2) highlighting family strengths, (3) instilling hope, and (4) reframing resistance.

Joining

First used by Minuchin (1974) as he developed structural family therapy, *joining* is probably the most universal—or the most borrowed—of family therapy terms. Not surprisingly, the personal rapport or empathy that therapists develop with those they are trying to help remains the single most proven variable determining the effectiveness of psychotherapy (Garfield & Bergin, 1978). However, when a family therapist begins to grapple with this process within a larger systemic framework, the number of people involved may make this a significant challenge.

Minuchin and Fishman (1981) view joining as an attitude:

> Joining a family is more an attitude than a technique, and it is the umbrella under which all therapeutic transactions occur. Joining is letting the family know that the therapist understands them and is working with and for them. Only under this protection can the family have the security to explore alternatives, try the unusual, and change. Joining is the glue that holds the therapeutic system together. (pp. 31–32)

This process begins with the first family contact and continues as the foundation for effective family therapy. Rather than an event, it is more a process of understanding and building rapport with each member of the family. While some family members may be more central than others, an understanding of all members is often necessary if family therapists are to be successful. General psychotherapy models share the goals of empathy and positive regard for clients; however, family therapy integrates these goals with systemic thinking. The result is a type of *systemic empathy,* in which the clinician is able to identify and describe the unique roles and dilemmas experienced by each family member.

Thus, the joining process can best be conceptualized as an interactional pattern that is repetitive throughout the entire course of family therapy. When a family therapist first becomes acquainted with the family, a certain formal stage may exist, but ongoing sequences of therapy require an understanding that is continually expanded as new information challenges the original perceptions of therapist and client alike. Therefore, it is helpful to think of joining as *a characteristic that pervades all other stages of the therapy process.* At any time, the therapist is either well joined or poorly joined. The following exemplifies how different elements of family therapy process contribute to the family therapist's ability to join with family members.

1. *Questions regarding the importance of ethnicity* help family therapists join when they respond with an appreciation of the family's language, customs, heritage, or beliefs.
2. *Transitional mapping* helps a family therapist join through identification of a family member's age, empathy with the family's stage of life, or understanding of the dilemmas the family faced with various transitions.
3. *Genograms* help a family therapist join through a recognition of significant family members who may not be present in the session. Their nicknames, circumstances, and impact on present family members may lead the family therapist into the client's private world.
4. *Structural and strategic approaches* help a family therapist join through assessing the family's hierarchy and making sure that those in authority are sufficiently engaged.
5. *Contextual family therapy* encourages multidirected partiality, which is the art of consecutively siding with and showing an understanding of each member's position in order to develop trust and fairness in relationships (Bernal & Flores-Ortiz, 1991).

6. *Ericksonian and constructivist approaches* are often noted for encouraging humor, playfulness, and creativity. Also, they view resistance in a positive light—as a helpful message about the client's uniqueness.

While these are not exhaustive, they are meant to stimulate the reader's creativity to find spontaneous and endearing ways of relating to family members that will contribute to trust and rapport. Many family therapists find it useful to join through the use of metaphoric comparisons from the client's world. Metaphors can tap into the client's worldview by using the client's language related to her or his interests. For example, a therapist who routinely obtains a genogram and a relationship history provides a rationale to each client for the necessity of such information gathering. A young couple who likes to go boating was provided this rationale for an assessment:

In order for me to help you, it is important for me to get to know you and understand something about the important people and events in your life. Couple therapy is often like teaching someone how to sail. By gathering information on your extended family, I learn something about what kind of boat you each have, from the type of sail that it has, to its size and shape. Your families equip you with many skills for sailing through the waters of life. In addition, some of the experiences you have with your families help you to develop certain strengths in areas as you meet similar challenges along the way. By learning about your relationship history, I learn something about the weather conditions that you have sailed through in the past and in the present. In addition, the direction of the wind and the speed of the currents are important for the sailor to know about. A good sailor must learn to take many different factors into account while planning the journey. Once I understand something about the gusts of wind in your life and the many directions that your boats have taken you, I can help you to fine-tune your sailing skills for the current waters and your future life together. Your present complaint is likely to be a result of a coincidence between several of these elements, just as a storm might come up in the water and you must struggle to learn and master some new sailing technique.

In the above example, the therapist took into consideration the couple's stage in the life cycle; this was a young couple in the first stage of married life. If the couple had been married 20 years, a different metaphor might have been more appropriate. A later stage in the life cycle would suggest that these people have been struggling with the same problems for a longer time. What they may need is some new way to address their conflict, if the old ways have not worked in 20 years. Thus, a more appropriate metaphor for such a couple might involve a new mode of transport: learning to canoe or deciding to take the train.

Guidelines for Joining   The methods therapists use to join with a family are often just beyond their conscious awareness and appear to be much like those used in ordinary human relationships. The past few decades of pop culture have produced several expressions to describe the phenomenon: The slang expressions "on the same wavelength," "in the same groove," and "on the same track" all refer to joining. Family therapists place a high priority on being *attentive* and *responsive* to family members. Connecting with them is both an attitude and a skill. To connect with the family, the family therapist must convey *acceptance* of family members and *respect* for their way of seeing and doing things. It is critical to *validate* each family member and acknowledge his or her experience and effort. The therapist must let family members know that they are understood and their views are important. In addition to using the strengths from each model of family therapy, the following tips can be used to help the therapist join with family members:

1. Greet each member of the family by name and make friendly contact with each. Ask each member about work, school, extended family, place where he or she lives, and so on.
2. Respect family leadership and caregivers. The therapist must begin with parents or caregivers when asking each member about his or her view of the problem.
3. Acknowledge each member's experience, position, and actions. ("So, Ms. Brown, you think your son ran away because he was angry at you.")
4. Normalize experiences, views, and actions. ("It is common for people in this situation to feel the way you do.")
5. Validate positive things you can say about a family member whenever possible. ("Ms. Jones, I know you have tried your best to help your son. It shows how much you care about him.") Reinforcing or validating a family member will often confirm that individual and help other members to view the problem differently.

In some cases, the therapist may join with the family by connecting with one of its members. This process is called *selective joining* (Colapinto, 1991). The therapist may often choose to affiliate with the most peripheral member in the family; or in some cases, the therapist will make special efforts through using similar language and tone of voice to get closer to the family member who will most likely influence the outcome of family therapy. Boyd-Franklin (1989) has wisely pointed out that African American families often rely on their own perception of "vibes" given off by the therapist. This nonverbal and subjective element in the interaction will influence their level of trust versus mistrust in therapy. We can see that vibes are related to the level of candor, authenticity, and acknowledgment of the unique challenges of another racial or ethnic group.

When Boszormenyi-Nagy (1966) developed the strategy of multidirected partiality, one of his goals was to address the challenge of connecting with each member of the family. In his work, he systematically interacted with each family member, in order to understand each position and to communicate that understanding for each member to ratify or clarify. As he did so, he was able to gain a clear picture of what each member thought about the presenting problem and what issues might become obstacles to change. In working with entire family groups or networks from the larger community, the skill of connecting with each member of the system will become a trademark of the evolving family therapist. To accomplish this, curiosity about the client's theory of change is often a critical component for success.

Client's Theory of Change   Recent research is highlighting the importance of therapists honoring the client's theory of change. This is a vital part of the client's worldview. Duncan and Miller (2000) suggest that *client theories of change* can be thought of as the ideas and opinions they bring into therapy about the *nature of the problem, its cause, possible solutions,* and the *role of therapy* in the process. Within these theories lies the basis by which clients judge therapist credibility and treatment success. For example, Hayes and Wall (1998) found that treatment success was strongly related to a match between how client and therapist thought about who is responsible for the problem. The challenge for beginning practitioners is to suspend their personal views while they learn to understand and work from the client's point of view. We do not think of this as agreement. Instead, we see the client's theory of change to be similar to a person's body measurements if we were tailors or dressmakers. We gather measurements to make the best fit possible. Our own body measurements are irrelevant in the process, unless we make the mistake of trying our clothes on the client! Instead, family therapists would assess who in the family is most influential to the change process and who is the customer for change. Then, using circular questions, we would explore their theories about change. Duncan and Miller (2000) offer these helpful questions:

What ideas do you have about what needs to happen for improvement to occur?
Many times people have a pretty good hunch not only about what is causing a
    problem, but also about what will resolve it. Do you have a theory of how
    change is going to happen here?
In what ways do you see me and this process as helpful to attaining your
    goals? (p. 84)

In addition, these authors warn us to see the client's theory of change as one that evolves *with* the therapist. Thus, these explorations begin the matching process but do not immediately produce a silver bullet. Instead, they generate "conversation structured by the therapist's curiosity about the client's ideas, attitudes, and speculations about change" (p. 84). These conversations become a foundation for the therapeutic alliance. It has been suggested that when assessing the client's theory of change, the therapist might take notes in order to record the client's language and track her or his line of thinking. These therapists show their notes to the client and offer the client a copy if desired (collaboration). By careful use of client language to construct goals, family therapists can keep the process client-centered rather than therapist-centered. As these notes are taken, the clinician can also highlight important information about family strengths in spite of the severity of the problem (Karpel, 1986; Henggeler et al., 1998; Zeig & Lankton, 1998).

Highlighting Family Strengths

A good relationship with the family is not only characterized by having empathy, understanding problems, and honoring the worldviews of others. It also depends upon how the practitioner highlights family strengths. Knowledge of family strengths will help the therapist understand how families cope with problems and how they promote growth and development. Assessing a family as having virtues—rather than adopting a deficit (problem) model—gives the family hope that it can solve its own problems. While this may seem obvious to most clinicians, it is frequently overlooked when family therapists become more intent on solving the family's problem, rather than developing a good relationship with the family.

Most family therapists use language that describes and labels competencies in clients. For example, Michael White (1986) will suggest that clients are experts on themselves. This emphasizes client strengths and downplays the authority of the therapist. Brief therapists such as O'Hanlon (1987) have elaborated on the Ericksonian technique of looking for exceptions. For example, a brief therapist, after listening to a description of the presenting problem, might ask the client to describe the times when things are going well. This is representative of a trend toward competency-based treatment in which strengths and successes are systematically investigated as a central element in the treatment process. More traditionally, this same element was found in the early models of family therapy. Minuchin and Fishman (1981) outlined their own emphasis on client strengths as they integrated their values with other leaders in the field:

> In every family there are positives. Positives are transmitted from the family of origin to the new family, and from there to the next generation. Despite mistakes, unhappiness, and pain, there are also pleasures: spouses and children give to each other in ways that are growth-encouraging and supportive, contributing to each other's sense of competence and worth. . . . The orientation of family therapists toward "constructing a reality" that highlights deficits is therefore being challenged. Family therapists are finding that an exploration of strengths is essential to challenge family dysfunctions. The work of Virginia Satir, with its emphasis on growth, is oriented toward a search for normal alternatives. So is the work of Ivan Nagy [Boszormenyi-Nagy], with its emphasis on positive connotations and his explo-

ration of the family value system. Carl Whitaker's technique of challenging the positions of family members and introducing role diffusion springs from his belief that out of this therapeutically induced chaos the family member can discover latent strength. Jay Haley and Chloe Madanes' view that the symptom is organized to protect the family and Mara Selvini Palazzoli's paradoxical interventions all point toward family strengths. (p. 268)

In a different way, Whitaker (1982) considered the goals of family therapy to be an increased sense of competency and self-worth. Symptoms were considered an attempt toward growth. While each model executed this objective in a different way, the trend toward a positive, affirming mode of practice became the norm in family therapy. This approach is a key element found in all models.

Guidelines   Focusing on the family's strengths and resources contributes to the development of self-confidence, inspires hope, and enhances growth within the family. Each family has unique strengths that may be buried or forgotten. The therapist must explore and probe to discover these strengths. Family members must be encouraged to discuss how they have coped with problems. The following guidelines will help beginning clinicians to join with the family by identifying the family's strengths:

1. *Emphasize positive statements reported by family members* (for example, "My mother listens to me when I have a problem"). It is also important to observe behaviors that reflect sensitivity, appreciation, or cooperation between family members.
2. *Encourage family members to share their story about themselves.* Pay particular attention to those aspects of their story that reveal how the family has coped successfully with problems.
3. *Note family interactions that reflect strength and competency* (for example, "I like the way you help your daughter find her own answers to the problem"). Underscoring positive family interactions helps the interviewer to identify other strengths and competencies.
4. *Emphasize those times that family members enjoy together.* What are they doing? What makes it enjoyable? These questions offer opportunities to discuss strengths and capabilities.
5. *Reframe problems or negative statements in a more positive way* (for example, "Your anger shows how much you worry about him"). Reframing consists of changing the conceptual or emotional viewpoint so as to change the meaning of the problem without changing the facts. The situation doesn't change, but the interpretation does.
6. *Emphasize what families do well.* All families have areas of strength (such as patience, skills, and coping behavior). By asking questions, the therapist can learn how families utilize these strengths to solve problems (for example, "What works best with your child?" "Tell me about the times you were able to get him to _____. What did you do?" "How were

you able to get him to _____?" "What does that say about your ability to get him to do that in the future?").

Miller, Duncan, and Hubble (1997) also provide an excellent summary of how a therapist might be more aware of these very important factors. Their suggestions include "listening for and validating client change whenever and for whatever reason it occurs during the treatment process . . . highlighting the contribution to change made by the client . . ." (p. 80).

These suggestions can be seen operating in many integrative approaches to family therapy and reflect the growing trend that we have observed in which family therapists attend to the natural resources of the client. These resources may be (1) signifiant relationships or events, (2) daily routines or hobbies, (3) a history of challenges and successes, or (4) detailed descriptions of what life is like when family relationships are going well. Since many therapy services are offered outside the family's natural world, it is important for the family thera-pist to obtain a clear picture of life outside the therapy room. People, places, activities, thoughts, etc., are all important resources to ask about, especially as they contribute positively to the self-esteem of the client.

Effort, Caring, and Intent   Finally, when family therapists have difficulty perceiving client competencies, a positive relationship can still include attention to positives. Using the analogy of whether the glass is half full or half empty, a beginning practitioner should always be prepared to see the glass as half full by commenting on the effort, sense of caring, and good intentions of family mem-bers. Henggeler et al. (1998) suggest that parents can always be validated for be-ing part of the solution, regardless of their part in the identified problem:

> The therapist should strive to find "evidence" of client effort and improvement and positively reinforce such, regardless of how small. For example, a client should be reinforced for attending sessions, giving his or her best, and so on. During the initial phase of treatment, Maggie's mother felt considerable apprehension, frus-tration, and hopelessness. The therapist reminded the mother that she was mak-ing important progress in helping her daughter by meeting with the therapist and helping to plan for changes. (p. 29)

In addition, these authors warn that a focus on strengths need not be a Pollyanna approach. Instead, it can be a realistic assessment of challenges coupled with at-tention to the smallest attempts at improvement, regardless of their success. Sometimes those who are feeling discouraged just need to know that others rec-ognize their good intentions and persistence. These acknowledgments lead to another important task in the therapeutic relationship, that of instilling hope.

Instilling Hope

Repeated studies show that 40 percent of the variance in psychotherapy out-come is related to client attributes and *factors outside* the therapy process, 30 percent is related to the therapeutic *relationship*, 15 percent is related to the client's *sense of hope,* and another 15 percent is related to specific *techniques* and models of the therapist (Bergin & Garfield, 1994; Lambert & Bergin, 1994). Thus, amid this formula for success, increasing the sense of hope is an important function of the therapeutic relationship. The Milan team suggests that the therapist's stance should be "hopeful and curious" (Tomm, 1984). The therapist manifests these traits primarily through voice inflection, conveying positive intent and interest in what the family says. Cunningham and Henggeler (1999) borrow the term *gift giving* from Sue and Zane (1987) as a universal strategy to be used in MST. O'Hanlon calls his recent work *possibility therapy* to emphasize his focus upon positive possibilities. Each of these provides practitioners with ideas about how to instill hope during the therapeutic process.

Gift Giving   This occurs when the therapist provides the client with some immediate and direct benefit, such as normalization of feelings, guilt reduction, and an understanding of the complexity of problems. Especially in the beginning stage of treatment, this practice provides relief, hope, and motivation to continue in the process. Examples of gift giving include statements such as:

1. I'm amazed at how well you're coping with such a complicated problem. A lot of people in the same situation would have given up by now.
2. I can see that you blame yourself for some of these problems, but I think you sell yourself short. I think you've done the best you could do under the circumstances. My role is to help you find some relief from some of your stresses so you'll have more energy. I know you don't want to give up on your son.
3. You might be surprised to know how many people have the same challenges you do. These days, life is often hard for many good parents who are just trying to survive. Many parents lose their temper when they don't mean to. That doesn't make them bad parents.
4. I can see you really care about your daughter. If you didn't, you wouldn't be here. There are a lot of things I'll need to learn from you in order to understand how I can help. I'm looking forward to working with you.

Explore Possibilities   O'Hanlon (1999) describes possibilities as existing primarily in the future, but has also found positive possibilities in the past and present. His future orientation is one that uses careful language to help clients live in the future and to imagine the future that they desire. For example, upon asking about exceptions to the problem, when the family identifies one, it is possible to explore in detail what life might be like if that exception was repeated. As these descriptions of the future unfold, the clinician identifies small steps of action that can be pursued in the present. If a family member stays focused upon past events, the clinician might look for opportunities to offer a different interpretation of the events as the story is retold. The new view might focus upon the client's strengths and determination, or give credit for what the family has accomplished in spite of hardship. As small steps of action emerge as small steps of success, family members gain trust in the process and develop self-confidence and hope.

As practitioners gain experience developing therapeutic relationships, their journey of discovery will also contain small steps of action that lead to a sense of confidence and success. Because people are wonderfully unique and resilient, challenges to the relationship are often our best teachers. It is impossible for any clinician to be prepared to relate successfully to all people. The best preparation for beginning therapists is to embrace the element of surprise. On this journey of discovery, those who surprise us the most will be the most memorable and the most interesting, if we are open to the adventure. As a final element on the road to a positive and productive therapeutic relationship, it is important to consider those cases that do surprise and challenge our abilities. Rather than blaming or judging those clients for our challenges, it is possible to take traditional notions of resistance and think of them in more human, egalitarian ways.

Reframing Resistance

The term *resistance* has become a cliché in the field of psychotherapy. Most often, it connotes the client's lack of cooperation with the practitioner or a lack of progress in treatment. However, in family therapy, there is a strong bias toward the notion that *resistance is an interactional event* characterized by the professional's *lack of understanding* about what is important to the family. For example, battered women are often considered resistant when they fail to follow professional advice that places physical safety above psychological safety. While there is widespread agreement about the importance of physical safety as a human right, professionals are frequently guilty of blaming the innocent when they label clients as resistant or stubborn without understanding the history that has influenced their beliefs about self, others, and the world around them. It is our observation that in many difficult cases involving elder abuse, domestic violence, and child sexual abuse, distinct perceptual patterns have a significant influence over the behavioral patterns that develop in family life. Thus, it is incumbent on family therapists to understand the unique thought processes of clients rather than to label them resistant or stubborn. As a therapist's skill develops in this area, client resistance diminishes.

We realize that it may be difficult to join with a family in which members manifest characteristics different from the therapist's (for example, parents who abuse their children) or in which members show hostile or detached behavior. These challenges are understandable and can usually be overcome by highlighting principles of Milton Erickson. He developed a process called *utilization* to address this issue (Erickson & Rossi, 1979). He learned to use, rather than challenge, a person's way of relating. For example, he would reframe hostility as honesty and would encourage the client to use it in solving the problem. He would reframe detached behavior as cautious or careful and would search for a context in which this behavior would be advantageous. Rather than suggesting that a person is "in denial," it is possible to acknowledge the person's unique sense of timing (Hanna, 1997). With abusive or demeaning behavior, family members may be characterized as being in pain themselves. Once the initial interaction is bridged through this form of reframing, the therapist is in a better position to address impasses and understand family process.

During a therapeutic impasse, one way to address family process is to search for a positive connotation to some element of the problem. For example, Selvini Palazzoli et al. (1978) describe a 10-year-old boy who exhibited psychotic symptoms following the death of his grandfather. At the end of the first session, the therapist told the boy that he was "doing a good thing" (p. 81). The therapist further noted that the grandfather was a "central pillar of the family" and kept the family together. The boy was told that he had assumed his grandfather's role to maintain balance in the family and that he should continue this role until the next session. Here the therapist used *positive connotation* to maintain homeostasis in the family rather than to challenge it. The boy had taken the grandfather's place to maintain a gender balance in a family that, following the grandfather's death, was predominantly female. The use of positive connotation allows the therapist to join with the family at a time of crisis and to understand the problem in light of complicated systemic dynamics.

When symptoms have become chronic, even though numerous people are trying to help the family or individual to change, it is often wise to take a cautious position about the timing and amount of change: Restrain the family when it begins to show improvement. Restraining interventions are used to help the therapist move at a pace that is optimal for the family. In essence, the therapist is saying, "I'm not sure this change would be beneficial. I realize the problem has certain disadvantages, but there may be benefits to this situation that need to be identified first so that improvement in one part of your life won't lead to unforeseen consequences somewhere else. Can you think of any conditions that might get worse if this problem were to be resolved?" As families are encouraged and allowed to identify certain dilemmas that may have been covert, the therapist offers genuineness and warmth to the family in addressing these unforeseen consequences before change begins in earnest.

These examples are commonly referred to as "paradoxical interventions" (see Chapter 8). However, we offer them not as strategic manipulations that may satisfy a practitioner's need for compliance, but as suggestions for understanding human nature at the deeper level of personal and relational dilemmas that often makes change a complicated process for families. If beginning practitioners address resistance as an issue of therapist inexperience rather than as a personal attribute of the client, therapeutic impasses become signals that this deeper level of understanding is needed to break the impasse. Then it is possible to return to the common themes of theory reviewed in Chapter 3 and choose another area of emphasis until the understanding is achieved. This ability to shift direction and approach a problem in multiple ways is developed over time as the family therapist learns from a variety of clinical experiences. Paying attention to these learning experiences is part of developing the self of the therapist.

THE SELF OF THE THERAPIST

With respect to the therapeutic relationship, the most important knowledge about family therapy may be the knowledge that most models fail to supply. For example, many approaches fail to include a discussion of ethical considerations. We think all marital and family therapists should have a working knowledge of the code of ethics published by the American Association for Marriage and Family Therapy (2001). In addition, Brock (1997) has developed a questionnaire to help family therapists assess their vulnerability for ethical violations. We have included these in Appendix A. From here, practitioners should become aware of how these issues might emerge differently with different approaches. If a client is hesitant to involve certain family members, how does the clinician work systemically without becoming coersive? When seeing couples, what is the marital therapist's responsibility for confidentiality in the event that each partner is seen alone? These are examples of questions that are commonly addressed in many family therapy programs. The nature of ethical issues in family therapy can be different from other professions because we value working with and considering the importance of the relational network closest to the problem. Because of this dimension, discussions with supervisors regarding local laws and the code of ethics are important for all family therapists.

In addition to the application of ethical principles, all therapists should monitor their levels of stress and the emotional impact of their daily work. As Brock's assessment suggests, family therapy can have an unintended effect upon the well being of the therapist and personal crises can have an unintended effect upon therapeutic work. The interplay of personal and professional stresses must be monitored continuously as part of professional development. These stresses can also be managed by developing a set of therapeutic attributes that lower stress and make the work rewarding and enjoyable.

While there is debate in the field regarding which attributes are essential to the process of facilitating change, there is generally a consensus that certain personal qualities will likely enhance therapeutic effectiveness. Here, we present a variety of perspectives in this area.

Lankton, Lankton, and Matthews (1991) suggest the following four therapist characteristics:

1. A great pragmatic understanding of people and of coping with life's exigencies (empathy).
2. An ability to step outside of oneself into the world of another person while at the same time retaining an awareness of that pragmatic understanding of coping with life (sympathy).
3. An excitement about learning.
4. The ability to articulate, especially the differences between one's own experience and that of the client. (p. 274)

In a national survey, Figley and Nelson (1989) asked family therapy supervisors to list the most basic skills that should be taught to beginning family therapists. Their results might be surprising to some since personal characteristics were listed above specific skills.

> Our fellow educators/trainers seem to believe, based on these data, that the person of the therapist is as important as, if not more so than, the skill of the therapist. . . . It is probable that our respondents were aware that, for therapy training to be effective, a foundation of abilities, values, attitudes, and other traits is essential for effective family therapy. (p. 362)

In their survey, 5 of the top 16 ranked items were "possess integrity," "desire to learn," "intellectually curious," "flexible," and "take responsibility for mistakes."

Finally, we think experiential family therapists are the best example of those who pay attention to the self of the therapist as part of their training. They are described by Piercy and Sprenkle (1986) in the following way:

> Experiential family therapists participate actively and personally in therapy sessions; they do not attempt to hide behind a therapeutic mask. This means at times being vulnerable with family members and at other times being angry and upset. If the therapist expects the family to have the courage to be real, the therapist must also demonstrate that courage. (p. 53)

Since personal characteristics of the therapist determine how a particular intervention is delivered, therapists must be able to utilize skills that fit with their own personality. Lebow (1987) suggests:

> The ability to feel and be hopeful, empathic, assertive, confrontative, and focused is all a part of being a therapist. To the extent possible, such skills should be directly taught, supplemented by personal therapy, to help overcome obstacles to attaining a therapeutic position. Each therapist ultimately needs to find a mode (or modes) of operating that is (are) comfortable and blends successfully with the theory, strategies, and techniques utilized. (p. 8)

Thus, the therapeutic person described from all perspectives is multidimensional. In order to help the beginning practitioner find a starting point for self-development, we suggest that flexibility is needed for many of the others to follow. From a pragmatic point of view, it is flexibility that often opens the door for other learning to follow.

Flexibility

In defining therapist flexibility, it may be helpful to return to the research of Figley and Nelson (1989). Some of the attributes that family therapy supervisors regarded as important include "nonjudgmental," "respectful of differences," "understanding that one reality doesn't work for everyone," and "meet clients 'where they are.' " These are indicative of a family therapist who has learned to be flexible. Is the clinician a person who can modify his or her style to match that of the family? If the members of the family are boisterous, can the therapist join with them, rather than convey subtle disapproval? Has the clinician been influenced by theories that encourage stilted jargon, or is there room for a wide range of interactions—playfulness, empathy, firmness, and humor? The chemistry between the family therapist and the family will depend, in part, on the ability of the clinician to become comfortable with a wide variety of people.

In developing a greater sense of flexibility, constructivist views have encouraged practitioners to reconsider some assumptions that may limit flexibility and narrow the possibilities for creativity. Duncan and Parks (1988) elaborate:

> Simply stated, reality, like beauty, rests entirely in the eye of the beholder; there is no objective reality or truth inherent in a given situation. Reality, therefore, is constructed by each individual in each circumstance. The process of construction is based in complex sociocultural interaction between the ever changing larger society, the family, and the biologically/psychologically developing individual. The constructivist position is central to a selective integration model. In the absence of a specific view of reality, the therapist is free to entertain the "reality" of any content that seems applicable in a given clinical situation. Rather than imposing the therapist's theoretical reality on the client, a theoretical language or specific content is chosen because it best matches the client's conceptualization and presentation of the problem. (p. 156)

Similarly, Milton Erickson stated that he invented a new theory for each individual (Lankton & Lankton, 1983). If the beginning family therapist can recognize his or her own limited view of the world, it will be easier to experiment with different perspectives and how they may apply to different situations.

In addition to such theoretical flexibility, it is also important for the family therapist to learn a type of "political" flexibility that requires the clinician to adopt a cooperative and hopeful stance, regardless of the family's own idiosyncrasies. For example, in research conducted on the treatment of adolescent substance abuse, the Purdue Brief Family Therapy Model (the P.B.F.T. model) listed the following curative factors related to successful change (Lewis, Piercy, Sprenkle, & Trepper, 1991):

1. The family feels the therapist is "with them" or "on their side."
2. The therapist engenders hope.
3. The therapist diminishes the family's fear of change.
4. The therapist avoids resistance.
5. The therapist respects the family's uniqueness.
6. The therapist mobilizes the family's resources. (p. 41)

We think this political flexibility is promoted in most contemporary models of family therapy. However, developing these personal qualities and skills may be, as the saying goes, easier said than done.

Perhaps more than in any other mental health profession, we consider the hallmark of a competent family therapist to be the ability to develop a positive relationship with diverse people, sometimes people in conflict with each other. Add to this the challenge of engaging these diverse, conflicted people all at the same time, all in the same room! This unique aspect of family therapy provides a significant test for professionals entering the field. However, like many of life's obstacles, when mastered, we have reaped some of our greatest rewards. As mentioned in Chapter 3, there are those models of family therapy that encourage an exploration of personal phenomenology. Given the research data on the importance of therapeutic relationships, we make a case for stronger emphasis upon personal process during the training experience of a family therapist. Thus, when beginning practitioners are taking on so many challenges at once, we recommend the following guidelines to ease the stress of their self-development.

Tips for Self-Development

We advise students to learn as much about people as they do about models. As one learns more about people, it is also important for the practitioner to learn more about self in relationship to others. Learning about others from *their* point of view can be done in a number of ways. We often recommend movies that may expose students to a world different from their own. In a multicultural environment, it is not difficult to find movies that portray life in a variety of cultures. For example, the producer Spike Lee has become well known for his depictions of African American life in America. Appendix B contains a list of movies we have used in teaching students how to empathize with diverse people who have diverse stresses and strengths. Fiction and nonfiction also provide trainees with views of the world that can be examined apart from professional jargon and scientific terminology.

Finally, exposure to diverse professions and cultures also provides insight about others from their perspective. During a period of training, it is sometimes most helpful for the trainee to spend as much time as possible with nontherapists in order to remain connected to a broader culture. For example, one family therapist had friends in medical school and asked permission to join their work group in anatomy and physiology. While they dissected a cadaver, the therapist was allowed to work with them, seeing the heart and identifying veins, arteries, and nerves. At the same time, the therapist learned about the world of medicine—what is involved in becoming a doctor and how that professional culture is different from family therapy. The experience provided an adventure that led to increased flexibility in considering others' values, worldviews, and cultures.

In addition, the academic world can sometimes become an obstacle to the trainee's attempts to remain balanced and versatile. It may seem an ironic paradox, but nonprofessional leisure activities can often be the best teacher in providing a trainee with exposure to a variety of people, cultures, languages, and metaphors. The use of metaphor is especially effective when clients differ dramatically from the therapist in stage of life cycle, values, economic level, and ethnic background, to name a few. If the client is a farmer, the family therapist might want to be compared to the county extension agent. If the client is a physician, the family therapist might want to be compared to a medical specialist, perhaps a cardiologist. If the client cares a great deal about physical appearance, the therapist might want to be compared to a hairdresser. By searching for metaphors and analogies that come from the clients' world, the therapist attempts to join clients in their world, rather than expecting them to fit into the prescribed world of the therapist.

The challenge of relating to diverse people is also related to how family therapists respond to conflict—their own and others'. We encourage students of family therapy to explore their own patterns of thought and emotion in the face of interpersonal conflict. Identify those coping strategies most often chosen and critique them for their usefulness in professional settings. As one begins to gain awareness of this personal process, the next step involves exploring how these personal patterns may or may not fit with the inclinations of a given client group. An interesting example of how personal process interacts with client process is illustrated by a study conducted by Gonzales, Hiraga, and Cauce (1995). In observing mother–daughter interactions in African American and Asian American families, they discovered that non–African American coders rated the level of conflict higher for African American mothers and daughters than did the "in-group" coders or the mothers and daughters themselves. In applying this research to a family therapy experience, it is possible that the practitioner's experience may be quite different from that of the family. We think learning to account for these differences and developing the ability to step back from them in order to "go with the flow" of a family are defining elements of competence.

SUMMARY

As noted in outcome research, the client's perception of the therapeutic relationship is an important factor related to successful outcomes. As the role of the family therapist has become more active and involved, there has been an accompanying shift in attitudes. Implicit in the more traditional doctor–patient relationship was the assumption that the therapist was the expert and authority who would pursue a cure for the client's distress. However, as interventions such as positive connotation have become popular, the therapist–client relationship has become more egalitarian and central to effective family therapy. The therapeutic relationship can be maximized when the therapist is active in highlighting strengths, instilling hope, and reframing resistance and is flexible in accepting differences. This perspective requires sensitivity to the unique aspects of a person's life that can become resources. These unique aspects are discovered through the therapist's ability to relate comfortably to individual strengths and differences. To become "relationally versatile," the clinician must make a personal decision to respect and esteem diverse people.

In early models, the therapist focused more upon behavior and less upon phenomenology. In later models, the role of cognition, personal experience, and individual meanings emerges as a critical factor in the process of change. Nevertheless, interesting parallels also remain between early and integrative models. For example, while the structural therapist is active in directing behavior, it seems that the collaborative therapist is also active. Collaborative activity may involve directing the thoughts of one person toward another or guiding a group toward a creative brainstorming process. Thus, certain activities remain universal in family therapy, even though the destination or purpose of the journey may vary. We see these activities as the foundation for a therapeutic style that will be effective in working systemically and relationally.

We think that the process of developing the therapeutic relationship in family therapy is similar to learning to drive a car. Driving a car is a process that involves a collection of actions and thoughts—certain knowledge and ideas. The territory (types of cases) one drives through may be as different as Africa and England; nevertheless, certain aspects of the activity are always the same (joining, highlighting strengths, etc.). In addition, driving is a series of separate but related activities like watching the road, estimating distances, and steering the vehicle (self-development). Each may happen in situations where one is a passenger rather than a driver (positive interactions or informal conversation). However, when a person is the one doing the driving, she or he must coordinate these activities in a certain way (positive therapeutic relationship). Our review of the therapeutic relationship and self of the therapist has pointed to a variety of processes and personal characteristics that are encouraged across most models of family therapy. Just as driving a car has some universal elements, regardless of the roads, territory, or destination, we believe it is possible to think of systems and relational therapy in the same way.

As we conclude this section devoted to connections between theory and practice, we leave the "parking lot" of training and proceed onto busy streets and highways. (Perhaps we can say that the rubber hits the road!) It is here that countless variations—from new surroundings to road construction—challenge the driver with endless and ongoing surprises. Even the most routine of drivers knows that the roads of life never stay the same. Thus, adaptability and the application of skills over time provide the learner with a way to manage variety. In addition, the activity once referred to as driving a car can now be transformed into many different activities such as going shopping, traveling, or racing.

In the next chapter, we will review the basic stages in the process of family therapy and provide a framework for integrating the themes of theory and practice that have been reviewed to this point. As we start the car and begin to move, we take along our theories, perceptions, and relational skills. We circle the parking lot—many times—and begin to see how each component interacts with the others, sometimes overlapping, sometimes proceeding in order. These movements and cognition become entwined as stages and interactions in the process. Now it is time to learn skills that apply to a variety of situations and driving conditions.

ORGANIZING TREATMENT: AN OVERVIEW OF SEQUENCES AND TASKS

Thus far, the basic elements of theory and practice have been identified across the various models of family therapy. Some of these elements relate to skills, attitudes, or qualities of the therapist, and some relate to specific concepts. In Part Two, we continue this integration. Family therapy can be thought of as an interactional and perceptual process with common elements that address problem or symptom resolution. These elements are presented within a sequential framework in which the therapeutic process is characterized as interactional, circular, and evolving over time. We outline this framework in the form of sequential steps to help the beginning family therapist manage the complexities of client contact. However, several of these processes can also occur simultaneously in "micro" sequences of therapist–client interaction. One person, called a therapist, and one or more persons, called clients, interact together. Efran, Lukens, and Lukens (1990) suggest that:

> If psychological assistance is to be effective, it must take place in the very same space in which our living and our problems are enacted—in meaningful conversation. In other words, that which we have labeled "psychotherapy" must begin to be

seen as a specialized form of dialogue—not as a medical treatment analogous to administering inoculations, performing surgery, or dressing wounds. (p. xv)

This evolves through many different stages, some of which may be limited to a certain order, whereas others repeat over time to form a pattern. These stages can be used as a map to chart the territory of most successful therapy experiences. They are:

Referral process
Intake process
Initial interview
Assessment and treatment planning
Beginning change
Maintaining change

While not every family therapy model addresses each of these processes consciously or explicitly, we suggest that each one occurs either simultaneously or consecutively as an influence on the larger process of therapy. These interactional processes, when combined with the common elements of theory and practice, form a general framework from which to apply the other skills taught throughout the remainder of this book. The next four chapters outline these steps in detail and provide the beginning practitioner with instructions for moving through the process.

STARTING OFF ON THE RIGHT FOOT

Referral and Intake

The Referral Process: Understanding the Natural Environment

The Intake Process: Organizing the Therapeutic Environment

Questions That Beginning Clinicians Often Ask

The beginning stage of family therapy is a critical time that requires the practitioner to be disciplined, deliberate, and wise. It takes great *discipline* to choose words and use language that will develop a positive relationship with those seeking help. It also takes discipline to manage the anxieties and uncertainties that come with starting any new endeavor. That's why a spirit of adventure is important to becoming a successful family therapist. With such a posture, the practitioner approaches therapy with an openness to the unusual and a curiosity about challenge. In addition, it is important to be *deliberate*— to plan and organize these first contacts in a way that will provide families with a sense of hope and trust in the process. All of this takes *wisdom,* the ability to follow the best course of action. Many models of family therapy consider every contact, no matter how brief, to be a therapeutic interaction in which the therapist either prepares for or promotes change. Thus, initial interactions in the course of seeking help are the beginning of the change process—even before meeting with a therapist. These first steps are known as the *referral process.* Once the referral has been made and a family therapist has been contacted, initial information is gathered by the therapist or the agency through an *intake process.* Once the intake has been completed, family therapists prepare to meet the family. This chapter concludes by preparing for this meeting with a discussion of frequently asked questions.

THE REFERRAL PROCESS: UNDERSTANDING THE NATURAL ENVIRONMENT

The referral is an interactional process in which, generally speaking, someone decides that a problem exists and someone initiates the idea that therapy is a possible resource and should be sought. Generally, there are two types of referrals. *Self-referrals* are those in which the intended client (either individual or family) makes the first contact seeking help. *Other referrals* are those in which someone other than the intended client makes the first contact. Exploring the interactions leading to the first contact provides key information needed to understand client motivation and the family's problem-solving process.

The appropriate time to gather this information varies across practice settings. For example, sometimes an agency's process may include an initial contact with one agency representative via telephone, an intake interview with a different staff person, and finally the initial interview with the assigned family therapist. When these intermediate contacts occur, the format often omits *detailed* referral information. Thus, in these situations, family therapists should be prepared to explore the referral process during the initial interview. However, when the practitioner is fully involved with either the first contact or the intake process, referral information may be gathered in detail during these stages. This introductory exploration can convey interest and caring on the part of the therapist.

The referral process will often include interactions within the family and between the family and other systems. Understanding these interactions can help the clinician to answer the following questions:

1. Which relationship should be the central focus?
2. Which parties are most relevant to a successful outcome?
3. Who is the most motivated participant in the therapy process? Who is most reluctant?

These questions, which can be answered indirectly through conversation with the family, direct the family therapist toward an exploration of the referral process. When individuals are being interviewed alone, it is important to assess whether their motivation for counseling is internal or whether they have been sent by family or friends who want them "fixed."

With the frequency of court-ordered therapy in the United States, it is important to explore and understand the *step-by-step sequences of interaction* that led the client to schedule an appointment or make a telephone call of inquiry. At the very least, the family therapist obtains information about who has taken the initiative. Ideally, the family therapist obtains crucial information about the family members' level of motivation and their influential external relationships and about whether therapy is even appropriate in some circumstances. Obviously, a court-ordered case will have implications for the motivation of the client to do therapy. While other models rarely address this aspect of the therapeutic process, it is our opinion that the beginning family therapist will encounter puzzling superficiality or courteous compliance without personal involvement unless the influence of the referral process is ruled in or out as a major issue.

In addition to court-ordered cases or public agency referrals, there are circumstances in private-practice settings where relatives, family members, clergy, and service providers have recommended or even initiated counseling, while excluding themselves from the process. For example, the parents of a young married couple may send them to marriage counseling and even pay for the process. The Milan team has consistently addressed the referral process in the case where therapy was initiated by someone who claims to be uninvolved in the life of the problem, such as a member of the clergy or a sibling (Selvini Palazzoli, 1985; Selvini Palazzoli, Boscolo, Cecchin, & Prata, 1980b). The Milan team found that examining the relationship between the referring person and the family must take precedence over traditional therapy—that is, over merely examining relationships within the family or even exploring the problem itself. In this way, differences in motivation may be addressed during early stages of the therapeutic process. By tracking the perceptual and interactional process, the therapist gains information for subsequent use in developing mutually satisfying goals that are sensitive to individual needs.

Assessing Client Motivation

Similar to the Milan team, O'Hanlon and Weiner-Davis (1989) also address referral concerns by establishing who is the "customer" of therapy—that is, who is actually requesting that a change be made. Questions such as these can aid in establishing who is the customer:

Who first noticed that this was a problem? This identifies the pattern of perception.

Who agrees or disagrees that this is a problem? This explores the "politics" or the issues of power surrounding the definition of the problem.

Whose idea was it to seek therapy? This identifies the pattern of initiation.

How was it brought to your attention? This identifies the interpersonal process involved in seeking help.

When you began to think about seeking help, who or what gave you the thought that coming here might help? This helps the therapist understand how familiar the family may be with the "culture" of therapy and what it involves.

When it is discovered that an outside party has suggested counseling, it is likely that the definition of the problem will have to focus initially on the relationship between those being interviewed and the referral source. This might be the family versus another system or the individual versus family, friends, or employer. Thus, if a family has sought therapy because the school is concerned about Johnny's behavior, the family therapist must decide how much the family agrees or disagrees with the school's perception of Johnny. When the family disagrees with others in the problem-defining system, it is best for the practitioner to follow the family's lead in developing client-driven goals (see Chapter 6).

When couples appear to be seeking help together, if one partner is more motivated and one more reluctant to pursue therapy, the questions might be something like these:

When you thought about coming to counseling, how did you talk to him or
    her about it?
When she or he talked to you about counseling, what was your reaction?
Did you get "dragged" here against your will?

If a husband has come alone for counseling because his wife has given him an ultimatum, the therapist must determine who has defined the problem and whether the husband agrees or disagrees with her point of view. He may want to save his marriage, but he may be unable to fully represent his wife's point of view. The intricate politics that have led to her exclusion from the session must also be investigated: Does she have her own therapist and feel that he should take his turn? Has she already privately decided on divorce and identified the therapist as someone her husband can turn to when she "lowers the boom"? Does she think he is totally to blame for the marital problems? Has he been violent, so that she has had to separate in order to capture some degree of control over her life? Detailed questions about the referral process will often help the family therapist to expand the definition of the problem to include issues between the client(s) and outside parties.

Exploring the Relational Network

When callers are family members, the therapist should determine what role the referral source might have in the definition of the problem. *Do other family members agree or disagree with the referrer's view of the problem?* On discovering that someone besides those in attendance actually developed the definition of the problem, the family therapist must try to clarify the relationship between the family and the parties who have defined the problem. This remains the focus of treatment until the appropriate role of the family therapist with respect to the parties involved is clear. As the Milan team discovered, when the problem is being defined by a sibling, in-law, or service provider, that party should be included in the session in order to properly define the problem (Selvini Palazzoli, 1985). Since the family may disagree with the person's opinion but still initiate therapy, the family may define the real problem as a difference of opinion with this outside influence. With this as the defined problem, family therapists can then suggest that their role be that of helping both parties reach a shared goal that will transcend their differing opinions (Why don't we look for something you can both agree upon?).

Working With Other Professionals

Family therapists often receive referrals from various sources, including school counselors, psychologists, social workers, previous clients, and family members involved in the problem. When a family is referred by an outside agency (for example, a court or school), the family may be suspicious and less willing to attend the initial session. This is particularly the case when families are forced to attend therapy by a probation officer or the court (Boyd-Franklin, 1989). If professional referral sources (for example, social workers or school counselors) make the first contact, the following guidelines will help the clinician to begin on a positive note.

1. Explain the family therapist's role as one that can address disagreements and conflict between the family and others.
2. Gain a clear picture of whether there is disagreement between the referring party and the family's view. Encourage the referring party to explain to the client that the family therapist will take a neutral position.
3. Encourage the referral source to emphasize the family therapist's independence, in order to minimize client defensiveness. In such cases, the role of the family therapist may involve resolving conflict between the family and the larger system. That role can be carried out effectively only when family therapists establish a stated position of both neutrality with respect to the referral source and support with respect to the family.
4. Gather information about the problem and the referral source's attempts to alleviate it. Weber, McKeever, and McDaniel (1985) suggest that it is important to determine what the referring person is requesting (for example, consultation for self or therapy for the family).

The following dialogue illustrates these issues with professional referral sources:

> CASE MANAGER: I need your help with a family our agency is involved with. Can I talk to you about the family?
> FAMILY THERAPIST: Sure. What seems to be the problem?
> CASE MANAGER: Well, the husband attends our Adult Day Center and has Alzheimer's. I've been trying to get his wife to start planning for his long-term care needs, but she says they're doing fine and she doesn't need anything like that. She's really in denial.
> FAMILY THERAPIST: What type of help did you have in mind? Are you looking for a consultation for yourself or therapy for them?
> CASE MANAGER: I really think they need therapy. We just haven't gotten anywhere with them.

FAMILY THERAPIST: Have you discussed this idea with them?

CASE MANAGER: Yes, the wife said she would be willing to talk to you.

FAMILY THERAPIST: OK. Tell me what you said to her and the reasons you gave for recommending that she come here.

CASE MANAGER: I told her that I was concerned about her future with her husband's illness, and I thought it would be a good idea if she talked to someone about her options.

FAMILY THERAPIST: How did she respond to this?

CASE MANAGER: She said, if I thought it was necessary, she would be willing to come.

FAMILY THERAPIST: Did you mention earlier that you don't think you've gotten anywhere with them?

CASE MANAGER: Yes, she just won't look at the future.

FAMILY THERAPIST: Well, I wonder if we could think of this as a difference of opinion between the two of you. You want her to look at the future, and it seems like she doesn't want to.

CASE MANAGER: Yeah, I guess you could say that.

FAMILY THERAPIST: If this is the case, she may respond to me in the same way she has been responding to you, unless I'm able to establish a position with her that is independent of yours. Do you think you could raise the issue of this difference between the two of you and explain that I will be a neutral third party?

CASE MANAGER: Yes, I can do that. I told her I'd call her back after I talked to you.

FAMILY THERAPIST: Good. Why don't you describe me as someone who is interested in her point of view? Then, you and I should come to an understanding about my role. I've found that I can often help people reach a resolution by increasing their understanding of each other. Would you be open to additional information that might help alleviate your present concerns?

CASE MANAGER: Oh yes. If you can just get her to open up, that would really help.

In this instance, the family therapist should be prepared for the client to be cooperative but not necessarily motivated to pursue the case manager's agenda. However, because the case manager has been prepared for a new agenda—that of increasing their understanding of each other—the family therapist will not be hindered by the previous misunderstandings between the referral source and client. Very likely, the goal the client will be most motivated to pursue is one that enables her to feel more support from the case manager and more freedom to manage her life as she wishes. The family therapist can be prepared to suggest that the purpose of the meeting can be to help the case manager understand the client's needs.

Once information about the problem has been gathered from the professional, an agreement should be reached about how treatment information should be shared. Court referrals often require periodic reports summarizing the progress of treatment. School counselors and teachers may want to know, for example, how a child is progressing so that they can support these changes. In many cases, families may request a report or evaluation of their progress. If the case is court-ordered, the family must be informed regarding the therapist's responsibility to the court. However, in cases where there is no legal obligation to report, the intake worker should advise the referral source that the family has legal control over what information is shared. The intake worker should make a note of this issue, instructing the therapist to discuss these questions with the family.

The beginning practitioner can think of the referral process as an important influence upon the therapeutic relationship, goals, and ultimate outcomes. These suggestions for exploration are a troubleshooting guide to alert the practitioner to important elements in the natural environment of families that can be overlooked. When these elements are addressed, the clinician establishes a thoughtful and realistic basis from which to begin direct contact with families through the intake process.

THE INTAKE PROCESS: ORGANIZING THE THERAPEUTIC ENVIRONMENT

As we mentioned earlier, different clinical settings vary in how they organize referral calls and intake interviews. Wright and Leahey (1984) pay specific attention to the telephone contact preceding the first interview, suggesting that this first contact can have great impact on the further course of subsequent contacts. The first telephone contact has also been an issue of note for other clinicians, many of whom have developed guidelines and strategies for addressing systemic dynamics with the earliest possible contact (Brock & Barnard, 1988; Napier & Whitaker, 1978; Selvini Palazzoli et al., 1978). For family therapists working in agency settings, there may already be an intake process established, over which the practitioner has little control. However, sometimes it is possible for the clinician to make a preliminary telephone contact after the agency intake and before the first session; the family therapist can then provide important direction before the first meeting. For others who have the discretion to structure client contact according to their own preference, this chapter may serve as a step-by-step guide to the beginning stages of family therapy.

Presenting Problem

It is important to get a concise statement of the problem. When family members call, they are giving their view of the problem. Often family members will express concern through the use of labels. For instance, they may state feelings of "depression" or "anxiety" or refer to a child as "out of control." While these labels offer a general indication of the problem area, they have different meanings for different people. Therefore, it is important to *ask for concrete examples* for each label. For example, "out of control" may mean that the child "doesn't come home on time." Likewise, the intake person should ask *how the problem is affecting family members.* For example, if a mother calls and reports that her teenage son is "out of control," it is important to determine how his behavior is affecting her or other family members. For instance, she may report that she and her husband "disagree about how to handle this problem"; she may report that her husband is the only one who can handle him. Finally, it is important to summarize the referring family member's view of the problem ("So you see the problem as your son being out of control, that he won't come home when you tell him, and that you and your husband don't agree about how to handle him"). The following dialogue illustrates how intake information can be gathered from the referral person:

> INTAKE WORKER: Can you give me a brief description of the problem?
> MARY: My husband and I are not getting along.
> INTAKE WORKER: Can you tell me what is going on that makes you feel that way?
> MARY: We never go out. We just don't seem to have anything in common since Laura, our daughter, left for college.
> INTAKE WORKER: How long ago did your daughter leave?
> MARY: She's been gone for 2 years.
> INTAKE WORKER: Have you sought any help for this problem in the past?

Note that the intake worker questioned the referral person immediately following her description of the problem. By asking specific questions early in the process, the interviewer guides the process and moves on to the next important topic.

Previous Help

Assessing previous therapy will help determine what works and what does not work. A client's attempted solutions and previous successes are important places to start in preparing for the change process (Watzlawick et al., 1974). These are part of the client's problem-solving history. This information will help the therapist determine how the family viewed previous therapy. In addition, if any family members are currently in therapy, the therapist can ask the family to sign a release, so that information and services may be coordinated.

  If a family left therapy because the therapist wanted to focus on the marriage rather than the child, this information will assist the therapist in avoiding the same mistakes as previous therapists made. In such cases, therapists learn not to focus on the marriage until the parents raise the issue. In addition, work with other therapists may be related to this current request for help. However, even if previous therapy seems unrelated, the current therapist should always explore the effects of these other experiences on family members, by asking:

1. What was your experience like with _____?
2. Was there anything uncomfortable about that experience?
3. What things do you remember being helpful?
4. Why didn't you return there for help with this problem?

These questions often facilitate the joining process with families, by providing an opportunity for empathy. Do the family members think their current therapist will be just like the last one? Are there certain things that make them drop out of therapy? Can the current therapist discover what fits for this family by listening to the family members' descriptions of past therapy? This information is often crucial to future successes with any client who has had previous helpers. In fact, the same questions can be asked about informal helpers with equally fruitful results. Sometimes, informal helpers become unrecognized influences on the course of therapy unless they are identified during such a discussion. They may be those who have offered help or opinions about the problem in the past—friends, neighbors, clergy, or extended-family members. What suggestions have they made? How does the family feel about these informal helpers? If such parties have significant influences with the family, it may be wise to ask about the possibility of their inclusion in the first session. These discussions can begin an understanding of the pattern of help seeking and problem solving that has ensued prior to the current effort.

Family Information

Family information includes names of the client of record and partner or spouse, birth dates, level of education, and place of employment or school. Blank lines are also included for the children. It is critical to determine who is living in the home, as well as those who are related to the problem. It is also helpful to obtain information about previous marriages, divorce dates, recent deaths, illnesses, and any other significant changes that have occurred in the family system. This information may be useful in formulating hypotheses about transitions, particularly if a marriage has followed soon after a divorce or if there have been other significant changes in rapid succession. This information will help to determine who will attend the first session.

Including Others

All family members who live in the household should be asked to attend the first session. If the contact person is unwilling to bring the whole family, then therapists can meet with the family members who are most concerned about the problem. However, when significant others are excluded from the process, family therapists must ask questions during the assessment process to bring to light information about the missing parties' point of view and how much influence they have on other family members. Then, as understanding increases about each person's position in the system, the therapist should look for opportunities to address key family members and negotiate their subsequent inclusion (see Chapter 6).

Therapists and intake workers should listen closely to how the caller describes the problem. For example, a wife may say, "We just don't communicate," or "We don't get along." In some cases a parent may describe the problem in triangular terms: "She won't listen to us," or "He minds everyone but me." In such cases the therapist should clarify to whom the caller is referring and what the person's relationship is to the problem. Whatever the request for help, all family members who are related to the problem should be asked to attend the first session.

When the contact person is hesitant to invite others to the first session, the person may report that her or his spouse's work schedule prohibits attendance, or the person may explain that she or he is reluctant to impose upon extended-family members not living in the home. As mentioned previously, some may also sense an adversarial relationship with the referral source and refuse to include that person. In these instances, family therapists should prioritize the various parties who could be included. All family members living in the household are the highest priority, next would be influential extended family, and last would be referral sources. If the client of record has objections to all three possibilities, positive sources of support (friends, neighbors, etc.) should become the primary focus. When the client is a single adult living alone, it is often best to proceed with the initial interview individually. During this time, the clinician can determine who are the significant others and how others might be successfully included (see Chapter 6).

The following intake dialogue illustrates how the interviewer might address the reluctance to include other members of the household:

INTAKE WORKER: Is your husband willing to attend the first session with you?
WIFE: Well, . . . I don't know. He told me that he is perfectly happy and that it's my problem.
INTAKE WORKER: What do you think about his assessment?
WIFE: He's probably right. He usually is.
INTAKE WORKER: So, what do you think would happen if you asked him to come?
WIFE: I don't think he would come.
INTAKE WORKER: Have you ever been afraid that he would become violent with you?
WIFE: Oh, no! He would never do anything like that. He's just stubborn.

INTAKE WORKER: Let's think about some other issues for a moment. Even if he agreed to come, can you think of some ways that you might be more uncomfortable if he was included?

WIFE: Well, . . . I guess I would probably clam up. I don't like to make him mad, and every time I bring up how I feel, he gets mad.

INTAKE WORKER: So you're afraid that things would go just like they do at home?

WIFE: Yes.

INTAKE WORKER: I see. . . . You may be right. I'm wondering if you might be able to tolerate that possibility in order to get the very best help.

WIFE: What do you mean?

INTAKE WORKER: Our family therapists generally find their greatest success when they are able to hear all sides of the question. Even if your husband thinks the problem is yours, it would help the therapist to understand your husband's point of view. That way, since you plan on staying married, she could give you the kind of direction that would be good for you and your relationship. Sometimes, therapists give suggestions that seem good for the person but that turn out to threaten the marriage in some way.

WIFE: But I don't know how to make him come in.

INTAKE WORKER: Would it be possible for you to simply quote me? You could tell him, "The intake worker at the agency says your opinion is important to the process, to help me with my feelings. He knows you're not seeking any help right now, but he'd like to know if you would attend a session and give your opinion about what you think my problem is. He says it's customary for the therapist to meet the person's spouse before proceeding with individual work. Would you be willing to attend the first session with me?"

WIFE: OK. I'll try. What if he still won't come?

INTAKE WORKER: Let us know what happened, and we'll ask your assigned therapist to contact you for further direction.

In this dialogue, the intake worker explores the reluctance from the husband's and the wife's point of view. Although the wife was focused more on her husband's reluctance, her own unspoken reluctance may be a significant factor as well. Without trying to change the husband's mind (something the wife may do repetitively), the intake worker suggests a rationale that meets her overall goal (help) without escalating the conflict between them. If the intake process reveals the presence of violence in the relationship or the wife's intention to follow through with divorce, the initial interview may be conducted individually. Once this is accomplished, it may be possible to engage violent men in individual counseling for themselves using the strategies of Jenkins (1991).

Scheduling Information

It is helpful to know what the scheduling requirements are (times available to be seen) and who will be attending the first session. Once this information is gathered, an appointment date should be set for the family. The date, time, and location of counseling should be provided. Families should be instructed when to arrive and given all relevant information about the intake procedure and fees. The family should also be made aware of the cancellation policy if there is one.

Hypothesizing

Information gathered from referral and intake helps the therapist formulate hypotheses for the initial interview or for additional assessment sessions to follow. *Hypothesizing* has been used by the Milan team as a formal part of their strategic plan. It best describes the individual and collective process by which questions are formulated about the data gathered. Specific theories often encourage family therapists to bring certain ideas with them to the therapeutic experience. However, these assumptions may limit their ability to see other possible realities. Just as data gathering can become theory-specific, so can the hypotheses generated by the therapy. Therefore, we want to encourage a style of hypothesizing that is creative and flexible rather than limiting and rigid. Instead of being told what to hypothesize, the beginning family therapist should learn to formulate a hypothesis and then test it through an organized set of questions such as those found in Chapter 3. By asking the right questions, students and trainees can examine and test hypotheses rather than transform their hypotheses into unquestioned truths that might not fit their families' experiences.

The process of hypothesizing is also related to co-creating a definition of the problem. Certain theories generate certain definitions of problems. However, family members often have their own definition, whether private or public, which has a bearing on how the family responds to therapy. More important than what the therapist thinks is what the family thinks and how the therapist interacts with them around these variant definitions. Thus, we think it is important to brainstorm questions that can guide the clinical interview, but it is important to keep flexibility and the perception of client competencies woven into the interactional fabric that ultimately determines which definition of the problem becomes shared by therapist and family.

Most schools of family therapy share a basic hypothesis about physical and emotional problems. Hanna (1997) suggests that "all problems have a relational component" (p. 104). This hypothesis assumes that some relationship within the family or with some significant other (even a teacher, employer, or neighbor) is a relevant part of either the problem or the solution. This hypothesis leads to the identification of relationship conditions that are important to consider. The following case is an example.

A man in his mid-fifties sought therapy for depression. His wife agreed to accompany him and be helpful. In pursuing a relational hypothesis, the therapist pursued the client's own description of his internal process and the couple's description of how they each responded to his depression. Instead of attempting to convince them that depression is really an interactional problem rather than an individual problem, the therapist chose to acknowledge the internal reality of the man's depression while exploring the couple's attempted solutions and their own interactional process. This discussion eventually led to the identification of perceptual and behavioral sequences that all agreed were problematic. The wife thought of her role as his emotional caregiver. Each time he expressed his despair ("I feel lousy"), she tried to make him feel better ("Cheer up and look on the bright side"). To him, these responses were implicit disagreements with his internal experience. Feeling misunderstood, he became more entrenched in his own position. As the therapist helped them examine and change this interactional pattern, the man was not robbed of his internal experience and his wife was not blamed for his depression. Instead, they were directed toward a plan that could facilitate the healing process. In this instance, the result was a lifting of the depression as the spouses began to cooperate in a new way. However, had the depression persisted, the couple, equipped with new relational skills, could then pursue additional solutions with their relationship strengthened rather than strained.

In this case, the hypotheses of the client were included in an expanded definition of the problem, which grew to include relational factors. Since the couple's hypotheses about the depression had included such things as the man's job change and a strained relationship with his only daughter, these were easily incorporated by becoming the issues that their new relational process could address more effectively.

Another example of a relational hypothesis deals with a universal concern for all therapists: what some call resistance. As we mentioned in Chapter 4, resistance is often described as client rigidity or lack of cooperation. However, a relational hypothesis of resistance suggests an interactional definition that involves the therapist as a participant in the problem. Such a hypothesis helps the beginning family therapist examine his or her own interactional process with the client rather than indicting the client. Interactional hypotheses can help the practitioner change perceptions and behaviors that may have unwittingly elicited resistant behavior. Like the wife of the depressed man, many family therapists can learn how to be more helpful by examining and changing their part of certain problematic sequences.

Thus, a hypothesis is the *beginning*, but not the end of how the therapist will view the problem. We have suggested that those themes shared by most models of family therapy are illustrated in Chapter 3. These themes are a good place to start when it comes to generating hypotheses from intake and referral data. For example, a young couple seeks therapy, each complaining that the other places his or her career above their marriage. The following hypotheses are all possible views of the problem that lead to corresponding questions:

1. They have not learned to negotiate closeness or distance in their relationship—a major developmental task of the beginning family (structure): *How much time do you spend together? When you first married, how did you decide about the use of time?*
2. They did not successfully clarify beliefs, roles, and expectations—a developmental task of courtship and mate selection (individual experience): *Before you married, what discussions did you have about the type of relationship you wanted?*
3. Over time, there has been some structural change in their relationship that they cannot understand or resolve (transitions): *Since your marriage, what major events have occurred in your lives?*
4. Their communication and problem-solving styles have not brought about successful conflict resolution (more of the same or the solution becomes the problem): *When this disagreement comes up, how do you handle it? What happens when you try to talk about it? Who first brings up the subject?*

The therapist can develop questions like these from intake forms or from intake interviews, then pursue these hypotheses until concrete information eliminates or verifies their relevance. In addition, the situation can be assessed as to whether interactional change (the way they behave) or cognitive change (the way they think) will be the focus of the therapist's interventions.

Box 5.1 is a sample intake interview form. Box 5.2 presents sample case material on the intake form. From the information in Box 5.2, the following hypotheses can be generated prior to the first session:

1. A rapid remarriage may have left no time for the new marital subsystem to successfully organize parenting responsibilities or for the biological parents to resolve custody and visitation issues.
2. There may be divorce-adjustment issues and grief issues lingering for Robert and his mother.
3. There may be conflict between Jerry and Robert.
4. There may be some historical interactions between Robert and his mother that have become an ongoing pattern.

While there are additional possibilities, these serve as examples of developmental, structural, and interactional hypotheses that family therapists can use to begin their exploration of the family. These hypotheses provide a sense of

5.1   *Intake Form*

Date _____

Referral information

Client of record   Last _____ First _____ M.I. _____

Parent/Partner/Spouse Last _____ First _____ M.I. _____

Parent/Partner/Spouse Last _____ First _____ M.I. _____

Street _____ City _____ State _____ Zip _____

Phone #s: Home _____ Work _____

Other _____ Phone _____

Referral source: Org. _____ Name _____ Phone _____

Clinical information

Problem description _____

_____

_____

_____

Previous relationships: Client of record _____ Dates _____

Partner/Spouse _____ Dates _____

Current marriage date: _____

Previous therapy

Name	Org.	Address	Dates
_____	_____	_____	_____
_____	_____	_____	_____
_____	_____	_____	_____
_____	_____	_____	_____

Family information

Last name	First name	Birth date	Ed.	Employ/School
_____	_____	_____	_____	_____
_____	_____	_____	_____	_____
_____	_____	_____	_____	_____
_____	_____	_____	_____	_____

Scheduling information

Appointment date _____ Time _____ Therapist _____

5.2   *Completed Intake Form*

Date <u>5/13/95</u>

Referral information

Client of Record   Last <u>Starks</u>   First <u>Robert</u>   M.I. _____

Parent/Partner/Spouse   Last <u>Russell</u>   First <u>Barbara</u>   M.I. <u>S.</u>

Parent/Partner/Spouse   Last <u>Russell</u>   First <u>Jerry</u>   M.I. <u>L.</u>

Street <u>2553 Hawthorne Ave.</u>   City <u>Batesville</u>   State <u>IN</u> Zip <u>47006</u>

Phone #s: Home <u>451-8484</u>   Work <u>276-3533</u>

Other _____   Phone _____

Referral source: Org. <u>Hawthorne Elem.</u> Name <u>M. Briggs, Counselor</u>

Phone <u>821-4793</u>

Clinical information

Problem description <u>Mrs. Russell stated that her son, Robert, is failing</u>
<u>the 4th grade. He also resists rules at home. This started after her</u>
<u>remarriage last year. She thinks Robert is depressed about being away</u>
<u>from his biological father who moved out of state last year.</u>

Previous relationships: Client of record <u>widowed</u> Dates <u>spouse died</u>
<u>3 yrs ago</u>

Partner/Spouse <u>divorced</u>   Dates <u>married 1980, div. 1991</u>

Current marriage date: <u>October 1994</u>

Previous therapy

Name	Org.	Address	Dates
<u>Mrs. Russell</u>	<u>The Family Ctr.</u>	<u>1337 W. Main St.</u>	<u>May, 1990</u>
			<u>2-3 sessions</u>

Family information

Last name	First name	Birth date	Ed.	Employ/School
<u>Russell</u>	<u>Barbara</u>	<u>9-1-43</u>	<u>H.S.</u>	<u>Sec., Ford Motors</u>
<u>Russell</u>	<u>Jerry</u>	<u>10-5-40</u>	<u>H.S.</u>	<u>Sales, Lincoln Ins.</u>
<u>Starks</u>	<u>Robert</u>	<u>10-10-85</u>	<u>4th gr.</u>	<u>Hawthorne</u>

Scheduling information

Appointment date <u>5-20-95</u>   Time <u>4 pm</u>   Therapist <u>Jim Austin</u>

direction until other information is available. Once the initial interview occurs, these hypotheses should be presented to the family and either eliminated or expanded based upon the family's response. In the practice of MST, reviewed in Chapter 2, Cunningham and Henggeler (1999) suggest that this process is a form of "scientific mindedness." That is, therapists check out their assumptions with the family before taking them as true for the family. For example, in the first session, the therapist may discover that Jerry works many evenings, leaving little opportunity for conflict with Robert. However, when he is home, Robert seems to respond more obediently to Jerry than to his mother. This information may eliminate hypothesis 3 and strengthen hypotheses 1, 2, or 4. By checking out hypotheses with the family, therapists learn flexibility in remaining tentative about assumptions until the family provides more evidence for them.

As the referral and intake stage comes to a close, there are questions that beginning family therapists often ask as they prepare for the initial interview. These questions represent common clinical situations that may have a significant impact on the course of therapy. In preparing for the first interview, the following section provides some guidelines to help practitioners address such issues.

QUESTIONS THAT BEGINNING CLINICIANS OFTEN ASK

1. How Should I Handle the Issue of Alcohol if I Suspect It Is a Part of the Problem?

When family members identify alcohol as part of the presenting problem, this issue must be addressed if therapy is to be successful. The therapist must assess the function of alcohol and its relationship to the problem in the family. Is the family concerned that one of its members is abusing alcohol? How has the family dealt with this problem? How are family members affected by the alcohol abuse? Do those affected family members have a plan for addressing the issue? Treadway (1989) suggests that if the therapist and family are therapeutically joined, they may raise issues of chemical abuse. He emphasizes the importance of the twin objectives of remaining allied (joined) with the substance abuser and remaining neutral about the chemical-dependence problem. The beginning therapist should understand that discussion of the alcohol use provokes defensiveness on the part of the client unless those two objectives have been achieved.

Terms such as *problem drinking* or *alcohol use* are preferred to *alcoholic.* Treadway also suggests that the therapist and client develop a controlled-drinking contract (e.g., time-limited abstinence). If clients are unable to comply with this plan, they should be referred to Alcoholics Anonymous (AA) and obtain a chemical-dependence assessment. If other family members object to this type of plan, the clinician can use their objections as an opportunity to intervene with the family and begin encouraging the new patterns of thought and behavior necessary for successful recovery.

When the therapist suspects alcohol is contributing to the problem but family members do not identify it as part of the problem, the issue should be considered as a preliminary hypothesis that must be explored and validated before focusing treatment in that direction. Tracking interactional sequences and exploring the referral process can elicit information about the evolution of the presenting problem. As this is done, the practitioner can assess alcohol use by asking if any member was using alcohol or drugs before, during, or after the sequences described. Steinglass, Bennett, Wolin, and Reiss (1987) encourage clinicians to make a distinction between families who have become organized with an alcoholic identity and those who happen to have an alcoholic member. Their research sheds much light on various types of alcoholic families, suggesting that the stereotype of a dysfunctional family does not represent the diverse levels of competence and strength that may exist among families affected by alcohol.

2. How Should I Deal with a Suicide Threat?

A suicide threat brings with it tremendous responsibility. The first step in dealing with a suicide threat is to understand the extent of the client's thinking. Do such clients have a well-thought-out plan for conducting the suicide? What keeps them from completing this plan? What effects does the suicide threat have on the family? What message is the client trying to send by expressing this threat? Is the suicide threat linked to other losses in the family? Is the client attempting to help another family member avoid a painful transition? Beginning therapists may be tempted to offer the person advice or argue against suicide. At the beginning of a conversation about suicide, it is important to explore and ask the preceding questions with concerned curiosity. If the therapist takes too strong a position, the determined client may decide to go underground and withhold information to maintain personal control. If the therapist remains concerned and exploratory at the outset, the client is more likely to share fully regarding the extent of his or her progression toward an actual attempt.

Once therapists have listened to and explored the client's experience, they may proceed toward an intervention strategy. If the danger of suicide presents itself during an individual session (due to previous attempts or the presence of a specific plan), therapists should discuss a no-suicide contract that will stay in force until a family or network intervention can be organized. Family members and significant others should be notified immediately. The family and others (e.g., referral person, agency personnel, or physicians) should be convened to build a coalition to cooperate around therapeutic goals. One group of family therapists developed an in-home crisis intervention strategy that avoided hospitalization in 42 of 50 cases (Pittman, DeYoung, Flomenhaft, Kaplan, & Langsley, 1966). Madanes (1981) provides guidelines for addressing suicidal adolescents, and Scalise (1992) reports the successful structuring of a family suicide watch in the case of a suicidal adolescent. In the case of suicidal adults, the family therapist should engage spouses, significant others, or extended-family members in discussions regarding any significant life-cycle transitions or changes in family roles that might assist in understanding how the suicide threat may be a response to some unrecognized problem (Pittman et al., 1966). Efforts should be made to involve the network in treatment. Making sure that all the members of the therapeutic system (family, friends, caseworkers, etc.) commit to the goals and the successful completion of treatment is a critical feature of this therapy (Landau-Stanton & Stanton, 1985).

3. What Should I Do if I Discover Family Violence?

Increased awareness of family violence has drawn the attention of family therapists to their responsibilities in this area. The therapist must be aware of behaviors that indicate physical abuse. For example, a mother may appear depressed although seeking help for her children rather than herself. Families often feel shame that makes it difficult for members to discuss the abuse. Some therapists are legally bound to report violence to the appropriate agency (e.g., adult protective services) if they suspect it. It is important to inform clients properly of any legal responsibility early in the initial interview, so that if abuse or violence becomes apparent, clients do not feel betrayed by the therapist.

As the issue of reporting is addressed with clients, family therapists should explain the procedure as it is carried out in the given community. In some communities, if clients are already voluntarily seeking therapy, the consequences of reporting may be minimal, with little disruption to the family or the therapy. However, in other cases, there may be more formal involvement with the legal system. In view of this diversity, beginning practitioners should thoroughly investigate local procedures under a variety of circumstances to be as accurate as possible in explaining the process to families. In addition, it is important for practitioners to understand the legal definition of abuse in their community to avoid unnecessary reports.

In all cases, it is best to maintain a position of partnership with all family members, with special emphasis on maintaining an empathic bond with the abuser. The process of reporting can then be an opportunity to join with the family by highlighting the courage it takes to discuss the violence and by suggesting that many people are never able to muster the courage to do so (Jenkins, 1991). By emphasizing what courage has already been shown, the therapist can lay a positive foundation for the reporting process.

In some cases, therapists are able to persuade clients to personally make the call in the office as a manifestation of their commitment to improving the relationship. By speaking directly with authorities, clients are able to take greater control over their lives, and correspondingly, they often feel empowered and respected. They receive information directly from social services and do not have to be dependent on the therapist for interpreting the process. Families who remain reluctant to participate in reporting may be helped by encouraging an anonymous telephone call for information, followed by the actual report. If danger is not imminent, it may also be possible to delay the report until the clinician and family can agree on how the report will be made. In these cases, however, the issue should not be confused; the question is not whether a report will be made, but only how the report will be made—who will call, what will be said, and so on.

In defining the problem, the therapist must view the violence as the problem rather than as a symptom of something else. While other dynamics such as gender socialization, communication patterns, or faulty belief systems may encourage violence, family therapists must remain firm in defining the initial problem as violence, with the hope of creating a safe foundation for examining the related dynamics. However, without addressing the safety issues first, a climate for further growth cannot occur.

4. How Should I Handle Family Secrets?

Family secrets usually become an issue in two ways. First, there are times when family members or referral sources want to disclose information about other people to the therapist (thereby forming a covert coalition). Second, there are times when family members disclose information about others in individual sessions that they are unwilling to discuss in the presence of those involved.

Such revelations need not be disruptive if the therapist takes a few precautions. One is to decide how such information may affect the therapist's relationship with other family members. For example, Keith and Whitaker (1985) give an account of a young practitioner who received a telephone call between sessions about a family member's alcoholism. He decided to share the information with the family. Subsequent sessions were preempted by a suicide attempt on the part of the identified patient. Keith and Whitaker suggest that families have their own wisdom about how much information they can tolerate.

In this case, they argue, the clinician violated the family's threshold for emotionally charged information. These professionals suggest that it may be unnecessary to reveal secret information if the therapist abides by the family's intuitive judgment on such issues. They make the assumption that there is no such thing as a secret in families because members know at some covert level and have merely agreed not to address it openly.

The Milan team has chosen to avoid receiving disclosures altogether (Selvini Palazzoli & Prata, 1982). Instead, the team maintains a strict rule that if the discloser must share the information, it is not kept confidential and he or she must be willing to be exposed as the source of the information. In receiving between-session phone calls, the team begins by stating that anything disclosed must be discussed in the next session. Then, callers have the opportunity to decide how much to say. If family members are unwilling to change their rules of communication, the Milan team is unwilling to become part of a covert coalition. With this approach, maintaining the neutral position of the therapist (process) takes priority over gaining additional information (content).

These examples illustrate issues of context and therapist bias. However, in cases where individuals share personal information that is difficult to share in conjoint sessions, family therapists must make decisions about structure that depend on the stage of the therapeutic process. Since we are discussing the initial interview, the therapist should take into account whether a client's spouse will eventually be engaged and how the therapist will delay the potential alignment with the client until both parties are present. When individuals come in without other family members, the order of the initial interview presented here is designed to help the therapist stay away from detailed and intimate content until the structure of the individual's significant relationships can be identified. In addition, it is helpful if the therapist explains to the client that the order of the initial interview leaves the most detailed information for last to obtain a general picture of the client's relational world. Then, if an individual is willing to invite a partner, the therapist can suggest that the details of problem definition be saved for the next session. In later stages of the therapeutic process, clients may request individual sessions in which they begin to disclose information on a different level from that shared in conjoint sessions. The therapist must assess family and couple dynamics to determine how these disclosures should be handled given the current goals of the therapeutic process.

When the information disclosed concerns abuse or safety issues in the current relationship, therapists must assess whether their relationship with the abuser is strong enough to confront the abuse directly without escalating danger for the spouse. In the worst case, more individual sessions with the victim might be required to develop an initial safety plan. Sheinberg (1992) has addressed treatment impasses at the disclosure of incest by integrating constructionism and feminism into strategies that respect all sides of three major dilemmas: social control versus therapy, pride versus shame, and loyalty versus protection. Her work makes an important contribution to addressing secrets of this nature.

If the information disclosed is important but not related to physical or sexual safety, it is best for the therapist to go slowly, taking the time to understand the complex issues of secrecy, privacy, and confidentiality. In particular, family therapists should consult a collection edited by Imber-Black (1993), who makes a detailed study of the topic. In this work, she encourages clinicians to understand their own biases about the sharing of information and to grapple with the complexities that make many unique situations call for careful understanding by the professional. For example, people who are HIV positive must develop strategies for maintaining their privacy that minimize potential discrimination. Some choose never to disclose their diagnosis to certain family members. Others choose to deal with their shock and depression before disclosing to their children. This delay enables them to be more available to the needs of those children as they adjust to and cope with new circumstances. Understanding the dilemmas that accompany each circumstance is an important goal during the initial stages of treatment.

THE INITIAL INTERVIEW

A Template for General Tasks in Family Therapy

General Tasks in Family Therapy Sessions

Negotiate Structure

Explore Client Experience

Address Relationships

Develop a Shared Direction

Summary

As families and therapists begin their work together, we have seen that each side of the interaction takes a path unique to them. We explore the referral process to understand the natural problem-solving process of families before entering treatment. We learn whether help seeking has involved their informal (nonprofessional) relational network, a professional network, or both. As part of this learning process, we ask specific questions about interactions—the thoughts, feelings, intentions, behaviors, and perceptions of relevant parties. This teaches us about clients' potential motivation for therapeutic work. In the best case, referral and intake will lead to a group of relevant individuals attending the first session to discuss an identified problem. One model of family engagement uses the term *concerned other* to refer to a variety of people who could potentially attend a problem-solving session (Garett, Landau-Stanton, Stanton, Stellato-Kobat & Stellato-Kobat, 1997). In some cases, however, the first session will be another opportunity to explore the relational network related to problem solving and invite participation of important persons.

In Chapter 4, we reviewed the development of beginning therapists and how they might prepare to work with unusual situations that are new to their experience. It is usually during the initial interview that the world of the client and the world of the therapist meet. Using our metaphor of driving a car, as these two vehicles approach, circumstances will lead to either a collision or a coordinated series of movements in different lanes of the highway. If the therapist has engaged in self-development and personal preparation, there may be the option to follow (join), lead (intervene), or drive parallel with the other (explore) on this journey that now becomes more complex than merely controlling a single vehicle. There may be traffic jams or isolated country roads. Discovering the potential for growth in either territory (identifying family strengths) is part of the adventure.

Pragmatically, we remind the practitioner that the actual tasks of this interview will depend upon what information has already been gathered during referral and intake. At the end of this chapter, we will provide an outline in Box 6.3 of the first stage of therapy that summarizes our suggestions for the process from the time of referral through the end of the first session. In addition, this chapter will also provide a template to use for general sessions of family therapy in Box 6.4.

GENERAL TASKS IN FAMILY THERAPY SESSIONS

A review of family therapy literature reveals that several approaches share some common elements of the initial interview. Breunlin (1985) noted a beginning phase of family therapy in which the therapist organizes the referral system, convenes the family, begins the helping relationship, assesses the family, and develops a definition of the problem. Haley (1976) described the initial interview in four stages: social, problem definition, interactional description, and goal setting. According to Segal and Bavelas (1983), the goal of the initial interview is to gather specific behavioral information regarding the nature of the complaint and the client's attempted solutions; this resembles Haley's interactional stage. The general pattern for many schools of thought involves the evolution of the therapeutic system where family and therapist come together in an exchange of information to determine the who, what, where, when, and how of family therapy.

As the trainee prepares to practice, we think it is helpful to develop a plan that will provide a sense of direction. Many models have their own protocols for conducting each session. For example, Todd and Selekman (1991a), in their work on adolescent substance abuse, provide a useful model for integrating structural–strategic family therapy with narrative and solution-focused approaches. They recommend starting with traditional structural–strategic approaches and implementing narrative, solution-focused, or paradoxical modes of practice when impasses occur.

The integrative approach we suggest builds upon common themes from family process and common elements from practice that have been identified here. It is based upon our review of family therapy literature and personal experiences with minority and agency-based populations. From previous chapters we know that *the therapeutic relationship is an important element that should be monitored during each step of the process.* We also know that *the referral process contains important clues to clients' motivation.* The following is our recommendation for ordering the other important elements that should be addressed to maximize clients' success. As an individual session proceeds, the process should be organized around the tasks of negotiating structure, exploring client experience, addressing relationships, and developing a shared direction. As with other stages and interactions covered thus far, each of these tasks may proceed in order or may overlap during complex exchanges with the family. These four tasks suggest that the family therapist should:

1. Organize treatment clearly and collaboratively.
2. Explore experience and context from the micro to the macro level.
3. Seek behavioral, perceptual, and relational change.
4. Develop a direction that considers the needs of important family members.

We believe these dimensions provide a map to integrate theory, practice, and the family therapy skills covered in the remainder of the book. With these four objectives in mind, we now illustrate how the initial interview can accomplish these tasks.

NEGOTIATE STRUCTURE

In an initial interview, the professional takes responsibility for exploring what family therapy will be for an individual or family—how it will be organized and how decisions will be made about the process. In subsequent sessions, the negotiating structure would include discussions about the organization, expectations, and purpose of each meeting. These should be summarized at the outset to provide an avenue for the client or therapist to ask for changes in the process. For example, if certain members are absent, the impact of this fact must be explored and a decision made about how the process will proceed in light of this change. In the event that a crisis has occurred between meetings, this task provides an avenue to decide what from the previous meeting is or is not still relevant. As the first task of each meeting, it can be thought of as a mutual agreement for that session.

Clarifying the Role of the Therapist

The family therapist and the family each bring a set of expectations to the therapy hour. These expectations relate to each party's role, the procedures that will be followed, and the conditions that each party expects to be met by the other. Perhaps the family has a media-related stereotype of a counselor, therapist, or social worker. Perhaps the family therapist also holds certain stereotypes or has a desire to maintain a certain image with the family. What if the two sets of expectations do not match? To use Bateson's terms, all communication has report (content) and command (process) levels: The report level is the verbal information transmitted; the command level is the nonverbal manifestation of how the sender is defining the relationship (Ruesch & Bateson, 1951). Therefore, the family therapist and family each define the nature of the relationship, but neither may be *openly* communicating their expectations to the other. For example, the family therapist may have chosen a role as neutral negotiator for the family. Meanwhile, the family may have defined the therapist as a referee or even an ally. As these implicit expectations unfold through nonverbal behaviors (process), the implicit conflict may interfere with explicitly stated goals (content). Once the implicit information is brought forward, roles can be clarified in a way that enlists cooperation more fully. As an example:

A woman sought help from a family therapist, and their work involved a pattern in which she brought up a different problem each week. Puzzled and frustrated, the therapist wondered about how the woman might be defining the role of the therapist. In the next session, the therapist inquired about the pattern and what it could mean. After some hypothesizing by the therapist, the woman was able to explain that involvement was more important to her than problem solving. She thought that if she didn't bring in some problem to talk about each week, the therapist would discontinue treatment. Having clarified how she was defining the relationship (command level), the therapist could help the woman feel more in charge of therapy and how long it continued. Once the problem of involvement was clarified, they could move on to more important issues.

As family therapists learn how to effectively clarify the role of the therapist, it may also be helpful to review Table 1.1 for examples of therapeutic roles that are adopted by various models of family therapy. These can be used to reconcile differences in expectations and to explain the role the therapist decides to assume.

Describing the Therapeutic Process

Once therapists have begun the initial interview, they should orient the family or individual to the process of therapy—that is, the staff involved and the specific techniques employed to pursue goals. It is important at the outset to provide at least a minimal structure of the therapeutic process. Just as a travel agent might provide an itinerary for a family vacation, the therapist might provide an overview of the initial interview in the following ways:

Today, we'll talk about things that concern you (your family) and discuss what you want to do about them. I want to know what is important to you, and I assume you might like to know what I can do to help. We can pool our ideas and come up with some ideas about where to go from here. If you're not in the middle of a crisis, I usually spend a few sessions learning everything I can about what works best for you. If you are in a crisis, we can decide what you might need immediately. After that, we'll develop a plan of action. If you try something and it doesn't work, we'll talk about it and figure out what else might help.

The description of the therapeutic process will vary depending on the family's previous experience in therapy. Families who have not been to therapy or who are uncertain of what to expect will require more specificity. On the other hand, with families who have had previous therapeutic contact, it will be important to explore their expectations for service. After hearing about the family's previous experiences with counseling, family therapists may need to clarify how this experience may be the same as or different from that with other practitioners.

One of the questions clients might ask is whether the therapist will reveal what is said in the session to others (for example, parents, a probation officer, a social worker). Before the question arises, family therapists should say that what is discussed will be held confidential *except under certain conditions.* A promise without this qualification can undermine trust. There are cases (usually with children or adolescents) where it is in the clients' best interests that information be shared. There are also laws in many states that mandate reporting under certain circumstances. If clients find their statements have not been confidential when the therapist promised total confidentiality, the trust is damaged and the therapist loses effectiveness. Consequently, these qualifications should be included. For example, the therapist might say:

I will try to keep what we talk about between the four of us, but if one of you said you were planning to do something that would be harmful to you or someone else, I would tell someone else and try to keep anyone from getting hurt. I promise that I'll let you know if I'm going to tell anyone what we've talked about. And sometimes, if I think it would be helpful for someone to know something you've told me, I may ask you if it's okay for me to mention it. For example, if you told me you were having trouble in school, I might ask you if you minded my discussing it with your teachers. It is also important for you to know that the law also requires that I disclose information in certain cases. These include. . .

6.1   *Describing the Process of Therapy*

Who will attend? (referral source, extended family, others)

What will each person's role be? (consultant, client, provider of information)

What are the treatment goals? (presenting problem and desired relational changes)

What are the process goals? (assessment then treatment, further exploration to define problem, brainstorming, experimentation)

When will sessions be held? (frequency or pace)

How will sessions be conducted? (in-session directives, circular or systematic questioning, out-of-session tasks, genograms, specific interventions, psychoeducation)

When will the arrangement be renegotiated?

What fees, resources, space, time, and help are needed?

Who else needs to be made aware of the plan?

Are there any barriers or costs to the plan?

Other questions concerning the therapist's role or the therapeutic relationship may come up throughout therapy sessions and should be answered as they arise. What's crucial in explaining the therapeutic process is to relieve anxieties that clients might have, to give them some expectations about what is likely to happen when they come, and to help them feel at ease in the therapeutic situation. Box 6.1 provides a series of questions to help the practitioner review aspects of the process with families.

EXPLORE CLIENT EXPERIENCE

Each session should afford all participants the opportunity to respond to questions about their thoughts, feelings, actions, intentions, and senses. The initial interview should obtain descriptions of interactional sequences and of each person's perception of the problem over time. As therapy proceeds from session to session, systemic themes (i.e., transitions, intergenerational process, gender, etc.) can be chosen as the focus of these explorations (see Chapter 3). Discussions can also include pragmatic reviews of attempted solutions, the identification of behaviors related to success, and the telling of stories that form the basis for a client's worldview.

Defining the Problem

In the early years of family therapy, problem definition was a continual struggle. Clients would come in asking for help with a child's behavior or their own predefined mental illness, but family therapists, anxious to convert their client families to systemic thinking, would be quick to persuade families to think of their child's behavior as a family problem or their mental illness as a marital problem. This approach only served to communicate blame to other family members. Today, many constructivist theories speak of *co-creating the definition of the problem* (O'Hanlon & Weiner-Davis, 1989), and integrative models such as the Purdue Brief Family Therapy (PBFT) model speak explicitly about avoiding resistance and respecting the family's uniqueness. By asking families to clarify what they would like to see happen in family therapy, therapists have the opportunity to rid themselves of any hidden agendas that might define the problem in ways that conflict with the family's way of thinking (theory of change).

To begin a dialogue about the problem with a family or individual, the family therapist might ask the following circular questions as a way of exploring clients' definitions while obtaining relational information:

1. What brings you here?
2. What would be helpful for us to discuss?
3. Who first noticed the problem and how long ago was this?
4. What led you (or another person) to conclude that this was a problem?
5. Who else agrees or disagrees that this is the problem?
6. Who else (inside or outside the family) has an opinion about the problem?
7. Have you or anyone else thought of any other possibilities regarding what the problem might be?
8. Are there times when the problem isn't occurring? What is going on at those times?
9. What are the differences between times when the problem does and doesn't occur?
10. What would happen if things don't change?

As we have seen, families sometimes come to counseling with a definition that has been created by others in the system. The therapist may be able to influence the definition of the problem away from a pathologized view. Sometimes families are relieved at this and are able to express their hopes and fears. However, if families feel strongly about a certain view of the presenting problem ("I'm bipolar," or "My family is dysfunctional"), family therapists must negotiate a cooperative relationship above all else, rather than one that unwittingly becomes subtly adversarial due to philosophical differences. An example of this is when a family comes in seeking help for a chemically dependent member. If the family therapist suggests that the problem is really a family problem, the family members are likely to leave the session thinking to themselves, "But we still think the problem is *his* drinking!" They may be reluctant to return. Instead, it is possible to develop a problem definition that *unifies* diverse opinions, such as "His drinking has affected your relationship, and you wish things could be better between you."

Thus, in the initial session, the therapist explicitly accepts the family's definition of the problem while implicitly exploring additional ways to describe it using relational terms. As the family members answer these questions, it is important to accept their description of the problem without criticism or premature advice. It is also essential to validate the importance of each member's contribution ("That's a very good point. You seem to have thought a lot about this issue"). If family members interrupt each other, remind them that they will each have an opportunity to express their views.

If an individual has come to the session alone, the definition of the problem might evolve from questions not only about the individual's opinion but about those of his or her significant other ("If your wife was here with us, what would she say?"). If a couple or family has come for family therapy, the definition might incorporate each person's opposing view of the problem. For example, if a husband says the problem is too little sex and his wife says the problem is too little communication, the family therapist might suggest that the problem is the couple's inability to meet each other's needs. The newly formulated problem definition must include the diversity expressed by the *relational network*.

Once descriptions of the problem emerge, the practitioner should ask questions that bring about greater specificity. Clients will often express global concerns through the use of labels (depressed, angry, nervous, and so on). While labels offer a general indication of the problem area, they often mean different things to different people. For example, a family member may say, "I don't want to go to school," which really means she is unhappy. A therapist might use the following questions to help each family member clarify the problem:

1. What do you mean by_____?
2. Give me some examples of_____?
3. Describe a situation when you_____?
4. How does this affect you now?
5. Tell me about the last time_____happened.

The goal is to help each family member to be *specific and concrete,* so that the problem defined will become more solvable. As the family members share their views, therapists can use this information to clarify client motives and expectations.

Understanding Expectations

Quite often, clients may have *hidden agendas* that they are unable to make explicit. These are unspoken intentions of which clients believe others might disapprove. In the earlier example, the woman was afraid to express her perceptions of how she thought therapy was organized. In marital therapy, an unfaithful spouse may come to the first session simply to assuage his or her guilt, having already decided to leave the marriage. Without ever intending to salvage the relationship, this client may hope that the therapist will become someone for the abandoned spouse to lean on. However, the client may be unable to disclose that intention unless the family therapist *raises the possibility first.* Similarly, a single parent may seek family therapy for his or her child when the parent is still grieving the loss of the marriage. In the first case, the hidden agenda has a great influence on the course of therapy, especially if it remains unknown to the family therapist. If it can become known, it may become the focus of therapy since it is actually the primary motivation for seeking services. In the second case, the hidden agenda may not greatly affect the course of therapy since divorce-adjustment work could be done in a way that simultaneously benefited parent and child. If the parent does not validate a therapist's hunch, there is nothing lost in staying with the stated agenda.

In addition, families often have expectations regarding who will actually be seen in sessions (the child alone, each spouse separately, and so on), how the problem will be defined, and what topics will or will not be discussed. While it is difficult to second-guess all the possible expectations, the therapist can try to join sufficiently so that families feel comfortable in disclosing even their most sensitive agendas (for example, "I'm hoping you can tell me if my marriage is worth saving"). Sometimes it may help to make some tentative guesses about what clients may be expecting; other times it may only be necessary for the family therapist to provide an atmosphere that is comfortable for sharing all possible responses. When the therapist shows an acceptance of the most unusual, the family will be more forthcoming with hidden agendas (i.e., "Sometimes people think I'm a little crazy, so you'll have to bear with me. . ."). However, there will be additional opportunities to clarify these expectations as the therapist learns more about relevant relationships.

ADDRESS RELATIONSHIPS

As individuals' experiences form a collective picture of behaviors, perceptions, and relationships, a therapeutic dialogue should develop in which the practitioner maintains a focus upon the *important and relevant relationships* connected to either the problem itself or possible solutions. Specific interventions from preferred models are part of this task. If a person is being seen individually, interactions should still maintain a focus upon relationships, not behaviors or perceptions alone. As in problem defining, we recommend that systemic therapists ask about the experience of significant others not present. By including a variety of views in the discussion, the process remains tied to relational factors and maintains a broader view of the interactional context. In

6.2

Questions to Track Interactional Sequences
Who did what when?
What did he or she actually say or do?
What was happening right before this?
When he or she said or did that, what happened next?
And then what happened?
Then what did they do?
While this was going on, where were _____, _____,
_____ (other family or household members)?
When he or she does that, then what happens?

Questions to Clarify Meanings and Messages
What was actually said?
What were you thinking when he said that?
When you said _____, what were you thinking?
When you thought _____, how did you come to that conclusion?
   (Where did you get that idea?)

addition, the therapist should make it a routine practice to obtain a *clear, close-up picture of the interactions* in relationships that coexist with the problem.

Tracking Interactional Sequences: The "Microscope" of Family Therapy

Regardless of the school of thought, much of the activity of a family therapist is focused on gathering interactional information about the family. Embedded in interactional sequences are thoughts, emotions, intentions, and behaviors that become targets for change within the relationship. This is why we use the analogy of the microbiologist: Tracking sequences is the "microscope" of the family therapist. We identify each element as a potential point of intervention in a relationship (see Chapter 7). In addition, focusing on these sequences begins to transform the description of the problem from an individual attribute (for example, "He's depressed") to an interactional definition ("When he's depressed, we don't agree on the solution").

Box 6.2 summarizes examples of how to track communication in interactional sequences. The approaches used in tracking a family's interpersonal patterns are similar to relationship techniques derived from client-centered therapy (Rogers, 1961). The therapist's open-ended questions, ability to reflect content and feelings, and attentive demeanor help establish a supportive relationship with the family. More complex techniques of tracking center on the therapist's efforts to "listen with a third ear." The therapist responds to thoughts and feelings that family members may be unable to acknowledge. When family members begin to talk, they usually describe the *content* of the problem. For example, a parent might say that a child "won't come home" or "won't do what I tell him." While therapists may listen to what family members say about each other (content), they are equally concerned about the *process*—how family members interact with each other. Do family members talk for each other? The therapist who focuses only on the content will not be able to assess the interactional pattern that contributes to the problem. Colapinto (1991) states:

> Following the content and the process of the family interaction, like the needle of a record player follows a groove, is the basic structural procedure to collect information on the family map. As the therapist listens to and encourages the contributions of family members, observes their mutual dances, and asks for clarifications and expansions, he or she begins to draft first answers to structural questions: Whether family members can converse without being interrupted, whether they tend to interact in age appropriate ways, how they organize each other's behaviors, how they deal with or avoid conflict, what alliances they tend to form. (pp. 431–432)

The therapist can also assess such patterns of interaction by asking Milan-style questions related to sequences (see Table 2.1 on page 38). When a family member begins to describe a problem, the therapist must explore with whom this problem exists and how the sequence unfolds. The following dialogue illustrates how this may be accomplished.

THERAPIST: Tell me what the problem is today.
MOTHER: He won't listen to me.
THERAPIST: Who won't listen to you?
MOTHER: My son, Eric.
THERAPIST: What does he do to indicate that he doesn't listen?
MOTHER: He just sits silently and watches TV when I tell him to do something.
THERAPIST: And what do you do when he does that?
MOTHER: Sometimes I go in and make him listen to me.
THERAPIST: How do you do that?
MOTHER: I go in and shut off the TV to get his attention.
THERAPIST: And then what happens?
MOTHER: He usually throws a tantrum.
THERAPIST: So what happens next? How does your husband get involved?

What is important here is that the therapist is thinking about the pattern of interactions that surrounds the problem *even if there is only one family member in the session.* The interactional description of the problem tells us who should be talking to whom about it. For example, can a mother and stepfather discuss the problem in the presence of their child? Rather than reporting *about* the problem, the family therapist asks them to describe how they respond, thus gaining a *picture* of the interactional sequence before and after the problem. If the therapist cannot visualize exactly what happened, more detailed questions should continue. To successfully learn this skill, family therapists should systematically use Box 6.2 and Table 2.1 to obtain a *detailed and specific picture* of these interactions. Special attention should be given to repetitive behavioral sequences that occur around the problem and the specific people involved. Family therapists can use this information to decide whether any important people are missing from the session.

Expanding the System: "There Is No Such Thing As a Person Without a Relationship"

Deciding whom to include in sessions is often difficult for the beginning family therapist. While some pioneers were noted for their insistence upon seeing the entire family (Boszormenyi-Nagy & Framo, 1965; Napier & Whitaker, 1978), others were noted for seeing individuals (Bowen, 1978). We think it is important to remember Whitaker's (1986) assertion that "there is no such thing as a person without a relationship." To our way of thinking, this should be a central premise of all family therapy. However, in deciding on issues of inclusion, it is also important that the expectations of the client be understood at the beginning, in order to negotiate effectively *without coercion*.

The focus of family therapy includes important relationships outside of formal family ties. For some, relationships between family and school may be targeted for intervention (Amatea & Sherrard, 1989). For others, nonblood kin may be more influential than their biological family (Boyd-Franklin, 1989). Therefore, any system or any set of relationships may be identified as the primary context for problem solving. As a relational network becomes the focus of the interview, the family therapist develops an approach that fits with the nature of these relationships as they emerge through families, friendships, or various community ties. We believe beginning practitioners will develop greater effectiveness if they give careful thought to a series of questions throughout this section. The first set concerns the influence of others.

1. **Who is defining the problem?** If it is a spouse or parent not in attendance, involving that person is a priority.
2. **Is the client living with significant others in the household or dependent on others in significant ways?** If so, involving them as sources of information and support should be strongly considered. It is important to engage spouses for such problems as depression, anxiety, and eating disorders. Many times they are willing to come, but it simply did not occur to them to do so. At other times, they may need to know

they are not being blamed but, rather, are considered a therapeutic influence upon the healing process.

3. **Does the client explicitly name others as a legal, psychological, financial, or relational part of the presenting problem?** To ensure a peaceful resolution, the client must believe that the therapist can remain on his or her side while also engaging the other party. If convincing the client of this proves to be beyond the skill level of the clinician, working systemically may involve playing devil's advocate, developing interactional strategies, or asking questions that provide multiple points of view.

4. **Has the person definitely decided upon a divorce?** If not, informed consent could involve the information that individual sessions may contribute to further distance in the marriage. Many times, one spouse who is reluctant to involve the other can clarify her or his own fears over including the husband or wife. Addressing these fears can become a preliminary goal until the person is assured that the therapist will be able to conduct conjoint therapy in a manner that is comfortable for the reluctant spouse. While the skill level of the therapist may be a factor in this issue, later chapters will address basic skills for conducting conjoint sessions.

5. **Are there significant others who appear to have ongoing knowledge of the day-to-day occurrence of the problem?** If so, a preliminary goal of gathering multiple points of view is important even if those other parties are unwilling to attend. Many times, however, parties who are involved but not necessarily perceived as part of the problem may be willing to attend as consultants. When expectations can be addressed and respected, it is possible to involve a number of people as sources of information or support, as long as the clinician respects their position as nonclient—someone who was not asking for help or change.

6. **If others were involved in sessions, would the person seeking help become more or less alienated in the process?** Situations of violence, emotional abuse, and extreme alienation may be contraindications for involving other parties on whom the client may be dependent. The clinician's skill level, the client's goals, and other contributing circumstances will have to be explored in total to determine the most beneficial course to take.

Depending upon who attends the first session, discussions may involve re-peated *references to significant people who are absent* from the session. This is often the case when individuals come alone. If so, these references should prompt the therapist to return to the possibility of including others in some way. Explore the client's ideas about what kind of service to expect and about whether including others would conflict with the family's or individual's perception of help. Quite often it is only a general stereotype about psychotherapy that has led to a person's expectations. Because family therapy is different in scope and philosophy, we think clients deserve the opportunity to become educated about their options in seeking help. These questions can become the basis for therapist and client to negotiate an expanded system that is safe, productive, and supportive. This second set of questions suggests an in-session exploration of concerns the clients have about process and specific feelings they may have about expanding the system.

1. How did you decide who would participate in today's session?
2. Maybe you are more comfortable without _____ here. Are there some reasons why you would prefer to leave them out?
3. What do you think might happen if _____ was invited?
4. If I encouraged you to invite them, would it be so uncomfortable that you might not return?

The answers to these questions help the family therapist to find a starting point from which to explore important relational issues. For example, the therapist can learn about the person's sense of disempowerment in her or his relational network (for example, "I'm afraid you will side with my husband against me"). Then, it is possible to address each area of discomfort with a plan such that the proposed conjoint session could avoid the client's worst fears.

Certainly, there are many situations in which a person's own framework for help would be violated and such an insistence would be inappropriate. Conversely, there are times when a family therapist will consider the attendance of others to be essential to a positive therapeutic outcome. If the attendance of others seems imperative, before taking a strong position, the family therapist should conduct a self-evaluation. This third set of questions helps the therapist develop a careful, detailed, and respectful plan for expanding the system.

1. Have I elicited and acknowledged fears the client has about inviting others to join us?
2. Have I reassured the client that I can orchestrate a constructive outcome when others are included? Has my reassurance included *detailed descriptions* of what I will say and do?
3. Do I know enough about these other people, and do I have the skills necessary, to set goals that guarantee the outcome of such a meeting?
4. Am I ignoring messages (verbal or nonverbal) from the client about what is essential to him or her?
5. Am I operating out of a model that narrows my perception of how I can be helpful? Does the client have important information to which I should defer, rather than insisting on a certain structure?
6. Have we explored alternative ways of bringing the influence of the expanded system into our sessions, such as speaker phone calls or the use of empty chairs to represent important others?

The answers to these questions can help the practitioner weigh priorities and skills. In many cases, clients can be shown how inclusion of others will be helpful. Of particular value is the work of a research project in which family therapists helped drug abusers to involve their family of origin in therapy (Van Deusen, Stanton, Scott, Todd, & Mowatt, 1982). In these cases, the therapist might say something like this:

There are many paths we could take to reach your goals. As a family therapist, I've found that some pathways may seem suitable to individuals at the time, only to find later that their spouse feels more alienated after an individual therapy experience or that the clients wish that their friends could understand them the way the therapist does. Because of these situations, I always try to find the road that will be good for the person and good for the person's important relationships at the same time. The best way to find this balance is by involving those other people, either in person, by telephone, or in some other way. Then we can look for a "win-win" direction that is good for everyone.

It has been our experience that, sometimes, the invited people become motivated clients in their own right if the therapist helps them to personalize what they may gain from the process. At other times, they may come and provide helpful information without agreeing to further involvement. Still others may come and be successfully enlisted as consultants as long as the family therapist refrains from overt or covert attempts to make them into clients. These possibilities should be suggested to individuals in the first session. However, if clients are still opposed to inviting others after they have explained their reluctance and they have been given reassuring explanations, it is imperative that the therapist accept the clients' position.

Once the position of the client is fully addressed, the next issue is that of addressing how others may feel about being invited. Family members may often be reluctant to attend therapy sessions, especially *if they fear being blamed for the problem.* In particular, fathers and husbands characteristically have been reluctant to discuss matters that they regard as private with someone outside the family. These problems can often be detected when a woman describes her perceptions of her husband's reluctance ("My husband would never talk to a therapist," or "He doesn't believe in counseling"). The beginning therapist must understand the protective nature of these responses and deal with them in a supportive manner. It is often effective to ask permission to assume the husband's point of view in the relationship. Then, therapist and family member can gain empathy for another's position and develop a plan for addressing those fears. Sometimes the contact person needs to know that the therapist will not criticize or blame those who are invited. At other times, the therapist will need to clarify that the purpose of including others is not to join the side of the client in some ongoing conflict. Instead, the role of the therapist can be repeated: to develop a win-win experience for all sides.

Evidence-based approaches to adolescent drug abuse are now finding great success from using this reluctance as *the starting point in successful treatment* (Cunningham & Henggeler 1999; Coatsworth, Santisteban, McBride, & Szapocznik, 2001). Instead of hoping that a family member, on his or her own, will persuade others, the therapist forms a partnership with the contact person and coaches that person on how to approach others. Often, therapists support this process with a direct contact. Such an approach has evolved as service providers have explored the first set of questions we posed above and found that those defining the problem and those crucial to the solution are as important as the client. When children and adolescents are involved, this is often the case.

In cases of adult substance abuse, David Treadway (1989) elaborates for the case where the drinking husband is the reluctant partner. This strategy helps the therapist gradually involve the reluctant family member in therapy:

> The other way I elicit the husband's cooperation is by asking him if he cares about his wife's anxiety and distress and if he would like to be helpful to her. This defines my work as help to her rather than an attempt to change him. I want him to take the position of aiding her in getting help with her part of the problem. Many drinkers will go along with this idea, because at least for the moment it takes the heat off them. For once their wives are being challenged about their own behavior. Anticipating and blocking the drinker's reactivity are essential to effective intervention with the spouse. (p. 40)

At the very least, the family therapist can take the results of these discussions as important information that can *invoke the influence of the expanded system* without actually including additional parties. Ongoing discussions can explore these issues so that the family therapist gathers important information about specific sensitivities in significant relationships. Identifying these obstacles can deepen the clinician's understanding of a client's personal reality. Accepting this reality enables the therapist to maintain a successful joining process. This acceptance then becomes the basis for formalizing a treatment plan that will unify therapist, client, and the influences of the relational network.

DEVELOP A SHARED DIRECTION

The therapist searches for language, metaphors, themes, or goals that will unite family members in forward motion, build upon their strengths, and instill hope. Dialogues about direction with clients should discuss their perceptions and provide a summary of the therapist's perceptions. In the initial interview, as the problem becomes described in relational terms, *unifying goals for treatment* should be developed through an exploration of desired outcomes and processes. The family therapist searches with the family for phrases upon which everyone can agree. At this point, the therapist should make recommendations about the process for working together. Does the family hope for a quick turnaround (such as in a crisis), or does the family prefer a period of exploration that helps to clarify the issues in a new way? Are the members of the family more pragmatic in their approach to problem solving, or do they value deliberation, education, and insight? As therapist and family decide on the course of action that best suits them, *treatment goals* should state the desired outcome of therapy, and *process goals* should state the desired procedures used to accomplish them. Thereafter, suggestions for the next session should be negotiated.

Setting Treatment Goals

In the goal-setting stage, the therapist helps family members decide what they want changed. For example, the therapist might begin by asking, "How would you like things to be different in this family?" or "What is it that you would like your son to be doing instead?" The responses eventually become goal behaviors ("If your husband doesn't pay attention to you, how would you like him to show that he is paying attention?"). Later, when tracking the interactional sequence that is maintaining the problem, the therapist might say, "And when he yells at you, what would you like him to do instead of that?" or "It sounds like when he talks to you that way, you get angry and threaten him. How could he talk to you differently at that moment so you don't get angry with him?" Often, when tracking the interactional sequence, the therapist is asking family members to describe how they would like another family member to respond differently within the sequence of behavior preceding or following the identified problem. In earlier phases of the interview, the clinician is requesting only that family members give a general statement of what they want to be different. Later, in the first interview, the therapist can help family members become more specific in formulating observable goals.

In most cases, client goals begin as abstract desires (for example, "I want help dealing with my low self-esteem," or "We want to communicate better"). The family therapist helps the family to clarify such desires until behavioral and perceptual elements of the problem are identified as specific goals ("I want to be able to go to a party and have something interesting to say," or "When we discuss finances, we'll be able to resolve the conflict to our satisfaction"). The treatment plan may include the assessment process, which clarifies the nature of the problem and outlines a subsequent plan of action, or it may consist only of the sequence of interventions set in motion as a result of the assessment process. In either case, the treatment plan should address the family's goals and hypotheses generated during the assessment process.

In some cases, the family's goals may be different from those of the therapist. A parent may wish to take care of a legal problem or illness, whereas the therapist may be concerned about the parent's relationship with the children. Parents often feel overwhelmed because they have multiple problems. The therapist should respond to the family's concern around these basic needs before inviting parents to consider an additional view about parent–child relationships. A good treatment plan requires the therapist to analyze hypotheses in order to (1) prioritize areas of change, (2) make goals concrete and specific, and (3) build on existing strengths.

Prioritizing Areas of Change   If the family presents several problem areas, the beginning therapist must start to set priorities for treatment. The therapist may often establish intermediate goals, each of which represents a step toward the final goal. This process helps make the family's problem more manageable. These criteria are critical in making this determination:

1. Which problem is most pressing to the family?
2. Which problem has the greatest negative consequence if not handled immediately?
3. What forces (people, situations) stand in the way of problem resolution?
4. What are the consequences of change? Will anything get worse if the problem gets better? If so, should we develop a plan for coping with change?

It is often helpful if the therapist brainstorms and writes the family's responses on an easel for everyone to read. Once the options are explored, the therapist should ask family members to decide on an order to the goals.

Making Goals Concrete and Specific   Once goals are prioritized, they should be stated clearly so that everyone can agree when the goal has been reached. For example, if parents report that they want their child "to pay attention," then the therapist must question the parent to determine what the child will be doing "to pay attention." Likewise, labels such as "unhappiness" and "anger" must be stated in such a way that they can be resolved.

The following suggestions represent several different ways to help family members describe changes (goals) in more observable terms:

1. *Ask each family member to describe how he or she would like things to be different.* The therapist might ask, "What changes would you like to see in this family?" or "How would you like things to be different?"
2. *Ask family members to describe changes in positive rather than negative terms.* The therapist might comment, "I know you don't like the way your son said that. How would you like him to say it?"
3. *Ask family members to be specific about what they want changed.* The therapist might ask a question such as one of these: "What do you mean by _____?" "What would your son be doing to show you that he can be trusted?" "How would you know that your mother cares about you?" "What would be one way he could help you?" "How would she show you that she has an improved self-concept?"

Building on Existing Strengths   Goal setting should evolve out of family strengths rather than weaknesses. Focusing on the family's deficits without considering its strengths makes it difficult to establish a relationship where both the therapist and the family can be optimistic about change. Emphasizing strengths helps alter the family's self-image and gives family members hope that their goals can be attained. In this, we adopt the following assumptions:

1. Families have resources and strengths to resolve problems.
2. Families often are aware of alternative ways to alter a problem.
3. Families will be more likely to implement a solution to the problem if they suggest it.

If therapists start treatment according to these assumptions, they can lead the discussion to focus on those areas that are working. The therapist will want to start by looking for small positive changes before examining bigger changes. When family members are able to make small positive changes, they are more hopeful about handling bigger changes (O'Hanlon & Weiner-Davis, 1989). This can be done by focusing on those aspects of the family that seem most changeable:

What would be a small sign that things are changing?
What might be one thing you could do to change?
What are some things you could do now to handle the problem?

The therapist will also want to focus on times when the problem is not occurring:

When are the times that you are able to handle the problem?
Are there times when the problem isn't occurring?
What are you doing differently in these situations?
What seems to be different when things are going well?

Understanding when they are able to manage the problem helps family members to get in touch with their strengths and resources. Since family members often feel hopeless, it is important to put them in charge of deciding on changes (goals). A final strategy for building on strengths is to interpret the family's definition of the problem in a different way, to give it new meaning. This new interpretation helps the family members get in touch with their own strengths. When a mother says, "I can't get him to do anything. He won't listen to me," the therapist shifts the focus to what she does out of her sense of "caring." If this makes it difficult for her to set firm limits, the therapist then can help her to expand her sense of caring to include additional behaviors. The Milan team referred to this as *positive connotation*. Milton Erickson referred to this as bypassing a person's *learned limitations*. When the mother perceives herself as caring, rather than weak, she has a new way of thinking about the problem that lowers her defenses. When the therapist creates an environment based on strengths, family members are more likely to set goals that can be met successfully.

Setting Process Goals

Breunlin (1985) notes that structural–strategic family therapists are comfortable intervening on the basis of a partial assessment of family functioning, whereas therapists using other models prefer a more thorough assessment before developing interventions. It is our belief that both methods are of value and the choice should be guided by client expectations. In every initial session, we think it is important for the therapist to *assess the level of crisis* by asking these questions:

1. Do you feel so hopeless or desperate about this situation, that you must see some change today in this session?
2. What do you think will happen if you don't see some change occur from this meeting?

Once the level of crisis is assessed, options for agreeing upon a process can be explored. If clients are in a crisis, the therapist should respond to the person feeling the most desperation. Is the person in a position of leadership in the family? Will her or his position play a critical role in the outcome of therapy? If so, others should be enlisted to participate in a plan of crisis intervention that uses the earlier section on setting treatment goals to develop an immediate, short-term plan of action.

If clients are not in crisis, we have good results when clients are asked for their preference between behavioral and perceptual changes related to their significant relationships. For example, when questioned about whether she preferred a therapy experience in which she was encouraged to make specific behavioral changes (through homework) or whether she preferred an experience in which she was able to reflect upon various aspects of her situation (insight), one woman chose the reflective mode. The therapist first used questions to reflect upon her family's genogram and then began making tentative suggestions about the possibility of discovering new patterns. After 4 weeks, the woman reported an incident of spontaneous behavior change at a routine family gathering. Thus, in the initial interview, if a client wants to work on certain interactional sequences or wants homework, the process goal may be *experimentation.* That would signal an emphasis on a quick strategic turnaround rather than a longer developmental process.

When client expectations point toward a longer assessment, process goals are aimed at developing a more specific definition of the problem. They can be labeled as *exploration* or *clarification.* For example, if an individual states the goal as "I want to stop hating my father" or "I want to have a better relationship with men," the therapist may pursue present-oriented interactional information only to discover in later sessions the existence of childhood sexual abuse. Therefore, if the problem definition is still vague at the end of the initial interview, family therapists are encouraged to negotiate a process goal in order to maintain a sense of direction with the client. In this way, the therapist helps the client anticipate a two-step process of problem resolution: clarification of context and development of strategies. An example of this follows:

Mary Ann, it sounds like there are many factors that enter into your desire to "stop hating" your father, and I want to make sure I fully understand your relationship with him before we develop more specific goals. You've been very helpful today, and I'm wondering if we could take another session to explore all of your feelings about this issue. If you decide to return, I would like to continue clarifying this situation until we are able to develop specific problem-solving strategies for you to try. How does this sound? After you've had some time to think about this, let me know next time if you would like to suggest anything different.

When a family or couple is being interviewed, the process will be similar. Families are usually so intent on getting results that they have become oblivious to their own process. This is why certain situations can benefit from a shift to process goals. Such goals can be explained to the family as a first step toward eventual problem resolution, to be followed by a second step in which strategies for change are developed. In the first step, focusing on the perspective of the family, the therapist can ask questions that begin to associate specific behaviors and perceptions with the description of the problem. This micro information can then be used to develop specific goals and strategies for change in the intervention phase of therapy. The family therapist might negotiate such a two-step agreement by stating the following:

It sounds to me like you have an idea about what the problem is but are struggling with how to go about resolving it. In the past, I've found it useful to help people develop a very specific understanding of the behavior, thoughts, and feelings that they would like to change. After that, it's much easier to help them develop solutions. If you decide to return, I would want some time to explore more details about the problem [perceptual change], so that all of us can come to some agreement about what should change. After that, if you're satisfied with the direction we're heading, we can pursue a specific plan of action [behavioral change].

If clients already have a clear set of behavioral goals when they enter family therapy, the negotiated goals may be easily determined to provide therapist and client with a clear sense of direction at the end of the first session. Because goals are tied to a certain sense of timing as the practitioner moves through the stages of family therapy (quick turnaround or slower exploration), these also become closely tied to the type of treatment plan that the family and the family therapist develop.

Developing Treatment Plans

Most agencies require therapists to develop a treatment plan early in the process. Personal services are most effective when families have the opportunity to take responsibility for the terms under which the services are rendered. Even in court-ordered cases, service delivery can be administered cooperatively. For example, a violent husband who has been ordered into treatment as part of a deferred-prosecution agreement may not have a choice about frequency or duration of sessions, but there may be some element of the content or process that he can choose, such as the topics to be discussed (hopes, aspirations, goals, patterns, relationships), the role of the therapist (director, guide, consultant), and goals (behavioral change, perceptual change, or both). These can be included in the plan.

An initial treatment plan might be a request to include certain people as sources of information during the assessment process, with the expectation that a different type of plan will be agreed upon for later stages of treatment. Another plan could define the role of the therapist as a consultant rather than a referee in the case of a highly emotional couple. Still another plan with an individual seeking help for depression might formalize the client's choice regarding which topic to pursue: family-of-origin influences having a bearing on the client's depression or strategies for day-to-day coping with the depression.

Each treatment plan should be individualized and should fit the unique characteristics of the family and interactive culture. Table 6.1 summarizes some typical goals and the relational issues that may be associated with those goals. We have deliberately listed *goals* instead of *problems* as an invitation for the practitioner to practice changing problem-oriented language into goal-oriented and future language. To use the table, take a presenting problem and decide what type of goal it suggests (physical, emotional, interpersonal, societal). Check to see if one of the examples comes close to categorizing it. Next, use the corresponding language of relational issues to conceptualize treatment. We have placed the goals according to a hierarchy of need, suggesting that clinicians should prioritize problems according to those most essential for survival (Weltner, 1985). Treatment plans should reflect these priorities. Often, a problem will encompass more than one level. For example, a suicidal client may present a situation in which the clinician must target safety issues and emotional issues simultaneously. In this way, the table can be used to develop a manageable order for complex problems. These should be considered as tentative suggestions, as there are situations in which one category might be cross-referenced with another. For example, sometimes physical

TABLE 6.1	COMMON GOALS AND RELATIONAL ISSUES		

Type of Goal	Example	Relational Issues to Address
Physical	Food Clothing Shelter Safety	Leadership Clarity of roles Protection
Emotional	Self-esteem Resilience Hope	Secure attachment Belonging Differentiation Personal authority
Interpersonal	Cooperation Shared responsibility Balance of power Productivity Intimacy	Communication Rules Beliefs Boundaries Balance Roles Secure attachment
Societal	Prosocial behavior Success with peers Success with job, school Social support Community support	Isolation Oppression Justice Relational ethics

goals might be related to relational issues in the societal category (oppression, isolation, justice). As the table reflects, at other times, a number of problems might be related to the same relational issue, such as secure attachment.

Once family therapists shift the language of problems and goals to relational terms, treatment plans should also include a description of how the goal will be addressed (intervention). To do this, Hanna (1997) first categorizes a problem according to its historical nature. *Situational* problems are new conflicts with no pre-existing history. *Transitional* problems are those related to normative life stages or non-normative changes in families that have had successes in earlier stages, but who have been unable to make the current adaptation. *Chronic* problems are those that can be traced to difficulties that may have started as situational in an earlier time frame, but have persisted through a transitional time period, and now have such an extensive history that they have become an organizing influence on additional emerging problems. By placing the problem in its developmental context, the clinician can begin to hypothesize about what therapeutic posture will be most successful with the family (direct or indirect). In general, we have found that the more chronic the problem, the more indirect the intervention should be. This is because chronic problems are often entwined in a sense of historical shame. Success is more likely when the clinician can bypass the shame by lowering defenses as much as possible (White, 1983; Selvini Palazzoli, 1986).

TABLE 6.2	TYPES OF PROBLEMS AND INTERVENTIONS		
	Possible Model of Family Therapy	**Interventions**	**Systemic Outcome**
Situational	Structural Cognitive behavioral Solution Focused	• Psychoeducation • Coach communication • Assign tasks • Explore options • Give support	Reorganization, adaptation and coping
Transitional	Strategic Experiential Intergenerational EFT CLS	• Address grief/loss • Develop rituals for healing • Resolve conflict • Address attachments • Explore meanings • Make the covert overt • Use metaphors	Mobilize resources for change
Chronic	MST Milan Approach M.R.I. Narrative	• Develop positive connotations • Implement paradox • Develop rituals for restructuring • Deconstruct beliefs and function of the symptom • Co-author new stories	Address underlying issues through lowering defenses

Table 6.2 provides suggested interventions and corresponding models of family therapy for these types of problems. For specific treatment plans that are based upon specific models of family therapy, Gehart and Tuttle (2002) provide some treatment plans that follow a given model's concepts. The interventions can be listed on treatment plans and revised as treatment progresses (see Chapter 8 for detailed information on these interventions). The models of family therapy start with those that are the most pragmatic and direct (behavioral) and progress toward those that are either indirect or focused upon internal experience. Often, the desired outcomes from chronic problems will include those of the other two. For example, situational problems will rarely involve underlying issues; however, moving upward, chronic problems often involve underlying issues, resources for change, and coping. However, the table suggests that the best place to start with chronic problems is with indirect strategies that minimize confrontation, negative labeling and straightforward directives. If the family responds to those approaches, it might not be necessary to become more direct.

TABLE 6.3	TREATMENT PLANNING PROCESS

Presenting Problem	Corresponding Goals	Relational Issues	Interventions	Models
Parent-child conflict (situational)	Cooperation	Conflict management	Psychoeducation	Solution focused
Hostile conflict (transitional)	Cooperation Resilience	Meanings of anger Quality of attachments	Individual sessions Coach communication	Intergenerational EFT
Long-term care (situational)	Safety Shared responsibility	Leadership roles	Psychoeducation Explore options Give support Assign tasks	Structural
Violent outbursts (chronic)	Self-esteem Cooperation Prosocial behavior Success with peers	Belonging Isolation Rules Boundaries	Circular questions Positive connotation Narrative Rituals	MST

Table 6.3 provides some examples of the entire treatment planning process beginning with the presenting problem, corresponding goal, relational objectives, and intervention strategy. For example, in one family where there is parent-child conflict, the treatment plan might call for conflict management skills. In another family with a similar problem, but more hostility, the plan might call for separate sessions with the parent and child, to establish trust. Sometimes a treatment plan can be presented in the initial contract for service. However, in those cases, clients already have their problem defined in concrete, behavioral terms, and the process of problem resolution is straightforward. For example, if the family is seeking a consultation in order to decide on a strategy for the long-term care of an elderly parent, the goal might be to decide who will be responsible for which tasks, after some psychoeducational sessions regarding the impact of long-term care on families. This direction could be decided upon in the initial session and described to the family as part of the therapeutic contract. In another case, parents might be seeking help for the long-standing behavioral problems of their daughter. Their goal might be for her to stop violent outbursts at school. A common treatment plan for such a presenting problem

would be to explore the relationships between the family and the school, between the daughter and her peers, and between individual family members (MST). The family therapist, the family, and the school might form a collaborative team to address the relational issues. Then the family therapist could facilitate cooperation among all parties in developing corrective strategies. This direction might develop over the first two assessment sessions. Then the treatment plan could be formalized, once the family approves the treatment and process goals.

In order to account for the essential elements of a successful treatment plan the clinician should review these questions:

1. Do I know what the client's original expectations were for the therapy process?
2. Have I provided a rationale if the process departs from those expectations?
3. Have we defined the problem in relational language?
4. Does the client have an understanding of the process goals and of what specifically will occur from session to session and how these activities will address the presenting problem?
5. Have I enlisted each member in the process, clarified the role of each family member, and addressed any objections or questions?

Beginning practitioners sometimes try to maintain client commitment in indirect ways—by persuasion or lectures about why clients should return for treatment. At other times, therapists may expect clients to continue attending and paying for sessions in spite of lingering reservations. These situations may be avoided by thoroughly exploring and validating the concerns and reservations that clients express in the first session. By assuming a "one-down" position, the clinician is able to empower the client to feel a sense of entitlement when it comes to dictating the terms of therapy. The clinician always has the right to refuse to see a client, but the client must also be allowed the right to express concerns when services do not seem helpful.

A practitioner's setting may influence whether a treatment plan is written or verbal. Fees, liability, releases of information, and other legal aspects of therapy are usually written in order to become legally binding. In some instances, clients are provided with statements regarding their rights to obtain records or to file grievances. It is empowering for clients to know that the therapist expects to renegotiate and to evaluate the process on the basis of the client's personal experience. Too often, therapists develop expectations that clients will blindly participate in the process without holding therapists accountable for their part of the contract. When no-shows occur in clinical settings, it is usually because an *unspoken* concern has not been addressed. Many consumers are more compliant when they are in crisis, only to find later that they need to renegotiate but are too intimidated to do so. Dropping out of therapy becomes the most expedient option.

Thus, a treatment plan is the result of sifting information related to the definition of the problem, the motivation to seek therapy, the likely participants, and their expectations for treatment. As this sifting takes place, the nature of the therapeutic process begins to evolve from the important elements that surface. The result is an agreement that specifies the role of the therapist, each family member's role, intermediate and long-range goals, and an initial plan for achieving the goals. Just as the therapist uses Box 6.1 to help explain the way therapy is organized, so might the questions in the box be used at the end of the session to cover important details of the future treatment plan. While these first roles, goals, and plans may be changed many times throughout the therapeutic process, grappling with them in a systematic way during the initial interview helps the family therapist begin the process in an organized manner.

SUMMARY

From Referral Process Through Initial Interview

As beginning practitioners prepare for the first stage of treatment, they may review Box 6.3 to decide what issues to address and when. The box outlines the key issues reviewed in this chapter and in Chapter 5, with integrative notes to identify what model of family therapy has influenced our suggestions. This outline brings together key elements across models that have been reviewed thus far. Our integration of these elements is based upon the belief that each first and second generation model of family therapy has strengths that can enhance the process at critical stages in the process. Thus, Box 6.3 suggests *when* these strengths can be most helpful within the initial stage of therapy. The order of the process assumes that the family therapist should exercise flexible leadership in which they assume responsibility for organizing the treatment experience and for discovering the best fit for the client. Thus, the process is driven by the desire to individualize treatment for each family. To develop a roadmap for the process of individualization, we suggest that problems are embedded in a multisystemic process that unfolds over time, just as a journey unfolds with many levels of process across a progression of events. The use of these models of family therapy provides enough variety to find the right fit for the breadth of human experience. They cover important elements of problems, relationships and the process of change. Also, our integration suggests that there is no need to develop a polarized position with respect to modern and postmodern perspectives of therapy. We think postmodernism is best considered as a *refinement* of therapeutic process, *not* a rejection of first generation models. In this sense, both perspectives highlight a number of issues that help the practitioner with a smooth entry into the process. As these issues are addressed, the outline can serve as a guide for the practitioner to know when to move on to the middle stage of treatment, that of beginning and maintaining change.

6.3 The First Stage of Family Therapy: From Referral Through Initial Interview

I. Referral Process (Milan Team)
   A. Step-by-step process that led the client to make an appointment
   B. Client's motivation for coming
   C. Problem-defining system (CLS)

II. Intake Process
   A. Statement of the problem
   B. Family information
   C. Concerned others
   D. Schedule
   E. Hypotheses and relevant questions for first session (MST, Milan Team)

III. Initial Interview
   A. Negotiate Structure (Structural, Behavioral, Experiential)
      1. Discuss organization, expectations and purpose of the session
      2. Describe the therapeutic process
      3. Clarify the roles of those in attendance
   B. Explore Client Experience (Solution focused, Narrative, Milan Team)
      1. Join with the client according to their expectations and level of motivation
      2. Explore each person's opinion about the problem, *including those who are not present*
      3. Explore history and onset of the problem (Milan Team)
         a. situational
         b. transitional
         c. chronic
      4. Explore exceptions, those times in which the problem does not occur (Solution focused)
   C. Address Relationships (Structural, Intergenerational)
      1. Track interactional sequences related to the presenting problem
      2. Determine the views of other important people missing from the session
      3. Address the inclusion of important people
      4. Define the problem in relational terms

The First Stage of Family Therapy:
From Referral Through Initial Interview
(continued)

D. Develop a Shared Direction
    1. Set treatment goals
    2. Set process goals
        a. Assess level of crisis
        b. Decide on the pace of intervention
            (1) clarification (MRI)
            (2) exploration (Narrative)
            (3) experimentation (Strategic,
                 Behavioral, Intergenerational)
    3. Develop a treatment plan
        a. Presenting problem
        b. Relational goals and issues
        c. Intervention strategies matched to history/onset
            of problem
        d. Role of the therapist
    4. Highlight strengths and instill hope (Narrative, Solution
        focused)
    5. Propose options and elicit feedback (Strategic, MRI)

Box 6.4 contains a general outline that can be used as a planning tool from session to session. In cases where both referral information and intake information are gathered in the first session, the therapist may want to explain the first session of therapy as one of exploration leading to a definition of the problem. Then, the second session can be used to address remaining topics leading to a treatment plan. In other cases, the therapist can propose a plan that allows for an assessment period followed by recommendations from the clinician. At the end of this assessment period (from one to four sessions), the family members can decide whether they would like to continue.

Conducting an assessment, whether brief or thorough, should be considered an intervention in itself. However, bringing the exchange from mere conversation to the level of intervention requires the discipline and wisdom we mentioned at the beginning of this chapter. Carefully chosen language and thoughtful questions must follow a deliberate order in the conversation. Chapter 7 discusses the assessment process in more detail and how its effectiveness is directly related to these skills. As beginning practitioners become acclimated to the process of therapeutic questions, they more fully understand the experience of those who have come seeking help.

6.4   Session Outline: Basic Tasks in Family Therapy

I.   Negotiate Structure
   A.   Discuss organization, expectations and purpose of the session.
   B.   Negotiate any desired changes in the process.
   C.   Clarify the roles of those in attendance.

II. Explore Client Experience
   A.   Explore clients' opinions about the last session.
   B.   Assess any changes (in thinking or in behavior) since last session.
   C.   Follow up on any homework assignments.
   D.   Organize assessment around those levels of experience from Chapter 3 that have greatest relevance to the treatment plan:
      1.   Individual beliefs, feelings, intentions, behaviors, perceptions
      2.   Organizational leadership, boundaries, alliances, goals
      3.   Intergenerational relationships, traditions, beliefs, loyalties
      4.   Transitions/Development of individuals and family members
      5.   Racial and Cultural marginalization, migration, assimilation, strengths, resources, traditions
      6.   Gender roles, beliefs, stereotypes

III. Address Relationships
   A.   Track interactional sequences related to the presenting problem or to any issues raised from session to session.
   B.   Choose relational interventions related to relevant levels of client experience from Chapter 8.
   C.   Represent the views of important people missing from the session.
   D.   Address the inclusion of important people.

IV. Develop a Unified Direction
   A.   Summarize the session and address each person's needs.
   B.   Assign out-of-session tasks.
   C.   Highlight strengths and instill hope.
   D.   Propose options and elicit feedback.

RELATIONAL ASSESSMENTS

Exploring Client Experience

In Chapter 6, we reviewed some ways to organize information from the initial interview into a treatment plan. As we stated then, sometimes a clinical situation will be straightforward and a plan can develop easily by the end of the first session. If the practitioner is able to easily match a treatment mode with clients' expectations, the first interview may be an initial assessment from which treatment is planned. However, since many agencies require the clinician to conduct initial mental health assessments, there is often not enough time to fully explore the relational aspects of the problem or to develop a corresponding strategy for intervention. In these cases, the family therapist can set the stage for an in-depth relational assessment by developing an initial treatment plan with the client that calls for

1. An assessment of the problem or symptoms (medical model).
2. An assessment of the influences and impact of the problem (relational/contextual).
3. An assessment of possible directions for treatment (solutions).

In our work, we believe that all problems have a relational component and all solutions have a relational component (Hanna, 1997). Thus, each of these steps can involve relational information in tandem with the necessary diagnostic information that is required in the workplace. As agency requirements are met, practitioners can gradually shift their focus to a more in-depth relational perspective. With this arrangement, managed care requirements are met as the practitioner learns how to use *assessments as interventions.* Since this skill has always been one of the strengths of a systemic approach, we devote the majority of this chapter to helping clinicians learn how to conduct assessments that create change. At the end of the chapter we provide suggestions for how to combine relational assessments with mental health assessments.

In family therapy, relational assessments have two important considerations. First, information seeking should complement the joining process by communicating interest, concern, creativity, and a desire to fully understand the experience of each family member. Gaining a sense of "systemic empathy" for each participant is an important goal. This sense of empathy must capture the *complexity* of each person's perspective, the *relationships* that have influenced that perspective, the *dilemmas* that may have evolved from these relationships, the unique *order of events* as they emerged in the family drama, and each person's stated *goal* or reason for participating in the session.

Second, whatever information the therapist seeks should be related to intervention—to what will eventually bring about change. Change can take place within the levels of communication conceptualized by Bateson at M.R.I., namely, content and process. The content and process of interactions can be thought of as evolving over time, moving from the past to the present and into the future. In describing their problem, clients may place greater emphasis upon one of these time periods. While structural, strategic and behavioral models of family therapy emphasized the importance of staying in the here-and-now, intergenerational and experiential models often explored the emotional and developmental aspects of the problem in the past. Generally, second-generation models of family therapy developed a balanced approach to the issue of history by taking an interest in narratives (narrative), comparative changes over time (Milan), exceptions in the past (solution focused), and exploring the context of the problem until it makes sense (MST). These methods of assessment help to determine whether the problem is situational, transitional or chronic.

Thus, dimensions of the assessment process should capture the content and process of each person's journey (interactional), shedding light on past and present influences upon the family that can be emphasized to bring about change in the future (temporal). In general, questions bring about discussions that become a forum for shifts in emotion, thought, and behavior. Such changes are strengthened and amplified by additional interventions that reorganize key family relationships around these changes. In this chapter, we review specific concepts and methods involved in organizing the interactional and temporal levels of information obtained. Then, we illustrate how these suggestions can be incorporated into the initial stages of family therapy.

INTERACTIONAL PATTERNS: CONTENT AND PROCESS

When family members come to therapy, they usually focus on the content of their concerns. Parents may say that their child does not come home on time or is hyperactive. A couple may describe their relationship as empty. The therapist listens to what family members say about each other (content) and asks how family members interact when the problem arises (process). A distinguishing characteristic of family therapists is their interest in relational process rather than content alone. Therefore, the beginning practitioner must begin to gather data on multiple levels. Through observation, in-session interactions can reveal the nature of intrafamilial relationships as well as the nature of the therapist–family relationship. Through questions and sequence tracking, the clinician also learns about out-of-session relationships and personal perceptions. As information is gathered regarding perceptions, behaviors, and relationships connected to the problem, the therapist may begin to develop hypotheses about which area of change is the most appropriate to target.

Communication theorists at the M.R.I. often look for beliefs that may hinder problem resolution in the present. One of their concepts—the utopian syndrome—refers to problems that develop due to a client's idealistic view of how the world should be. For example, a widow hoping to cure her depression through therapy is invited to consider how her depression may be a natural response to loss and not a problem to be solved. It may actually be her response to her own grief that is the problem. Only in a utopia would humans fail to feel the impact of death and loss. To integrate with other dimensions, we can see that change might occur as a result of exploring the content of the client's thoughts and providing her with a new reality. This reality would then be a basis for helping her address her isolation from others.

Another concept—the solution becomes the problem—suggests that some presenting problems grow out of a belief that "more is better." Thus the problem escalates when an attempted solution has an exacerbating effect. In this instance, the therapist can discover this phenomenon by tracking interactional sequences between people and gathering specific behavioral information about attempted solutions for the original problem. On the basis of these concepts, therapists help the client analyze the content of thoughts and the process of problem solving in the present so as to discover alternative solutions that were previously overlooked.

The Milan team's model also balances attention to content and process. The team's approach is based on the Batesonian concept that information regarding differences or comparisons within the family can bring about change in family life (e.g., the therapist might ask, "How are Mom and Dad different from each other?"). Some questions were designed as interventions to bring forth information (content) regarding the systemic functioning (process) of family members that was new or different from the family's normal way of viewing the problem (i.e., to reframe the situation). Informational interventions can be thought of as eliciting *systemic insight* into the therapeutic arena so that a family can view itself from a distance. This metaperspective, as articulated by the Milan team, often includes questions regarding family roles, rules, and beliefs that may be related to the life of the presenting problem. This information then becomes the basis for hypotheses and directives that affect out-of-session relational changes in a family.

Temporal Patterns: Past, Present, Future

While the past and present provide background information regarding the context of the problem, the future becomes a stage for more flexible options. Haley and Minuchin recognized the importance of information regarding the family's current stage of life and focused their observations on present in-session behavior. Framo's approach seeks information about past interactions and perceptions to understand the development of current relationships. Boszormenyi-Nagy gathers information about past relationships between the child and his or her parents to understand the unconscious needs of parents. The Milan team is often interested in tracking the life of the problem from the past into the present, with interventions focused on the client's ability to impact the future (Boscolo et al., 1987).

Regardless of whether data gathering focuses on the past or the present, the therapeutic direction is always future-oriented; the therapist facilitates hopeful connections between the original problem and future solutions. Later in this chapter, the reader will be helped to strike a balance between gathering information from the past and present. However, the balance must also include guiding families into "forward thinking" (White, 1986) by gathering data about projected perceptions and behaviors in the future. Positive possibilities may be evoked by such questions as "What would you imagine your life to be like when you no longer have this problem?" or "What things would you like to be doing when this is no longer a problem?"

These questions illustrate how the family therapist is required to think about multiple levels of experience and alternate between levels to gather relevant information about the family system that contributes to positive change. Data gathering can be thought of both as an ongoing process that pervades all other stages of the therapeutic process and as an early formalized stage in some cases.

Most family therapists have been exposed to assessment techniques from a combination of early and second-generation models. Bowen (1978) popularized the use of genograms for collecting family-of-origin information. Structural and strategic therapists engage in tracking interactional sequences as a way of learning about common relational patterns (Minuchin, 1974). Social constructionists inquire about the evolution of family issues over time as described in stories that the family relates (Boscolo et al., 1987; Sluzki, 1992; White & Epston, 1991). We will explain each of these procedures and illustrate how they may be systematically employed to gather microassessment and macroassessment data.

GENOGRAMS

In the early days of family therapy, Bowen began to diagram a person's family of origin by means of a three-generation family tree that came to be known as the *genogram*. This diagram starts at the bottom with the identified patient's generation, including siblings, and moves up through the generations to each parent's family of origin, including parents and siblings. As the field has progressed, numerous practitioners from a variety of orientations have adapted the genogram to their use. As McGoldrick and Gerson (1985) note:

> In family therapy, genogram applications range from multi-generational mapping of the family emotional system using a Bowen framework, to systemic hypothesizing for Milan-style paradoxical interventions, to developing "projective" hypotheses about the workings of the unconscious from genogram interviews, to simply depicting the cast of characters in the family. (p. 4)

In addition, Kuehl (1995) has used the genogram to concentrate on solution-focused material such as exceptions that manifest the breaking of an undesirable pattern across generations (e.g., "You seem to have decided not to repeat your grandfather's mistakes. How did that happen?"). He has also used genograms to normalize current behavior by depathologizing it in the context of generational influences (e.g., "It's understandable that you are coping in this way, given the family challenges surrounding you"). Hardy and Laszloffy (1995) use the genogram to explore influences of the therapist's culture. Such influences as race, class, and gender are explored to highlight "pride–shame" issues that may impede a balanced therapeutic posture ("What aspects of your culture of origin do you have the most comfort 'owning,' the most difficulty 'owning'?") (p. 234)

The genogram is a diagram of three generations of a family. Figure 7.1 describes examples of common notations used to construct one. It includes family members (and their relationships to one another); ages; dates of marriage, death, divorce, and adoption; and places of residence. Women are symbolized by circles and men by squares. Horizontal lines are used for couples and dates. Marriages are noted by solid lines; common-law unions are noted by dotted lines. Vertical lines extending down from couple lines connect parents and children. For further instructions on the conventions of genograms, consult McGoldrick and Gerson (1985) or Carter and McGoldrick (1989a).

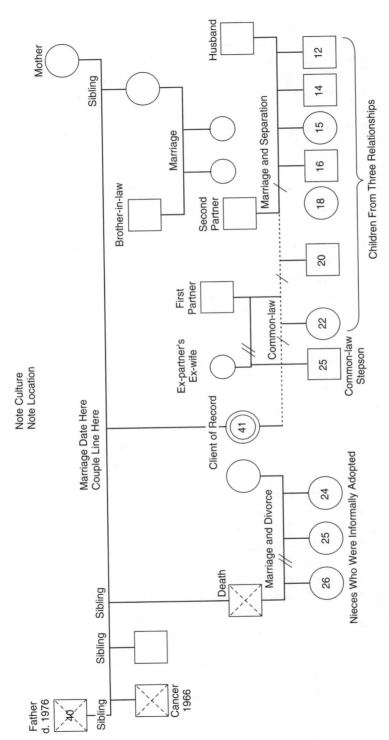

FIGURE 7.1

Genogram of an extended family network

In Figure 7.1, we see that the client has experienced untimely deaths of males and has assumed child-rearing responsibilities for an entire network. In Figure 7.2, we see that the father is 56 and the mother is 54. They were married in 1978 and both had previous marriages. Divorces are noted by the double slash on the line joining marital pairs. The two-generation family can be expanded to include grandparents on each side. The birthplace of each person is listed. The birth year, death year and cause of death (when applicable), marriage year, ages of living and ages at time of death are listed. These help to track sequences. The dotted circle indicates who was in the household prior to the divorce and before the launching stage began. We can reflect upon whether the history of losses on both sides or racial issues are relevant to the divorce, especially because of the race issue attached to the abortion. Cultural issues may enter in, given the different locations represented intergenerationally. In addition, the nature of their remarried family, the effects of a child's Down syndrome and actual causes of death are relevant to explore. Table 7.1 presents a summary of suggested questions that can provide the family therapist with information at both the microlevel and macrolevel of family functioning.

We suggest that genograms be constructed with the family as a type of public note-taking that can help the family begin visualizing its own system. Since a family therapy model seeks to expand the area of focus regarding the presenting problem, a genogram is helpful in expanding the interpersonal area of focus from individual to family and from family to extended family. As the family therapist becomes aware of certain relationships that are important to the client of record, relevant areas of discussion can be determined through the construction of a genogram, and potential sources of family support are usually identified. In family sessions, the genogram helps family members consider where the presenting problem fits into the larger context of their three-generation heritage. In individual sessions, the family therapist learns to understand clients through a knowledge and understanding of their families. When the practitioner wants to know "where a client is coming from," the genogram becomes a vehicle for such an understanding in a most literal way because most clients come from a family with a tradition and a history.

To make successful use of a genogram, the family therapist must be able to articulate a rationale for its construction that is meaningful and reassuring to the client. In cases where the presenting problem may seem unrelated to family or extended family, practitioners can explain that a diagram of the family helps the family members understand significant relationships that might be a resource in addressing the presenting problem. The therapist begins by posing the question, "What people are most helpful to you when this problem is bothering you?" As family members respond, the therapist can ask permission to diagram the relationship of these important people. In these instances,

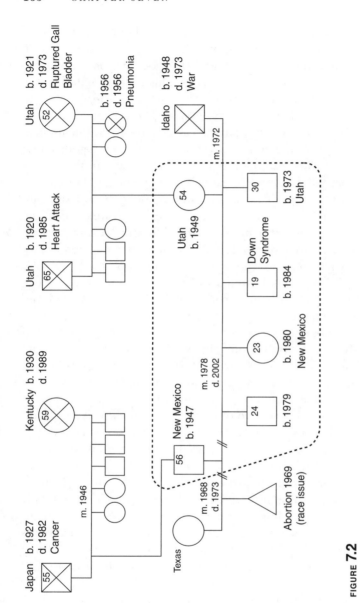

FIGURE 7.2

Genogram depicting issues of race, culture, loss

TABLE 7.1	CIRCULAR QUESTIONS AND GUIDELINES FOR GENOGRAMS	

Questions	Directions for Therapists	Explanation
How is your family different from other families you know?	Begin writing brief words on the genogram that represent the responses to this question. Construct the genogram in front of the family and use public note-taking as a form of acknowledging each person's comments.	Explores family members' sense of difference from others in general and from others in their reference group (e.g. If Asian, the family can be asked, "How is your family different from other Asian families?"). This provides a window into the family's macroculture and microculture.
How are Mom and Dad different from each other?	List adjectives near the corresponding person on the genogram. When negative labels are given, try to reframe in a neutral, positive, or empathic way. Use these questions as an opportunity to tease, joke, and set people at ease. Many people will be privately fearing judgment, criticism, and psychological analysis; therefore, the less "therapeutic" the environment, the better.	Explores perceptions of parental interactional styles, provides clues as to whether there is polarization or cohesion between parents and reveals the roles each may assume.
How is (each child) different from everyone else in the family?	List adjectives near the name of each person. As the interview continues, take notes and diagram any information that will help in answering the general assessment questions of this section.	Siblings always have a sense of uniqueness from each other (even twins). This uniqueness provides clues to family roles, issues of fairness and various alignments.
Who is most like Dad? Who is most like Mom? What makes you say that?	Encourage story telling. Jot a few words beside the person mentioned that summarize the story.	Examples of comparisons lead to narratives about individual differences, strengths, possible coalitions and beliefs.

(continued)

the genogram may be sketchy, noting minimal information in a short amount of time. However, if the questions elicit important information, the family therapist can ask if this line of questioning seems to be a useful direction for understanding clients' experience. Nonverbal behavior of family members often suggests whether they are engaged in the process.

TABLE 7.1	CONTINUED	
Questions	**Directions for Therapists**	**Explanation**
How does your family express affection?	Ask how they communicate positive feelings to one another. Ask how they know when a given family member is feeling positive toward them.	Specific examples of how affection is demonstrated provide a window into the family's affectional and communicational style.
Who gets the most angry? How do you know when that person is mad?	Reframe anger as pain, fear or feeling overwhelmed. Ask who else gets angry besides _____. Ask what they get angry about. Whenever the family characterizes any member as being an extreme in any way, follow up the comment with, "Who is the next most _____?"	Narratives about anger identify pain in the family. Expanding to "who else" prevents scapegoating and traces the pattern of pain that may often go unacknowledged (alternate story).
Who runs the family? Who gets the last word? Is there anyone outside the family who has a great deal of influence on members?	Use humor and keep the pace one in which questions suggest a sense of normalcy, not pathology. Give each member a chance to respond.	Perceptions of overt and covert power are critical to know and understand. Then the leadership of the family can be more fully engaged in treatment.

Source: Adapted from Hiebert (1980).

Other rationales can be provided based on the particular direction of the therapist. The following are examples of certain approaches and the rationales that can be used by the therapist for constructing genograms:

Problem-solving approach. "By mapping your family, I can explore the ways you have solved other problems and see what types of solutions are most comfortable for you."

Solution-oriented approach. "When I draw a family tree, I look for ways that other people in your family have solved similar problems. This may give us some new ideas" (Kuehl, 1995).

Cultural or family-of-origin approach. "It sounds like part of your difficulty is related to a clash between two worlds, the world of _____ and the world of _____. I'd like to diagram these influences and see how we can begin to change these problems."

Boyd-Franklin (1989) notes that African American families or others may be anticipating judgmental views from the therapist when a genogram is constructed. Thus, a period of joining should occur so that the family is reassured that the genogram will not invite criticism of diverse extended-family structures. With these families, it is best to preface the genogram with an explanation, such as:

> *In order to help you, it's important for me to understand something about the significant people in your life and what they mean to you. It's my usual practice to diagram family and personal relationships so that I can get the big picture of a person's life. I think all families have unique strengths and a variety of relationships. They often have survived some hard times together. Would you be willing to let me get acquainted with the members of your family by putting them on a diagram?*

In cases where clients were adopted or transferred through many foster placements, the genogram can be adapted with dotted lines, arrows, or specific symbols to depict the multiple settings and relationships that have become the norm for their development. However, even with early disruptions, some clients may still have a desire to know and understand their family roots. Thus, the main objective of a genogram may be either to chart biological patterns of behavior and relatedness or to discover and diagram any relationships that shaped the development of family members, including thoughts, behaviors, and values that were embedded in those relationships. In either case, the result is a visual representation of important relationships in which similarities and differences are identified. These patterns are used to pinpoint attitudes or behaviors that may be involved in perpetuating or solving the presenting problem. Often, such details are elicited through the use of circular questions.

CIRCULAR QUESTIONING: IN RELATIONSHIP TO WHAT?

Although the Milan team was the first to speak of circular questions, family therapists from a wide range of models now use the term generically in referring to questions that make "connections among actions, beliefs, and relationships of individuals within the system" (Campbell, Draper, & Crutchley, 1991, p. 346). Table 7.1 offers examples of circular questions that seek out perceptions of difference in family life. Systemic therapists find that circular questions elicit a broad range of information about family dynamics, including individual roles that make family members unique; marital patterns of power, communication, and intimacy; and coalitions among subsystems within the family. This "information about differences," as Bateson (1972) once labeled it, becomes the family therapist's foundation for understanding the family as a social system. As this understanding evolves, hypotheses and interventions are formulated.

The important focus for the family therapist is to gather information that compares one piece of information about perceptions, roles, and relationships with another (information about differences). As clients make statements, the therapist should be processing the information according to relationships, contrasts, and comparisons. The following sample dialogue illustrates this point:

MOTHER: Becky is driving me crazy! I can't go on this way!

THERAPIST: (seeking a comparison) I can see this is very upsetting for you. Is there anyone else who is upset by Becky's behavior?

MOTHER: Yes. My mother is very concerned.

THERAPIST: (seeking a relationship) How does she become affected by Becky? Tell me about their relationship.

MOTHER: She tends Becky every day after school while I'm at work. By the time I pick Becky up, my mother's at the end of her rope.

THERAPIST: So, something happens between the two of them that leaves your mother upset. (seeking a contrast) Was there a time in the past when things were different?

MOTHER: Not recently. We've had trouble with her for a long time.

THERAPIST: (still seeking a contrast in time) What about in the *distant* past? How far back in time do we have to go to find a time when things were different?

MOTHER: Oh, my! (thinking) I guess when she was tiny—2 or 3 years old—she was so cute, and she loved her grandma. I guess things changed when she started school.

THERAPIST: How were the three of you getting along then?

Each piece of information about relationships, comparisons, and contrasts could be explored more fully in a real interview. The point here is to use therapeutic conversations to develop a broad view of those who have some relationship to the problem, an understanding of differences and similarities related to the problem, and a preliminary hypothesis about how the problem developed.

Fleuridas, Nelson, and Rosenthal (1986) provide guidelines for teaching circular questions at each stage of the therapeutic process:

> This form of questioning serves as an efficient process for soliciting information from each member of the family regarding their experience of: (a) the family's presenting concern; (b) sequences of interactions, usually related to the problem; and (c) differences in their relationships over time. This provides the family and the therapist with a systemic frame of the problem, thereby enabling the therapist to generate hypotheses and design interventions (or additional questions) which interrupt dysfunctional cycles of interrelating and which challenge symptom-supporting myths or beliefs (cf. Minuchin & Fishman, 1981; Papp, 1983; Selvini Palazzoli et al., 1978, 1980b). (p. 114)

In addition, circular questions may compare people across generations ("Who is most/least like the identified patient?"), developmental time periods ("Has it always been this way? When did things change? What was it like before?"), and meanings ("Who agrees/disagrees that this is the problem?"); explore differences in perceptions of relationships ("Who is closer to Mom, your brother or your sister?") or differences of degree ("On a scale of 1 to 10, how were you able to solve problems this week?"); focus on before and after distinctions ("Did she get angry before you told her or after you told her?"); and pose hypothetical possibilities ("How would things be different if you spent more time together?") (Boscolo et al., 1987). These questions help track family members as they evolve through different experiences, developing beliefs and attitudes about family life as they go.

In Table 7.1, the circular questions used with genograms focus on contrasts in the interviewee's perceptions of family relationships, roles, and emotional climate. The first question, "How is your family different from other families you know?" gives respondents an opportunity to provide information about the interface between this family and the outside world. If certain obvious differences exist (e.g., a child with Down syndrome, racially different, religiously different), the therapist may make the question more specific to elicit the most useful information. For example, having a child with Down syndrome gives a family different experiences and a different identity from those of other families. However, all families with such a child do not seek family therapy, and many cope with their sense of difference in creative and insightful ways. If a family answers with the obvious difference first, it may also be important to ask, "Compared with other families affected by Down syndrome, how is your family different?" or "Compared with other Amish families you know, how is your family different?" These questions elicit clues about the client's sense of difference at personal, familial, and cultural levels. They often generate interesting information that acquaints the family therapist with themes and unique factors relevant to treatment planning.

The other questions in Table 7.1 follow a similar logic, proceeding to smaller and more intimate levels of observation. As these questions of difference outline the family members' unique perceptual blueprint, the therapist can develop an exploration of how these perceptions and beliefs impact behavior. They can be explored on both a microlevel and macrolevel by using questions that focus on sequences of immediate interaction and on sequences of important changes through time.

TRACKING INTERACTIONAL SEQUENCES: FACTS VERSUS ASSUMPTIONS

As an assessment proceeds, the family therapist may discover certain relationships at the microlevel that seem to have ultimate importance in the client's mind. For example, in the previous dialogue with the mother of Becky, the therapist may ask this mother which relationship (i.e., Mother–Becky, Grandmother–Becky, Mother–Grandmother) seems most relevant to the problem at hand. When these relationships are discussed, the therapist must gain a description of facts, not merely assumptions (O'Hanlon & Weiner-Davis, 1989). This can be done by tracking interactional sequences that occurred during important moments in the relationship:

THERAPIST: How would you describe your relationship with your father?

CLIENT: I'd say it's strained.

THERAPIST: (draws a line on the genogram between father and daughter and writes "strained") How is it strained?

CLIENT: Oh, it goes way back. He always tries to make me feel guilty. I can never do anything right.

THERAPIST: (Writes "guilty" on the genogram next to daughter) When you say he always tries to make you feel guilty, what does he do or say that gives you that impression?

CLIENT: Well, when we talk on the phone, he'll say something like, "I sure would like to see you more often," implying that I don't visit him enough. Then, if I do come to visit, he complains that I haven't stayed long enough.

THERAPIST: (writes "wants to see her" on the genogram next to father) So, when you're on the phone with him and he says he wants to see you more often, what do you say back?

CLIENT: I try to explain to him that I'm busy and can't just pick up any ol' time to travel all that way.

THERAPIST: And then what does he say?

CLIENT: He usually starts to lecture me about how families ought to be close.

THERAPIST: And then what do you say?

CLIENT: I don't say anything. I just let him go on and on.

THERAPIST: So you clam up.

CLIENT: Yeah.

THERAPIST: And you're probably thinking to yourself—what?

CLIENT: Here we go again!

THERAPIST: Okay. So this is a familiar pattern with the two of you.

CLIENT: Oh, yes!

THERAPIST: Well, let's backtrack for a minute. When he first says he'd like to see you, what is going on right before that part of the conversation? Anything in particular?

CLIENT: Mmm. Usually just talk about what he's doing and what I'm doing.

THERAPIST: So in the earlier part of the discussion, you're talking and interacting with him, telling him about yourself, and then it changes when he makes his statements.

CLIENT: Yes. It usually starts out okay and then goes downhill.

In this discussion, the client is making an assumption about her father's intention based on what he says to her. The therapist does not challenge her assumption at this point, but merely seeks to illuminate the facts—in this case, what her father actually says to her. Then, as the facts become known, they are put in sequence with her responses, and the entire sequence is placed in the larger context of their conversation and the way it evolved over time. In the same interaction, the therapist could also follow up on the client's statement that her father complains when she comes to visit. The word *complain* could be written on the genogram and explored in the same way because it connotes a negative intent on the part of the father. By gaining microinformation about what is actually said and what happens before and after the father's statement, the facts and assumptions begin to separate.

As the facts are described, the clinician can start to identify patterns of thinking and assumptions that may be hindering the development of a new pattern. The daughter believes that her father wants her to feel guilty. If the therapist has developed a supportive relationship, it might be appropriate to begin challenging her assumption during this phase of an assessment (e.g., "Is it possible that your father is trying to send you a different message besides wanting you to feel guilty?"). On the other hand, the client may have more concrete evidence through other experiences with her father that his intent is that of inducing guilt. In this case, behavior patterns can be challenged as attempted solutions that have become unsuccessful ("When you clam up, does this solution give you the result that you want?"). In any event, the decision to intervene must be based on what the presenting problem is and whether the client perceives the intervention as relevant to stated goals. If the presenting problem was a child-focused problem, genogram discussions and the tracking of interactional sequences may provide information to help the clinician develop a broad understanding of the client's relational patterns, but interventions should be related to the problem (e.g., "Do you ever find that your son tries to make you feel guilty like your father does? How does he do that?"). Then, as similarities and differences are identified, the client's responses can be indicators of whether she is ready to consider alternative views.

If the presenting problem was directly related to the father–daughter relationship, the therapist may still want to complete the genogram, learning about the nature of other family relationships and tracking other important sequences before deciding on a treatment strategy. Sometimes, clients respond to the genogram with their own ideas about what is the best way to address the problem or who in their three-generation system could be most helpful with the problem. At other times, more developmental information may be needed to put a presenting problem into the context of family process over time. This may be done by tracking longitudinal sequences.

TRACKING LONGITUDINAL SEQUENCES: NARRATIVES ABOUT CHANGES OVER TIME

In gathering information about developmental progress across different stages of family life, it is often helpful to diagram a horizontal time line that illustrates the family's story during significant time periods or that provides a chart of the family's life at the macrolevel of observation. Hiebert, Gillespie, and Stahmann (1993) use a time line for marital and premarital counseling as a means of tracking the interpersonal "dance" of each couple and identifying the developmental roots of their presenting problem. Stanton (1992) uses a time line to discover clues about what might have triggered the family's problem. Hanna (1997) uses a time line to dissect the accumulation of stresses over time that have brought a family to the point of crisis. In transitional family therapy, Suddaby and Landau (1998) make use of consecutive time lines in which they explore the progression of hardships followed by the progression of successes and positive stories. They suggest that this technique

> allows the family to construct a perspective of normal response to stress, rather than viewing themselves as failures across time. When helping the family to see this positive, transitional perspective, the therapist should not be simply implementing a strategic maneuver, but rather showing his or her own heartfelt respect for how the family has dealt with the repetitive stress and trauma. (p. 289)

All these applications adopt the premise that the identification of developmental patterns of interaction is an important step in developing hypotheses that are born out of client experience and that address nodal events related to key patterns. We believe these events and patterns may give rise to significant thoughts and beliefs that continue beyond the event and lead to subsequent difficulties. As these difficulties unfold, they may appear unrelated to previous events. However, we often discover that they are bound in relevance by certain patterns that originated with a prior nodal event. To change the patterns, it is often empathic and helpful to discover how they originated.

Other family therapists also emphasize assessments with a historical element. Hargrave and Anderson (1992) conduct life reviews based on questioning to validate an older person's life history, but without the use of a visual chart. Fleuridas et al. (1986) provide examples of time-oriented circular questions exploring changes and transitions in the past that may be affecting the present. In these cases, the focus on historical information helps family members reflect on significant experiences that may stimulate their own natural abilities to heal or change.

The advantages of using a visual time line are similar to those of using a genogram. Because families often feel stuck in a problem when they enter family therapy, a chronological account of important transitions can restore an element of movement and flow to the family's self-perception. If a genogram has already been constructed, it is a logical transition to take information already recorded there and begin putting the significant events in sequence. The in-session process thus transforms awareness from the family as a system to the family as a larger story that extends beyond the presenting problem. Marriages, births, deaths, illnesses, job changes, graduations, and other significant events often cluster at certain points in a family's life story. These clusters may be developmental times at which certain themes in the family developed. By tracking the sequences of these events through time, the therapist is able to broaden the family members' perception of how they came to be stuck and to summarize important information in a graphic manner. Consider the following example:

Randy and Betty were rebuilding their relationship after Randy served a jail sentence for drug dealing. They had both been married previously and met while Randy was in recovery from substance abuse. A review of their early relationship revealed his sobriety and exemplary recovery as an important attraction for Betty. She was attending Al-Anon after having been married first to an emotionally distant, autocratic man and second to an alcoholic. Randy was attracted to Betty because of her strength and determination. They dated for over a year. However, the month before their wedding, Randy began using prescription drugs again. Betty was unaware of his relapse until their wedding day when he offered her drugs on the way to their honeymoon. She was devastated.

Figure 7.3 is a time line of Randy and Betty's early relationship. As it was constructed, the therapist highlighted strengths of the couple (spiritual talks, flexibility), tracked interactional sequences, and explored each person's evolving perceptions of the other during courtship. As the relationship progressed beyond engagement toward marriage, the therapist began asking the couple about whether they thought anything should have been different. Randy acknowledged that they became isolated. Betty reported not knowing about the pain medication.

As the time line brought the therapist and family up to the present day, it provided the clinician with an opportunity to reflect on this couple's courage and endurance as important qualities needed to overcome obstacles in the future. Since a time line shows progression over time, it becomes an unspoken voice for the inevitability of change. These narratives about strengths and resilience in the face of adversity are important outcomes that therapists should

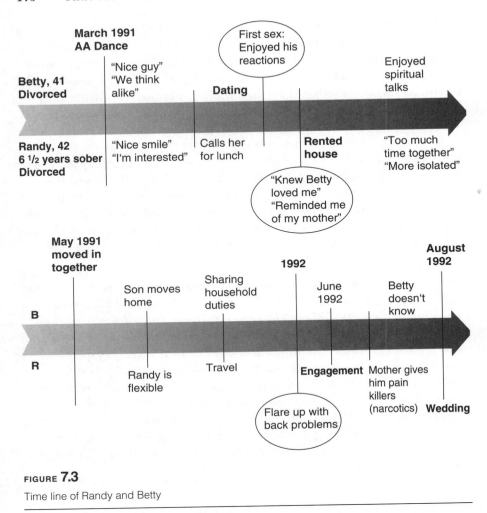

FIGURE 7.3

Time line of Randy and Betty

pursue when constructing time lines. In this case, the therapist could empathize with Betty and Randy's pain, highlight their strengths, and puzzle with them about how to address the problems they identified.

Deconstruction

In addition, dissecting microprocesses in the family provides developmental information that is important to the change process. Just as in tracking sequences of behavior, when family therapists track sequences of thought and emotion, they are putting relationships under the microscope. White (1990) suggests a process of *deconstruction* in which a client's core belief (e.g., "I'm no good," "She's lazy," "We can't go on together") is addressed through careful and detailed questioning of how that belief developed. Questions might follow this sequence:

1. When you say _____, I'm wondering how you came to that conclusion?
2. Who are the people that have influenced your thinking on this?
3. What experiences have led you to think in this way?
4. Would you be interested in comparing your point of view with that of others?
5. If you began to think differently, would there be a backlash from important people?
6. How would you cope with such a backlash?

Each question might evolve into a lengthy conversation. People and experiences can be noted on a time line. Future projections about coping can be noted beyond the present time. In this way, perceptions, behavior, and relationships are identified as part of the problem. These elements are dissected to develop opportunities for relational change as part of the solution. In some cases, treatment will paradoxically involve a plan to cope with change before actually addressing the original problem (see Chapter 8 for more discussion on paradox).

Developing a Rationale for the Time Line

Clinicians must provide a rationale for the time line that emphasizes their neutral point of view and their desire to understand how the family came to be in its present position. The following sample rationale could be used in an initial interview to develop the contract.

Listening to your account of the problem that brings you here, I have been impressed by your sincere desire to solve it. In spite of your best efforts, things have not changed, and you seem to be stuck. When people try as hard as you have to solve a problem, but to no avail, there is usually something missing in their understanding of what the problem is. I can usually help people solve this puzzle by reviewing the experiences they have been through together, each person's point of view (content), and how they have come to this point (process). By looking at the big picture of their life, we are able to discover some new direction that proves successful. I would like to propose a few sessions in which you give me the chance to review important experiences with you. Then, we can see what solutions will best fit for you in view of your unique experience.

As with genograms, other rationales can be presented based on the therapist's chosen perspective, whether problem solving, solution-focused, or cultural. If a person is deconstructing a client's beliefs, a time line may become a natural extension of noting important experiences. In such cases, a rationale may only need to explain a reason for extending the time line into other conversations. The most important task is learning how to relate this process to the presenting problem in a meaningful way. Chapter 6 suggests possible strategies for setting goals and developing therapeutic contracts. These may also be helpful in developing a rationale for genograms and time lines. When the initial goal is clarification or exploration, these assessment procedures provide a time-limited sense of direction. When the goal is experimentation, these tools are used to gather ideas about previous successes and behavioral sequences.

Creating a Sense of Movement

For the beginning practitioner, creating a sense of movement along the continuum is the primary goal. Therefore, it is important to develop a different rhythm for each family or individual that captures the uniqueness of the movement through time; in some cases, lengthy discussions occur at some points along the time line, and only superficial coverage is necessary at other points. However, the clinician must make sure that certain emotional points in time do not derail the discussion before it reaches the present; otherwise, the sense of movement may not be achieved. As significant events are explored but left unresolved, the therapist can develop a list of themes and experiences that family members identify as most influential. After the time line is complete, the identified issues can be explored more fully using questions that seem most relevant from Chapter 3. This list of issues noted by clients can form the foundation of a treatment plan.

One of the advantages of using a time line is that it helps the family therapist keep a sense of direction during stages of exploration when emotional issues may be raised before a therapeutic direction has been explicitly defined. It becomes understood, through constructing the time line, that both therapist and family are moving forward, from past toward future. The time line allows an emotional issue to be explored in its original context as a point along a continuum rather than as an end in itself. In this way, microinformation through deconstruction generates empathy; macroinformation through mapping nodal events generates perspective.

Summarizing Details

Boxes 3.2 and 3.3 in Chapter 3 give examples of questions in developmental interviewing that elicit microinformation, but it is not necessary to write details or complete sentences on a time line. Key words, themes, or events with the month and year are adequate. Too many details clutter the family members' visual perception of their movement over time and leave them feeling just as overwhelmed. Therefore, if the clinician helps a couple have a lengthy discussion about a misunderstanding that occurred 15 years earlier when the couple's first child was born, it is enough to note the event together with important reframings, questions, or alternative views that emerge from the discussion.

Hanna (1997, p. 112) uses the following questions to assess the relationship between events, behaviors, and perceptions. This information can be summarized on a time line:

1. What was the first (or next) significant event you shared as a family?
2. When this happened, how did each of you react? What was the sequence of these reactions?
3. After it ended, what conclusions did you draw about yourself and others?

For couples and families, the usual starting point for a time line is when the couple first meets, with progression from left to right through courtship to the birth of each child and so on. For individuals, the usual starting point is at birth, unless the presenting problem is child-oriented or work-related, in which case the time line may start at some significant marker in the sequence of a person's life—college graduation, divorce or marriage, or some other important change. To illustrate how the time line can be used with genograms and circular questions, the following case study provides an integration of the assessment process.

Case Example: The Wilsons

The Wilsons were a White, middle-class family who sought family therapy after their son, Bob, 15, was caught smoking at school twice and was subsequently dropped from the basketball squad at school. Bob's parents were John, 42, and Kristin, 39. He also had a sister, Sue, 14, who attended the first session. John was a hospital social worker, and Kristin was a nurse. They had been married for 19 years. Both were raised in small rural communities. They met and married while attending college.

Figure 7.4 shows a genogram of the Wilsons. It summarizes information gathered in the initial sessions of family therapy with all members present. Figure 7.5 is a time line of the Wilson's family story, noting transitions that have affected the family. Family members reminisced over happier times in the past. They were able to compare earlier stages with current circumstances.

FIRST SESSION: Intake and Initial Interview

DEFINING THE PROBLEM: *Everyone is asked to comment, but the therapist notices that Kristin is the most verbal and Bob is the least verbal during this stage of the process. After some initial small talk, the therapist asks "What brings you here?" The family responds by giving various accounts of Bob's recent problems at school and by noting how each family member feels about the recent progression of events. Bob was caught smoking at school twice, was suspended for 3 days, and was dropped from the*

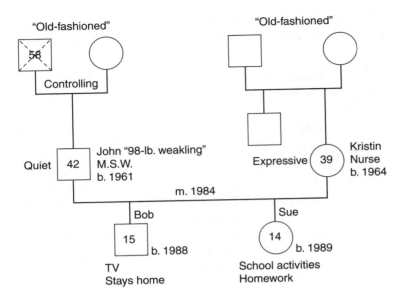

FIGURE **7.4**

Genogram of the Wilsons

basketball team after playing in the first two games. John and Kristin express their concern and state that they wish Bob would "open up."

TRACKING INTERACTIONAL SEQUENCES: With the focus on present events, the therapist investigates interactional patterns of the family as the problem developed. "How did you find out about Bob's smoking?" "What did you do when you found out?" "Bob, what did you do when your mother confronted you?" "Sue, where were you and what were you doing while all this was going on?" "John, how did you find out and what did you do?" Information comes forth about Bob's tendency to withdraw, John's tendency to lecture, Kristin's tendency to interrogate, and Sue's tendency to stay busy when there is conflict.

PRECIPITATING EVENTS: Attention is shifted away from the topic of "What did Bob do?" (present-oriented) to the topic of "What has been happening to Bob?" (recent past). This shift diminishes his shame and provides a developmental perspective on how problems evolve from a sequence of events. Since Bob appears reserved and uncomfortable during this part of the discussion, the therapist decides to engage him in conversation that might be less threatening.

"It seems unusual for a guy of 15 to already be starting on the basketball team. How were you able to do this?" At this point, Bob opens up and tells the story of how the coaches noticed his unusual height and *coordination while he was still in middle school. Anxious to have him play, they began to encourage him to try out for the team the summer before he started high school. He began attending practices and easily made the team. However, as the season approached, he began to feel bad although he couldn't explain why.*

His parents state that they do not understand why he would be feeling bad when things seemed to be going so well. However, they believe that he has negative feelings about himself and quote him as saying, "Things don't matter. I wish I could fry my brains out."

GOALS: *All members are able to agree on the same goals. This is acknowledged by the therapist as a strength. The therapist asks what the family would like to see happen. The parents state their goals for therapy as wanting Bob to feel better about himself and wanting to improve communication and intimacy in the family. Bob and Sue both agree that these would be good goals.*

CONTRACT: *At this point, the family therapist responds to the family's story by describing the assessment process and clarifying expectations for change: "It sounds as if all of you care about each other and want to solve the puzzle of how to help Bob. It also sounds as if no one is certain about what the real problem might be. In view of this, one possible direction is to take a couple of sessions to explore the problem in greater detail. Once we have a definition of the problem that we all feel comfortable with, our efforts at developing solutions will be more effective and we can move on to developing a plan of action. How does that sound as a starting place?" The family agrees to a plan for three assessment sessions, after which subsequent sessions would be devoted to developing a plan for helping Bob.*

Since the family's goals are abstract (intimacy and communication) at this point rather than concrete behavior goals, the therapist suggests an interim process goal of exploration, which will produce more concrete goals to work on during the intervention stage.

DATA-GATHERING PHASE (GENOGRAM): *The members of the family are invited to shift their attention away from the immediate problem in the present to a discussion about general family relationships and extended-family influences. With time left in the first interview, the therapist explains that it would be helpful to understand the family relationships most important to the family members as a group and to see the way grandparents may have solved similar problems.*

Using John and Kristin's marriage as the central relationship, the therapist proceeds to sketch a skeleton genogram that includes Bob and Sue as the youngest generation and shows both sides of the extended family. Listing only the names, ages, deaths, and hometowns of parents, the therapist has time afterward to ask circular questions about individual differences in the nuclear family and about the parents' experiences in their own families of origin (see Figure 7.4).

- *How are family members different from each other? John is quiet; Kristin is more expressive, suggesting a possible complementary marital relationship. She states, "We have a hard time expressing gut feelings." Bob watches a lot of TV and stays home more. Sue is immersed in school activities and homework.*
- *What was each parent's experience in his or her family of origin? Kristin expresses regret that her own family did not care more about her and tells the story from her younger years of how her family, hardworking farmers, never came to see her perform when she was a cheerleader. John describes his family as very controlling of him and recounts an important experience: his decision to finally assert himself with his parents and change majors in college.*

As Kristin and John share their experience, Bob expresses surprise at his father's account of standing up to the grandparents. Bob and Sue describe their grandparents on both sides as "old-fashioned." John also explains how he had been a "98-pound weakling" as a youth and therefore can't understand why Bob is not enjoying his enviable athletic ability; John would have given anything to have had Bob's height and strength. At this point, Bob is silent, eyes looking at the floor.

At the end of the session, the family therapist thanks the family members for their openness in sharing information and indicates that the next session would be an opportunity to explore the development of their family and the events that might be related to Bob's current feelings.

Second Session: Tracking longitudinal sequences

TIME LINE: *The rationale for tracking longitudinal sequences (Figure 7.5) is that Bob's difficulties could possibly be related to various changes—recent or past—that may have affected him in ways no one was aware of. Thus, it would help the therapist if the family members could describe the various transitions they had been through together. What do the members of the family consider to be the major changes they have experienced together in the areas of personal development, job experience, and family roles?*

The parents report success as a beginning young family: They were happy with each other, John's work, and their young children. From 1989 to 1991, there was some stress in the family. Sue developed a serious fever as a baby, Bob broke his arm when he fell off his bicycle, and Kristin began to work part-time so they could buy their first home. The family weathered these challenges through hard work and sacrifice.

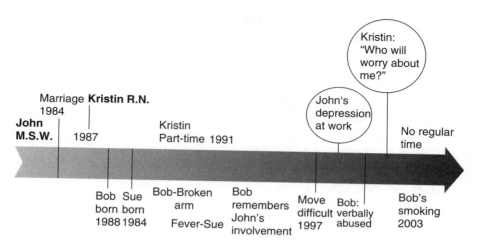

MARKING AND DISCUSSING TIME PERIODS: *The horizontal time line is divided into major time periods and labeled as the family discusses each stage (e.g., "1997: move"). Short descriptions note important issues (see the words below in boldface) as the chart moves from left to right, from past to present. Family members are included by placing parents' experience above the line (e.g., "Dad: depression") with children's experience below the line (e.g., "Bob: verbally abused"). As the time line progresses toward present-day concerns, the therapist uses the visual diagram to stimulate a reflection and reconceptualization of the problem as developmental–interactional in nature.*

In **1997,** *John got a better job offer, and the family contemplated a major* **relocation.** *Soon, the members of the family were reestablishing themselves in a new city, with new jobs for the parents and a new school for the children. From this time forward, life proved more difficult. John's job required many more hours, and he was assigned patients with terminal illnesses. In addition, the salary increase he was promised after 3 months was put on hold because of the financial instability of the hospital. He became depressed and sought individual counseling for his* **depression.** *After 2 years, rumors were prevalent about possible mergers, layoffs, and terminations because of the hospital's continued financial difficulties. John reports that his main way of coping was to tell himself that things would get better if he could only* **work harder** *and get a promotion. He found himself trying harder, but with* **no results.**

In the meantime, Kristin was hired at a different hospital and was assigned to a critical care ward. She works with patients whose conditions are listed as serious or critical. Bob remembers his mother talking about her work and how anxious she felt about the stresses there, but he was completely unaware of his father's depression. Sue also indicates that she was unaware of her father's depression. Kristin reports that John talked a great deal to her about his depression, to the point that she remarks, "I wish someone would **worry about me** once in a while." In the last 4 years, the children had become more involved in school activities: Bob played hockey and basketball in middle school, and until recently played basketball in high school; and Sue has developed her hobbies and musical abilities. The parents state that time spent with the children now is usually after dinner and on some weekends when Kristin is not working. John and Kristin also say that their time together is usually when the children are busy or early in the morning. It has been years since they have scheduled any **regular time** for themselves.

COMPARING LIFE- STAGES: What are the main differences between various life-stages for this family? Asked how their past had been different, all the family members agree that the period before 1997 had been much happier for everyone. The therapist notes nonverbal cues that indicate the impact of the assessment process on Bob, who has become more verbal and involved. Bob is very active in this discussion, reminiscing that his **dad** had been **more involved** with the family during those days. He also defends John in some surprising ways, given the fact that Bob has had a great aversion to his father's lectures. The family agrees that Kristin is more involved with the children during the week, and John is home on the weekends but uninvolved with the children while Kristin works.

USING, IDENTIFYING, AND EMPHASIZING FAMILY STRENGTHS: The therapist points up the family's strengths while externalizing the problem away from Bob. Life got hard. Patients at the hospital were struggling with life-and-death issues, and everyone at home began to feel the effects of each parent's stress. Now assessment begins to overlap with intervention. The therapist ends the session by commenting extensively on the transitions, reflecting for this family a picture of itself that includes many successes, the family's closeness and caring, the unexpected stresses after 1997, and the unintended consequences of these stresses as John's depression and Kristin's anxiety began to shape family interactions.

Third Session: A Return to the Presenting Problem

CULTURAL ISSUES, INTERACTION PATTERNS, FAMILY STRUCTURE, AND THE MEANING OF THE SYMPTOM: An exploration of cultural issues, interaction patterns, family structure, and the meaning of the symptom begins with a discussion about the symptom: Bob's smoking. It emerges that Bob had started smoking during the summer that the coaches began recruiting him for the team. When asked about the summer practices, Bob relates experiences in which he felt **verbally abused** by the coaches and thought about quitting. When asked what he thought might have happened if he had quit, Bob says he knew his dad would have been disappointed. John indicates that he had no idea that Bob was feeling this way.

Cultural issues and family values: How do the parents feel about smoking in general? The parents are emphatically against Bob's smoking. John had smoked earlier in his life and quit for health reasons. The family is very religious and has firm values about living a temperate life. This is an area where John had frequently lectured Bob, and there had been many attempts to get Bob to stop smoking.

Family interaction and structure: How does the family handle other issues? By this time, Bob is much more comfortable discussing his relationship with his parents directly. He complains about how his mother "nags and interrogates" him about his schoolwork when he comes home. In response, he retreats and goes to his room or becomes distant by "vegging in front of the TV."

TRANSFORMING ASSESSMENT TO INTERVENTION THROUGH REFRAMING: By the end of the third session, the therapist moves further into formal interventions by beginning to make implicit family process more explicit: "It seems that there are some things going on in the family that have been invisible until now. One is the fact that Bob was struggling and feeling overwhelmed by the coaches, but no one in the family knew. Another is that John has been depressed at work, but only Kristin knew, and she has become overwhelmed by his depression and the stress of her work. Even though Dad envies Bob's size and ability, I wonder if Bob is really more like Dad on the inside, sensitive and caring, which makes it harder to tolerate harsh treatment from the coaches. At the risk of being called a quitter at school and disappointing Dad at home, maybe getting caught smoking was the best way for him to change the direction of his life. By the same token, it sounds like Kristin has needed more support than she has been able to get in the family, and she has dealt with her struggle by trying to get Bob to do things that would be more helpful to her. When we meet next time, I would like to get your reactions to these ideas and see if you're ready to develop a plan of action for meeting your goals."

The formal assessment for which the family had contracted concludes with the third session. As the process unfolds, it becomes an opportunity for the family members to shift their focus from the immediate intensity of the presenting problem to a more reflective focus on their life together. In addition, the therapist is able to continue the joining process, to identify strengths, and to experiment with reframing to determine the clients' cognitive flexibility. The degree to which they are open to the reframing becomes information used in *developing a treatment plan. Would direct or indirect interventions be more useful with this family? Would perceptual change, behavioral change, or both be needed for this family to achieve its goals?*

Hypotheses

To adopt a pragmatic approach, the beginning clinician must understand something about how different hypotheses relate to the change process. In the case of the Wilsons, the therapist made the following tentative hypotheses:

Gender-Related

1. Bob may have felt trapped into playing basketball by the expectations of the coaches and his father. His lack of self-esteem may be related to interactions with other males and his resulting feelings of inadequacy.

2. Bob's mother may also have expectations of him that he perceives as overwhelming.

3. Since Kristin stated, "I wish someone would worry about me once in a while," she may be a catalyst for change in the area of gender patterns if her feelings are a manifestation of disempowerment in her marriage.

Culture-Related

4. The Wilsons both come from rural, religious backgrounds. Conformity to parental authority is expected. Bob may be breaking with tradition and feeling the effects of parental disapproval; however, both parents seem firm about adherence to family traditions.

5. Both parents have jobs in the helping professions. They believe in the values of respect, empathy, and promotion of self-esteem within their family. These values may become catalysts for change in their relationship with Bob.

Intergenerational

6. Bob's grandparents have not been resources for this family. Both parents report a lack of closeness with their families of origin. Lingering conflict over their own disengagement may make it difficult for them to be comfortable with Bob's individuation.

7. John's adolescent image of himself as a 98-pound weakling may prevent him from empathizing with his son and may thus contribute to Bob's discouragement. The pain that John still experiences over his inadequacies as a youth may become a catalyst for resolving personal beliefs that complicate his relationship with Bob.

8. There are cross-generational similarities in the temperament of Kristin and Sue, John and Bob. Perhaps Bob's low self-esteem is related to John's style of coping.

Transitions

9. The family successfully completed early stages of development but experienced overwhelming discomfort after 1997 as a result of job stress that precipitated a change in lifestyle and a significant sense of disengagement among all members. Bob's low self-esteem may have developed during this period of stress, in which his parents had little energy to address the tasks of families with adolescents and prevents the family from grieving their losses since 1997.

Family Structure

10. There may be a complementarity in the marital and parental subsystem that leaves Kristin overfunctioning for John and Bob but underfunctioning for herself. Her sense of overresponsibility for Bob may be the force behind her "interrogations" of Bob that leave him feeling criticized and suffocated. John's underinvolvement may leave Bob feeling abandoned.

11. The interaction pattern that surrounds Bob's depression usually runs as follows: Bob comes home from school. Mother becomes involved by questioning Bob's homework. Bob retreats. Father becomes involved by lecturing. Bob retreats. Sue returns from school activities, and the family focuses on her accomplishments.

Individual Development

12. Bob is different from his father athletically, but similar to him in temperament. Bob's aversion to the subculture of male competition could be looked on as a strength and as a way in which he is loyal to his father's humanitarian values.

13. Bob's intent is to please his father. However, he feels abused by coaching strategies, embarrassed with his friends, and misunderstood within his family. Seen in this context, his actions (smoking and withdrawal) could be regarded as resources in that they served to help him out of his dilemmas at school with the coaches and at home with his mother and father.

Since some of the hypotheses were related to resources for change and some were not, it is appropriate to ask which of these hypotheses fit best with the family's goals. *The presenting problem was the fact that Bob was caught smoking and suspended from the basketball team. The parents stated that they wished Bob would open up and discuss his problems. Because of the parents' background (i.e., their expectation of conformity to parental authority) and disengagement from their family of origin, the therapist might hypothesize that they do not have a model for encouraging Bob to open up. This may be exacerbated by the pain that the father still carries from his adolescence. Acting on this hypothesis, the therapist might explore the parents' family of origin to understand how the past gets played out in the present. What current belief systems and new frames of meaning from the culture and family of origin can the therapist find to assist the Wilsons in resolving the problem? On the other hand, the therapist may also hypothesize that unrealistic gender expectations are contributing to the problem. This might lead the therapist to emphasize Kristin's desire to get help as a strength or to explore alternative ways in which Bob can meet his masculine needs or his mother's expectations.*

The therapist may also view Bob's problem as a metaphor for the parents' job stress and may wish to explore some alternative ways to cope with that stress. Or the therapist may hypothesize that the problem is structural—that if Kristin curbed her impulse to be helpful, Bob could learn to be more responsible; or it may be that Mr. and Mrs. Wilson need to work together and help Bob become more responsible. The therapist must also consider individual strengths, such as Bob's loyalty to his father, and internal resources when choosing an intervention.

Knowing the parents' stated goals for therapy—wanting Bob to feel better about himself and wanting to improve communication and intimacy in the family—the therapist may review the list of hypotheses and see which ones might relate to their stated goal. Hypotheses 3, 5, 7, 12, and 13 all recognize potential resources and strengths that might lead to change. Since intimacy and communication are often blocked by problematic interactional sequences, the therapist used Hypotheses 3, 5, and 6 to motivate the family to accept some tasks that would indirectly address Hypotheses 10 and 11. By appealing to the parents' strengths and good intentions, the therapist made an assignment for Kristin to quit asking Bob about his homework at any time during a 2-week experiment. In the meantime, Bob could decide in the next 2 weeks what he would initiate and talk about on his own regarding his progress in school. The parents were asked to find one night a week that was exclusively reserved for themselves and to set aside time in which Kristin was given a chance to vent her feelings and John would be willing to do more listening to her.

In addition, the therapist decided to address Hypotheses 12 and 13 directly by reframing Bob's behavior, his reason for smoking, the dilemma he had found himself in, and the strength that he had been exhibiting. After 2 weeks, the family reported Bob's depression was lifting, and he and Kristin had no conflicted encounters about homework. He had successfully initiated conversation on his own about school progress, and Kristin was relieved and satisfied with this. Family members desired to continue with the current experiment and were also asked to add another dimension to their plan: John was asked to find some time to talk with Bob about how John felt as a young man when he began smoking. He was to share his memory of his feelings toward parents, peers, and others at the time he started smoking. Then he was to share his feelings and thoughts when, as an older man, he decided to quit smoking on his own. The parents agreed to maintain their plan and asked if they could attend the next session alone. During this final session (the sixth), they reported continuing improvement in their relationship with Bob and used the time to discuss their own relationship—the imbalance and disempowerment that Kristin had been feeling and ways that they as a couple could restructure their lives for improved satisfaction. The Wilsons reported success in accomplishing their goals; there were no further school problems with Bob.

ASSESSMENT AS INTERVENTION

We think that all family therapy models share certain assessment procedures that make them effective in facilitating change. They each gather certain information about the family in the form of stories and nodal events that families relate to the therapist. Regardless of whether the therapist's theme is life cycle, intergenerational relationships, or nuclear family structure, the therapist takes the family's story and begins to evolve an alternative story. Thus, it is possible that any assessment from any model of family therapy is a plausible foundation for the remainder of the change process.

In the case of the Wilsons, an analysis of how change actually occurred must take into consideration the impact of the structured assessment process and the in-session interventions embedded in the questions and dialogue that took place during the genogram and through tracking their longitudinal sequences. Also included in the change process were the tasks and assignments that helped members of the family modify their behavior between sessions. The assessment was an opportunity for family members to tell their story and have an audience in the form of the therapist, who could reflect their story with only slight modifications (e.g., through reframing). The intervention stage was an opportunity for behavior change to start and, if successful, stabilize during the last weeks of the treatment period.

The process evolved through several stages, each with its own sense of mystery about what the family would bring to it. With experience, the practitioner can develop a sense of timing and rhythm in being able to move comfortably from one stage to the next. After narratives provide the therapist with a sense of understanding for each person's predicament and the family's movement through time, the salient issues can be organized and addressed as relational issues. The next chapter provides direction on various methods used to facilitate relational changes. By this stage in the therapeutic process, the therapist has focused on how interpersonal dynamics relate to the problem by eliciting descriptions of client experience. These descriptions are the basis by which participants begin to see that all problems have behavioral, perceptual, emotional, and relational components. In family therapy, relationships are sometimes the background of a problem and sometimes the foreground. We have noted that as clients have their experience known and understood, they become more open to a change in the story or in relevant relationships as they have known them. Their understanding of the problem evolves into one where they can see that certain relational aspects need to change. To help them, the therapist can devote a group of sessions to a number of pragmatic processes that encourage relational change.

RELATIONAL ASSESSMENTS AND MENTAL HEALTH ASSESSMENTS

Before we leave our exploration of client experience through relational assessment, it is important to reflect upon mental health assessments in general and how family therapists fit into the larger culture of mental health treatment. As we have seen from Chapters 1 and 2, family therapy became an alternate approach to mental health problems as mental health treatment became more prevalent and mainstream during the last half of the twentieth century. Today, traditional mental health treatment approaches use a *medical model* that involves *diagnosing* a problem using the Diagnostic and Statistical Manual of Mental Disorders, fourth edition (DSM-IV, American Psychiatric Association, 1994). This approach is now accepted among healthcare providers, insurance companies and many community agencies. Although the profession of marriage and family therapy has remained unique in its relational/contextual views of mental health problems and their corresponding solutions, family therapists generally practice in environments where it is necessary to provide a DSM-IV diagnosis and assess mental status, suicidal ideation and other risk factors.

Debates in family therapy are still common regarding the advantages, disadvantages, values, and philosophies that underlie these two approaches (Hansen & Keeney, 1983; Kaslow, 1996). Family therapists agree that it is important to assess safety issues and follow state laws related to the protection of others, but the issue of what *else* is important to assess still brings much discussion among some clinicians. On one side of the discussion, there have been those who have advocated for the DSM-IV to include problematic relationship categories as legitimate targets of treatment (Wynne, 1987; Yingling, Miller, McDonald & Galewater, 1998). An assessment tool appears in Appendix B of the DSM-IV, entitled *Global Assessment of Relational Functioning* (GARF). This is the result of long and persistent efforts of the Group for the Advancement of Psychiatry Committee on the Family (1995). We think this tool represents an important step toward developing a common language in our profession that can be used to provide relational information for Axis IV of the DSM-IV (psychosocial and environmental problems). We have included a copy of the instrument in Appendix C. The GARF provides three generic categories of relational functioning that can guide the practitioner in categorizing the *type* of psychosocial problem. These categories are *problem-solving, organization* and *emotional climate.* Together, they represent three dimensions in organizing assessment information that can help the practitioner to be brief, accurate and informative when summarizing important relationships. They also work well with any model of family therapy and we find that they can be used easily with either problem-based or strength-based perspectives. Thus, our goal is to help the beginning practitioner find a pragmatic place from which to succeed *within* our current mental health service delivery system. Bertram (2001) refers to this balance as "walking the MFT walk while talking the DSM talk."

If we return to our suggestions for treatment planning in Chapter 6 and add these dimensions from the GARF, we can use the case of the Wilsons to illustrate how these ideas fit together. Returning to Table 6.1, we see that the family's goals were emotional (Bob's self-esteem) and familial (intimacy). From Table 6.2, we can suggest that the problem was transitional. We make this judgment based upon the fact that the family had a number of strengths and reported earlier life stages in which they overcame challenges together and enjoyed a positive emotional climate during those times. However, since several family members reported a gradual erosion of positive emotion, the problem seemed more than situational, since a history of the erosion had developed over a period of years (see Chapter 10 for a discussion of *pile-up*). The problem was not viewed as chronic because there was a significant history in which the problem did not exist. From the models of family therapy listed in Table 6.2, the therapist chose strategic, experiential and intergenerational family therapies. Experiential concepts were the basis for exploring Bob's sense of self-esteem in the family. Intergenerational information was used to understand beliefs and attitudes and to address issues of loss and transition. Both of these approaches are direct. Strategic interventions were used to reframe meanings, change interactions and direct new patterns of relating. These interventions were more indirect. Since the problem was considered transitional, a mix of direct and indirect interventions was used. Indirect interventions are often more comfortable for adolescents. John and Kristen shared the same goals and level of motivation for help. This made many direct interventions ap-

TABLE 7.2	WILSON CASE HYPOTHESES AND THE GARF		
Problem solving	**Organization**	**Emotional climate**	
Transitions	Gender	Gender	
Family structure	Culture	Culture	
	Family structure	Intergenerational relationships	
		Individual development	

propriate.

Using the GARF, the therapist gave the family an initial rating of 68, based upon their strong sense of organization, their lack of satisfaction with reported problem-solving (attempted solutions) and the inconsistency in their emotional climate. On these dimensions, they made great progress with Bob and his sense of well-being. They were exploring additional progress within the marital dyad, but had not completed those changes when therapy ended. Thus, the initial rating suggested a *somewhat unsatisfactory* experience for the majority of family members, but that experience improved in relationship to how the family related to Bob. The therapist gave them a closing rating of 78. We can guess that if John and Kristen made the progress they desired in their marriage, the rating would move into the *satisfactory* range (80 and above).

Table 7.2 shows which hypotheses from the Wilson case may be relevant to GARF areas. As clinicians develop their hypotheses, they can summarize them according to GARF concepts for case records and treatment planning. There are arguments that can easily be made for the relevance of all possible combinations of concepts with GARF categories. This is one strength of the instrument, as it doesn't limit clinicians from a wide range of perspectives, but instead, helps to organize the breadth of information for brief summaries and for progress reports.

SUMMARY

To summarize, family therapy assessment can be thought of as a series of interactional processes that are guided by flexible, strength-based clinicians who observe content and process, track sequences that span past, present, and future interactions, and deconstruct the development of thoughts, emotions, intentions, and behaviors in relationships. Like all other relationships, the therapeutic relationship evolves through developmental stages as clinician and family discover new definitions of the problem and corresponding solutions. The family therapist organizes the structure of therapy, joins with each family member, and gathers information that focuses on the family's potential for change. Initial treatment plans combine relational and mental health information. As new information emerges, the therapist develops interventions that match the history of the problem, the family's developmental level and the therapist's skill level. These interventions are often chosen from a collection of early and second-generation family therapy practices. They provide a foundation from which to begin and maintain the process of change. The next chapter instructs practitioners in how to implement a variety of these techniques.

BEGINNING AND MAINTAINING RELATIONAL CHANGE

Family therapists must be facilitators of relational change. Such a process can take many forms since, most often, the clinician chooses, adapts, and combines interventions from various schools of thought. The result, however, should be a strategy for a specific family in a specific culture at a specific stage in the family's life. While a variety of strategies are available, the following are the major categories of therapist behaviors and processes that represent interventions that target behavioral change, perceptual change, and relational change: (1) managing in-session process, (2) reconstructing belief systems, and (3) exploring new behaviors.

MANAGING IN-SESSION PROCESS

All families evolve interactional patterns that vary in their degree of flexibility and permeability. Some family patterns may be too rigid (inflexible) and therefore make it difficult for family members to adjust to new situations. The permeability of a family pattern or subsystem pattern refers to the amount of access that family members have across boundary lines (e.g., children's access to parents). Some families' patterns are too permeable and allow too much access (or interference by other family members or society). In that case, the therapist must block such patterns to permit new, more functional patterns to evolve.

As the therapist begins to accommodate to the family system, he or she observes behavioral or transactional clues to areas of possible dysfunction. The therapist may then want to focus on these areas and formulate hypotheses for testing. For example, to explore parental interactions, the therapist might focus on the behavior of one of the children, who is interrupting the parents' conversation. Accordingly, the therapist suggests that the parents "get the child to behave" so that the discussion can continue. If the child continues to interrupt the parental interaction, the therapist intervenes with a variety of techniques (Minuchin & Fishman, 1981). The therapist may wish to focus on a particular topic, build intensity by lengthening the time of interaction, or limit participation to specific members as a way of boundary marking. Other conditions might require the therapist to unbalance the system or to make the covert overt to alter family interactional patterns. Each of these options is considered in turn.

Focusing

Focus refers to the therapist's selection of an area to explore from the vast quantity of information presented by the family. Initially, the therapist focuses on the content of family communication—what the family is saying. Soon, though, the focus shifts to the process—how the family members interact with each other. For example, parents may report that their child is "out of control." Without disregarding this content, the therapist is concerned primarily with observing how family members interact with each other: Do family members speak for each other? When the child begins to speak, does Mom or Dad interrupt? Do parents argue about how to solve the problem? Focusing on the process helps the family function better as a system.

The following techniques are helpful in focusing:

1. **Look for areas of content that might illustrate how family members typically interact with each other.** Some problems are too small or too large; that is, some problems are of such little concern or so severe that family members are unwilling to discuss them. It is sometimes important to look for recurring themes such as "Mom doesn't trust me" or "Dad has to make the decision." These areas often say the most about the family's interaction pattern.

2. **Avoid jumping from one area of content to another.** Beginning therapists often make the mistake of searching for the area that resolves the family's problem. Consequently, they move from area to area and never focus on what the family gives them to understand the family's process.

3. **Ask permission before focusing on a specific area.** By asking the family's permission, the therapist ensures that the family has control over the content and gains useful clues to the family's interaction pattern.

As an illustration of focusing, consider the case of a family who comes to therapy because the daughter is so "disagreeable." The mother and father present themselves as perfectly happy and compatible, except for their daughter's behavior. Early in the session, the therapist begins to notice that each parent's description of how he or she responds to the daughter's unpleasantness appears to displease the other parent. The parents' expression of disagreement is a detail that does not fit with the content level of their report. The therapist slowly expands the conversation about how they disagree. As the session unfolds, the therapist develops a hypothesis: This family doesn't know how to express disagreement. By focusing the therapy on this theme, the therapist could work to change the family structure by reframing the family's beliefs about disagreements—that is, by persuading the family members that family disagreements are normal and even beneficial.

Increasing Intensity

Intensity is a term used to describe the degree to which an emotion is being felt in the session. Family systems have coping styles that evolve to reduce anxiety by absorbing or deflecting outside intrusions. These protective mechanisms become dysfunctional only when the system's boundaries are so impenetrable that information necessary for change is deflected or when the family's boundaries are so permeable that individual boundaries must compensate for the lack of system security. Either way, some families have a low threshold for experiencing anxiety and attempt to modify the therapist's message by fitting it into their preestablished response patterns.

It is important to emphasize that transmission of a message to the family by the therapist does not mean that the members of the family are ready to act on the message. They may have heard the message and responded to it in a positive manner but failed to make any changes. Therapists, therefore, should cultivate a personal style that accommodates intensity by widening their range of potential responses beyond those that are deemed appropriate by cultural norms. Drama, timing, and intensity are not part of daily discourse, and a family therapist must be comfortable with the tension such behaviors can create.

Techniques for building intensity include (Minuchin & Fishman, 1981):

1. **Use a simple repetition of the message.** Simple repetition creates intensity because the therapist focuses on one theme, resisting the family's attempts to avoid the message. The therapist may continue to repeat the question or highlight the same message in a variety of ways until he or she gets the desired response. The therapist may also create intensity by repeating messages that appear to be different yet focus on a single direction for change.

2. **Encourage continuation of the interaction beyond the family's comfort limit.** This pushes the family past the regulatory threshold that

usually warns members they are entering an area of discomfort. In some cases, the extension elicits the necessary conflict or yields access to normally unavailable family resources (e.g., warmth and tenderness). In either case, the family breaks out of its predictable path and experiences new patterns of relating.

3. **Avoid accepting the family's expectation of how the therapist should relate to the family.** For example, the therapist may insist that all family members attend the session even though some family members insist they cannot come; or in some cases, the therapist may appear confused when the family requests an expert opinion.

4. **Manipulate the physical space of the therapy session.** By moving closer to a family member or moving two members closer to each other, the therapist is able to take advantage of the emotional response inherent in a change in personal boundaries. Because family members grow up learning the comfortable distance to maintain with other members, closer proximity creates momentary tension. If the tension is similar to the therapeutic message, the therapist is able to increase intensity.

To illustrate how a therapist might utilize these techniques, consider a parent with a teenager who doesn't get to school on time. The therapist might repeat the message by (1) letting the child wake himself and (2) letting him walk to school if he misses the bus. These messages are different, but both send the message that the parent needs to encourage the teenager's responsibility. The therapist might encourage the mother and child to move closer together when they discuss the issue, thereby violating the normal comfort zone. The therapist continues to keep the parent and teenager on the problem despite their attempts to avoid the issue.

Boundary Marking

Boundary marking comprises a series of operations with the common goal of changing the family's structural boundaries. As the therapist begins to accommodate to the family system, he or she observes behavioral and transactional clues that aid in identifying the existing boundary structure of the family. Sometimes the therapist will block interruptions by family members so that transactions can be completed. In some cases, individuals or subsystems (parents or children) might participate in a separate session with the therapist to strengthen this behavior. For example, a therapist may meet with an adolescent boy to help him understand his mother's concerns and discuss some ways he can respond to these concerns. Likewise, the therapist may meet with the mother to help her recognize the son's needs for autonomy. Once individual sessions are completed, a conjoint session could be held to discuss these issues.

The therapist can mark boundaries in the following ways:

1. **Rearrange the seating.** The therapist can rearrange the seating to allow family members to carry out their functions. If a child is sitting between her parents, the therapist might move her further away so that the parents can discuss their issues without interruption.
2. **Reframe the problem.** When therapists reframe or reinterpret a family's view, they are reconstructing reality. Families often get locked into problems because they see the problem from only one perspective. A discussion of how to reframe the problem is included in the next section.
3. **Block interaction patterns.** The therapist can block inappropriate interactions by (a) moving closer to the family member, (b) raising a hand to stop the interaction, and (c) giving a directive. Staying in close proximity to family members permits the family therapist to disrupt an interaction by physical contact (a touch of the hand).

For example, a family consisting of a single mother, 20-year-old twin daughters, and a 15-year-old daughter who had been truant from school was referred to a family service agency. In the initial session, the therapist turned to the 15-year-old and inquired whether she had trouble waking up in the morning. At this point, the twins began to complain how difficult it was to wake her and how they had to use extreme measures to pull her out of bed. Assuming a weak parental and sibling subsystem, the therapist changed the seating arrangement by putting the mother and the 15-year-old next to each other, with one twin next to the 15-year-old and the other next to the therapist. He suggested that the twins were taking over the mother's job and neglecting their responsibilities. When the therapist focused on the mother's expectations for her 15-year-old daughter, she was interrupted by one of the twins. At that point, the therapist raised his hand to block the twin and reframed the interruption as a need to avoid her own responsibilities by helping the mother.

Unbalancing

In family therapy, unbalancing comprises those operations by which the therapist attempts to tip the balance of power within a subsystem or between subsystems. Specifically, the therapist uses unbalancing techniques purposefully to align or affiliate with a particular family member who is in a position of low power. By asking for help, the family grants power (or influence) to the therapist, who then uses that power therapeutically. The only time that this power may not exist is when the family is externally ordered to therapy, as by a court referral.

The family members often grant power under the assumption that the power will be exercised equally or that they personally will not feel its weight—that is, only the "sick" member will be asked to change. On the contrary, in therapy, the therapist's power is often used to support one family member at the expense of the others in an attempt to alter the family structure, thus creating new alternatives that allow for greater complexity and flexibility in the family system.

The therapist can unbalance the family system in the following ways:

1. **Align with a family member who has less power.** The therapist aligns with a family member not because he or she necessarily agrees with that member's position but because he or she wants to lend power to a family member to modify the structure. The therapist might say, "I can see why you would feel that way," or "She needs to be convinced of your position."

2. **Refuse to recognize a family member.** This technique is extremely powerful because it challenges the excluded family member's need to belong. A disengaged, oppositional, or controlling member of the family may begin to fight the therapist for a way back into the family. Because therapists control the interaction, they can influence how a family member comes back in; that is, the price of admission may be participation or tolerance or whatever facilitates an improved system.

An example of unbalancing can be found in the case just noted above—of the single mother, twin daughters, and 15-year-old "troublemaker." The therapist used his power to unbalance the inappropriate parental subsystem. He empowered the mother to fire the twins from their parental role, even though the action and resulting loss of role placed temporary stress on the twins. He also did not let up on the pressure when the twins tried to reinvolve themselves. The family therapist is able to maneuver in this manner because the treatment plan focuses on the whole family system or organism and not on its individual members.

When the therapist sides with a family member—saying, in effect, "I agree with you. They need to be convinced of your position"—it is important to note that the content of the interaction matters less than the structural issues; that is, the therapist aligns with a family member simply as a means of modifying the family structure. For instance, the therapist may align with a depressed wife in her complaints about her husband's work habits not because the therapist also objects to the work habits, but because the therapist hopes to unbalance the marital subsystem.

Making the Covert Overt

Families seeking help are often characterized by vague communication and unclear role expectations. When a problem arises, the family often adheres to the same old rules and customs. Satir (1972) describes dysfunctional families as closed systems "in which every participatory member must be very cautious about what he or she says" (p. 185). Honest self-expression is discouraged and considered deviant by these families. Such families often reach an impasse during a life-cycle transition. When passing through this transition, interactions become more rigid, and symptomatic behavior may develop. If therapists are to be effective with these families, they must make the covert messages overt.

Satir (1972) suggests several ways to encourage honest and open communication:

1. **Ask family members to speak in the first person singular and take the "I position."** When a family member uses referents such as "we" or "they" (e.g., "We don't like to go to Father's house"), the therapist should ask the family member to speak for himself or herself ("Tell me what you want to do"). "I" statements are a good indication of whether family members are taking responsibility for themselves. The therapist can often encourage the family member to take an "I position" by first saying, "I feel . . ." and then allowing the family member to complete the sentence with his or her own feelings (e.g., "I feel unhappy"). Family members who are able to state their own feelings are taking responsibility for themselves.

2. **Ask family members to level with each other.** When family members level with each other, their tone of voice matches their words and bodily expression. The therapist can get family members to level with each other by asking them to be specific ("Be specific and tell him what you want him to do").

3. **Help family members sculpt the structure of the family.** Family sculpture may be used throughout the therapeutic process to increase family members' awareness of perception and thereby alter family relationships. To implement this technique, the therapist positions each family member in a composite living sculpture as other members see him or her. Satir (1972) also asks family members to express feelings through exaggerated facial expressions such as extreme smiling or frowning at each other. Family members may also be encouraged to express the way things are or the way they would like them to be. In some cases, family members may be asked to role-play their feelings.

These techniques help the therapist raise the family's self-awareness to a new level. When clients are helped to address issues that they normally observe but do not discuss, they begin to *metacommunicate* (Watzlawick et al., 1967)—to communicate about their own interpersonal process. As this occurs, individual family members begin to accept the reality that each family problem involves more than their own singular points of view.

As practitioners attend to in-session process through directive structural interventions, families are helped to develop more order in their interactions and a clearer understanding in their communication. They begin to develop more self-control (e.g., to refrain from interrupting others), and parents begin to see effective leadership modeled by the therapist. These interventions address the microprocess of the family on a behavioral level; the therapist may also assess the need to address the microprocess on a perceptual level. This entails addressing the language and beliefs that the members of the family incorporate into their understanding of the problem.

RECONSTRUCTING BELIEF SYSTEMS

The influence of social constructionists on traditional structural–strategic models of family therapy has prompted an increased interest in how beliefs, values, myths, and perceptions restrain family members from choosing alternative behaviors and solutions (Bateson, 1972; Selvini Palazzoli, et al., 1978; White, 1986). Selekman and Todd (1991a) noted the limitations of their structural–strategic approach with a certain subgroup of adolescent substance abusers. Generally, when there had been multigenerational drug abuse or past treatment failures, they found indirect interventions to be more effective. Interventions that address perceptions and beliefs are generally more indirect than structural interventions. Next, in this section, we review a few basic interventions that help the beginning practitioner address problematic aspects of the family's belief system and language patterns. The strategic use of language affords a new understanding of family problems.

Identifying Current Belief Systems

Several family therapy models have emphasized the importance of belief systems in contributing to the problems that families bring to therapy (Hargrave & Hanna, 1997). Indeed, self-defeating thoughts typically lead to feelings of self-pity, anger, and blame. None of these reactions are constructive. Rather, they lead a person to feel that things should not be as they are because he or she doesn't like them that way, or they make the person feel inadequate or incapable. In either case, the anxiety, depression, or feelings of inadequacy prevent family members from behaving in a constructive fashion to change the situation. Different family members process cognitions or beliefs in different ways. For example, suppose that a person walks across the room, trips over someone's foot, and falls to the floor. One person's first reaction may be extreme anger. Another person may feel little or no anger. The different reactions are due to different belief systems. The first person probably thought something like, "That rude, inconsiderate clod! He has the nerve to trip me! I know he did that purposely." On the other hand, the second person may have thought, "Oops, I'd better start watching where I'm going. He didn't mean to trip me. It was an accident." The therapist should be sensitive to these differences and respond accordingly.

Family members' belief systems are often at the core of the problem. Snider (1992) discusses this issue as follows:

> Some clients present themselves with a symptom such as depression or anxiety. After evaluation, it becomes clear that their agenda is to change someone else's

behavior to get them into therapy. I saw one woman who presented symptoms of depression. After reviewing her situation, it became clear that she thought her husband should be in therapy. Her presumption was that if he changed then she would not have any problems. . . . Sometimes people seek therapy because they are alone and lonely. I saw an elderly widow whose children lived in other parts of the country. She had a successful experience in therapy many years earlier. She presented symptoms around a difficulty in relationship with her children. After discussion, she acknowledged that there was nothing wrong with her relationship to them except the distance between them. She needed to talk and felt that this would be an appropriate entree. Her fantasy was that I would help her find a way to get her children to move back to the same city. (p. 145)

Understanding the family members' belief systems helps the therapist to understand the underlying problems and formulate goals for change. In identifying current belief systems, the therapist should explore the presence of constructive and nonconstructive beliefs related to the problem.

The therapist can identify current belief systems in the following ways:

1. **Identify beliefs that contribute to the problem.** Helpful questions include: "What do you think when _____ is going on?" "What makes it better?" "What makes it worse?" "What goes through your mind during this time?"
2. **Ask family members to complete incomplete sentences.** Such sentences might begin: "I think . . ."; "I believe . . ."; "I should . . ."; "My husband thinks I want . . ."; "When my wife comes in the door, I think . . ."
3. **Identify family members' self-talk.** Everyone engages in some kind of internal dialogue. This dialogue, or self-talk, expresses the family members' belief system. The therapist can identify self-talk through the following questions: "What do you say to yourself at this time?" "When she uses that tone of voice, what do you tell yourself?" "What are you telling yourself before this happens?" By identifying current beliefs and thoughts that contribute to the problem, the therapist can identify thought patterns that must change before constructive action can be taken to correct the problem.

Reframing the Meaning of Symptoms

Reframing—sometimes known as *relabeling*—refers to a change or modification in the family members' thoughts or views of the problem. When therapists reframe a family's view, they are suggesting a change in the family's definition of the problem. Reframing often shifts the focus from the identified patient or scapegoat and onto the family system in which each family member is an interdependent part (Watzlawick et al., 1974). Thus, reframing alters the way the family thinks about the problem.

In reframing, the therapist must first alter the family's view of reality. By using the technique of focusing, the therapist takes bits and pieces of what the family supplies and provides information that forms a new perspective. The therapist attempts to create a therapeutic reality from a family reality. For example, parents may describe their son as "defiant" or "hard to control," whereas the therapist may view the son as "independent" or "discriminative." By voicing these alternative descriptions, the therapist helps the parents see their son in another way. Such a reconstruction is only possible, however, if the family has a worldview that includes such a possibility. For example, the therapist may reframe a child's tantrums or uncontrollable behavior as a signal that the parents have taught their child how to express independence, but this may be ineffective if it is too far from family or societal norms.

The therapist can also accomplish reframing by taking the symptom and giving it universal qualities. For example, a child who is having difficulty following rules may be redefined as "having difficulty growing up." If a therapist is working with a family whose religious culture emphasizes a dominant patriarchal order, the therapist might challenge the image of a distant, emotionally controlled father by saying, "Surely you realize that it is only the courageous patriarch who is able to show tenderness to his family." By drawing on universal symbols, the therapist is able to pair a dysfunctional family belief with a universal belief that offers a new frame or view of the problem.

In addition to these strategies, the therapist can also reframe the meaning of the symptom in the following ways:

1. **Relabel problem behaviors to give them more positive meanings.**
   Giving new labels often provides family members with a new way of thinking about the problem so that it can be resolved. For example, therapists can relabel "jealousy" as "caring" and "anger" as "desiring attention."
2. **Relabel deficits as strengths.** All behavior can be viewed positively and negatively depending on the person's perspective. For example, a child who has trouble getting things done may be viewed as a "thinker" or a "perfectionist" depending on the circumstances. Family members are more likely to accept a reframe if their strengths are emphasized.
3. **Reframe the context of the problem.** Reframing the context of the problem permits the family to decide with whom a given problem behavior is appropriate (Cormier & Cormier, 1991). Every behavior has costs and benefits. Thus, when a wife complains that her husband leaves during their arguments, the therapist might help the couple identify those situations (contexts) where leaving is useful (e.g., when there is a threat of violence).
4. **Give homework to reinforce new beliefs.** Cormier and Cormier (1991) believe that homework helps family members practice aspects of the problem that go undetected. For example, a husband and wife might be required to observe those times when the husband attempts to walk away from a situation. What was going on? What was each thinking at the

time? What happened afterward? The therapist can then discuss this information to help the family discover new beliefs and perceptions of the problem.

Reframing helps family members get unstuck from rigid thought patterns that contribute to the problem. A new perspective helps the family members look for alternative solutions to their dilemma.

Stressing Complementarity

The therapist often finds it useful to help family members understand that they are interconnected in ways that make one member's actions complementary to another's. For example, a therapist might underline a couple's complementarity by congratulating the wife for the husband's change in behavior. The therapist in this case is teaching the couple that they do affect each other and that they have the potential to do so constructively. This intervention also allows the husband to reconnect with his wife by encouraging him to praise her for helping him express his feelings. Complementarity also helps the members of the family understand their relationship over time. During an assessment, if family members begin to describe each other as opposites in some way, the therapist should note these as potential examples of complementarity. Some common examples occurring in most families are shy versus outgoing, dominant versus submissive, stable versus unstable, and emotional versus rational. While these labels may need to be reframed for the family, the dynamic of complementarity can still be addressed.

Jorge Colapinto (1991) describes the process of complementarity as follows:

> Family rules develop primarily through a process of correlated differentiation: The behaviors of any two family members mutually accommodate in such a way that one develops selective aspects of himself or herself, while the other develops a complementary trait. Typical examples are the harsh and soft parents, the active and passive spouses, the left brain and the right brain siblings. When all the members of the family are considered, the resulting image is like a jigsaw puzzle, where the irregular borders of the various pieces fit—complement—each other. Carrying the metaphor further, the salient borders of each piece represent the traits expected from each member (harshness, passivity, left brain) while the concave sections represent traits not expected. In well-functioning families, complementarity takes the form of effective teamwork. (pp. 422–423)

Complementary relationships become a problem when they fail to provide flexibility for individual members. Traditional fixed male and female roles often have costs that lead to problems. A father who insists on making all the decisions may take away the mother's executive role when she is home with the children. At the same time, the father may feel overly responsible, which doesn't permit him to enjoy or play with the children. When these patterns become fixed, families experience problems in moving through developmental transitions.

The therapist can emphasize complementary roles in the following ways:

1. **Ask a family member to relate his or her behavior to what another family member is doing.** For example, a husband who describes himself as "jealous" may be asked what he is noticing about his wife when he begins to feel jealous ("What things do you see or hear her doing when you begin to feel jealous?").

2. **Congratulate a family member for another member's accomplishments.** For example, a wife may be congratulated for helping her husband express his feelings. Here it is important to look for small changes in a family member's behavior that contribute to another family member's behavior (e.g., a smile that another family member notices and reacts to).

Complementarity broadens the family's perceptual framework by emphasizing the interpersonal nature of the problem. Thus, rather than focusing on a problem residing within the individual (e.g., jealousy), the therapist focuses on current interactions that contribute to the problem (e.g., the husband's behavior). Moreover, the therapist can emphasize complementarity to punctuate interactions that alleviate the symptomatic behavior (e.g., the therapist congratulates the husband for the wife's change in behavior). The therapist is thus teaching the family members that they do affect each other and that they have the potential to do so constructively.

Using Metaphors

A metaphor is a word or phrase that represents another condition by analogy. Metaphors can be used to characterize family relationships or a condition, such as a symptom. In using metaphorical tasks, the therapist chooses an activity (e.g., writing bad checks) that resembles the problem (say, a daughter's conflict with her mother). The activity must be one that family members can discuss and in which they can produce change. The therapist typically assigns tasks—such as having a heated discussion and obtaining separate checking accounts—that will produce a change in the desired area—for instance, increasing autonomy (Haley, 1976). If the mother and daughter are able to accomplish the task (i.e., get separate checking accounts and pay their own bills), they will be more likely to accomplish separation around the more difficult issues later on.

There are six steps to designing appropriate metaphors (Cormier & Cormier, 1991):

1. **Examine the nature of the family member's problem.** The symptom may often be a metaphorical label for conceptualizing the problem. A metaphorical message usually contains an explicit element (e.g., "I have a headache") as well as an implicit element (e.g., "I want more attention," or "I am unhappy"). The therapist must identify the problem or theme and develop a metaphor that parallels it.

2. **Choose a representative "character" for the metaphor (e.g., an animal, personal symptom, or inanimate object).** It is helpful if the therapist has a character to use in developing the metaphor ("So, when you come in the door, you are like a bull in a china shop").

3. **Select words in the metaphor that match the family member's visual, auditory, and kinesthetic frame of reference.** For example, the second author of this book recently suggested to an electrician and his wife that their marriage needed to be "rewired." Similar metaphors could be used with a mechanic ("Your marriage needs a tune-up") or a doctor ("You need a new prescription").

4. **Develop an interactional process in the metaphor to match the interactional process in the problem.** The cycle of interaction in the metaphor should parallel the pattern of interaction around the problem. For example, the family's interactions about the child's problem will be similar to the family's pattern regarding the mother's problem when one is a metaphor for the other.

5. **Expand or embellish the character to promote behavioral change.** For example, a therapist may knock on the table as if it were a door as a metaphor for a new marriage.

6. **Develop a story that includes an element of mystery.** For example, the therapist may tell a story of a person who miraculously overcame a disease and went through a transformation that brought a new meaning to her life.

In some instances, the therapist may use metaphors to represent patterns of communication. The therapeutic use of metaphor helps reframe a family's reality by simply tracking the family's communication from the content to the process level. Minuchin (Minuchin & Fishman, 1981) is a master of such tracking skills, using metaphors for family process as diverse as "You're his alarm clock," or "You're her memory bank." Often, he will derive a metaphor from a family member's occupation. With a nurse (content), he might say, "Your relationship needs first-aid" (process); with a teacher, "You need a lesson plan in discipline." If there is a point of family pride, as with a family whose policy is "never a late payment," he might say, "You are indebted to each other." When illustrating a family rule, as with a family that has a strong work ethic, he might say, "Playtime should never be done slipshod!" Using metaphors is a form of accommodation because it is effective only when therapists are able to tune themselves in to the family language rather than imposing their own.

In strategic family therapy models, the therapist gives a directive metaphorically without making explicit what he or she wants the family to do. When therapists give a metaphorical directive, they are encouraging family members to behave in a way that resembles how they want them to behave in the symptom areas, such as assigning a couple to have a gourmet meal as a metaphor for a better sex life (Haley, 1976). The instructions for the meal parallel the proposed process for improving their sexual relationship.

Introducing Paradox

In the early stages of family therapy history, the use of paradox generated much controversy. Hanna (1995) suggests that the paradox associated with strategic models of family therapy often had elements that could be perceived as manipulation and dishonesty. Such strategies were considered by some to be disrespectful of clients. However, as the field has progressed, paradox has become a way of understanding the change process with all of its complexities. For example, Weeks (1991) suggests that much of psychotherapy in general has the following paradoxical elements:

1. The therapist takes charge by placing the client in charge.
2. The therapist maintains a positive view of symptoms through accepting and understanding the client.
3. Change is not directly attributed to the therapist but to the interaction with clients, inviting them to attribute the change to themselves.
4. Clients are encouraged to "work through" a problem, not flee from it. They are asked to move toward the symptom and examine it. "Don't change quickly. Be who you are."
5. Responsibility for change is put back on the client, either directly or indirectly.
6. What was once uncontrollable eventually becomes controllable.

Contemporary family therapists make use of paradox as an element that encourages perceptual changes in subtle ways. For example, a number of strategic models encourage families to "go slow" with the change process. The therapist explains that there can be "side effects" to the change process and so it is sometimes helpful to approach change cautiously to properly prepare for any of its negative effects (Lewis et al., 1991). The deconstruction process of White (1990) also follows this direction (see Chapter 7). The person is invited to explore the backlash that might occur in significant relationships if change occurs. The process then turns to an exploration of how one might cope with change rather than continuing to focus on the change itself.

These recent applications of paradox suggest that change sometimes happens in indirect or "slow" ways because there are, in fact, some disadvantages to change. Our rule of thumb is that when some things get better, other things might get worse. We have watched many clients become animated and engaged in a discussion of the possible disadvantages of change. These disadvantages, such as a change in the way people view a person, the uncertainty of one's self-perception, or even depression (e.g., in the case of substance abuse recovery), constitute real dilemmas that should be taken seriously as a precursor to the actual change.

When family therapists encourage discussion of these legitimate dilemmas, such a paradoxical direction can be seen as a deeper form of respect and empathy for the client's unique drama (Hanna, 1995). These discussions also help change beliefs about the problem for both therapist and client.

An example of the respectful use of paradox came during work with a 28-year-old woman who was obese. She wanted to lose weight and had tried for many years, but to no avail. A genogram and time line were effective in explaining how her weight problem emerged shortly after her parents' divorce and how conflict with her mother began to center on her pattern of overeating at that time. However, when the family therapist began asking about the disadvantages of losing weight, more specific information came forth about how her friends might consider her a threat in vying for certain men and how the messages her weight was sending to each parent might be silenced. At this point, the therapist helped her compensate for these projected effects of change by developing strategies to maintain a secure circle of friends and by communicating more directly with her parents about her needs. She began to see that her weight problem was a relational problem, not merely a problem of "willpower."

EXPLORING NEW BEHAVIORS

Generating Alternative Solutions

Generating alternative solutions is central to the problem-solving process; the goal is to identify as many potential solutions as possible. This process is based on the following three assumptions: (1) There are a number of potentially effective ways to handle a problem; (2) families are often aware of some alternative ways to alter a problem; and (3) generating solutions increases the likelihood of selecting a manageable solution to the problem. Families are more likely to implement a solution if they suggest it. When the family generates alternative solutions, it helps the family take greater ownership of the solution and work collaboratively with the therapist.

In generating alternative solutions, the therapist uses a brainstorming procedure. There are three basic rules for good brainstorming: (1) If the therapist or family member suggests an alternative solution (e.g., "Maybe I need to set a time aside for homework"), each party refrains from critiquing the other; (2) the therapist and family can take an idea and improve on it; and (3) all parties should attempt to generate as many solutions as possible. The more solutions generated, the more likely it is that an effective solution will be found.

The therapist can generate alternative solutions in the following ways:

1. **Explore possible solutions to the problem.** The therapist might say, "Let's think of some ways you could handle this situation," or "What are some things you could do now to handle this problem?"

2. **Encourage family members to improve on another member's idea.** The therapist might say, "What do you think about John's suggestion? Do you have anything you want to add to it?"
3. **Ask family members how two or more ideas can be combined to form a better idea.** In some cases, two suggestions can readily be combined into a better idea ("So, Mary, you want to wait to talk about the problem after dinner. And, John, you want to be relaxed. What might be a good time and place to talk this issue over?").

Resolving Conflict

A set of well-developed strategies for dealing with disagreements when they arise comprise skills in conflict resolution (Stuart, 1980). Conflict resolution has proved effective in treating marital conflict (Jacobson & Margolin, 1979). The process has two distinct phases: problem definition and problem resolution. In the problem definition phase, the critical issue or problem— for example, "You don't care about me"—is defined in operational terms. An operational definition of the problem is much more likely to lead to an effective response.

The problem resolution phase emphasizes behavior change rather than insight. It is best to choose a solution that can be implemented by the family with a minimum of help. Solutions should be kept simple, since complex plans often fail because the costs (in time and energy) outweigh the benefits (say, parenting skills).

There are several things a therapist can do to help families choose the best solution:

1. **Choose a solution that is acceptable to family members.** Once the family has generated alternative solutions, the therapist can help the family select one of them. Family members have the option of striking out any that are unacceptable. The remaining solutions can be subjected to a cost–benefit analysis for all family members. The best solution is then selected from the most promising alternatives. Note that the best solution will produce an outcome that requires some accommodation from all family members.
2. **Decide how the solution will be implemented.** How will the solution be put into practice, and who will work with the family to carry it out? Because specificity and consistency are essential to success here, it is often helpful to prepare a written plan or contract listing what procedures will be followed and where the plan is to be implemented, as well as conditions, resources (both personal and material), and the amount of time that it will be in effect. The plan ensures that the family and therapist follow the agreed-upon steps and do not change their

practices midway through the program. It also reminds the members of the family of the resources they will need. The following questions can be used to develop a written plan:

- What is the chosen solution?
- What are the steps to carry out the solution?
- Who will work with the family members to help them carry out the plan?
- When will the plan begin and end?
- Who else should be involved in this plan?
- When do we meet again?

3. **Evaluate the proposed solution.** How will family members carry out their agreed-upon responsibilities? Are responsibilities or tasks being carried out according to the specifications in the contract? These questions can best be answered through data such as self-reports, collateral reports from social workers or teachers, and so on. Once information is collected, the therapist should hold a meeting with the family to discuss progress toward the goals adopted.

4. **Renegotiate the contract if necessary.** The evaluation may suggest that the contract should be renegotiated. Do the results meet the desired level of satisfaction for the family? If not, are more cost-effective solutions available to reach the goals? What have the members of the family learned from the attempted solution that can help them find a better way to resolve their problem? What adjustments (changes in behavior) must be made to reach the desired goals? In some cases, the family's level of satisfaction may not increase as the goals are attained. Here the therapist should help family members decide whether negotiated agreements—what they will talk to each other about and under what conditions—will be more satisfying over time or whether the family should set new goals.

Coaching Communication

Regardless of the therapist's orientation, coaching communication is a core component of therapeutic change strategies. Coaching communication is effective for couples (Rappaport, 1976), parents and adolescents (Crando & Ginsberg, 1976), and divorced parents (e.g., Brown, Brown, & Portes, 1991). Related programs often last from 3 to 15 weeks and contain the following core components.

Modeling   The first step in helping a couple communicate more effectively is to demonstrate, or model, the appropriate communication skill; that is, the family therapist shows each spouse what the response looks like or how it sounds. Therapists themselves model behavior throughout the treatment process. Modeling has been effective in teaching information—seeking behavior (Krumboltz, Varenhorst, & Thoresen, 1967), reducing feelings of alienation (Warner & Hansen, 1970), and improving attitudes toward drug abuse (Warner, Swisher, & Horan, 1973).

Another common practice is to provide live or symbolic models (e.g., on audiotapes or videotapes) who show, in sequential steps, the specific behaviors necessary to solve the problem (Hosford & de Visser, 1974). Taped or filmed models have been used successfully (Hansen, Pound, & Warner, 1976). The models only demonstrate the desired behaviors; there is no opportunity for interaction between the models and the spouses. However, the taped models may help stimulate discussion, which is important to prevent rote imitation by the spouses. If new behaviors are to be effective, spouses need to learn a variety of responses for a particular problem situation.

The therapist may also wish to develop models for each of several sessions. For example, the therapist could develop tapes that teach each spouse to (1) listen, (2) express a compliment, (3) express appreciation, (4) ask for help, (5) give feedback, and (6) express affection (Goldstein, 1973). Each skill could be modeled and practiced during a session if the spouses' skill levels allow. Each modeling sequence could thus represent a closer approximation of the final behavior.

Effective modeling includes the following procedures:

1. **Model a clear delineation of the desired behavior.** The behavior must be identified clearly so that family members know precisely what the therapist is actually modeling. If the modeling sequence is too vague, there is little likelihood that any learning will take place. For example, rather than trying to model "awareness" to a family member, the therapist should operationalize this by identifying and labeling emotions. To teach relationship skills, the therapist might break the relationship down into "expressing" and "responding." These areas might be broken down further into subskills such as responding to anger, affection, and so on. It is always beneficial to operationalize the skill to be learned; that is, the skill should be such that it can be seen and heard. After operationalizing the skill, the therapist explains what the model (in this case, the therapist) will be saying or doing and tells family members what they should look for. For example, if a family member is having difficulty asking for help, the therapist might say, "John, I need you to _____ when I'm feeling down."

2. **Model behaviors that hold the family members' attention.** Familiar and relevant experiences are more likely to hold attention and facilitate learning. In addition, models are generally most effective when they are the same sex as a family member and similar in appearance, age, and so on. Because of this, the therapist may want the family to identify personal

resources (friends) who could serve as models. If the family member is having difficulty entering a social situation, a friend who is accepted in that situation and who is similar to the family member might be asked to model or demonstrate how to get involved. The therapist might say, "I would like you to show Mary what to do when she wants to have a conversation with others." A model who verbalizes his or her own uncertainty (e.g., "I'm not sure, but here is one way to try it") and offers subsequent problem-solving or coping strategies can be helpful in eliciting the family members' attention. Another useful technique is to emphasize those behaviors to be modeled. The therapist might ask the model to speak more loudly during the relevant responses or to repeat a key passage ("Would you repeat that, please"). Tone of voice and mannerisms can also be used to gain the family members' attention.

3. **Ask family members to discuss what they have observed.** Unless family members are able to understand and retain the essential characteristics of the model's behavior, the intervention is of no avail. When the modeled behavior is particularly abstract, retention may be facilitated if either the model or therapist discusses the important features of the model's performance. For example, a model demonstrating how to express affection to a family member could discuss different ways to show affection. The therapist could evaluate the family members' understanding by asking them to summarize the main features or general rules of the model's performance.

4. **Reinforce the modeled behavior.** The therapist must provide incentives that encourage family members to perform the modeled behavior. When modeled behavior is not reinforced, imitation does not occur. The likelihood that imitative behavior will occur increases with the probability of receiving reinforcement. To reinforce the modeled behavior, the therapist might respond to the model's statements with positive comments ("That's an interesting point," or "That's a thoughtful idea"). By observing that the model is reinforced for expressing an opinion or solving a problem, the family members learn the most effective response in that situation.

Instruction   Once the family has attended to and understood the model's behavior, the therapist should provide instructions before the family begins practicing the new behavior. The therapist can focus attention on the relevant and essential aspects of the model's performance. The instructions may be spoken or written by the therapist or be provided in the form of an audiotape or videotape. The therapist might say, "Watch how I show appreciation to your wife," and then model the appropriate behavior, adding, "Now I want you to show appreciation for something your wife has done recently."

Instructions can be provided in the following ways:

1. **Prompt specific behaviors for family members to try.** The therapist is now essentially serving as a coach who prompts specific behavior for the family to try. Instructions generally may be positive (do this) or negative (don't do that). The therapist gives numerous specific examples. Instructing a wife to give feedback to her husband, the therapist might say, "Look directly at your husband and tell him how it makes you feel when he doesn't call to say he won't be home. Don't just accuse him of being inconsiderate."

2. **Help family members decide when to give feedback to each other.** The therapist might discuss when to give feedback—for example, "when you have time to sit down" or "when you are not so angry"—since family members may know what to say but not when to say it. By going over the demonstration, the therapist can pinpoint behaviors by the model (therapist, friend) and discuss why such behaviors can serve as a cue to a family member to perform a specific behavior.

Practice   Having received instructions on what to say and do, the family is ready to practice the behavior; practice is an essential part of the learning process because people learn by doing. Family members role-play new relationships or problem-solving behaviors. If either spouse shows resistance to this idea, the therapist can provide examples of the usefulness of practice. The crucial point is that each family member must feel that he or she is not just learning a role that is artificial and unusable. Consequently, the role-playing situations should be as realistic as possible and should include verbal responses with which each family member feels comfortable.

The following are important guidelines:

1. **Prepare the family member for practice.** The family must accept the idea that practice is an appropriate way to develop new coping or problem-solving behaviors. If the family shows some resistance to this idea, the therapist can provide examples where practice has proved useful. Experience, drills, rehearsal, recitation, homework, and exercises all involve practice. The therapist might say, "Maybe we could practice expressing appreciation to your son. I'll role-play your son, and we'll see how it goes. If you have trouble thinking of something to say, I'll help you."

2. **Start with a situation that the family can perform with little difficulty.** Practice is more successful when the initial situation is familiar to the family. For example, in a parent–adolescent conflict, the therapist might ask both parties to start by "talking about something that happened at school today." If they are unable to do this, the therapist might ask them to engage in less threatening activities such as sitting next to each other. Regardless of the activity, the therapist should begin with a nonthreatening situation.

3. **Break the behavior down into small steps.** These steps should range in complexity from simple (e.g., giving a compliment) to the complete new behavior (e.g., asking for help). In this case, the social interaction varies according to the level of difficulty.

4. **Prompt family members when they can't think of what to say or do.** The therapist can provide a sentence that fits within the context of the interaction (e.g., "It's important to me to know how you feel"). It is essential that the prompt occur only when the family member pauses or hesitates (generally for about 5 seconds). In addition, the therapist can use hand signals to raise or lower the family member's voice or to signal to come closer. Prompts should be faded as family members become able to practice the behavior unaided. At this point, the therapist should praise the family members for expressing the desired behavior in their own words.

Feedback   When family members have practiced the skills, each must receive feedback on her or his performance. Such feedback provides an incentive for improvement. Information received about poor performance can be potentially as helpful as knowledge regarding positive performance.

The following guidelines are important in providing feedback:

1. **Solicit the family's ideas about feedback prior to practice.** The therapist might say, "I'll observe you and try to give you some helpful hints." When a family member denies or disagrees with feedback from the therapist ("That's not the way it sounded to me") or attempts to justify a response ("The reason I said that was . . ."), then feedback was probably not solicited or agreed on prior to practice.

2. **Describe rather than evaluate the family members' behaviors.** For example, the therapist might replay a videotape of what a family member said and comment, "Here you say 'My mother thinks I should. . . .' Do you remember we agreed you would say, 'I think I should . . .'?" The therapist's feedback statements should avoid blame. Statements such as "That just doesn't sound right" or "I don't know why you can't do that" fail to provide helpful information.

3. **Reinforce a family member's response and at the same time prompt similar responses.** For example, the therapist might say, "That's a good question to get him to talk to you. Sometimes, however, your husband may not want to talk about his job. Can you think of some other questions you could ask him?" By prompting additional questions, the therapist not only helps reinforce the spouse's use of questions in a practice session but also facilitates its generalization to other situations and people.

The therapist should provide opportunities for the family members to practice their skills at home and should supply guidelines or worksheets to facilitate such practice. Therapy is more effective when family members are able to practice skills successfully in everyday interactions.

Assigning Tasks

Tasks attempt to change the sequence of interaction in the family. They may help a family become more organized, establish operational boundaries, set rules, or establish family goals (Madanes, 1981). Tasks might include (1) advice, (2) explanations or suggestions, or (3) directives to change the interactional sequence in the family (Papp, 1980). For example, in the case of a family with a mother and daughter who are overinvolved and a father who is peripheral, the therapist might give the following explanation to the mother: "Your daughter needs to treat you with respect. She will be able to do that when you have your husband's support. Right now, he gets called on as the bad guy when you aren't able to deal with her. This is a critical time when your daughter needs to spend more time with her father." Unfortunately, advice may not be successful because family members often know what to do but don't know how to do it.

In many cases, the therapist must convince the family to follow the directive or task. This may be difficult unless each family member sees some payoff. Persuading a family to perform a task depends on the type of task, the family, and the kind of relationship the therapist has with the family (Haley, 1976). For example, there may not be a payoff for adolescents to talk in a session if they aren't certain that their parents care about them or if they can get their way without talking. In this case, the therapist's directive must provide some benefits (e.g., more privileges or parental concern) for the adolescent as well as for other members of the family.

Haley (1976) offers several suggestions to therapists for getting families to follow their tasks or directives:

1. **Discuss everything the family has done to try to solve the problem.** In this way, the therapist can avoid making suggestions that have already been tried. The therapist should lead the family to the conclusion that everything has been tried but nothing has worked. At this point, the therapist is in a position to offer the family something different.

2. **Ask family members to discuss the negative consequences if their problem is not handled now (i.e., "What is going to happen if this problem is not resolved?").** Aversive consequences are probably different for different members of the family. Nevertheless, examining the negative consequences of the problem for each family member emphasizes the intensity of the problem. A mother and her adolescent daughter, for instance, get into conflicts; both cry and are unhappy, and neither gets her way. The mother doesn't get the kind of respect she deserves, and the daughter doesn't get any privileges. It is important for the therapist to emphasize these consequences and to project what might happen if the problem is not resolved.

3. **Assign a task that is reasonable and easily accomplished.** To ensure that the family members can complete the task at home, it is often necessary to get them to complete the task in the session. For example, the therapist may want an adolescent daughter to have a conversation with her mother without interruptions by her father. Therefore, the therapist may ask the daughter to talk with her mother in session while the father reads a magazine. The therapist might suggest an activity that both of them might enjoy doing together. If the father interrupts before the mother and daughter complete the task, the therapist may wish to devise something else for the father to do, such as running an errand, so as to improve the chances that he does not interrupt when mother and daughter attempt to complete a conversation at home. The therapist can also ensure that the task is accomplished by providing adequate instructions. In this instance, the therapist focuses attention on the relevant and essential aspects of each family member's performance. Before the family begins the task, the therapist might instruct the father that it will be difficult for him to stay out of it and that he needs to occupy himself in some other way.

4. **Assign a task to fit the ability and performance level of the family members.** In the film *Family With a Little Fire* (Minuchin, 1974), the task is focused on the scapegoated child's fire setting. The therapist, Braulio Montalvo, asks the mother to spend 5 minutes each day teaching her daughter how to light matches correctly. He also instructs the parental child who stands between mother and child to watch the other children while the mother is teaching the child. This task is suited to each family member's level of ability.

5. **Use authority to get the family to follow the directive or task.** Sometimes the therapist must use his or her knowledge and expertise to get the family to comply. It is important for the therapist to accept the role of expert rather than asking the members of the family what they think they should do. The therapist might say, for example, "From my experience, I'd say that this is a critical time for your son, and he needs time with his father." The therapist is really saying, "On the basis of my expertise, I believe that it is important for you to do this." Sometimes the therapist may ask whether the family or family member trusts him or her. If the family or family member says yes, the therapist might say, "Good. Then I want you to do this because it is important. Trust me." Here the therapist uses trust to gain control of the interview.

6. **Give clear instructions to each member of the family.** Everyone should know what his or her responsibilities are. If a therapist asks a father and daughter to do something together, then exact dates and times should be specified. By deciding in advance on a time, the father and

daughter make a commitment to perform the task. Establishing a time also decreases the likelihood of interference by something else, such as work or TV. The therapist and the family should also decide who will take care of the other children and what the mother will be doing during that time. The therapist might ask family members to describe what they will be doing so that they are all clear about their roles. Family members should be encouraged to discuss anything that might interfere with the completion of the task.

Developing Rituals

Rituals can address a number of therapeutic goals related to rigid family rules and omitted developmental tasks in the life cycle. The Milan team (Selvini Palazzoli et al., 1978) designed specific strategic instructions in the form of family rituals. The ritualized prescriptions were designed for "breaking up those behaviors through which each parent disqualifies and sabotages the initiatives and directions of the other parent in his relationship with the children" (Selvini Palazzoli et al., 1978, p. 3). Such prescriptions can be repeated with the same format for any type of family. Rituals are used instead of interpretation, which is often ineffective in altering the rules of the system. At the end of an assessment period, the therapist helps the family develop a ritual. The following is a common Milan-style prescription:

> On even days of the week—Tuesdays, Thursdays, and Saturdays—beginning from tomorrow onwards until the date of the next session and fixing the time between X o'clock and Y o'clock (making sure that the whole family will be at home during this time), whatever Z does (name of patient, followed by a list of his symptomatic behaviors), father will decide alone, at his absolute discretion, what to do with Z. Mother will have to behave as if she were not there. On odd days of the week—Mondays, Wednesdays, and Fridays—at the same time, whatever Z may do, mother will have full power to decide what course of action to follow regarding Z. Father will have to behave as if he were not there. On Sundays, everyone must behave spontaneously. Each parent, on the days assigned to him or her, must record in a diary any infringement by the partner of the prescription according to which he is expected to behave as if he were not there. (In some cases the job of recording the possible mistakes of one of the parents has been entrusted to a child acting as a recorder or to the patient himself if he is fit for the task). (Selvini Palazzoli et al., 1978, p. 5)

Selvini Palazzoli et al. (1978) note that the ritualized prescription operates at several levels. First, the rules of the game are changed to prevent interferences from occurring. Second, parents are blocked from competing for the therapist's approval since their efforts only serve to deflect attention from the problem (relationship). Finally, the therapist gains information regardless of whether the family follows the prescription. This information can be used to design subsequent interventions.

The following guidelines are helpful in designing rituals:

1. **Prescribe one or more aspects of the problem. Those problematic thoughts and behaviors then form the content of the ritual.** For example, a boy who threw frequent "out-of-control" temper tantrums was asked to continue having his tantrums but to have them in a special place at home and only after school when he really had time to throw one.

2. **Provide a rationale for the ritual to increase the likelihood of compliance.** For example, the therapist might suggest to the family that structuring the temper tantrums in this way helps family members gain control of the problem or helps the therapist better understand the problem.

Another type of ritual, suggested by Imber-Black, Roberts, and Whiting (1988), helps families address unresolved developmental issues by grieving traumatic losses, completing developmental milestones, or celebrating and stabilizing progress. Such rituals form a part of many religious and societal traditions, but may have been overlooked as a family's problem was developing. For example, if families have suffered a traumatic death or loss, the therapist may develop special grieving rituals for the family to facilitate the further healing necessary to break a dysfunctional pattern. These rituals are most effective when the influence of the loss on the presenting problem has been recognized and the family becomes the author of the ceremony, determining the participants and the desired meaning of the ritual.

Sometimes, families skip important developmental milestones that later become metaphors for the presenting problem. For example, when couples elope or forgo a honeymoon, family therapists may use this as a metaphor for skipping some important developmental task, such as creating a strong marital attachment. As the couple identifies elements of the marriage that were skipped and need to be developed, the planning of a honeymoon or special anniversary celebration can symbolize the completion of relationship tasks facilitated during the course of therapy.

Other rituals celebrate the completion of therapy as a rite of passage (Epston & White, 1992); for example, a triangulated child may be helped to disengage from the position of "marital therapist" and be given a new position as "liberated sixth grader," free to explore how children grow up when they don't have to worry about their parents' marriage. A concluding ritual then allows the family to celebrate such achievements in the company of significant others. Thus, the culmination of therapy is not seen as being a private termination or as implying loss of the therapeutic relationship. Rather, such rituals help families to stay focused on the changes they have made. These rituals also normalize therapy by incorporating societal traditions into the process.

SUMMARY

The Anatomy of Therapeutic Change

In this chapter, we have explored a number of suggestions for facilitating relational change in families. One of the concepts from general systems theory is that the whole is greater than the sum of its parts. In family therapy, this means that a family is more than just a collection of people. Instead, a family is a unique group of people with a dynamic, evolving history together that creates organizational complexity and includes elements of content and process in its communication. This communication, in turn, leads to interpersonal patterns that include thoughts, behaviors, emotions and intentions. These interpersonal patterns can be deconstructed into the various themes from Chapter 3 (gender, race, culture, structure, intergenerational relationships, individual experience). These are a few of the many elements that comprise our concept of relationships.

Similarly, we think that the process of relational change is much greater than the sum of the suggestions we have offered in this chapter. As a starting place, they provide beginning clinicians with some basic techniques. However, the interplay of the themes from these interventions make the whole complex. For example, assigning successful tasks requires that the therapist have credibility with clients and that the task is appropriate to the unique culture of the family. Increasing intensity also requires a solid and positive therapeutic alliance and a climate of safety felt by clients. Thus, it is helpful to remember that suggestions from this chapter will not be successful unless the therapist is developing competent relational skills such as those we described in Chapter 4.

In addition, there is another level of complexity that makes our work challenging and rewarding. When we think of ourselves as made up of separate parts, we might miss the fascinating energy that often contributes to our greatest successes. For example, in Chapter 2, we noted a growing trend that recognizes the importance of emotion and attachment in relationships. If we place these basic skills alongside this growing emphasis in the field, we can see a number of ways in which first and second generation family therapies impact emotion, even though the writing from a particular author might not have made the link explicit. As an example, this can be seen when we assign some intergenerational tasks to a client and we witness a transformation of the troubled relationship with an aging parent. This transformation will be manifest in the new emotions that develop from these changes. Thus, when we speak of changing behaviors, beliefs or communication, we encourage the beginning therapist to see these as inseparable from emotions. Considering these elements as the web of interpersonal process, we think good therapeutic plans impact all these factors in some way (Remember the awareness wheel in Chapter 3?). However, we also believe that what makes a therapist successful is the ability to know what might be the most relevant entry point, given the unique contexts of family members. For example, some families are comfortable speaking directly about their feelings and others are not. Given these differences, one plan may call for behavioral interventions that delay speaking about difficult emotions until the therapist ascertains a feeling of safety from family members. A different situation might prompt the therapist to immediately confront the strong emotion in a conflicted marriage before the relationship deteriorates further. Finding a flexible balance within this range of possibilities is our goal for the developing, creative family therapist.

As therapists seek to be flexible in managing the therapeutic process, the middle stage of therapy is often a good opportunity to evaluate the process, examine the fit between the family and the treatment plan and make any midcourse corrections that seem important. To continue with our metaphor of driving a car, we were in first gear during referral, intake, and initial session (the process is deliberate and careful); and we shifted into second gear during assessment, treatment planning, and initial interventions (our speed picked up, but we were far from settled). If we have a direction that produces a good fit with the client, we might be ready to coast into third or fourth gear. However, to carefully ascertain how the elements are fitting together, family therapists must understand how evaluations can be helpful to the overall success of our clinical work. Chapter 9 will review types of evaluations in the therapeutic process and will make suggestions for how developing practitioners can begin to use evaluations to improve and document their work.

three

THE FUTURE OF FAMILY THERAPY: EVALUATIONS, RESEARCH, AND COLLABORATION

The field of family therapy is no longer new. While other mental health professions have a longer history in the industrialized world, we can see that there have already been several "generations" in the development of our field. The pioneers of the 1950s and 1960s taught students who practiced in the 1970s and 1980s. Those students, taught third-generation family therapists like ourselves. We, in turn, are introducing the practice and profession of marriage and family therapy through efforts such as this book. As fourth-generation family therapists prepare to practice, we are reminded that the world of mental health treatment is changing even as we write. These changes come in response to many societal influences. For example, business practices in managed care companies have forced clinicians to grapple with becoming accountable for the concrete outcomes of their work. Other funding sources have become just as concerned about how their tax or charitable dollars are used. Mental health consumers are also becoming more conscious of whether therapy produces the results they need. Trends in psychology and social work are also having an influence upon the culture of psychotherapy. Psychologists have begun to study the "common factors" of successful models of psychotherapy in order to develop unifying themes from which to practice (the focus of this book for our field). The field of social work has seen ecological models of practice included in research projects that tackle complex problems such as delinquency.

These societal shifts are changing the face of psychotherapy and the way it is practiced. In addition, family therapists have seen encouraging results from research efforts, but the number of studies is still small compared with those in other mental health professions. Thus, every family therapist must put away the notion that business and research are contrary to clinical work. Instead, we encourage our trainees to see that there are a number of ways to explore the change process in family therapy. Learning to use these additional lenses to address therapeutic outcomes is an important step of personal growth for every clinician.

As accountability, outcome research, and social change challenge all mental health professions in similar ways, interdisciplinary collaborations are occurring in many areas of service delivery to meet these demands. No single discipline is thought to have the entire solution when complex problems involve multiple symptoms (e.g., parental depression and joblessness), multiple settings (e.g., home, school, medical clinic), and multiple people (e.g., adolescents with substance abuse problems and parents with mental illness).

Thus, in this final section, we offer suggestions for integration at a different level. Instead of addressing how to integrate the variety of models in family therapy, we examine ways to include outcome research, process evaluation, and interdisciplinary collaboration in clinical practice. These activities can become inspiring opportunities to expand the influence of family therapy beyond the therapy room and the 50-minute hour. Family therapy's systems–interactional approach to problem solving provides a grasp of complex problems that works well with the traditions of other professions. We think the future of family therapy will be defined by these areas of growth that are already occurring in the field. As the final step in our journey, be prepared to travel in "foreign lands" and "exotic places." Our metaphor of driving may have one meaning when the roads are paved and the language is familiar. However, if we have a luxury car and we suddenly find ourselves on the dusty roads of Kenya, we may find driving to be traumatic! At such times, changing vehicles can be a relief and even exhilarating. We leave you with this picture as we explore the future of family therapy.

EVALUATIONS AND RESEARCH IN FAMILY THERAPY

Evaluating Therapeutic Process

Documenting Outcomes of Family Therapy

Assessments for Termination and Follow-Up

Measuring Family Process

Evaluations in Training

Summary

As a group, clinicians are rarely apt to call themselves researchers or scientists. Thus, the idea of evaluation is often met with a lack of enthusiasm. Very often, practitioners are so immersed in the implicit subtleties of therapeutic experience that they dismiss scientific inquiry as irrelevant to clinical work. Particularly with beginning therapists, their energy is often directed exclusively toward learning what works with their clients ***from their perspective*** and they do not consider outside perspectives to be important. In addition, experienced clinicians often hold the belief that scientific rigor fails to acknowledge the human aspects of therapeutic experience. However, exciting trends in mental health and family therapy are changing these biases and opening new doors of creative clinical work. Seasoned clinicians are now engaging in research about the process and outcomes of therapy. In Chapter 2, we discussed the new tradition of evidence-based practice and provided examples of what these dedicated clinicians are doing. This research is teaching us about how to maintain our human creativity while documenting the successful outcomes of our work.

In the traditional use of the term, ***clinical evaluation*** may be associated with inconvenient paperwork and documentation in many agencies. Just as research often connotes an interest in the explicit, observable, and quantifiable parts of human experience, so too may evaluation be seen as a distraction to the energizing part of the work. However, if these activities are both defined as **systematic inquiry,** family therapists are more likely to see that clinical research can have great relevance to their work; one example is the growing trend toward adding qualitative methods to our research skills. For example, ethnographic studies on client perceptions can provide therapists with a mirror of their professional role (Newfield, Kuehl, Joanning, and Quinn, 1991). In addition, Selekman and Todd (1991b) argue in favor of "empirically-based clinical practice." From studies on family therapy effectiveness with adolescent substance abuse, they conclude that family-based research shows what type of intervention is most effective with what type of family. In their review, chronic, discouraged families did not respond well to "zealous optimism and pushy methods" (p. 321). This research supports our suggestion that indirect interventions are more appropriate for chronic problems.

Thus, clinicians can participate in systematic inquiry to evaluate their outcomes in family therapy and to support their treatment plans. This need not compromise the spontaneity of clinical work. In fact, some qualitative research can be performed informally as part of the therapeutic process to improve the therapeutic relationship. Any time family therapists ask the same question in each case, they are engaging in systematic inquiry. When therapists notice similarities between families, presenting problems, and eventual solutions, this is a form of research. As clinicians begin to observe and understand these patterns, their work can be influenced by new information. For example, they can begin to routinely ask families at the end of successful treatment what they remember as the most or least important topics discussed during sessions. Even though the answers may be diverse, family therapists can use the information as a mirror from which to view their work. They may decide to emphasize or minimize aspects of the process on the basis of such client feedback.

An example of formal inquiry in clinical practice might be the categorization of completed cases according to presenting problems, type of family, number of sessions, type of intervention, and outcomes. Over time, the practitioner can begin to determine whether certain characteristics emerge as similarities or patterns that can be anticipated at the beginning of treatment to improve treatment effectiveness. For example, studies in adolescent drug abuse found that a structural–strategic model worked well with a variety of intact and single-parent families as long as they did not have parental or multiple drug abuse, unresolved losses, or financial or community problems. However, when these problems were present, an indirect approach such as that used by the Milan team was more successful (Selekman & Todd, 1991b). Family therapists are currently learning more about the relevance of quantitative and qualitative research. As this continues, they will be able to identify parts of their clinical experience that are naturally occurring methods of research.

EVALUATING THERAPEUTIC PROCESS

As we suggested in Chapter 4, the therapeutic relationship is central to the facilitation of change and should be monitored on many levels as family therapy progresses. This evaluation should include the perceptions of the practitioner and of the family. Without feedback from each side of the interaction, it is difficult for clinicians, supervisors, or researchers to account for strengths and weaknesses in the interpersonal process between therapist and family. What is the relationship like? Is it accomplishing the desired goals? Is it authoritarian, cooperative, or collegial? This assessment may focus on each person's role and expectations in the relationship as well as on the way these are manifest in therapeutic interactions. What type of communication patterns can be described in therapy sessions? Are therapist and family able to "communicate about their communicating" with each other? This type of evaluation is subjective in nature and should be used regularly to avoid misunderstandings and to troubleshoot when the clinician feels a lack of therapeutic progress; it should also be used in situations where the clinician anticipates a potential problem from a subsequent part of the treatment plan.

The Family's Evaluation

Family members may be privately evaluating the therapist with respect to trustworthiness, empathy, safety, helpfulness, and so on. This level of evaluation is based on subjective criteria chosen by each person and is often related to first impressions of interpersonal comfort. At this level of evaluation, discussion must be initiated by therapists because the topic can be intimate and threatening for family and therapist. To ask families about how they are experiencing the process elicits information that may imply how therapists are doing their job. Nevertheless, beginning family therapists can minimize their sense of threat in such an interaction by regarding the clients' perceptions as information about what is most comfortable for them. Therapist competence is then related to a willingness to ask the questions and not to the content of the answers. Family therapists can conduct this type of evaluation in a spirit of reflection, communicating self-confidence and concern about the well-being of the client. Is the family feeling comfortable with the process? Does the process seem beneficial and hopeful? Is it too structured? Too unstructured? Too authoritarian? Relevant? Not relevant? We think this is an example of systematic inquiry that is part of sound clinical expertise.

An interesting research project that addressed client perceptions of family therapists was conducted by Newfield, Kuehl, Joanning, and Quinn (1991) with families who had participated in family therapy as part of a study of adolescent substance abuse. In this qualitative study, independent interviewers asked participants to describe their experience of the family therapy process, their perceptions of the therapist, and their views of the outcome. The purpose of the project was to obtain qualitative information about therapy from a lay point of view. The investigators characterized professional clinicians as members of a culture (with a distinctive language and expectations) that is different from the culture of those who seek their services. This attention to the interplay of different cultures is borrowed from the field of anthropology. The main questions focused on what occurred in the process and what the implications of these occurrences were. The results of this research suggested that clients were most satisfied with treatment when therapy matched their conceptualizations of the problem. Consequently, an anthropological view of the therapeutic experience uses the natural language and expectations of clients to understand the process rather than technical theories that are rooted in the culture of the profession.

Often, beginning practitioners are most threatened by openly expressed anger, criticism, or despair from family members. However, we find it useful to help trainees anticipate their most feared stumbling blocks and develop a repertoire of questions and responses that encourages open discussion of client experience. For example, some clinicians give clients permission to express disagreement or discontent ("It's normal for family members to become upset over some aspects of the therapy process. Can you think of anything so far that has been upsetting or confusing for you?"). Family members may be uncomfortable with some part of the process (e.g., questions or responses from the therapist that inadvertently offend someone). When this is discovered, the therapist can legitimize their experience ("I'm sorry for the misunderstanding; you did the right thing to let me know about it") or put their feelings into a larger perspective ("I can understand how you would come to feel this way. You're not the only one who has had this type of experience, and sometimes we professionals need help in knowing how you're feeling about our work together"). Very often, anger can be reframed as pain, thereby alerting the practitioner to some aspect of the process that has become threatening for a family member. Dominance can be reframed as fear, which alerts the therapist to a covert sense of vulnerability. When clients express despair ("This isn't doing any good"), the therapist can inquire about expectations and priorities of the client that may need to be addressed more directly. Despair may also prompt the therapist to explain the process more fully and to shift the target of change—for example, from behavioral to cognitive or from cognitive to behavioral. Family members who are more literal or concrete (result-oriented) often want behavioral change to be manifest first. Family members who are more intuitive (process-oriented) often want emotional change that impacts their internal experience.

It is recommended that practitioners ask for client perceptions of therapeutic process before and after various stages of assessment and treatment. For example, if a family has agreed to cooperate with the construction of a genogram in an initial interview, the practitioner may still want to ask family members at the beginning of the second session if they feel comfortable proceeding in that direction (e.g., "On a scale from 1 to 10, how comfortable are you with our plan for today?"). By acknowledging that some families are uncomfortable with the process or do not think it is a relevant exercise for their particular problem, the therapist provides the family members with an opportunity to discuss their thoughts, second thoughts, or questions about the process. It also gives the therapist an opportunity to search for a rationale that makes sense to the family or to search for a different approach.

Careful observation of nonverbal messages is another important vehicle for gauging client perceptions. Many family members are too threatened to make direct disclosures about their experience. In that case, the observation of behavioral patterns and sequences over time provides useful information on how the process fits the clients. For example, family therapists may discover that clients respond to some direction, advice, or task with a "yes, but" pattern. This pattern can be interpreted as a nonverbal message that the direction or task does not fit. In addition, such a pattern should be thought of as a courteous power struggle between therapist and family member, which should be avoided through therapist flexibility. When the therapist can take a one-down position and state a desire to change the process so that the family feels more comfortable, the family is encouraged to trust the therapist more and to be more direct.

One way of learning from nonverbal messages involves noting how families respond to homework and out-of-session tasks. De Shazer (1985) lists five possible responses that clients may make to a given task assignment and five suggested responses from the therapist. Even when a family does something opposite to the task or fails to fulfill the assignment at all, therapists are encouraged to view the family's response as a message that the family members are instinctively doing what is best for the family. By such nonverbal observation, the therapist learns to understand messages that are sent through behavior instead of words.

As family therapists become skilled at eliciting microevaluations from family perceptions, they discover that such evaluations become interventions. These turning points of change in the therapeutic relationship become models for change in family relationships. In addition, the effectiveness of the therapeutic relationship is influenced by perceptions that develop within the therapist. These will now be examined.

The Therapist's Evaluation

The therapist may be evaluating clients with respect to level of cooperation, severity of the problem, and so on. In addition to focusing on the family's perception of the process, clinicians must also pay attention to their own perceptions and misperceptions of the process. If a therapist is feeling stuck but finds that the client is satisfied with the process, what does that say about the theory that the practitioner is using as a lens? By the same token, if both therapist and client are feeling dissatisfied with the process, blame can be centered on the process and not on either party. Then, both parties can work together to cooperatively resolve their dissatisfaction. Besides modeling problem-solving skills, the family therapist also demonstrates a willingness to admit mistakes and to explore misunderstandings. When the client is feeling dissatisfied, but the practitioner believes that all is well, it is important for clinicians to distinguish assumption from fact or, in constructivist terms, to distinguish their personal reality from the reality of the client.

When reviewing their own perceptions, family therapists should remember that their behavior is often an extension of their beliefs and intentions. Using the awareness wheel from Chapter 3 (Miller et al., 1988), it is possible for the clinician to identify what thoughts and intentions may have been operating during problematic interactions. A therapist who has chosen a specific model of family therapy may also compare his or her own perceptions with the assumptions adopted by the model. For example, suppose a therapist's goal is to address a client's weight problem from an intergenerational point of view. The fundamental assumptions of that model include an acknowledgment that past relationships and interactions affect present relationships and interactions and the assertion that thoughts and intentions are often taught by one generation to another. If the therapist inquires about family and cultural values, significant intergenerational relationships, and the evolution of the client's experience in the family of origin, these behaviors reflect an intergenerational point of view. However, if the therapist becomes concerned with a client's weight problem without explaining how the weight is *related* to intergenerational dynamics, the therapist's conduct might fail to impact the client's reality. This omission can lead to problematic interactions in which a client's reality may be based upon one reality (e.g. "It's a problem of willpower") and a therapist's reality may be based upon a different reality (e.g. "It's a cultural and intergenerational problem that requires changes in the thoughts and emotions that underlie behaviors").

Therapists should also take the opportunity to evaluate their own perceptions when they leave a session feeling angry, defeated, or confused. At these times, reflecting on expectations for self, client, and the process itself is in order. Is the therapist expecting too much from the family? Is the therapist becoming dependent on client behavior for a feeling of success? Has the therapist remembered to utilize strengths and idiosyncrasies of the family in the proposed solution to the problem? Has the therapist found a way to value the unique and sometimes contrary style of a family? By means of these questions, which constitute a form of self-supervision, clinicians are able to develop learning and process goals that can further their own cognitive and behavioral development. In addition, the traditional supervisory process can shed light on therapists' perceptions of the process. Objective evaluations can also provide an external review of the therapeutic process.

Frequency of Process Evaluations

In many instances, periodic evaluations of the process prevent impasses from occurring. Coleman (1985) suggests that treatment failures are often related to a variety of factors, including theoretical issues, process issues, motivation and consumerism, goal setting, the therapeutic alliance, personal issues of the therapist, and relationships with larger systems. If an impasse has occurred, an evaluation of these factors might provide a constructive resolution. For many beginning family therapists struggling to put their nascent skills to work, it is a challenge to initiate an evaluation. Since negative evaluations make learning difficult, it is human nature to avoid the possibility of criticism until more confidence is gained. However, such evaluations can be as simple as reviewing the history of therapy to date. Beginning practitioners can also use the outline from Chapter 6 to analyze the beginning stages of therapy. Was any important topic skipped? Was the information about previous treatment history detailed? Was the discussion about goals and expectations candid? What might the client still be hesitant to disclose? What does the family need for the therapeutic relationship to become more comfortable? As clinicians begin to experiment with periodic evaluations of their own process through the eyes of the family, they discover the importance of such information in facilitating therapeutic progress.

While discussions about the therapeutic relationship may often be informal and impromptu, it is also possible to evaluate therapeutic interaction in a formal way for supervision or research. Supervisors may observe therapeutic exchanges firsthand to understand the nature of the therapeutic relationship. In some training programs, sessions are recorded on audiotape to enable beginning practitioners to review their communication patterns and to monitor their grasp of various skills. For example, a formal evaluation might consist of the practitioner reviewing a tape of a family therapy session and counting how many circular questions were asked of the family. If there was a part of the session when the therapist felt stuck, the evaluation could also include a review of circular questions to see which ones could have been asked during the period of difficulty.

In addition, therapeutic process can be formally evaluated through models of interactional analysis that are used for research. The couple communication program can be used for this purpose since communication may readily be broken down into each category of the awareness wheel and then quantified by noting the frequencies in each category. The relational coding scheme is another model that analyzes communication into categories such as questions, support, assertions, talk-overs, and so on (Ericson & Rogers, 1973). An analysis of therapeutic interaction with this method categorizes each message from each person and quantifies how many of each type of statement were made. In additional analyses, this coding scheme produces data that describe the sequence and patterns of each exchange over time. For example, if the client made frequent assertions that were often followed by the therapist asking frequent questions, this recurring pattern could be noted by the formal analysis.

Thus, it is possible to conduct formal and informal evaluations of each person's experience in the therapeutic process, the nature of specific microinteractions within the relationship, and the ongoing relationship and its effectiveness. In focusing on therapeutic process in these ways, the beginning practitioner begins to see that the process of family therapy is, indeed, a complex set of interactions that accommodates multiple points of view and is experienced on multiple levels. These interactions become the means used by the clinician to bring about change. Such change is measured at another level of clinical evaluation, which usually focuses on treatment outcomes.

DOCUMENTING OUTCOMES OF FAMILY THERAPY

There are several formal methods for determining whether goals have been met in therapy: measuring behavioral changes, using goal attainment scales, and focusing on self-reports. These methods may be used separately or in combination to determine whether goal behaviors have been successfully reached.

Measuring Behavioral Changes

Of the various evaluation designs the therapist may utilize, the most useful for tracking specific behavioral changes are time-series designs, where data are collected over different points in time. Some of these have been developed for experimental purposes and, therefore, may not be practical for the therapist, who, in many cases, must change the family's behavior in the shortest possible time. Only those designs that are of practical use in family therapy are discussed here.

The AB Design   The simplest time-series approach is the AB design. Here the therapist or family first records baseline rates of target behaviors (positive interactions, arguments, etc.). Having plotted the baseline level of behavior, the therapist and family set an objective. It is helpful to specify the number of consecutive days on which the criterion must be achieved to provide an objective determination of when the goal has been reached. The therapist or family gathers a second set of data during the implementation phase of the program. Data may be collected continuously throughout the program or at specific times. For example, during baseline, a couple averaged only 3 minutes of positive interaction per day for 1 week. On the basis of this information, the therapist and family decided the couple should set a goal of at least 15 minutes each

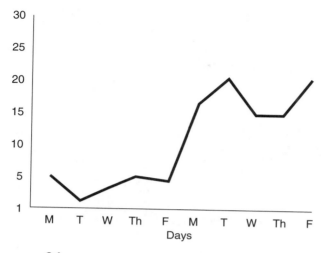

FIGURE **9.1**

Time-series graph

day for positive (problem-free) interaction. Figure 9.1 illustrates that the goal was reached. The AB design in this instance provides an easy means of evaluating one behavior of one family in one setting. The therapist may only need to collect baseline data for several days (until there is some consistency in the rate), then set a reasonable objective, and continue collecting data to measure changes. By graphing data, the therapist and family can set realistic goals and monitor those goals on a daily basis.

The therapist should be mindful that other events might also be influencing the behavior of the family. For example, although the couple set aside time for positive interaction, both spouses may have been getting encouragement from friends and family to do more things with each other. However, even though this design does not control for error resulting from competing events, it is an acceptable means for determining whether an objective has been met.

The Multiple Baseline   In some instances, therapists may be interested in more than one target behavior for a particular family, or they may want to measure changes on a specific behavior for more than one family or situation. In that case, a multiple baseline is used. For example, a second target behavior for the couple just discussed was the amount of time spent arguing with their son. When they reached the first goal (15 minutes per day of positive interaction), the family, under the therapist's guidance, set a second goal: to reduce the amount of negative interaction with their son from 25 to 5 minutes daily.

Figure 9.2 illustrates an increase in the couple's positive interaction time when exposed to the first intervention (i.e., structured time for positive interaction), while the amount of negative interaction time with the son (which is not

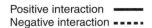

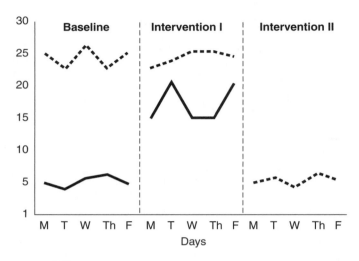

Positive interaction ━━━
Negative interaction ■ ■ ■ ■

FIGURE 9.2

Multiple baseline graph

being treated) shows little change. The latter quantity only decreases when the second intervention is introduced. By exposing each target behavior—positive couple interaction and negative interaction time with the son—to the intervention, the therapist can determine if the intervention is actually responsible for meeting the goal; that is, each family behavior should change only as it is exposed to the intervention and not before. It should be noted that the behaviors studied in the multiple baseline are not necessarily isolated. For example, positive interactions probably affect negative interactions and vice versa.

There are many instances when the target behavior occurs in more than one situation (home, school, work, neighborhood, etc.). In this case, the therapist can use the multiple baseline to evaluate the target behaviors of the family in different situations. For example, negative requests (complaints or demands) by a child can be monitored both at home and at school. If parents are able to successfully reduce the child's negative requests at home, while the level of negative requests remains the same at school, then a similar intervention can be implemented at school with the assistance of the therapist and the family. The multiple baseline is useful here in determining the success of an intervention when the problem occurs in more than one setting.

Comparative Data From Taped Interviews   Although the graphing procedures just described were applied primarily to discrete behaviors that can be easily observed and recorded, the same principle can be applied to data that are more difficult to observe and quantify. For instance, the therapeutic goal may be to improve marital satisfaction as measured by the number of positive statements each spouse makes about the other. Marital satisfaction can obviously be measured in other ways; the important thing is that all goals be operationalized so that there is some way of measuring progress. For instance, if the goal is stated only as improvement in the relationship, this may mean different things to different people, and it is difficult to measure success. Assuming that the number of positive statements that each spouse makes about the other is a reasonable measure of marital satisfaction, the therapist can tape interviews and record the number of positive versus negative statements. Using the first session or two as a baseline, the therapist can then chart this behavior as intervention is implemented.

Even when objectives are operationalized, there are varying ranges of objectivity. For example, the therapist must often depend on clients' self-reports of behaviors such as anxiety, marital discord, and drug use, and there may be no way to verify the accuracy of such reports. Still, if the evaluation data are to be obtained by the self-recording of client behavior, there is some evidence that the very act of self-recording is itself effective in promoting the desired behavior.

The therapist must follow several guidelines when using behavioral observation:

1. **Use repeated observations to evaluate behavior change.** Repeated measures provide a more accurate evaluation of therapeutic goals. Infrequent observations often reflect random changes in behavior and fail to provide an accurate representation of behavior before and after treatment.
2. **Ask family members to practice self-observation.** For example, a family member might be taught to observe and record the number of angry thoughts he or she has about another family member.
3. **Record behavioral observations on a prepared form.** The form should include the date, session number, family member's name, observer, operational definition of the problem, times of observation, length of interval, and setting or activity.
4. **Provide a graphic summary of the behavior.** The therapist should enter the time of recording (minutes, days, etc.) on the horizontal axis, from far left to far right, and the number of target behaviors on the vertical axis.
5. **Determine whether further observations are necessary.** If baseline or pretreatment data are characterized by extreme variation or a gradual increase or decrease, further observations should be collected until some stability is noted. Of course, these considerations must be weighed against the need for prompt treatment; if the problem behavior is severely disturbing (as in the case of violence), treatment should supersede behavioral observation. Too much time spent in collecting baseline data may reduce the time available for treatment, which is of greater importance.

There are several limitations to self-observation as a means of recording behavior change. First, family members may change their behavior during the period of observation to please the therapist. This is particularly true for family members who have a need to please others. Second, some family members may not follow through with monitoring behavior change because of the time or effort required to keep accurate records. This is often the case when the therapist has not chosen a focus that is meaningful to family members. Finally, since self-observation can often produce a behavior change, the data may not accurately reflect the situation in the absence of observation (Barlow, Hayes, & Nelson, 1984).

Using Goal Attainment Scales

A second method for evaluating behavioral change specifies the level or amount of change—how much families must do to reach the desired goal. In this case, the level of attainment determines whether the goals have been successfully reached. Cormier and Cormier (1991) offer an example:

> Suppose a client wants to increase the number of assertive opinions she expresses orally with her husband. If she now withholds all her opinions, her level of change might be stated at a lower level than that defined for another client who already expresses some opinions. And if the client's husband is accustomed to her refraining from giving opinions, this might affect the degree of change made, at least initially. The counselor's and client's primary concern is to establish a level that is manageable, and that the client can attain with some success. (p. 233)

Achievable goals should be determined by the current level of problem behavior, the desired level of goal behavior, available support and resources, and the desire to change. One way to establish achievable and measurable goals is through the use of goal attainment scaling. This procedure (Kiresuk & Sherman, 1979) involves four basic steps and ends with a written product mutually agreeable to the therapist and the family.

1. **State the goal in measurable terms.** Goals should be stated clearly and should be decided on mutually by the therapist and family. It is important to select goals that can be changed.
2. **Assign a weight to each goal.** Some goals are more important than others and should be weighted to show their comparative value. These weights are relative and may be ranked on a scale of 1 to 3, where 1 is the least important and 3 is the most important. It should be noted that it is the relative rather than the absolute weight that is imperative (some goals may be assigned the same weight).
3. **Determine the expected level of attainment.** The central questions that must be asked are:

   What is the current amount or duration of behavior?
   What is a reasonable or expected level of goal attainment?

To answer these questions, the members of the family must have some knowledge of their current level of behavior (baseline). This information should be entered in the column "Expected level of attainment."

4. **Determine other levels of attainment.** Once the expected level of attainment has been determined, the next step is to determine levels that are "more than expected" and "most favorable outcome." Likewise, the therapist and family must specify a "less than expected" and "most unfavorable outcome." In some cases, the appropriate levels might be only 1 or 2, as in the case of alcohol consumption, violence, or curfew. These levels should be entered in the lefthand column.

Table 9.1 is an adaptation of goal attainment scaling, which is titled "Goal Attainment Review." This shows a completed goal attainment review for a family. Note that the goals are stated in performance terms and specify the criteria for success. Consequently, measurement is relatively simple, and evaluation of goal attainment is straightforward.

Goal attainment reviews have several limitations: (1) Families often have difficulty in knowing what to expect from therapy; stating goals in objective terms or measurable terms may be very difficult. (2) Family members often have difficulty presenting problems and specifying what is an "expected" or an acceptable level of attainment; moreover, they may have even more difficulties specifying "less than expected" levels of attainment. (3) The therapist and family may have difficulty completing a goal attainment review during the initial intake session. Adequate time must be allotted to complete a goal attainment review. As we mentioned in Chapters 6 and 7, sometimes the initial treatment plan outlines an assessment process that leads to an outline of concrete goals. Thus, the clinician must be prepared to engage in goal attainment scaling after proper assessment but before intervention is fully underway.

Focusing on Self-Reports

Self-reports are simply what family members say about their condition in the interview; that is, improvement is determined by what family members report to the therapist. This approach assumes that if the family is improving, family members will report the improvement ("Everyone seems to be getting along better"). Likewise, little improvement is characterized by statements such as "Things are about the same" or "I can't see any change." Self-reports are the easiest way for the therapist to evaluate changes in the family.

Here are some considerations:

1. **Develop some specific questions to evaluate the family's progress.** Questions such as "How are things different than they were before?" or "How did things used to be, and how they are now?" help determine the effectiveness of therapy.

2. **Ask family members to scale their improvement.** The therapist can ask the family members to describe their ability to handle the problem on a scale from 1, "not able to handle the problem," to 10, "able to handle the problem." These questions can be asked prior to, during, and following treatment.

3. **Ask family members how satisfied they are with therapy.** The therapist might ask, "Was therapy helpful? How so? What was most helpful to you?"

4. **Ask family members to describe what still needs to change.** When asking them to identify anything that still needs to be done, the therapist may need to remind them of some issues that were raised but not worked on during sessions.

TABLE 9.1	Case Name <u>Mary Goddard</u> Case Number <u>MA-03285</u>		Date <u>3/28/93</u> Phone Number <u>477-8240</u>	
	Goal Attainment Review* **(Client Constructed Outcome Goals)**			
	Contract Goal 1	**Contract Goal 2**	**Contract Goal 3**	**Contract Goal 4**
Weight of Goal (1–3) Expected Level of Attainment (1–2)	Weight = 3 Attainment = 1	Weight = 3 Attainment = 2	Weight = 2 Attainment = 2	Weight = Attainment =
G U I D E **T O** **G O A L S** — MUCH LESS THAN EXPECTED RESULTS = 0	Robbie will not complete his homework every night.	Robbie will complete his assigned work at school 2 or fewer days per week.	Robbie will argue with his mother more than 1 time per day.	
EXPECTED OR MOST LIKELY RESULTS = 1	Robbie will complete his homework every night.	Robbie will complete his assigned work in school 3 out of every 5 days.	Robbie will argue with his mother no more than 1 time per day.	
MUCH MORE THAN EXPECTED RESULTS = 2		Robbie will complete his assigned work in school 4–5 per week.	Robbie will argue with his mother fewer than 1 time per day.	
P R O G R E S S — 3-MONTH REVIEW Treatment ____ Terminated <u>x</u> Discontinued ____	Case terminated 6/16/93 Progress ____ Follow-up <u>1</u> Date <u>6/22/93</u>	Progress ____ Follow-up <u>1</u> Date <u>6/22/93</u>	Progress ____ Follow-up <u>2</u> Date <u>6/22/93</u>	Progress ____ Follow-up ____ Date ____

| TABLE 9.1 | Case Name <u>Mary Goddard</u> | Date <u>3/28/93</u> |
| | Case Number <u>MA-03285</u> | Phone Number <u>477-8240</u> |

Goal Attainment Review*
(Client Constructed Outcome Goals)

	Contract Goal 1	Contract Goal 2	Contract Goal 3	Contract Goal 4
Weight of Goal (1–3) Expected Level of Attainment (1–2)	Weight = 3 Attainment = 1	Weight = 3 Attainment = 2	Weight = 2 Attainment = 2	Weight = Attainment =

F O L L O W - U P

6-MONTH REVIEW Treatment _____ Terminated _____ Discontinued _____	Progress _____ Follow-up _____ Date _____	Progress _____ Follow-up _____ Date _____	Progress _____ Follow-up _____ Date _____	Progress _____ Follow-up _____ Date _____
9-MONTH REVIEW Treatment _____ Terminated _____ Discontinued _____	Progress _____ Follow-up _____ Date _____	Progress _____ Follow-up _____ Date _____	Progress _____ Follow-up _____ Date _____	Progress _____ Follow-up _____ Date _____
12-MONTH REVIEW Treatment _____ Terminated _____ Discontinued _____	Progress _____ Follow-up _____ Date _____	Progress _____ Follow-up _____ Date _____	Progress _____ Follow-up _____ Date _____	Progress _____ Follow-up _____ Date _____
15-MONTH REVIEW Treatment _____ Terminated _____ Discontinued _____	Progress _____ Follow-up _____ Date _____	Progress _____ Follow-up _____ Date _____	Progress _____ Follow-up _____ Date _____	Progress _____ Follow-up _____ Date _____

*The Goal Attainment Review is a derivative of the GAS.

Although self-reports are a common type of outcome evaluation, family therapists should be aware of their limitations. First, self-reports are open to bias because family members may report what they believe will please the therapist. Thus, self-reports are quite subjective and may not accurately represent the family's progress in treatment. Second, family members may be able to report how they feel today but may not be able to reliably describe their behavior between sessions. Day-to-day behavioral changes are often difficult to recall without some written record. Finally, self-reports are nonstandardized and are often determined by therapeutic leads (nonverbal cues) that seek to elicit a certain description of behavior change. Different leads at different points in therapy may result in different descriptions of progress.

ASSESSMENTS FOR TERMINATION AND FOLLOW-UP

Two criteria should be used in determining whether to continue therapy. First, family goals should be met. In some cases, the family or others (teachers, social workers, friends, or relatives) may feel the problem no longer exists. However, if family data fail to support this, therapy should continue until family goals have been met. Second, the goal may have been met, but the family or others in the environment may not be satisfied with the change produced, in which case a new goal should be established. Sometimes, the family may wish to pursue another related goal. When goals have been reached and no new goals have been set, the therapist and family can focus on the maintenance of behavior change.

In some cases, families terminate by not returning. This may occur for several reasons. Family members may feel that therapy is not working, or they may become upset with the therapist. Occasionally, members of the family may be unwilling to change some of their behavior. Unless the therapist works through these concerns early in therapy, termination may occur.

There are several guidelines the therapist should follow when terminating with the family:

1. **Plan for termination in advance.** The therapist should be careful not to withdraw therapy abruptly because in such cases the problem behavior generally returns to the pretreatment level. Families should be given an approximate estimate for the length of therapy. The use of a contract specifying a fixed number of sessions ensures a periodic review of therapy (Barker, 1981). Setting a specific time for termination helps the family and therapist plan for change. The therapist should be flexible about the frequency of sessions, which depends on the nature of the problem. The frequency of sessions should decrease when initial goals have been met (Wright & Leahey, 1984).
2. **Plan to gradually withdraw therapy.** If families have been heavily dependent on therapy (as sometimes happens in cases of severe crisis),

they are less likely to resist termination if therapy is withdrawn gradually. One method of gradual withdrawal is to increase the amount of time between sessions (perhaps to between 3 and 5 weeks). This step should be taken if families are unsure they can maintain the desired changes. Todd (1986) discusses this withdrawal process as follows:

> As therapy begins to be successful in achieving the agreed-upon goals, the sessions are usually spaced at wider time intervals, such as moving to alternate weeks and progressing to once a month. This allows the spouses to do more of the work themselves and helps ensure that they can maintain the changes without the therapist. (p. 81)

Wright and Leahey (1984) suggest that families are more likely to believe they have the resources to deal with this problem when the therapist gives them credit for change. If families believe they were responsible for alleviating the presenting problem, they are likely to be more confident they can handle future problems. Statements such as "You handled this; you'll be able to handle a similar problem if it comes up" help the family believe in its abilities outside of therapy.

3. **Summarize the major themes.** In terminating, the therapist should summarize the major themes of therapy (e.g., growing up) and observe closely to see whether the family agrees or disagrees with the summary statement. If the family disagrees, the therapist should note this and give family members the opportunity to discuss their views. On some occasions, the therapist may ask the family to summarize the therapy.

4. **Ask members of the family to decide what needs to happen for them to return to therapy.** It is important for the therapist to help the family members decide when they no longer can manage the problem and need to return to therapy. The therapist might say, "What would be the first sign that you no longer can handle this problem?" Tomm and Wright (1979) ask, "What would each of you have to do to bring the problem back?" (p. 248) Such questions should help family members understand the specific changes they have made in therapy. The therapist should help the family understand that returning to therapy does not mean the family has failed. Instead, a follow-up session can be framed as a booster shot to help the family maintain desired changes. Then, if further services are sought, the therapist can reiterate that this is not an indicator of failure; instead, additional therapy sessions are likely to be brief because the family has demonstrated an ability to solve its problems (Todd, 1986).

5. **Reassure family members that they have the strengths and resources to deal with future problems.** In some cases, a family presents a new problem at the time of termination. If the problem is not serious, the therapist must reassure family members that they have the skills to deal with this problem on their own without therapeutic intervention. If therapists have difficulty letting go of the family (e.g.,

the therapist may get special nurturance and support from the family or may need the family to work out some unresolved issue), they should discuss such matters in supervision to minimize client dependence as well as their own.

Conducting Follow-Up Evaluations

Once termination has been discussed, follow-up allows the therapist to find out how the family is progressing and to discuss new problems if any have developed. Follow-up can be short term (2 to 4 weeks) or long term (3 to 6 months) after termination of treatment. When setting a date for follow-up, the therapist should assess the amount of time the family will need to maintain goal behaviors without therapeutic intervention.

There are several reasons for follow-up contact with the family. First, many families, particularly those who require intensive services, need a booster shot following termination. For example, family preservation programs that offer intensive in-home family crisis intervention often provide weekly or biweekly follow-up visits in the home. The purpose of these visits is to support desired behavior changes or to troubleshoot any problems that the family may have in implementing the program (Kinney, Haopala, & Booth, 1991). Second, follow-up helps assess the effectiveness of the intervention program, particularly the long-term effects of therapy. Third, planned follow-up encourages the family to monitor its own change program and thus benefit from contact with the therapist.

There are several ways the therapist can conduct follow-up:

1. **Conduct a follow-up interview in the home or office.** Follow-up interviews provide an opportunity for the family to discuss what is working and what still needs to change. Interviews are useful for reinforcing desired changes and problem solving if necessary.
2. **Make a telephone call.** Telephone calls can be useful in assessing the effectiveness of the intervention, and they also provide a cost-effective way of determining whether a follow-up interview is warranted.
3. **Mail a questionnaire to the family.** This is another way to assess the effectiveness of the program. Unfortunately, families may only report what they think will please the therapist; this method may lack objectivity.

MEASURING FAMILY PROCESS

In addition to evaluating the content and process of therapy, family therapists may be called upon to provide evaluations that relate specifically to client variables occurring in a variety of situations. Traditionally, therapists have adopted the role of expert and evaluated their clients. This may happen during the initial assessment phase in treatment and is sometimes formally accomplished by administering objective instruments. In addition, third parties, such as schools and social services, may desire some type of evaluation related to client behavior if they initiate referral. Because of this, even if family therapists hope to maintain a focus on the family's strengths, it is virtually impossible to escape situations where the goals of the client or others dictate that therapists provide an evaluation in their role as expert.

Family process measures are often designed as paper-and-pencil questionnaires that provide family therapists with a family member's self-report of his or her own behaviors or perceptions. Of the various instruments commonly in use, we discuss the Family Adaptability and Cohesion Evaluation Scale (FACES), the Locke-Wallace Marital Status Inventory (L-W), the Dyadic Adjustment Scale (DAS), the Marital Precounseling Inventory (MPI), and the Divorce Adjustment Inventories (DAI).

The Family Adaptability and Cohesion Evaluation Scale, third edition (FACES III), is based on the Olson circumplex model (Olson, Porter, & Ravee, 1985). This inventory measures family members' perceptions of family process and provides a score on the two dimensions of adaptability and cohesion. Adaptability refers to flexibility of roles, rules, and relationships during times of stress. Cohesion refers to the sense of emotional bonding experienced by family members. FACES III is the most recent version of the inventory and is widely used to discriminate between control groups and families with varying degrees of dysfunction. Family therapists often use FACES III for research and in obtaining a baseline of family functioning prior to treatment.

The Locke-Wallace Marital Status Inventory (Locke & Wallace, 1959) contains a set of true–false items that are used to assess steps toward dissolution of the marriage. According to Weiss and Perry (1979), the test was designed to provide an intensity scale (for example, Guttman scale) such that any given step would necessarily include all preceding steps. Thus, before one sought legal aid for a divorce, it would be reasonable to assume that one had thoughts about divorce and engaged in behaviors preparatory to that of seeking legal advice (p. 17). Because this inventory describes intensity, it is possible for the clinician to use the information in deciding whether crisis intervention is needed or whether a less dramatic treatment plan is warranted.

Spanier (1976) included many items from the Locke-Wallace inventory in his assessment scale. Weiss and Perry (1979) altered the items omitted by Spanier so that both measures are incorporated into one questionnaire called the Dyadic Adjustment Scale. The DAS is somewhat more modern in its wording than the Locke-Wallace inventory and provides four factor scales: Dyadic Consensus (e.g., problem solving), Dyadic Satisfaction (e.g., "good feelings" and "sentiment" in the relationship), Dyadic Cohesion (e.g., outside interests, exchange of ideas, cooperation), and Affectional Expression (e.g., sexual and emotional expression). The DAS is an easy instrument to score and may be very useful to the behavioral family therapist because it conceptualizes the marital relationship as a set of specific behaviors that may be targeted for increase or decrease.

The Marital Precounseling Inventory (Stuart & Stuart, 1972) is administered prior to treatment to aid treatment planning. The inventory is 11 pages long and provides assessment information in the following areas: daily activities of both spouses, general goals and resources for change, spouse satisfaction and targets for change in 12 areas of marital and family functioning, rationales for decision making, and level of commitment to the marriage (Stuart, 1976). The MPI serves several purposes. It provides the therapist with data for planning a treatment program, and it also helps orient the couple to treatment. Each spouse can often anticipate issues that will be discussed. At the end of treatment, the inventory can be completed to evaluate therapy.

The Divorce Adjustment Inventories (Brown, Eichenberger, Portes, & Christensen, 1991) provide both child and parent ratings of divorce adjustment. The DAI for parents consists of 31 Likert scale items that offer a numerical range of responses related to family functioning, children's coping skills, and social support systems before and after divorce. The DAI for children consists of 25 Likert scale items that assess the child's adjustment to divorce. Clinicians are able to help parents facilitate the adjustment of their children through the use and discussion of results.

These instruments serve a variety of assessment functions. First, they provide objective measures of overt and covert behavior important to the satisfaction of the relationship. Second, instruments often reveal information that family members might be reluctant to provide in an interview; for example, a spouse may find it embarrassing to discuss sexual issues in the interview. The therapist can often use this information to help family members focus on critical issues that might otherwise be avoided. Finally, instruments often provide an ongoing measure of subjective satisfaction that cannot be obtained through direct observation.

When using self-report scales and inventories, there are several considerations:

1. **Select instruments that measure specific areas of family functioning.** This is of critical importance. For example, the DAI (Brown et al., 1991) contains subscales that measure parental interaction and parent–child interaction, both critical variables in divorce adjustment.

2. **Select instruments that have been validated on similar populations.** If the instrument of choice is normed on a population similar (in terms of socioeconomic status, race, ethnic group, etc.) to the client family, the scores can be compared with those of the norm group. If norms are not available for the client family's group, interpretations are likely to be unfair and negatively biased.

3. **Use the scales or checklists in conjunction with other evaluation data.** By using scales and inventories to corroborate other evaluation data—observations, goal attainment scales, and self-reports—the therapist can be more confident that change has actually occurred.

The biggest limitation in using scales or inventories is that they are global and often fail to pinpoint specific concerns of the family; that is, marital adjustment or satisfaction scales may provide an index of marital quality but may not be an adequate measure of the problem the family brings to therapy. Furthermore, scales and inventories may not be appropriate for minority families (if the appropriate cultural norms are not available), some family members who have little education, or families who are hesitant to disclose certain information before developing a comfortable relationship with the therapist. If a family has already suffered some degree of prejudice from a comparison with cultural norms, such instruments should be used with caution and with a neutral explanation of how results will be interpreted. For example, inventories that primarily describe internal family process can provide families with descriptive information about their relationships rather than a diagnostic score that indicates health or dysfunction.

EVALUATIONS IN TRAINING

Finally, evaluations may also extend to those that focus upon the skill development of the therapist. Formal evaluations of therapists are often model-specific; that is, they evaluate the trainee's mastery of the therapeutic process specified by a certain school of family therapy. For example, those learning structural family therapy might be evaluated according to their ability to mark boundaries or to set up enactments in a session. Those learning intergenerational family therapy might be evaluated according to how well they construct genograms and how effectively they facilitate intergenerational dialogue. Other models might emphasize the therapist's use of self or the therapist's ability to design specific directives and tasks.

Piercy, Laird, and Mohammed (1983) have developed a therapist rating scale that integrates several models of family therapy into a supervisory rating of the student or trainee. In this rating scale, each major school is represented as a cluster of behaviors that each family therapist can be challenged to master as part of his or her education and training. The rating scale provides a guide for the supervisor and therapist in setting training goals. Nelson and Johnson (1999) developed the Basic Skills Evaluation Device (BSED). This provides an integrative set of categories with specific dimensions. Both of these instruments are included in Appendix D for the use of therapists and their supervisors.

In addition to these formal methods of evaluating trainees, it is important for family therapists to monitor their own progress and development in personal ways. Clinicians can do this by being responsible for their own well-being as professionals and by becoming aware of times when their physical or mental health may have a negative impact on their ability to provide effective service. While this type of evaluation is often underemphasized as part of formal training, it can help practitioners focus on personal factors that make them vulnerable to job stress and burnout. In addition, when family therapists evaluate their own patterns of fatigue and stagnation, their own creativity and growth can be maximized.

SUMMARY

Evaluation is an important part of the treatment process, but it is often omitted by beginning family therapists. However, the process of therapy is sometimes stalemated without a mechanism to provide ongoing feedback and reflection about families and their therapy. While objective assessment instruments often provide quantitative information about family variables and therapy outcomes, informal feedback loops can provide qualitative information about the effectiveness of the therapeutic relationship and the fit between family, intervention, and clinician.

In the course of family therapy, evaluations and research can take place in many different ways. Evaluations of family process may occur during initial assessments if therapists employ formal measures such as objective questionnaires or research instruments. These forms of evaluation are used in planning treatment and in developing an understanding of family members' experience. Later in the process, research may take the form of documenting treatment outcomes that provide the impetus for a new treatment plan or termination supervision can make use of instruments that are suitable for research. If these forms are placed in an order corresponding to therapeutic process, the beginning practitioner could conceptualize the various forms of evaluation as follows:

1. Objective evaluations can be administered during the assessment stage of therapy to aid in understanding family process and in formulating treatment plans.
2. Ongoing microevaluations can take place session by session as a conversational feedback loop that informs the clinician how family members are reacting to the therapeutic process.
3. Outcome evaluations can gather qualitative (verbal) or quantitative (behavioral or numerical) information that helps the family therapist document the completion of goals or the need to revise treatment goals or plans.

4. Evaluations in training and research can document therapist skill levels
    and general therapeutic patterns.

When evaluation is integrated into the practice of family therapy, beginning practitioners become flexible and responsive to the individual needs of
families and family members. In addition, treatment planning becomes more
systematic and effective. Family therapists develop a shared reality with their
clients rather than a reality created in isolation from those who are expected to
receive the benefits. Although considered here as a skill to be learned by the
beginner, evaluation is also a threshold into intermediate and advanced practice. Learning from experience and refining skills on the basis of feedback are
fundamental to advanced practice. These same strategies are also important in
developing interdisciplinary collaborations. In our final chapter, we will review
the future of our field as we find many important ways in which family therapists can provide valuable services through teamwork with others.

Family Therapy Collaborations[*]

Marriage and family therapists practice in many different settings. Once the basic elements from Chapters 1 through 9 are understood and practiced, they can be applied to a host of problems as the foundation of many problem-solving strategies. Although the field began as the study of family relationships and the practice of relational change, an understanding of cybernetics, communication, human development, and intimate relationships can be applied to problems in organizations, medicine, and education. In this chapter, we provide an introduction to the practice of family therapy with professionals in different settings. We have had successful experiences working in schools and working in primary health care and collaborating with art therapists in both these settings. We will use these examples of collaboration to illustrate successful principles of collaboration.

COLLABORATION WITH SCHOOLS

Historically, family therapists have been keenly interested in promoting healthy family systems that will meet the needs of our children. As mental health services become needed by more and more children, settings for mental health practice are growing to include educational systems. Mental health work with children is

---

[*]By Suzanne Hanna, Claudia A. Ronaldson, and Joseph H. Brown.

taking family therapists out of the office and into the school. In addition to the needs of children, teachers are finding a need for innovative interpersonal strategies to reach students and parents. Family therapists are excellent resources for helping children make the transition from home to school and for helping teachers and parents work together. Boyd-Franklin and Bry (2000) document the need for diversity in family therapy practice based upon cultural, racial, and socioeconomic differences that are found among many mental health consumers. School-based family therapy is a good example of culturally sensitive practice that teaches the family therapist how to honor the different cultures of family and community. This is particularly important when the welfare of children is at stake.

Family therapists often encounter school problems directly, when schools recommend to parents that they seek help for themselves or their children. Family therapists may also encounter school problems indirectly, when families seek help for one problem and happen to mention that school issues are a problem for one of their children. In American society, where education is compulsory, school problems can become dominating factors that influence family life in important ways. Thus, it is important for family therapists to address these issues and offer school consultation services as part of treatment. When referrals are made from schools, it is important to explore how the family views the problem. Does the family agree or disagree with the referral process (see Chapter 5)? When families disagree with the school assessment, clinicians can offer to be mediators between schools and families. Therapists can maintain a balance between the two sides by defining their role as one of seeking a *win-win solution*—a solution that includes the desires of both sides in the final plan. Once this is done, asking the family's permission to discuss and understand the school's position will not be seen as taking sides. Many times, families will agree with the school because they have been struggling at home. In these cases, therapists can define their role as that of consultant to both sides, helping them discover ways of working together with shared strategies.

If the family indicates that it would like help with school problems, the therapist should assess relationships at multiple levels to gain a full picture of the problem in context. In addition to family relationships (student and parents, student and siblings), these multiple levels may be between:

1. Student and teacher
2. Student and peers
3. Teacher and parent
4. Parent and administrators

In assessing these relationships, Henggeler et al. (1998) suggest that attention be given to resources and concerns in order to build upon existing strengths in the problem-solving process (i.e., the student is in conflict with peers but likes her teacher). As we suggest in Chapters 5 and 6, these are important opportunities to expand the system and work collaboratively with other professionals.

If the family therapist is recruited by the school or referring agency, it is best to adopt the *role of consultant* and clarify with the school and family that a *problem-solving consultation* need not carry the stigma of mental health treatment (Hanna, 1997). This approach encourages school personnel to reframe the problem in simple terms and reassures the family that the consultant is not rushing to judgment about the severity of the problem.

Involving the Network

It is important to understand that the cultures of schools have evolved from circumstances that often bring great pressure to bear upon teachers because of trends that emphasize test scores and upon administrators because of increasing school violence. Although consultants will often understand that psychosocial influences weigh heavily upon the development of any given problem, they must also understand that educators may not view a problem from the same lens. We think a common problem of beginning therapists is that of trying to persuade or convince other professionals to adopt their position. Instead, as we have emphasized in Chapter 4, a successful working relationship will come from assessing another's worldview, respecting the other's culture, building rapport and trust, instilling hope, emphasizing the professional's strengths, and allowing for disagreements without becoming judgmental. Table 10.1 presents examples of common attitudes adopted by parents and teachers when a problem arises at school.

As Table 10.1 shows, the potential for agreement and disagreement between parent and teacher varies according to the particular situation. The top

TABLE 10.1	COMMON ATTITUDES TAKEN BY PARENTS AND TEACHERS

Parents	Teachers
I don't have a problem with my child at home.	I'm concerned about this child, but I don't need help in the classroom.
I don't want help at home with my child.	I think the problem is best solved at home.
I want help at home with my child.	I'm unsure if I should respond to family issues, the child's feelings, etc.
I have the same problem at home with my child.	I need help in the following area: _____.
I want help at home with issues other than my child.	I want the family to help more.
I want the teacher to have more help with my child at school.	I think the problem is best solved in the classroom.

two rows in the table represent levels in which the greatest conflict may occur. In these cases, it is most important for the consultant to adopt a win-win goal with both sides. Multidirected partiality, as discussed in Chapter 1, is an important skill in showing empathy and understanding for all sides. When therapists can truly place themselves in the position of the other, it is possible to sympathize with both sides and pursue explorations that may include a strength-based and solution-focused approach to solving the problem.

Gary was a 9-year-old Euro-American boy who was having a hard time paying attention in his fourth grade class, and the teacher and parents reached a heated impasse. The consultant joined with both sides and used direct classroom observation to explore ways in which Gary's strengths at home could be incorporated into the culture of the classroom. His father described his amazing ability to remember the smallest details about the solar system. By suggesting that everyone's position was legitimate (multidirected partiality), the therapist redirected each side's blame of the other and moved toward a mode of creative experimentation that was based upon the strengths of Gary, the teacher, and parents. A new plan of communication between home and school was developed, and the parents began providing materials for the teacher to use that brought Gary's strengths into the classroom.

Thus, a starting point is to work with all relevant parties *on their terms*. For example, if consultants want a positive working relationship with teachers, they can review Chapter 4, *with a teacher in mind,* to develop a positive and respectful foundation for problem solving. Many teachers feel rushed and exhausted just trying to keep up with the day-to-day pressures of instruction. Phone consultations and on-site observations (for children ages 3–10) by the therapist are more convenient for many teachers. The following points can help clinicians begin the process:

1. In all cases, make sure there are releases of information signed by family members in order to communicate freely with school personnel.
2. Contact the teacher and ask about the possibility of a consultation, an on-site observation, or both.
3. If an on-site observation occurs, report to the main office and identify yourself. Many schools require that visitors sign in at this point.
4. When feasible, negotiate with the teacher to conduct the observation first and then discuss and consult with the teacher afterward.

Once initial contacts are made, the consultant should review the position of each member of the system in order to decide upon an intervention strategy.

1. Describe the primary/targeted behavior.

   Is the behavior observed today different from that observed other days? If so, how? Better? Worse?

2. In what situations does the behavior occur?

Location	Time	Person	Instructional context
__Class	__Arrival to school	__Teacher	__Entire to group/mealtime
__Hallways	__Morning	__Resource	__Small group
__Cafeteria	__Lunch	__Assistants	__Individual
__Special classes	__Afternoon	__Bus driver	__Experiential learning
__Bus	__Recess/ break	__Other children	__Field trips
__Other_____	__Other_____	__Other_____	__Other_____

3. How intense is the behavior?

   __No problem __Low __Moderate
   __High __Very high __Catastrophic

4. How long does the behavior occur?

   __<2 min __2–6 min __6–12 min __12–20 min __>20 min

5. When the behavior occurs, what happens right <u>before</u> that might be influencing the behavior?

   __Child was involved in activity he or she enjoyed
   __Child was being given direction by an adult
   __Child was alone performing a task
   __Child was in transition from one activity to the next
   __Child was given a lot of praise
   __Child was given more attention by adults
   __Child was interacting with peers
   __Other _____

6. What do people do right <u>after</u> the behavior?

   Child in question _____
   Other children _____
   Teachers _____
   Others _____

10.1   *Continued*

7. What interventions has the teacher tried?
   __Redirect __Verbal reprimand/ __Ultimatum   __Time out
              warning
   __Ignore   __Taking something __Office referral __Other _____
              away
   Comments: _____

8. What was tried to help the child settle down?_____

9. What are the child's strengths? _____

10. What are his or her strongest interests? _____

11. What time of the day is the most positive for the child in the
    classroom? _____

12. How is the child doing academically?   IEP in place?: Y / N

13. How is the child doing with other services?
    A. Other service providers: _____
    B. Teacher's knowledge of any history of services (consultations with
       providers):

14. What are your thoughts about the causes of the child's misbehavior?

15. Do you have any thoughts about the best course of action?

16. Would you be interested in hearing other suggestions about this
    issue in addition to the ones you have offered?

17. What could be changed in the classroom environment that would
    make it easier for the child to have better behavior?

Implementing Intervention Strategies

When referrals involve a request for behavior modification plans at school, we
have found certain worksheets helpful in guiding a classroom observation. Box
10.1 is a guide for gathering information on school-related behavior. We adopt a
behavioral perspective, looking for antecedents and consequences of behavior
(see Chapter 1). Behavioral management plans are common in educational settings, and these can form a common language for consultants, parents, and schools
to use. Box 10.2 outlines a behavioral management plan. Such a plan might evolve
out of consultations with all relevant parties. While it is ideal if all relevant parties

10.2   *Behavior Management Plan*

Name of Child: _____ Age of Child: _____ Today's Date: _____

Child's Interests and Strengths (that can be used in increasing desired behavior or decreasing undesired behavior):

_____

_____

_____

Desired Behavior (behavior that the team would like to see the child develop, both short term and long term):

Short term: _____

_____

_____

Long term: _____

_____

Short term: _____

_____

Long term: _____

Who will do what, when, and where?

Who	What	When and Where
_____	_____	_____
_____	_____	_____
_____	_____	_____
_____	_____	_____

Evaluation:

Date_____ Progress made/changes needed: _____

Date_____ Progress made/changes needed: _____

can meet, it is not necessary if school personnel are under extreme time pressures and positive rapport has been established with the consultant.

The following are two cases in which consultants provided home and school consultations using the guidelines shown in Box 10.1. In this first case, parents and teacher were amenable to meeting together and developing teamwork:

A first grade teacher was concerned about Sara's pattern of lying and stealing from other children. Sara was blonde, blue-eyed, small for her age, and the oldest of three children. The therapist first helped the parents explore family circumstances related to the problem. The parents were able to recognize that the father's travel schedule had left the mother with added burdens at home. When he returned, he would inadvertently indulge his children because he missed them and wanted to enjoy them. The mother was perceived as the "bad guy," and Sara developed beliefs about herself from interactions in which her mother was under pressure and was trying to maintain order at home. The therapist helped the parents to design a series of experiences in which the father took a more active role in disciplining all the children and the mother planned some errands in which Sara could join her and they could "steal" some time together. At the same time, the concerned teacher was invited to develop an understanding with Sara that when she wanted something that wasn't hers, she could talk with her teacher and they would plan a way for her to have something special that was rightfully hers. The teacher allowed her class to check out special books and take them home. This became a way for Sara to have nice things without stealing.

During the teacher consultation, the teacher reported that she overlooked Sara's lies because she was small for her age and very endearing (consequence). In addition, the consultant discovered that Sara was quiet and would often get lost in the crowd, due to size and lack of assertiveness (antecedent). This information helped the therapist to understand Sara in both contexts and to draw some parallels between the two. A multisystems approach such as that practiced by Boyd-Franklin (2000) helped the clinician to develop and test hypotheses about Sara's emotional development and about the way each side could foster her growth. This is a good example of how many teachers and parents go the extra mile to benefit the children in their care.

In the next case, tensions were extreme between parent and teacher. However, the consultant was able to enlist the help of additional school personnel to bring about a new agreement between the school and family.

Jeff was an African American boy in third grade when he set a fire that destroyed his family's apartment. This was the third fire in 2 years that led to another relocation for his family. He lived with his grandmother for a year before the fires started. During his transition back to his mother's care, conflict developed between his grandmother and mother. His grandmother wanted him returned to her custody. She had friends who worked at his school, and they supported her position. As a result, Jeff's mother felt outnumbered and powerless when interacting at his school. The teacher's reports about Jeff were inconsistent with other teachers' observations and with information from the consultant's classroom observations. The consultant found Jeff to be competent and capable in completing class assignments. She also observed that he would often finish ahead of the other children and begin looking around the room for something else to do. However, the teacher insisted that a report should be filed to child social services indicating that Jeff was a danger to himself and others. An investigation ensued that united the grandmother and mother. During this process, the role of the consultant was initially to foster trust with the mother, who believed everyone was against her. As that alliance developed, the investigation ironically became an opportunity for the consultant to enlist the grandmother's support of her family. The mother and grandmother began to reconcile during consultations with the consultant, and all three developed a plan for helping Jeff change schools. The consultant discovered that student services personnel were willing to be advocates for change within the system. They provided a counterpoint with the family that led to a satisfactory change in which Jeff was transferred into a small classroom with one of the few male teachers in the district. This proved beneficial for Jeff, and his family continued to call upon the consultant for help with non-school issues. At this point, the clinician negotiated with the family to provide "family therapy."

One of the keys to success in this case was the therapist's ability to expand the system to include helpful school personnel who were outside the immediate conflict. As the issues of crisis waned and Jeff's family began to settle their differences to help him, the therapist enlisted the family in new ways of helping Jeff with any problematic behaviors that remained. The grandmother was affirmed for her importance in his life. The mother was complimented for her courage in advocating for her son. The therapist helped them form a team by suggesting parenting strategies that they could learn together. Box 10.3 contains principles of child behavior change that were used with the family to promote prosocial behavior from a strengths' perspective. These are adapted from Adlerian parent education materials (Dinkmeyer, McKay et al., 1997).

Such collaborations with schools, families, and family therapists are a growing innovation in the profession. Family therapists bring the strength of their interactional perspective with the wisdom of relational interventions to address conflicts and problems that drain energy from homes and schools. One of the ways therapists gain trust and credibility in these situations is by proving *how their services can make everyone's job easier and more successful.* Thus, a win-win situation is brought about by addressing the needs of

10.3   *Steps to Individual Behavior Management*

1.   **Determine the purpose of the target behavior.**
     Keep a journal for several days.
     What happens right before the behavior occurs? With whom? What happens after? With whom?
     What is the result of the behavior? Attention? Control? Revenge? Dependency?
     How might the aftermath be a reinforcement?

2.   **Divert the child from the problem situations by increasing positive reinforcement in other areas.**
     What are the child's strong points? Where lies potential? Begin a systematic campaign to convince the child of his or her strengths.
     When the child comes close to doing something right, call attention to the child as if he or she had already done it ("Good job, Jerry, you almost kept your hands to yourself. I can see that you were trying. I bet next time you'll be able to keep your hands quiet.").
     For competitive children, "dare" them to do what is right ("I bet you can't walk all the way to the cafeteria! Let me see if you can!").

3.   **Remove reinforcements from the old behavior.**
     Use nonverbal communication as much as possible.
     For attention seekers, use a pat on the shoulder or nonverbal signals.
     Avoid power struggles. Walk away from tantrums. Explain to other children that Maria is upset, but she will learn how to calm herself down. Reassure Maria that she can learn to calm herself.
     Acknowledge that aggression can be an expression of hurt feelings. Ask if something made the child feel bad. Show empathy. Brainstorm new ways to handle the child's hurt feelings in the future.
     Encourage children who display helplessness. Allow them to have natural consequences.

each member in the system (teacher, parent, child, etc.) and by finding a way for the tension between competing needs to lead into creative problem solving that is developmentally appropriate for everyone. This approach is equally effective when family therapists bring their skills to medical settings and health problems.

COLLABORATION WITH HEALTH CARE PROFESSIONALS

As health care continues to change, the need for lower costs, better patient care, and improved health outcomes continues to grow. Family therapists have been active in developing methods of consultation that are directed at these goals. In this role, they promote a coordinated partnership between (1) psychosocial providers and biomedical providers and (2) provider systems and family systems. Rolland (1994) suggests that the family can be an important part of the health care team. Often family therapists facilitate the involvement of family members in the treatment and recovery of medical patients for better health outcomes. McDaniel, Hepworth, and Doherty (1992) suggest that there is a unique and important role for family therapists in medical settings because of the:

> attention to medical illness and its role in the personal life of the patient and the interpersonal life of the family. . . family therapists are trained to work with difficult cases in an intense and sometimes prolonged manner. . . In the current healthcare system . . . the family, if it is involved at all, is likely to be viewed as an adjunctive aid in treating the patient, not as a group of people who need help in their own right. (pp. 4–5)

As research continues to improve our understanding of the human body as a collection of interrelated systems that operates socially *in* a collection of interrelated systems, the impact of health and illness upon individuals and their relational networks is of increasing relevance. For example, providing services that address these linkages is an important role for the family therapist working in health care settings.

Medical Family Therapy: Is This the Best Term?

Although McDaniel, Hepworth, and Doherty (1992) used the term *medical family therapy,* with the passage of time, we have found the term to be problematic when interacting with patients, families, and health care professionals. This is because the referral process and the precipitating circumstances are often related to illness or stress, and families do not think of themselves as candidates for mental health treatment, even though they may want help in coping or problem solving (Hanna, 1997). Walsh and Rolland (2003) also find the term confusing. They suggest that *medical* implies physician involvement. *Family therapy* implies either relational or mental health *treatment.* None of these may be part of the process. For these and the reasons mentioned in working with schools and families, we prefer that the activity be labeled as a *problem-solving consultation* until there is some indication that family and clinician are entering into a "traditional" client–therapist relationship. Walsh and Rolland (2003) also use the term *psychoeducational family consultation.* This term is useful in emphasizing how important education is to the empowerment of families in health care settings.

Thus, problem-solving consultations can be helpful in a variety of ways, and the well-being of the family can be preserved or restored, depending upon the level of need. Some of these needs may be those of the family, whereas others may be those of the physician or other health care professional. For example, doctors are often concerned about how well a patient can follow medical directives. With diabetes as an example, the demands to manage insulin levels at home can be difficult for some patients. Age of patients, pharmaceutical costs, quality of life, and severity of the disease can be factors in what doctors call *compliance,* or following the doctor's orders. Social isolation or family conflict over some part of the medical directives (as with adolescents with diabetes) can become added problems if not addressed. Using the same win-win approach that is successful in schools, the consultant can assess important relationships related to the problem of compliance and look for practical solutions that include a recognition of each person's needs.

From an educational perspective, the consultant's role can also complement that of the health educator. Often, nurses assume the role of health educator, that of providing information to families about an illness and its management. A psychoeducational family consultant can provide time to the family members to help them problem-solve how they may adapt and cope with life changes that are brought about from a medical condition. These changes may range from traumatic (i.e., spinal cord injury and paralysis) to inconvenient (i.e., broken leg that will take a few months to heal). They may also range in prognosis from good to poor or even fatal (i.e., metastasized cancer).

McCubbin (1980) found that families can cope best with the challenges of illness when they have information about *why an event happened, how it happened,* and *what they can do to cope* successfully. This is the role of the psychoeducational consultant. Using their knowledge of family structure and family development (Chapter 3), consultants can provide a road map for families in the face of unknown territory. If we return to our metaphor of driving a car, becoming a helpful consultant to a family is like being a tour guide who helps a group of people to find their way when life brings them to a foreign land. It is helpful if the consultant does some of the driving while the visitors become oriented to the new situation. This might be done by providing information about common challenges that illnesses can pose to family relationships and personal well-being. Engaging these visitors in discussions about how they might prevent their own health breakdown while coping with that of a family member can be useful. Another part of being a helpful consultant should involve providing these directions as options and exploring which directions would be most relevant for them at a given time.

LaVoie (1985) offers seven important points to keep in mind when providing help to families facing illness or loss:

1. The family life cycle, age and sex are more sensitive indicators of abnormal conditions than age and sex alone (Medalie, 1979). That is, the practitioner must be sensitive to the life cycle phase of the individual and family.

2. Family treatment of individual health breakdown should be considered. Family medical practitioners are moving in the direction of treating the family as a unit. Family therapists can consult with physicians regarding the family dynamics that led to the breakdown.
3. The chronic crisis-ridden family must be identified early so that intervention procedures can be initiated before major problems appear (Rainsford & Schulman, 1981).
4. Where possible, family coping strategies should be assessed; if found to be deficient, coping techniques should be introduced and practiced.
5. Families should be made more aware of their stage in the life cycle and of future events.
6. The social network of the family should be examined, since support systems are important buffers in coping with stress.
7. Since stress appears to have a negative impact on the immune system, individuals and families must learn to recognize stress build-up and to initiate stress reduction strategies as necessary. (pp. 65–66)

We have found this emphasis upon the family's stage of life to be especially important since it often provides an explanation for conflict that normalizes or removes blame from family members. Especially during times of normal transition when illness may complicate the family's normal adaptation process, explaining how life stage affects family interactions can provide the family with a road map that includes coping with the illness and fostering the healthy development of its members.

These suggestions form the basis of our approach to consultations for health issues. The spectrum of this work will range from prevention for the patient and family members to actual treatment in cases where research shows that interpersonal interventions can impact the recovery and management of an illness. For example, if a family member is diagnosed with Alzheimer's disease, the consultant may meet to help members of the family consider their own unique type of loss (Boss, 1999), to help them reorganize family roles when the patient has been central to their organizational scheme, and to help them develop strategies to cope with stress and promote optimal functioning of the family (Long, 1997). We think psychoeducational interventions bring together elements of mind, body, spirit, and relationships that are needed to bring about the best possible health outcomes.

Mind, Body, Spirit, and Relationships: A Framework for Health Care Interventions

Medical problems can sometimes bring shocking and life-changing circumstances into family life. These often prompt family members to reflect upon the spiritual aspects of coping with illness and of those losses associated with death. When we ask families to talk about how they have coped with challenges in the past, they often share unique aspects about their faith and spirituality. These are important resources to mobilize during times of challenging illnesses. Often spiritual resources are intergenerational gifts that are passed down through generations. As we discussed in Chapter 3, exploring intergenerational strengths and legacies can be an important starting point in mobilizing hope and courage for families in pain. Their future may be uncertain, but they may appreciate being reminded of traditions and values that help them to endure adversity.

Denise was a 40-year-old African American woman who had become severely depressed after she discovered that she was HIV positive. She had been the victim of a rape and later learned that her assailant had died of AIDS. She had a history of seizures, and her compromised immune system was discovered during a hospitalization 2 years later. Upon discharge, she was referred to an outpatient clinic to begin management of her HIV. Her depression was understandable, and the nurse suggested that she speak to the family consultant at the clinic.

Often, medical cases are referred in this way. When family therapists work in health care settings, client contact is most often made during routine medical visits. Consultants may speak with patients in the exam room before or after time with the doctor and then follow up with home or office-based work according to the needs of the patient.

The consultant listened sympathetically to Denise's story and explored her current support system. Her closest supports were her niece and a friend who was a nurse. They shared her grief and vowed to stay close to her during this ordeal. Her friend explained what she knew about HIV medications, and her niece was willing to become the guardian for her children if the need arose. The consultant used the genogram and time line we described in Chapter 7 to explore areas of strength and vulnerability with Denise and her family. In this case, the complexity of past history was important to know and understand. Also, the time line extended into the future to note Denise's most important goals.

Chapter 3 outlined aspects of individual experience that are important to track during medical crises. Genograms can be used to note personal resources, family strengths, patterns of illness, and causes of death in the intergenerational family. Time lines are particularly important when tracking the sequence and timing of multiple stressors that may have besieged a family in a short period of time. This is called *pile-up* and is an important factor in explaining how severe the effects of the most recent stressor may be (McCubbin, Dahl & Hunter, 1976). For example, if family members had already exhausted their emotional and spiritual resources due to a serious automobile accident and then a member of the family was diagnosed with cancer 3 months later, this knowledge is critical to develop a true appreciation of a family's stress and corresponding strengths. In addition, important encounters with health care providers can be explored on time lines to understand medical histories as sequential and interactive.

During initial consultations, medical history contained the story that Denise had been seizure-free for the past 2 years after she felt compelled to stop her medication. In her words, the Lord had protected her, and she had accomplished this through the miracle of prayer and faith. She attended her church weekly and in the midst of her current challenge had kept her faith in God. The consultant agreed that she was a "miracle woman" and that this history of miracles and faith could help her address the problems at hand (spirit). Initial consultations focused upon information about the disease since new drugs were helping HIV patients to live longer. She no longer needed to fear an immediate death. Her condition could be considered a chronic illness that needed safe management, rather than a fatal disease from which she would soon die. This education (mind) helped Denise's depression to lift, and she began to see how she could disclose her diagnosis to her four children and reassure them that she would not die immediately (relationships). She resolved to follow the doctor's directives in the management of her disease (body) so she could live to see her youngest son, age 14, graduate from high school. The consultant helped her develop strategies for disclosing her condition to her family, for improving her mental health, and for using her support system as part of her "management" team.

As in this case, strengths and vulnerabilities may encompass mental, physical, spiritual, or relational functioning. Mind, body, and spirit each have a strong impact upon the nature of relationships during times of coping and problem solving. Conversely, the strength of relationships through intimacy, commitment, sacrifice, and nurturing can greatly enhance the functioning of mind, body, and spirit. Schwenk and Hughes (1983) found that the incidence of chronic illness increases in family members of those with chronic illness. Thus, it is important to conduct a careful assessment of family strengths that can be highlighted as protective factors against this increased risk. Chapter 4 provides suggestions for exploring and identifying family strengths.

Often, those with medical problems are older, and they become more retrospective in their focus: They appreciate the opportunity to review their past strengths and accomplishments. Butler (1963) has suggested this as a primary mental health intervention for older clients, and we have found it therapeutic to organize the telling of narratives around a structured time line with the entire family of an older client, to facilitate shared coping and problem solving. Hanna and Hargrave (1997) have suggested that many models of family therapy are present-oriented and should be modified to meet the needs of persons in later life. Thus, constructing a genogram and time line on a large easel in front of the family lends itself to the role of a consultant who is exploring strengths and problem-solving strategies from the past as a starting point for addressing present difficulties. Younger families also appreciate the opportunity for the consultant to learn about them before they were affected by a life-changing illness. In these cases, the time line can be used to map grief and loss issues. By keeping questions focused upon strengths and methods of coping, consultants can control the level of intimacy in the interview. If families want the consultation to include a focus upon historical conflicts, past misunderstandings, and long-standing symptoms, a formal therapeutic relationship can be negotiated. Otherwise, a positive, affirming, pragmatic problem-solving relationship should be maintained by the consultant.

The following case illustrates how the consultant's role must be balanced between that of a therapeutic relationship and that of a psychoeducational consultant.

Harvey was a 65-year-old man with a 20-year history of paranoia and schizophrenia. He was the third generation of Irish immigrants who had come to America and settled in the midwest. He had been steadfast in his refusal of any mental health or physical health service. He was referred by a local social service agency when volunteers with the meals-on-wheels program tried to deliver his meals and became intimidated by his behavior. They refused to return, and intervention was sought through a home-based service program to mediate this conflict. The consultant found Harvey to have many medical complaints, one of which was trouble breathing. However, he was well known in the social service community, and other providers considered his report of symptoms to be part of his mental illness. The consultant negotiated a plan with Harvey to help others understand his needs. In the process, she found a family doctor at the university clinic who was willing to work with Harvey's complex interpersonal patterns in order to provide his medical care. The consultant did not try to treat Harvey's mental health issues. Instead, based upon his most consistent complaints, she worked to gain Harvey's trust, and he considered going with the consultant under certain conditions to the doctor's office. The initial appointment brought Harvey to the waiting room, but he was unable to tolerate sitting long enough to keep the appointment. However, on the second visit, Harvey found that he could tolerate the threat of confinement, and he allowed the doctor to examine him. Some simple, noninvasive procedures revealed a significant oxygen shortage in his blood, and he was immediately provided with ongoing oxygen for his lung disease. With this success, Harvey remained open to the consultations, which eventually led to a reunion with one of his seven children after 10 years of no contact.

In health care consultations, traditional family therapy training is initially used to solve immediate and practical problems. However, when the medical condition has a strong influence upon the family, the trusting relationship that has developed over practical matters often becomes the foundation for careful work related to grief and loss, life-stage transitions, intergenerational conflict, and family reorganization (Chapter 3). *The key to being a successful consultant in medical settings is to go slow and let the family members dictate their goals.* In addition, the relationships developed with health care professionals must be built upon the same principles of understanding we discussed in working with teachers and students in school settings. As consultants, our "clients" are often other professionals who want our help to address difficult problems. They deserve the same careful empathy and trust that we give to clients who seek traditional mental health services. As a further illustration of how family therapists can develop these collaborations, the following section will outline how family therapists and art therapists have joined together in providing innovative mental health services.

COLLABORATION WITH ART THERAPISTS

Along the continuum of behavioral and mental health practice, various allied health disciplines contribute to cutting-edge practice. Research shows that many innovative approaches from family therapy and art therapy are successful with groups who underutilize traditional clinic-based mental health services (Campbell, Liebmann, Brooks, Jones, & Ward, 1990; Henggeler et al., 1998; McGoldrick & Giordano, 1996). For example, family therapists address mental health problems such as mental illness and substance abuse from a pragmatic relational approach (Anderson, Reiss, & Hogarty, 1986; McFarlane, 2002; Stanton & Todd, 1982; Todd & Selekman, 1991b). Art therapists successfully address numerous problems including bereavement, domestic violence, antisocial behavior, and medical trauma (Wadeson, Durkin, & Perach, 1989; Koplewiez & Goodman, 1999).

In this section, we will explore some of the characteristics of another mental health profession and illustrate how family therapists can collaborate to develop innovative services for groups who are uncomfortable with traditional mental health services. Because psychotherapy developed within the White, middle-class, industrialized, world and family therapy has been influenced by this historical context, there are still many people who do not come to office-based counseling with the same goals, values, traditions, or worldviews as those of the therapists themselves. Often, people living in economically impoverished conditions are *sent* to counseling by someone with authority over them or their family (medical, educational, legal, or governmental). These referral sources often adopt goals for the family that are not adopted *by* the family. Thus, it is important to know how to address this unspoken disparity and to know when nonverbal communication should become the preferred mode of conducting therapy. Since art is a universal language found on a neighborhood wall or in a posh, upper-class gallery, it transcends many of the barriers that are constructed from differences in class, race, politics or sexual orientation.

> Art therapy is a human service profession using art, images, the creative process and patient responses to reflect an individual's development, abilities, personality, interests, concerns and conflicts. The practice is based on theories of human development and psychology to treat emotional conflicts, foster self-awareness, develop social skills, manage behavior, solve problems, reduce anxiety, aid reality orientation and increase self-esteem. (American Art Therapy Association, 2000)

As a profession, art therapy has a national association and promotes board certification. In addition, a number of states are becoming aware of the value of art therapy and have adopted certification or licensure regulations. The profession's history has a similar pattern to that of family therapy, in that art therapy sprang from a number of people from the 1940s on who were innovators in a variety of fields such as education, medicine, and psychology (Rubin, 1999). One of these pioneers was a sculptor from Poland, Hanna Yaxa Kwiatkowska, who developed a method of family art therapy and evaluation at the National Institute of Mental Health in 1958 (Kwiatkowska, 1978; 1967). There, she developed a close friendship with family therapy pioneer, Lyman Wynne and his wife Adele (see Chapter 1).

Achieving success in multidisciplinary collaboration depends upon the clinician's ability to value the contributions of other professionals and to look for win-win solutions when professional disagreements occur. Using the case of art therapy and family therapy, we can provide an example of how family therapists discovered the value of other professionals and how they addressed points of potential disagreement. From the definition of art therapy above, it can be seen that art therapy focuses more on individual growth and phenomenology; family therapy focuses more on relational growth and family process. While family art therapy combines both perspectives, many art therapists are trained in traditional individual and group theories of counseling, whereas family therapists are departing more from those traditions and adopting nontraditional lenses that do not focus upon pathology (diagnoses), defense mechanisms (denial, rationalization), or the attribution of certain intentions (avoidance, control, ego).

In spite of these conceptual and language differences, the two professions often share similar goals, especially in school-based settings. Thus, *staying focused on common goals* is useful in developing collaborations. In addition, we discovered a number of *shared values* such as putting an emphasis upon the client's narrative, deconstructing client experience, and creating a safe, accepting, and nurturing environment. The language of these values was also useful in creating a respectful and innovative collaboration. The *welfare of our clients* provided a unifying framework around which each professional could make his or her *unique contribution.* This may happen through in-service meetings in which individual professionals have the opportunity to teach others about the perspectives and interventions from their practice (Robbins, 1994) or through case management meetings in which team members share information and accept assignments related to their area of expertise (Ronaldson & Hanna 2001). These same forms of collaboration also existed in medical activities outlined earlier. If beginning clinicians do not find these activities existing at their practice site, they may suggest these and even volunteer to lead them if need be. We have found that many people are receptive to new ideas that have a mutual benefit to all the stakeholders.

In our collaborative projects for children, it was easy to see how art therapy and family therapy could become a *synergistic* combination, that is, how they could be combined to produce better results than either activity in isolation. We made the distinction between *multidisciplinary* (many professionals sharing a case but working independently) and *interdisciplinary* (many professionals working together and developing a common knowledge base while maintaining separate roles that occasionally overlap). Since synergy is a concept from general systems theory, it is consistent with our conceptual values to adopt this position. We think this notion lies at the center of successful interdisciplinary work. Our synergy involved the process of interprofessional education in which each learned about the other. In preparing family therapists for such collaboration, we outline some basics in art therapy that provide enhancements to their own practice. These include some elementary concepts from the field and foundational art activities that are relevant for family therapists.

Understanding Expressive Communication

Art therapy rests on the premise that all people are inherently creative and that the creative process mirrors the natural world and evokes processes that promote growth and balance. Rubin (1999) suggests that the practice combines "involved doing" and "relaxed reflection" together. Further, the combination of these two elements is more powerful than either alone. Lusebrink (1992) established the *expressive therapies continuum* (ETC), outlining levels of individual experience in dynamic interaction that could be used to guide the practitioner's work. These levels are placed on a continuum of complexity that corresponds with human development: *kinesthetic–sensory, perceptual–affective,* and *cognitive–symbolic.* The author uses the principles of systems theory to explain the relationships between these levels, similar to how a family therapist would use systems theory to explain relationships between family members. Ronaldson and Peacock (2001) have suggested the following principles in conducting successful art therapy:

1. The *process* and *content* of an individual's self-expression is valued over the aesthetic quality of the visual product.
2. The expressive therapies continuum provides a framework for establishing continuity between media, self-expression, and communication with others.
3. Nonverbal expression using visual images related to internal experience provides a catalyst for self-reflection, insight, and verbal response.

In addition to these principles, Box 10.4 lists corresponding outcomes to assess client satisfaction with the process. These outcomes assume that the process also involves joining with the client, explaining the value of the art process in therapy, and engaging the client in meaningful creativity and reflection.

 Desired Outcomes in Art Therapy

Self-expression is valued over aesthetic quality.
1. I felt comfortable with making art.
2. The therapist was very accepting of my artwork.
3. I was able to talk easily about my artwork.
4. The therapist respected my artwork and what I had to say about it.
5. My process of making art was pleasurable and satisfying.
6. I gained new information about myself and my problems from the artwork.

The ETC integrates levels of media, self-expression, and communication.
1. I had an opportunity to explore a variety of art materials.
2. I was able to understand myself and my family better after doing art together.
3. Using a variety of art materials and techniques helped me to look at my problems in different ways.
4. The therapist was knowledgeable about how to use different art materials.

The art process evokes self-reflection, insight, and verbal response.
1. The artwork stimulated my thinking about my problems.
2. The therapist did not interpret my artwork for me.
3. The artwork helped me to see things differently.

Although art therapists are noted for their innovative work with all ages and all types of psychosocial problems, our collaborations began over work with children in school settings. In these projects, we began to see that there is great value in combining family therapy and art therapy. The field of family therapy has often relied too much on "talk therapy," with too little attention paid to involving children in ways that match their attention span and developmental level. We found that art therapy had much to add to the family therapy process.

Developmentally Appropriate Practice

Early childhood educators are already very familiar with the term *developmentally appropriate practice*. This refers to educational practices based upon children's abilities as they develop rapidly during the first years of life. For example, in preschools, there are specific differences in many 3- and 4-year-old children. Their attention span, physical development, and cognitive complexity change significantly from one year to the next. A 3-year-old begins to speak in short sentences and may ask "What?" or "Why?" A 4-year-old learns to take turns and begins to understand the concept of time. With the exception of Michael White's playful interventions with children, current models of family therapy fail to consider how a family therapy session can privilege children's voices in a developmentally appropriate way. Most often, children are asked adult questions and are expected to give well-formed verbal answers. However, Koppitz (1968) suggests that children can express their experience through images long before they can verbalize them. One way to overcome this shortcoming is through family art therapy.

In a pioneering program that embraced both family therapy and art therapy, Robbins (1994) found that families and schools became better collaborators through a program called Family Builders in which family therapists and art therapists collaborated to provide school-based services. In another project, Ronaldson and Hanna (2001) reported that reluctant parents often became more engaged in problem solving about their preschool child when the child's art was shown and discussed. These projects used the concept of developmentally appropriate practice to unify professionals around the needs of children and to respect the wishes of parents to provide help to their child. The following suggestions present beginning therapists with an example of how a creative process from art therapy can give children and their families a concrete experience that provides a framework for communication and problem solving.

Accessing Relationships Through the Creative Process

A common art intervention is known as the kinetic family drawing, or KFD (Burns Kaufman, 1970). This intervention can be used when children are seen in individual sessions with art therapists or when family therapists have sessions that include children. Box 10.5 provides directions for conducting a family session using the KFD. As an introductory activity in which all members can participate, we find that when parents are anxious for treatment to be directed toward the identified child, this activity reassures them that treatment will focus upon those needs. Since family life is often filled with child-centered activities, stories, and goals, the KFD can help a family therapy session to mirror the natural environment and set the family at ease. Here are some suggestions for incorporating the KFD into a session.

1. Explain to the parents that children can often gain new skills and insights through art activities. To help their children, the clinician would like family members to do an activity together, and then they will discuss how this activity can contribute to some problem-solving strategies.
2. If adults are reluctant to participate with their children, offer analogies such as coaches in sports using diagrams to discuss their team's strategies,

---

10.5 *Instructions for Kinetic Family Drawing*

1. Provide the directive: "I'd like you each to draw a picture of your family *doing something together.*"
2. Limit your observations to permissive phrases such as "You can make your drawing any way you want," "Whatever you decide to draw will be just fine," "No one will be judging your work," or "Take your time."
3. Wait until all family members are finished before beginning a discussion. At that time, ask: "Who would like to start telling about their picture?"
4. "Tell me about the picture. Who is each person and how old is each one?"
5. "What is the family doing (it may be a past event, distant memory, or daily activity)?" "What is the best part of the activity for you?" "Do you have any other favorite memories about the activity?"
6. "What do other family members remember about this activity?"
7. Rotate descriptions and reflections until all the members have described and discussed their drawing.

or fashion designers sketching their future plans. In some cases, the therapist may need to give some examples of events, memories, or daily routines.

3. Encourage all the participants to draw their own picture independently and reassure them that the nonverbal *process* of communication is more important than the *appearance* of their drawing. For example, the game Pictionary is an example of how families can use drawings for fun and recreation.

4. Limit the media to blank paper and pencils or crayons for young children in order to simplify the process and to emphasize that the activity is more about creating a positive experience together. Usually, pencils are ordinary enough to avoid posing a threat for adults. The erasers are also important to help people feel comfortable with the process. Children are generally more familiar with crayons and might find pencils to be too formal.

5. Once the KFDs are complete, discuss the process as an example of how family members bring different perspectives about their life together. These perspectives can often generate more potential solutions to a problem.

We caution all beginning clinicians against making interpretations from the drawings. If the drawings are of concern to parents or the clinician, consultation should be sought from a registered art therapist who is board certified (ATR-BC). Art therapists are required to meet strict standards of practice and assessment to become board certified. Family therapists can locate an ATR-BC through the American Art Therapy Association website (AATA.org).

Instead of using the drawings as a platform for interpretation, our suggestion is to use these activities as a developmentally appropriate catalyst for discussion. From a narrative perspective, the KFD elicits each person's narrative about the family. The KFD can be followed by a similar exercise in which family members are asked to draw the presenting problem from their perspective. Thereafter, each member can discuss how she or he sees the problem. Drawings can communicate perceptions and feelings in ways that are symbolic and less threatening than stating them verbally. The clinician's role is that of reflection. Families are often so fraught with stress that they have little time for reflection. That single element is an asset to the therapeutic experience. Clinicians can model reflection by highlighting strengths, similarities, and differences in a nonjudgmental way and asking rhetorical questions that incorporate the images and metaphors from the drawings (refer to Chapter 8 for more discussion of metaphors). These activities become the basis for assignments and interventions that use the material that the child and family have presented.

Ray was a 5-year-old African American boy who was living with his grandparents. He had come to the attention of his teacher and the school because of his angry outbursts. The most concerning event was when he struck another child's lunch tray, sending the dishes and food crashing to the floor. An art therapy–family therapy team was assigned to work with the boy and his family. On alternating weeks, the art therapist saw Ray at school and focused on drawings that would access his kinesthetic–sensory level, since his problems were described in terms of physical action. Using this level for art interventions, in turn, provided a way to learn about Ray's perceptual–affective level of functioning. The therapist used Ray's drawings to discuss his feelings about his school relationships, the specific events leading up to his outbursts (antecedents), and eventually his feelings of loss since he was not allowed contact with his mother due to her drug use. During other weeks, the family therapist met with the grandparents, highlighted their strengths, and helped them explore strategies that would help Ray with transitions in the family. The art therapist explored Ray's drawings and learned that remarks were made before he hit the tray that left him with the impression that someone was criticizing him. The therapist helped Ray with other ways to express his hurt feelings. Since the teacher was also concerned with his lack of concentration in class, the therapist provided consultation to the teacher with strategies for helping Ray stay focused. They discovered that Ray's worst times occurred in the later morning, right before lunch (see Box 10.1). The consultant helped the teacher brainstorm strategies for scheduling certain assignments for Ray at that time, such as helping her with a task or going with her assistant to get supplies. However, the teacher expressed dismay at spending so much time on Ray when other children also deserved her attention. She had tired of the extra work he required and was not open to changes that would take more of her time. The consultant respected her position and explored what desired change would give her the most relief. They decided that delegating an assignment to her assistant during the later morning would be a compromise that could help her and Ray (win-win solution).

DEVELOPING A COLLABORATIVE TEAM

The above examples of collaboration came about because (1) physicians, educators, art therapists, and family therapists all recognized the value of working together on behalf of those who needed their services and (2) they were willing to change the way they practiced in order to improve clinical outcomes. While good intentions and sacrifice are important to the success of collaboration, additional skills and abilities are important to cultivate. Here are some suggestions for successful collaborations:

1. The therapist must develop good relationships with larger systems such as schools, hospitals, and social service agencies. A beginning therapist might call to make an appointment in order to learn more about the organization. In some cases, it might be helpful for the therapist to offer a free workshop or consultation on special cases.

2. Therapists should provide feedback to referral sources (school counselors, social workers, and so on) about current cases, when clients have given their permission.

3. Therapists should ask other professionals (collaborators) for their suggestions and ideas about cases. Would they be willing to provide assistance if asked?

4. Therapists should seek out professionals to form an interagency team that can deal with problems that come to the attention of various organizations.

In many settings (schools, hospitals, social service agencies, and mental health centers), the family is assigned to a case manager or team. While the therapist may treat the family, the case manager or team determines the nature of treatment. In these settings, the therapist may not have access to all family members nor have control over the welfare of the child. For example, in a school setting, the therapist does not have control over the educational plan for the child. The important issue here is how the therapist works with the team or network to empower the family.

A critical consideration is how the therapist can establish a collaborative relationship with team members to protect the boundaries of individual roles. Collaborative relationships are predicated largely on the problem-solving process. Team members (teachers, social workers, ministers, friends, and others) are encouraged to identify specific problems and generate solutions. The therapist facilitates full participation from all team members. Working with team members as mutual partners within their prescribed roles, the therapist establishes mutual trust with the collaboration team. Finally, positive changes in the family are more likely to be maintained when team members are fully involved. Given the importance of collaboration, practitioners should become aware of potential barriers before organizing a collaborative team. The list in the following section will prepare practitioners to address these possibilities in a proactive way.

Obstacles to Collaboration

In preparing for collaboration, the beginning practitioner is well advised to anticipate as many potential problems as possible (Amatea & Sherrard, 1989). Amatea and Sherrard (1991, p. 6) list the following obstacles to collaboration in school settings. Their original words appear in italics.

1. *Educators and therapists are engaged in different systems and traditions, which often makes communication and team work problematic.* For example, educators often handle the needs of the school and community, which requires them to develop rules and expectations for that group. By contrast, therapists deal with the specific beliefs and patterns depicted by the family members before them.

2. *Therapists can often become triangulated in the pattern of blaming and counter blaming between adults at home and school.* The school can often blame the therapist because the school perceives she or he is allied with the family. This may serve as an obstacle to working cooperatively with school personnel.

3. *Many therapists are unfamiliar with school contexts and learning/schooling issues.* Unless they are willing to become active learners about the realities of school life and educational practice from educators, they will not be able to collaborate effectively.

4. *The engagement of school personnel in addition to family members in the resolution of a child's problem requires a redefinition of traditional notions of family confidentiality and parameters as to what information is to be shared and with whom.*

5. *Insurance reimbursement is not organized to fund collaborative team efforts between family therapists and school personnel.* Collaborative team efforts often require additional time that does not get reimbursed by the insurance carrier.

When these obstacles are overcome, the collaboration process may become an intervention that effects change on its own. At other times, the collaboration sets the stage for other interventions that relate to specific hypotheses formulated by the family therapist through ongoing assessment.

Guidelines for the Collaboration Team Interview

The collaboration team interview has evolved from the ecostructural model of Harry Aponte (1976a) and has been described more recently by O'Callaghan (1988) and Boyd-Franklin (1989a). Brown and Vaccaro (1991) have developed a set of guidelines for the collaboration team based on these models (Box 10.6). The collaboration team interview is implemented currently with at-risk children and their families at public schools, social service agencies, and mental health centers.

The most essential consideration for the therapist in conducting the collaboration team interview is to remain neutral. Whether the therapist is inside or outside the system (school, social service agency, hospital, and so on), it is important not to be identified too closely with any particular part of the team. For example, if a therapist is too close to the staff in a school, the therapist may have difficulty in remaining neutral rather than siding with the school against

---

10.6   *Guidelines for Conducting a Family-School Collaboration Meeting*

---

1. Establish a positive climate for change by acknowledging each person's good intentions, contribution and significance.
2. Summarize the purpose of the meeting.
3. Ask each participant to tell how he or she sees the problem.
4. Discuss the strengths of the child.
5. Suggest that participants tell what results they hope to see.
6. Decide how this can be accomplished. Who will do what? When?
7. Decide if other people need to be involved in the intervention.
8. Discuss obstacles to the intervention (e.g., lack of transportation, schedule conflicts).
9. Define how the participants will know if the intervention has been successful.
10. Explore if a follow-up meeting needs to be scheduled. If so, when?

---

the family. The position of neutrality allows the therapist the greatest latitude for effecting change. The family therapist can do several other things to maintain a collaborative relationship with team members:

1. *Try to understand the family problem and the way each team member perceives it.* Inherent in this understanding is some discussion of the extent to which the problem is affecting the individual team members, as well as each team member's expectations for the family. In this context, the therapist can clarify the team members' biases and unrealistic expectations.
2. *Make use of the word we as consensus develops among the team members.* The word *we* helps to build a sense of cooperation and support among team members. The therapist should avoid criticizing fellow team members.
3. *Suggest attempted solutions on the part of team members.* Team members might want to refer the family to the family therapist without doing anything about the problem. For example, a school counselor might refer a child to a family therapist without attempting to address the problem itself. Unless the counselor has tried to solve the problem, the therapist might be unaware of its severity and uncertain of the

school's commitment to do something about it. Moreover, if the counselor has intervened, the therapist needs to know the results of the attempted solution.

4. *Work with individuals within their prescribed roles.* For example, classroom problems should be handled by the classroom teacher, conduct problems at home should be handled by the parents, and so on. Friends should be asked to provide support without usurping the executive role of parents. Respecting roles will help to establish a collaborative relationship with team members and avoid triangles and coalitions that interrupt the treatment plan.

Occasionally, the therapist might choose to shift to the role of advocate for a family if the family is having difficulty obtaining services or needs the weight of an expert to effect a change in the system. We have acted as advocates for families, primarily around issues of educational placement, when appropriate procedures were not being followed or testing data were not being interpreted accurately to parents (similar to the case of Jeff and his family). But it is preferable to move back to a more neutral stance as quickly as possible. To step in and act as an advocate for parents reduces their own sense of power and competence and creates a coalition with the parents that restricts the range of therapy and limits the therapist's role with the school personnel.

In summary, the increased emphasis on family preservation and home-based services has led to therapeutic practices characterized by collaboration between families and community organizations (schools, churches, and other agencies). Thus, the therapist must assist families to become aware of resources and support. Moreover, the therapist must move beyond simply making families aware of services and programs to helping them become effective and successful in accessing them. Using our metaphor of therapist as tour guide, as the family becomes more empowered with information and confidence to take action on its own behalf, the therapist can shift from driving the car to simply going along for the ride. Usually, this signals the time of termination.

SUMMARY

As the beginning practitioner starts to implement assessment, treatment, evaluation, and collaboration skills, confusion and anxiety inevitably set in. This is a normal part of the learning process. However, as in-session experience accumulates, practitioners will be able to review their own therapeutic behavior, assessing what parts of the process may need attention. Because the therapeutic process is complex and fast-paced, it is sometimes only in retrospect that the practitioner can make sense of it. Though the elements discussed here have been reviewed as separate skills, they are rarely that distinct in practice. Thus, professional growth often depends upon the therapists' willingness to reflect on the therapeutic process, which cannot be expected to conform to a step-by-step recipe; instead, beginning practitioners must endeavor to identify missing elements or possible options for improving the experience. Like driving a car, after the basics are mastered, it is the driver who determines how each adventure is approached, how each challenge is addressed, and what meaning will ultimately be given to the relationships that are encountered along the way. As family therapists, we encourage a journey that will contain enough courage to enter the unknown, enough hope to believe in positive possibilities, and enough compassion to find value in the uniqueness of all people. Bon voyage!

Ethical Considerations

AAMFT Code of Ethics

Effective July 1, 2001

© 2002 *American Association for Marriage and Family Therapy.* Reprinted with permission.

112 South Alfred Street, Alexandria, VA 22314

Phone: (703) 838-9808 - Fax: (703) 838-9805

The Board of Directors of the American Association for Marriage and Family Therapy (AAMFT) hereby promulgates, pursuant to Article 2, Section 2.013 of the Association's Bylaws, the Revised AAMFT Code of Ethics, effective July 1, 2001. The AAMFT strives to honor the public trust in marriage and family therapists by setting standards for ethical practice as described in this Code. The ethical standards define professional expectations and are enforced by the AAMFT Ethics Committee. The absence of an explicit reference to a specific behavior or situation in the Code does not mean that the behavior is ethical or unethical. The standards are not exhaustive. Marriage and family therapists who are uncertain about the ethics of a particular course of action are encouraged to seek counsel from consultants, attorneys, supervisors, colleagues, or other appropriate authorities.

Both law and ethics govern the practice of marriage and family therapy. When making decisions regarding professional behavior, marriage and family therapists must consider the AAMFT Code of Ethics and applicable laws and regulations. If the AAMFT Code of Ethics prescribes a standard higher than that required by law, marriage and family therapists must meet the higher standard of the AAMFT Code of Ethics. Marriage and family therapists comply with the mandates of law, but make known their commitment to the AAMFT Code of Ethics and take steps to resolve the conflict in a responsible manner. The AAMFT supports legal mandates for reporting of alleged unethical conduct. The AAMFT Code of Ethics is binding on Members of AAMFT in all membership categories, AAMFT-Approved Supervisors, and applicants for membership and the Approved Supervisor designation (hereafter, AAMFT Member). AAMFT members have an obligation to be familiar with the AAMFT Code of Ethics and its application to their professional services. Lack of awareness or misunderstanding of an ethical standard is not a defense to a charge of unethical conduct.

The process for filing, investigating, and resolving complaints of unethical conduct is described in the current Procedures for Handling Ethical Matters of the AAMFT Ethics Committee. Persons accused are considered innocent by the Ethics Committee until proven guilty, except as otherwise provided, and are entitled to due process. If an AAMFT Member resigns in anticipation of, or during the course of, an ethics investigation, the Ethics Committee will complete its investigation. Any publication of action taken by the Association will include the fact that the Member attempted to resign during the investigation.

CONTENTS

PRINCIPLE I: RESPONSIBILITY TO CLIENTS

Marriage and family therapists advance the welfare of families and individuals. They respect the rights of those persons seeking their assistance, and make reasonable efforts to ensure that their services are used appropriately.

1.1. Marriage and family therapists provide professional assistance to persons without discrimination on the basis of race, age, ethnicity, socioeconomic status, disability, gender, health status, religion, national origin, or sexual orientation.

1.2 Marriage and family therapists obtain appropriate informed consent to therapy or related procedures as early as feasible in the therapeutic relationship, and use language that is reasonably understandable to clients. The content of informed consent may vary depending upon the client and treatment plan; however, informed consent generally necessitates that the client: (a) has the capacity to consent; (b) has been adequately informed of significant information concerning treatment processes and procedures; (c) has been adequately informed of potential risks and benefits of treatments for which generally recognized standards do not yet exist; (d) has freely and without undue influence expressed consent; and (e) has provided consent that is appropriately documented. When persons, due to age or mental status, are legally incapable of giving informed consent, marriage and family therapists obtain informed permission from a legally authorized person, if such substitute consent is legally permissible.

1.3 Marriage and family therapists are aware of their influential positions with respect to clients, and they avoid exploiting the trust and dependency of such persons. Therapists, therefore, make every effort to avoid conditions and multiple relationships with clients that could impair professional judgment or increase the risk of exploitation. Such relationships include, but are not limited to, business or close personal relationships with a client or the client's immediate family. When the risk of impairment or exploitation exists due to conditions or multiple roles, therapists take appropriate precautions.

1.4 Sexual intimacy with clients is prohibited.

1.5 Sexual intimacy with former clients is likely to be harmful and is therefore prohibited for two years following the termination of therapy or last professional contact. In an effort to avoid exploiting the trust and dependency of clients, marriage and family therapists should not engage in sexual intimacy with former clients after the two years following termination or last professional contact. Should therapists engage in sexual intimacy with former clients following two years after termination or last professional contact, the burden shifts to the therapist to demonstrate that there has been no exploitation or injury to the former client or to the client's immediate family.

1.6 Marriage and family therapists comply with applicable laws regarding the reporting of alleged unethical conduct.

1.7 Marriage and family therapists do not use their professional relationships with clients to further their own interests.

1.8 Marriage and family therapists respect the rights of clients to make decisions and help them to understand the consequences of these decisions. Therapists clearly advise the clients that they have the responsibility to make decisions regarding relationships such as cohabitation, marriage, divorce, separation, reconciliation, custody, and visitation.

1.9 Marriage and family therapists continue therapeutic relationships only so long as it is reasonably clear that clients are benefiting from the relationship.

1.10 Marriage and family therapists assist persons in obtaining other therapeutic services if the therapist is unable or unwilling, for appropriate reasons, to provide professional help.

1.11 Marriage and family therapists do not abandon or neglect clients in treatment without making reasonable arrangements for the continuation of such treatment.

1.12 Marriage and family therapists obtain written informed consent from clients before videotaping, audio recording, or permitting third-party observation.

1.13 Marriage and family therapists, upon agreeing to provide services to a person or entity at the request of a third party, clarify, to the extent feasible and at the outset of the service, the nature of the relationship with each party and the limits of confidentiality.

Principle II: Confidentiality

Marriage and family therapists have unique confidentiality concerns because the client in a therapeutic relationship may be more than one person. Therapists respect and guard the confidences of each individual client.

2.1 Marriage and family therapists disclose to clients and other interested parties, as early as feasible in their professional contacts, the nature of confidentiality and possible limitations of the clients' right to confidentiality. Therapists review with clients the circumstances where confidential information may be requested and where disclosure of confidential information may be legally required. Circumstances may necessitate repeated disclosures.

2.2 Marriage and family therapists do not disclose client confidences except by written authorization or waiver, or where mandated or permitted by law. Verbal authorization will not be sufficient except in emergency situations, unless prohibited by law. When providing couple, family or group treatment, the therapist does not disclose information outside the treatment context without a written authorization from each individual competent to execute a waiver. In the context of couple, family or group treatment, the therapist may not reveal any individual's confidences to others in the client unit without the prior written permission of that individual.

2.3 Marriage and family therapists use client and/or clinical materials in teaching, writing, consulting, research, and public presentations only if a written waiver has been obtained in accordance with subprinciple 2.2, or when appropriate steps have been taken to protect client identity and confidentiality.

2.4 Marriage and family therapists store, safeguard, and dispose of client records in ways that maintain confidentiality and in accord with applicable laws and professional standards.

2.5 Subsequent to the therapist moving from the area, closing the practice, or upon the death of the therapist, a marriage and family therapist arranges for the storage, transfer, or disposal of client records in ways that maintain confidentiality and safeguard the welfare of clients.

2.6 Marriage and family therapists, when consulting with colleagues or referral sources, do not share confidential information that could reasonably lead to the identification of a client, research participant, supervisee, or other person with whom they have a confidential relationship unless they have obtained the prior written consent of the client, research participant, supervisee, or other person with whom they have a confidential relationship. Information may be shared only to the extent necessary to achieve the purposes of the consultation.

PRINCIPLE III: PROFESSIONAL COMPETENCE AND INTEGRITY

Marriage and family therapists maintain high standards of professional competence and integrity.

3.1 Marriage and family therapists pursue knowledge of new developments and maintain competence in marriage and family therapy through education, training, or supervised experience.

3.2 Marriage and family therapists maintain adequate knowledge of and adhere to applicable laws, ethics, and professional standards.

3.3 Marriage and family therapists seek appropriate professional assistance for their personal problems or conflicts that may impair work performance or clinical judgment.

3.4 Marriage and family therapists do not provide services that create a conflict of interest that may impair work performance or clinical judgment.

3.5 Marriage and family therapists, as presenters, teachers, supervisors, consultants and researchers, are dedicated to high standards of scholarship, present accurate information, and disclose potential conflicts of interest.

3.6 Marriage and family therapists maintain accurate and adequate clinical and financial records.

3.7 While developing new skills in specialty areas, marriage and family therapists take steps to ensure the competence of their work and to protect clients from possible harm. Marriage and family therapists practice in specialty areas new to them only after appropriate education, training, or supervised experience.

3.8 Marriage and family therapists do not engage in sexual or other forms of harassment of clients, students, trainees, supervisees, employees, colleagues, or research subjects.

3.9 Marriage and family therapists do not engage in the exploitation of clients, students, trainees, supervisees, employees, colleagues, or research subjects.

3.10 Marriage and family therapists do not give to or receive from clients (a) gifts of substantial value or (b) gifts that impair the integrity or efficacy of the therapeutic relationship.

3.11 Marriage and family therapists do not diagnose, treat, or advise on problems outside the recognized boundaries of their competencies.

3.12 Marriage and family therapists make efforts to prevent the distortion or misuse of their clinical and research findings.

3.13 Marriage and family therapists, because of their ability to influence and alter the lives of others, exercise special care when making public their professional recommendations and opinions through testimony or other public statements.

3.14 To avoid a conflict of interests, marriage and family therapists who treat minors or adults involved in custody or visitation actions may not also perform forensic evaluations for custody, residence, or visitation of the minor. The marriage and family therapist who treats the minor may provide the court or mental health professional performing the evaluation with information about the minor from the therapist's perspective as a treating marriage and family therapist, so long as the marriage and family therapist does not violate confidentiality.

3.15 Marriage and family therapists are in violation of this Code and subject to termination of membership or other appropriate action if they: (a) are convicted of any felony; (b) are convicted of a misdemeanor related to their qualifications or functions; (c) engage in conduct which could lead to conviction of a felony, or a misdemeanor related to their qualifications or functions; (d) are expelled from or disciplined by other professional organizations; (e) have their licenses or certificates suspended or revoked or are otherwise disciplined by regulatory bodies; (f) continue to practice marriage and family therapy while no longer competent to do so because they are impaired by physical or mental causes or the abuse of alcohol or other substances; or (g) fail to cooperate with the Association at any point from the inception of an ethical complaint through the completion of all proceedings regarding that complaint.

PRINCIPLE IV: RESPONSIBILITY TO STUDENTS AND SUPERVISEES

Marriage and family therapists do not exploit the trust and dependency of students and supervisees.

4.1 Marriage and family therapists are aware of their influential positions with respect to students and supervisees, and they avoid exploiting the trust and dependency of such persons. Therapists, therefore, make every effort to avoid conditions and multiple relationships that could impair professional objectivity or increase the risk of exploitation. When the risk of impairment or exploitation exists due to conditions or multiple roles, therapists take appropriate precautions.

4.2 Marriage and family therapists do not provide therapy to current students or supervisees.

4.3 Marriage and family therapists do not engage in sexual intimacy with students or supervisees during the evaluative or training relationship between the therapist and student or supervisee. Should a supervisor engage in sexual activity with a former supervisee, the burden of proof shifts to the supervisor to demonstrate that there has been no exploitation or injury to the supervisee.

4.4 Marriage and family therapists do not permit students or supervisees to perform or to hold themselves out as competent to perform professional services beyond their training, level of experience, and competence.

4.5 Marriage and family therapists take reasonable measures to ensure that services provided by supervisees are professional.

4.6 Marriage and family therapists avoid accepting as supervisees or students those individuals with whom a prior or existing relationship could compromise the therapist's objectivity. When such situations cannot be avoided, therapists take appropriate precautions to maintain objectivity. Examples of such relationships include, but are not limited to, those individuals with whom the therapist has a current or prior sexual, close personal, immediate familial, or therapeutic relationship.

4.7 Marriage and family therapists do not disclose supervisee confidences except by written authorization or waiver, or when mandated or permitted by law. In educational or training settings where there are multiple supervisors, disclosures are permitted only to other professional colleagues, administrators, or employers who share responsibility for training of the supervisee. Verbal authorization will not be sufficient except in emergency situations, unless prohibited by law.

PRINCIPLE V: RESPONSIBILITY TO RESEARCH PARTICIPANTS

Investigators respect the dignity and protect the welfare of research participants, and are aware of applicable laws and regulations and professional standards governing the conduct of research.

5.1 Investigators are responsible for making careful examinations of ethical acceptability in planning studies. To the extent that services to research participants may be compromised by participation in research, investigators seek the ethical advice of qualified professionals not directly involved in the investigation and observe safeguards to protect the rights of research participants.

5.2 Investigators requesting participant involvement in research inform participants of the aspects of the research that might reasonably be expected to influence willingness to participate. Investigators are especially sensitive to the possibility of diminished consent when participants are also receiving clinical services, or have impairments which limit understanding and/or communication, or when participants are children.

5.3 Investigators respect each participant's freedom to decline participation in or to withdraw from a research study at any time. This obligation requires special thought and consideration when investigators or other members of the research team are in positions of authority or influence over participants. Marriage and family therapists, therefore, make every effort to avoid multiple relationships with research participants that could impair professional judgment or increase the risk of exploitation.

5.4 Information obtained about a research participant during the course of an investigation is confidential unless there is a waiver previously obtained in writing. When the possibility exists that others, including family members, may obtain access to such information, this possibility, together with the plan for protecting confidentiality, is explained as part of the procedure for obtaining informed consent.

PRINCIPLE VI: RESPONSIBILITY TO THE PROFESSION

Marriage and family therapists respect the rights and responsibilities of professional colleagues and participate in activities that advance the goals of the profession.

6.1 Marriage and family therapists remain accountable to the standards of the profession when acting as members or employees of organizations. If the mandates of an organization with which a marriage and family therapist is affiliated, through employment, contract or otherwise, conflict with the AAMFT Code of Ethics, marriage and family therapists make known to the organization their commitment to the AAMFT Code of Ethics and attempt to resolve the conflict in a way that allows the fullest adherence to the Code of Ethics.

6.2 Marriage and family therapists assign publication credit to those who have contributed to a publication in proportion to their contributions and in accordance with customary professional publication practices.

6.3 Marriage and family therapists do not accept or require authorship credit for a publication based on research from a student's program, unless the therapist made a substantial contribution beyond being a faculty advisor or research committee member. Coauthorship on a student thesis, dissertation, or project should be determined in accordance with principles of fairness and justice.

6.4 Marriage and family therapists who are the authors of books or other materials that are published or distributed do not plagiarize or fail to cite persons to whom credit for original ideas or work is due.

6.5 Marriage and family therapists who are the authors of books or other materials published or distributed by an organization take reasonable precautions to ensure that the organization promotes and advertises the materials accurately and factually.

6.6 Marriage and family therapists participate in activities that contribute to a better community and society, including devoting a portion of their professional activity to services for which there is little or no financial return.

6.7 Marriage and family therapists are concerned with developing laws and regulations pertaining to marriage and family therapy that serve the public interest, and with altering such laws and regulations that are not in the public interest.

6.8 Marriage and family therapists encourage public participation in the design and delivery of professional services and in the regulation of practitioners.

PRINCIPLE VII: FINANCIAL ARRANGEMENTS

Marriage and family therapists make financial arrangements with clients, third-party payors, and supervisees that are reasonably understandable and conform to accepted professional practices.

7.1 Marriage and family therapists do not offer or accept kickbacks, rebates, bonuses, or other remuneration for referrals; fee-for-service arrangements are not prohibited.

7.2 Prior to entering into the therapeutic or supervisory relationship, marriage and family therapists clearly disclose and explain to clients and supervisees: (a) all financial arrangements and fees related to professional services, including charges for canceled or missed appointments; (b) the use of collection agencies or legal measures for nonpayment; and (c) the procedure for obtaining payment from the client, to the extent allowed by law, if payment is denied by the third-party payor. Once services have begun, therapists provide reasonable notice of any changes in fees or other charges.

7.3 Marriage and family therapists give reasonable notice to clients with unpaid balances of their intent to seek collection by agency or legal recourse. When such action is taken, therapists will not disclose clinical information.

7.4 Marriage and family therapists represent facts truthfully to clients, third-party payors, and supervisees regarding services rendered.

7.5 Marriage and family therapists ordinarily refrain from accepting goods and services from clients in return for services rendered. Bartering for professional services may be conducted only if: (a) the supervisee or client requests it, (b) the relationship is not exploitative, (c) the professional relationship is not distorted, and (d) a clear written contract is established.

7.6 Marriage and family therapists may not withhold records under their immediate control that are requested and needed for a client's treatment solely because payment has not been received for past services, except as otherwise provided by law.

PRINCIPLE VIII: ADVERTISING

Marriage and family therapists engage in appropriate informational activities, including those that enable the public, referral sources, or others to choose professional services on an informed basis.

8.1 Marriage and family therapists accurately represent their competencies, education, training, and experience relevant to their practice of marriage and family therapy.

8.2 Marriage and family therapists ensure that advertisements and publications in any media (such as directories, announcements, business cards, newspapers, radio, television, Internet, and facsimiles) convey information that is necessary for the public to make an appropriate selection of professional services. Information could include: (a) office information, such as name, address, telephone number, credit card acceptability, fees, languages spoken, and office hours; (b) qualifying clinical degree (see subprinciple 8.5); (c) other earned degrees (see subprinciple 8.5) and state or provincial licensures and/or certifications; (d) AAMFT clinical member status; and (e) description of practice.

8.3 Marriage and family therapists do not use names that could mislead the public concerning the identity, responsibility, source, and status of those practicing under that name, and do not hold themselves out as being partners or associates of a firm if they are not.

8.4 Marriage and family therapists do not use any professional identification (such as a business card, office sign, letterhead, Internet, or telephone or association directory listing) if it includes a statement or claim that is false, fraudulent, misleading, or deceptive.

8.5 In representing their educational qualifications, marriage and family therapists list and claim as evidence only those earned degrees: (a) from institutions accredited by regional accreditation sources recognized by the United States Department of Education, (b) from institutions recognized by states or provinces that license or certify marriage and family therapists, or (c) from equivalent foreign institutions.

8.6 Marriage and family therapists correct, wherever possible, false, misleading, or inaccurate information and representations made by others concerning the therapist's qualifications, services, or products.

8.7 Marriage and family therapists make certain that the qualifications of their employees or supervisees are represented in a manner that is not false, misleading, or deceptive.

8.8 Marriage and family therapists do not represent themselves as providing specialized services unless they have the appropriate education, training, or supervised experience.

TABLE A.1	ETHICS AT-RISK TEST FOR MARRIAGE AND FAMILY THERAPISTS

Ever wonder how close you are to blundering over the ethics edge and possibly harming your clients, yourself, and/or the profession? The At-Risk Test may tell you. Of course, you must answer honestly. Add up your score and compare the total with the key at the end.

1. Is it true that you have **never** taken an academic course on MFT practice ethics?   No = 0   Yes = 1

2. Honestly, are you *unfamiliar* with some parts of the latest version of our Ethics Code?   No = 0   Yes = 1

3. Do you think our Ethics Code *interferes* somewhat with the quality of your therapy, research, or supervision?   No = 0   Yes = 1

4. Have you *ever* sent a false bill for therapy to an insurance carrier?   No = 0   Yes = 1

5. Do you feel sexually attracted to any of your *present* clients?   No = 0   Yes = 1

6. Do you fantasize about kissing or touching a *present* client?   No = 0   Yes = 1

7. Do you comment to a *present* client how attractive he or she is or make positive remarks about his or her body?   No = 0   Yes = 1

8. Are you tempted to ask out an ex-client even though less than 2 years have passed since termination?   No = 0   Yes = 1

9. Do you commonly take off your jewelry, remove shoes, loosen your tie, or otherwise become more informal during therapy sessions?   No = 0   Yes = 1

10. *Presently,* do you meet a client for coffee or meals or for socializing outside of therapy?   No = 0   Yes = 1

11. Has a *present* client given you an expensive gift or frequently given you inexpensive gifts?   No = 0   Yes = 1

12. Are you stimulated by a *current* client's description of sexual behavior or thoughts?   No = 0   Yes = 1

13. Are you in the midst of a difficult personal or family crisis yourself?   No = 0   Yes = 1

14. During the past 2 months, have you seen clients while you were hung over or under the influence of drugs, even if only a little?   No = 0   Yes = 1

15. Does your personal financial situation cross your mind when considering whether to terminate therapy or to refer a client?   No = 0   Yes = 1

16. Do you feel manipulated by a *current* client such that you are wary of him/her or are angry and frustrated by him/her?   No = 0   Yes = 1

17. Do you provide therapy to a *current* student, supervisee, or employee?   No = 0   Yes = 1

18. Have you wanted to talk to a colleague about a *current* case but feared doing so would show your lack of skill or might lead to an ethics case against you?   No = 0   Yes = 1

19. Are you behind on case notes?   No = 0   Yes = 1

20. Do you talk about clients with other clients or gossip about clients with colleagues?   No = 0   Yes = 1

TABLE	(CONTINUED)
A.1	

0   Excellent, you are nearly risk free.

1–2 Review your practice. Read and follow the Ethics Code.

3–4 Review your practice for problem areas. Consider needed changes.

5–7 Consult a supervisor. You are engaging in high-risk behavior.

8+ Probably you are harming your clients and/or yourself. Seek therapy and supervision. Come to terms with your situation by making immediate changes.

Table by Gregory Brock

The items making up the Ethics At-Risk Test come from research and from Ethics Committee case experience. Send your comments and questions to Gregory Brock, PhD, 315 Funkhouser Building, University of Kentucky, Lexington, KY 40506-0054, U.S.A. Permission is granted to copy, distribute, or publish the At-Risk Test with credit given for authorship.

Films of Interest to Students of Family Therapy

Some films have several themes. Those are listed in more than one category due to the complexity of the plot and characters.

INTERGENERATIONAL

Avalon
Born on the Fourth of
    July
Catch Me If You Can
Joy Luck Club
Nixon
Nuts
Shine
Soul Food
This Boy's Life
Tortilla Soup
You Can Count on Me

UNATTACHED ADULTS

An Officer and a
    Gentleman
Autumn Sonata
Bull Durham
Frankie & Johnny
Pretty Woman
Stanley & Iris
The Graduate
Waiting to Exhale
When Harry Met Sally
You've Got Mail

MARRIAGE

A Beautiful Mind
Barefoot in the Park
Best Intentions
Chapter 2 (Remarriage)
Enchanted April
Goodbye Girl
Hannah and Her Sisters
Hours
Prelude to a Kiss
Scenes from a Marriage
Shadowlands
Who's Afraid of Virginia
    Woolf

CHILDREN

Grand Canyon
Hours
Mr. Mom
My Life as a Dog
Parent Trap
Shadowlands
The Education of Little
    Tree
To Kill a Mockingbird

ADOLESCENTS

Back to the Future
The Great Santini
The Karate Kid
Ordinary People
Running on Empty
Sixteen Candles

LAUNCHING

About Schmidt
Betsy's Wedding
Father of the Bride
Guess Who's Coming to
    Dinner
Moonstruck
October Sky
Steel Magnolias

AGING/DEATH

About Schmidt
Avalon
Cocoon
Cocoon: The Return
Dad
Folks
Fried Green Tomatoes

Harry & Tonto
Iris
Moonstruck
On Golden Pond
Shadowlands
Steel Magnolias
Straight Story
Strangers in Good
    Company
Terms of Endearment

DIVORCE

Kramer vs. Kramer
Mr. Mom
Mrs. Doubtfire
Parent Trap
War of the Roses

STEP-FAMILIES/
REMARRIAGE

Chapter Two
Emmy & Alexander
Shadowlands

This Boy's Life
Tortilla Soup
With Six You Get
    Eggroll
Yours, Mine, and Ours

GENDER

Fried Green Tomatoes
Full Monty
Moonstruck
Nuts
Ordinary People
Real Women Have
    Curves
Strangers in Good
    Company
Terms of Endearment
This Boy's Life
Waiting to Exhale

RACE

A Soldier's Story
Beloved

Boyz N the Hood
Do the Right Thing
Guess Who's Coming to
    Dinner?
Jungle Fever
Malcolm X
Roots
To Kill A Mockingbird
Waiting to Exhale

CULTURE

About Schmidt
Avalon
Joy Luck Club
Moonstruck
October Sky
Real Women Have
    Curves
Sophie's Choice
The Education of Little
    Tree
The Chosen
Tortilla Soup

Global Assessment of Relational Functioning (GARF)

INSTRUCTIONS

The GARF Scale can be used to indicate an overall judgment of the functioning of a family or other ongoing relationship on a hypothetical continuum ranging from competent, optimal relational functioning to a disrupted, dysfunctional relationship. It is analogous to Axis V (Global Assessment of Functioning Scale) provided for individuals in DSM-IV. The GARF Scale permits the clinician to rate the degree to which a family or other ongoing relational unit meets the affective or instrumental needs of its members in the following areas:

A. *Problem solving*—skills in negotiating goals, rules, and routines; adaptability to stress; communication skills; ability to resolve conflict
B. *Organization*—maintenance of interpersonal roles and subsystem boundaries; hierarchical functioning; coalitions and distribution of power, control, and responsibility
C. *Emotional climate*—tone and range of feelings; quality of caring, empathy, involvement, and attachment/commitment; sharing of values; mutual affective responsiveness, respect, and regard; quality of sexual functioning

In most instances, the GARF Scale should be used to rate functioning during the current period (i.e., the level of relational functioning at the time of the evaluation). In some settings, the GARF Scale may also be used to rate functioning for other time periods (i.e., the highest level of relational functioning for at least a few months during the past year).

Note: Use specific, intermediate codes when possible, for example, 45, 68, 72. If detailed information is not adequate to make specific ratings, use midpoints of the five ranges, that is, 90, 70, 50, 30, or 10.

81–100 Overall

Relational unit is functioning satisfactorily from self-report of participants and from perspectives of observers.

Agreed-on patterns or routines exist that help meet the usual needs of each family/couple member; there is flexibility for change in response to unusual demands or events; and occasional conflicts and stressful transitions are resolved through problem-solving communication and negotiation.

There is a shared understanding and agreement about roles and appropriate tasks, decision making is established for each functional area, and there is recognition of the unique characteristics and merit of each subsystem (e.g., parents/spouses, siblings, and individuals).

There is a situationally appropriate, optimistic atmosphere in the family; a wide range of feelings is freely expressed and managed within the family; and there is a general atmosphere of warmth, caring, and sharing of values among all family members. Sexual relations of adult members are satisfactory.

61–80 Overall

Functioning of relational unit is somewhat unsatisfactory. Over a period of time, many but not all difficulties are resolved without complaints.

Daily routines are present, but there is some pain and difficulty in responding to the unusual. Some conflicts remain unresolved but do not disrupt family functioning.

Decision making is usually competent, but efforts at control of one another quite often are greater than necessary or are ineffective. Individuals and relationships are clearly demarcated but sometimes a specific subsystem is depreciated or scapegoated.

A range of feeling is expressed, but instances of emotional blocking or tension are evident. Warmth and caring are present but are marred by a family member's irritability and frustrations. Sexual activity of adult members may be reduced or problematic.

41–60 OVERALL

Relational unit has occasional times of satisfying and competent functioning together, but clearly dysfunctional, unsatisfying relationships tend to predominate.

Communication is frequently inhibited by unresolved conflicts that often interfere with daily routines; there is significant difficulty in adapting to family stress and transitional change.

Decision making is only intermittently competent and effective; either excessive rigidity or significant lack of structure is evident at these times. Individual needs are quite often submerged by a partner or coalition.

Pain or ineffective anger or emotional deadness interferes with family enjoyment. Although there is some warmth and support for members, it is usually unequally distributed. Troublesome sexual difficulties between adults are often present.

21–40 OVERALL

Relational unit is obviously and seriously dysfunctional; forms and time periods of satisfactory relating are rare.

Family/couple routines do not meet the needs of members; they are grimly adhered to or blithely ignored. Life cycle changes, such as departures or entries into the relational unit, generate painful conflict and obviously frustrating failures of problem solving.

Decision making is tyrannical or quite ineffective. The unique characteristics of individuals are unappreciated or ignored by either rigid or confusingly fluid coalitions.

There are infrequent periods of enjoyment of life together; frequent distancing or open hostility reflects significant conflicts that remain unresolved and quite painful. Sexual dysfunction among adult members is commonplace.

1–20 OVERALL

Relational unit has Become Too Dysfunctional to Retain Continuity of Contact and Attachment.

Family/couple routines are negligible (e.g., no mealtime, sleeping, or waking schedule); family members often do not know where others are or when they will be in or out; there is little effective communication among family members.

Family/couple members are not organized in such a way that personal or generational responsibilities are recognized. Boundaries of relational unit as a whole and subsystems cannot be identified or agreed on. Family members are physically endangered or injured or sexually attacked.

Despair and cynicism are pervasive; there is little attention to the emotional needs of others; there is almost no sense of attachment, commitment, or concern about one another's welfare.

0

Inadequate information.

Evaluations for Supervision D

FAMILY THERAPIST RATING SCALE

Directions: Rate the relative effectiveness with which the family therapist engages in the behaviors listed below. Some of these behaviors might be associated with a school of therapy other than your own. Try to be neutral and rate the relative effectiveness with which the therapist performs each behavior regardless of whether you agree or disagree with the type of intervention. In other words, try not to rate the model of therapy, just the behavior as identified by the statement on the rating scale.

Not Present (0); Ineffective (1); Neutral (2); Minimally Effective (3); Effective (4); Very Effective (5); Maximally Effective (6)

0 1 2 3 4 5 6

STRUCTURING BEHAVIORS

1. __:__:__:__:__:__:__: Helps the family define its needs.
2. __:__:__:__:__:__:__: Stops chaotic interchanges.
3. __:__:__:__:__:__:__: Shifts approach when one way of gathering information is not working.
4. __:__:__:__:__:__:__: Uses short, specific, and clear communications.
5. __:__:__:__:__:__:__: Asks open-ended questions.
6. __:__:__:__:__:__:__: Helps clients rephrase "why" questions into statements.
7. __:__:__:__:__:__:__: Makes a brief introductory statement about the purpose of the interview.
8. __:__:__:__:__:__:__: Lays down ground rules for the therapeutic process.
9. __:__:__:__:__:__:__: Clarifies own and client's expectations of therapy.
10. __:__:__:__:__:__:__: Explicitly structures or directs interaction among family members.

RELATIONSHIP BEHAVIORS

1. __:__:__:__:__:__: Engenders hope.
2. __:__:__:__:__:__: Uses self-disclosure.
3. __:__:__:__:__:__: Demonstrates warmth.
4. __:__:__:__:__:__: "Communicates" the attitude that the client's problem is of real importance.
5. __:__:__:__:__:__: Tone of voice conveys sensitivity to the client's feelings.
6. __:__:__:__:__:__: Speaks at a comfortable pace.
7. __:__:__:__:__:__: Empathizes with family members.
8. __:__:__:__:__:__: Confirms family members' experience of an event.
9. __:__:__:__:__:__: Attempts to improve the self-esteem of individual family members.
10. __:__:__:__:__:__: Demonstrates a good sense of humor.

HISTORICAL BEHAVIORS

1. __:__:__:__:__:__: Directly asks about the current relationship between a spouse and his/her parents and siblings.
2. __:__:__:__:__:__: Explores the couple's mate selection process.
3. __:__:__:__:__:__: Emphasizes cognitions.
4. __:__:__:__:__:__: Assembles a detailed family history.
5. __:__:__:__:__:__: Avoids becoming triangulated by the family.
6. __:__:__:__:__:__: Attempts to help clients directly deal with parents and adult siblings about previously avoided issues.
7. __:__:__:__:__:__: Assigns or suggests that family members visit extended family members.
8. __:__:__:__:__:__: Maintains an objective stance.
9. __:__:__:__:__:__: Makes interpretations.
10. __:__:__:__:__:__: Collects detailed information about the etiology of the identified problem.

STRUCTURAL/PROCESS BEHAVIORS

1. __:__:__:__:__:__: Checks out pronouns to see who did what to whom.
2. __:__:__:__:__:__: Assigns tasks both within the session and outside it.
3. __:__:__:__:__:__: Concentrates on the interaction of the system rather than the intrapsychic dynamics.
4. __:__:__:__:__:__: Employs paradoxical intention.
5. __:__:__:__:__:__: Relabels family symptoms.
6. __:__:__:__:__:__: Reorders behavioral sequences (e.g., order of speaking, who speaks to whom).

7. __:__:__:__:__:__: Rearranges the physical seating of family members.

8. __:__:__:__:__:__: Helps the family establish appropriate boundaries.

9. __:__:__:__:__:__: Elicits covert family conflicts, alliances and coalitions.

10. __:__:__:__:__:__: Assumes the role of expert technician who observes and then intervenes.

EXPERIENTIAL BEHAVIORS

1. __:__:__:__:__:__: Uses family sculpting.

2. __:__:__:__:__:__: Encourages family members to find their own solutions.

3. __:__:__:__:__:__: Encourages individuals to share their fantasies.

4. __:__:__:__:__:__: Asks for current feelings.

5. __:__:__:__:__:__: Lets the clients choose the subject of the session.

6. __:__:__:__:__:__: Attempts to focus on process rather than content.

7. __:__:__:__:__:__: Uses role playing.

8. __:__:__:__:__:__: Responds to his/her own discomfort.

9. __:__:__:__:__:__: Uses own affect to elicit affect in family members.

10. __:__:__:__:__:__: Keeps the interaction in the here and now.

Family Therapist Rating Scale Profile

Therapist's Name _____   Comments _____

Date _____   _____

Rater _____   _____

		Structuring	Relationship	Historical	Structural/ Process	Experiential
6	60	–	–	–	–	–
	55	–	–	–	–	–
5	50	–	–	–	–	–
	45	–	–	–	–	–
4	40	–	–	–	–	–
	35	–	–	–	–	–
3	30	–	–	–	–	–
	25	–	–	–	–	–
2	20	–	–	–	–	–
	15	–	–	–	–	–
1	10	–	–	–	–	–
	5	–	–	–	–	–

Mean Rating of Behaviors Observed   Raw Score

Note: A profile of a family therapist's behavior may be constructed in two ways. In one approach, raw scores, the total points within each category, may be added and placed in the profile. However, it may at times be helpful to use the mean ratings of only those behaviors actually observed within each category. The above profile has been constructed to accommodate either method.

Basic Skills Evaluation Device©

The Basic Skills Evaluation Device was developed from data gathered to determine the basic skills for family therapy that are essential for *beginning level trainees*. After evaluating the data, the device was developed and tested on beginning trainees who were new to family therapy in COAMFTE accredited or candidacy master's or doctoral programs or students in PDI programs who had not developed family therapy skills. The device has not been tested on more advanced trainees or on experienced therapists. The author believes, however, that the device may have utility for these populations and encourages experimenting. The author is in the beginning stages of this next phase of instrument testing.

The Basic Family Therapy Skills Evaluation Device (BSED) was developed using empirical data from the Basic Family Therapy Skills Project, conducted by Charles Figley and Thorana Nelson. The items and descriptions were developed from information gathered from nearly 500 experienced marriage and family therapy trainers and supervisors.

The device serves several purposes, including that of evaluating therapist trainees in their first 500 hours of training. The scale is used at the experience level *of the trainee.* That is, "meets expectation" means "in your experience, compared with other trainees with this level of experience and training," which may differ from supervisor to supervisor. Included are descriptions for each training dimension based on data from the Basic Family Therapy Skills Project. Please use these descriptions when evaluating your trainees.

Included in the devise is a nongeneric theory section that you may want to use, filling in the blank for the theory that the trainee is currently working with.

Evaluate each trainee using your best judgment from the descriptions given plus your subjective ideas about each item.

General Guidelines Regarding Developmental Levels

Beginner   First 50–75 hours of experience; less, perhaps, if under intensive live supervision. The beginner will need more direction and structure, clearer session plans, and more freedom to go in a direction that may seem less productive, but which follows the trainee's plan for the session and the supervisor's plan for what the trainee is currently working on. For example, the supervisor may see an opportunity for a paradoxical or solution-oriented approach, but the trainee may be working on structuring the session with parents and children. The trainee can discuss case material based on one theoretical perspective, but may get confused if trying to use more than one. The trainee is eager for supervision and may feel confused or anxious in new situations.

Intermediate   Between 50 or 75 hours of experience and 350 or 400 hours. The trainee is comfortable joining with clients, can structure sessions and execute session plans, and is able to provide hypotheses or direction for therapy based on theoretical concepts. The trainee can be flexible during a session, changing the session plan easily and with little confusion. The trainee can discuss cases from multiple theoretical viewpoints and evaluate both treatment and self-as-therapist progress based on clear goals. The trainee may be uneven in evaluations of therapy and self. The trainee benefits from supervision, but may appear at times to not want supervision, wanting, instead, to be allowed to work on one's own unless asking for help.

Advanced   Between 350 or 400 hours of experience and 500 hours. The trainee is comfortable and does well in most therapy situations, managing most case situations smoothly and professionally. Supervision focuses on microskills and finer, abstract points of therapy and theory. The supervisor and trainee may engage in debate regarding theoretical perspectives and interventions. The trainee is able to evaluate both therapy and self. The trainee may appear eager for supervision and may express concern that he or she is inadequate as a therapist, unable to evaluate progress in therapy or supervision.

Conceptual Skills

Knowledge Base   The trainee has a basic understanding of family systems theory. The trainee is able to articulate principles of human developmental, family developmental, and family life cycle issues pertaining to the case. The trainee communicates an understanding of human interaction and normal family processes. The trainee can articulate how gender, culture, and class have an impact on the client and on therapeutic issues (including interaction with one's own gender, culture/ethnicity, and class). The trainee is able to determine and work within the clients' worldview. The trainee has an understanding of human sexuality. The trainee has a knowledge of assessment strategies (e.g., interviewing skills, various assessment devices, DSM IV).

Systems Perspective   The trainee understands and can articulate basic systems concepts. When talking about client problems, the trainee employs systemic concepts and perspectives, thus showing that he or she is thinking in systemic and contextual terms. Formed hypotheses are systemic. The trainee can articulate the difference between content issues and process issues. The trainee can recognize hierarchy problems.

Familiarity with Therapy Models   The trainee has a basic knowledge of family therapy theories. The trainee's goals, hypotheses, session plans, interventions, and evaluation strategies for terminating therapy are all linked to a specific employed and articulated therapeutic model (which may be an integrated model). The trainee also recognizes his or her own perceptions, client resources, and links between problems and attempted solutions.

Self as Therapist   The trainee can articulate his or her own preferred model of therapy. The trainee is also aware of how his or her communication style impacts therapy and is curious in learning about himself or herself. The trainee is aware of and able to manage his or her own anxiety in therapy. In talking about cases, the trainee is able to reframe or positively connote issues from cases for herself or himself. The trainee has an understanding of how to use a sense of humor in therapy. The trainee recognizes her or his ability to be flexible and curious and to think critically and analytically, expressing authenticity and accepting feedback. The trainee is able to recognize how her or his own developmental or other issues interact in therapy.

Perceptual Skills

Recognition Skills   The trainee shows the ability to recognize hierarchies, boundaries, dynamics of triangling, family interaction, and family behavioral patterns. The trainee can also recognize gender, ethnic, cultural, and class issues in client dynamics and in therapy.

The trainee is able to recognize clients' coping skills and strengths and can understand dynamics and patterns in presenting problems: The trainee recognizes how patterns associated with presenting problems may be similar to other patterns of interaction in clients' lives.

The trainee recognizes and can articulate her or his impact as part of the client/therapy system.

Hypothesizing   The trainee can formulate a systemic hypothesis and can generate general hypotheses as well as theory (or model) specific hypotheses. The trainee can formulate long- and short-term treatment plans based on hypotheses. The trainee is able to distinguish process from content at an appropriate level and include process issues in hypotheses. The trainee reframes patterns and problems appropriately.

Integration of Theory and Practice   The family therapy trainee is able to articulate theory as it is applied in practice, utilizing concepts appropriately, and describing interventions that fit with the theory and hypotheses. If using an integrated theory, the trainee is able to differentiate concepts and provide rationale for choices of hypotheses and/or interventions. The trainee is able to evaluate the appropriateness (positives and negatives) for a theory or integrated theory using concrete data from therapy cases.

Executive Skills

Joining   A trainee skilled in the technique of joining is able to engage each family member in a therapeutic alliance and relationship by establishing rapport through clear communication that conveys a sense of competency, authority, and trustworthiness while at the same time demonstrating empathy, warmth, caring, and respect. The trainee is capable of gathering information without making the client feel interrogated, laying down the ground rules for therapy, and setting up a workable treatment contract by exploring the client's expectations, point of view, and preparedness to make changes. These goals are accomplished in conjunction with setting appropriate boundaries and avoiding triangulation.

Assessment   The family therapy trainee demonstrates the ability to assess clients through use of genograms, family histories, suicide/depression interviews or inventories, and discussion of SES, employment, school, and developmental stages. The trainee is familiar with and skilled in basic interviewing techniques and strategies. Assessment is formulated and appropriate to an articulated theory of change. The trainee is able to clarify the presenting problem, explore previous solutions to the problem; gather information regarding sequences and patterns in the family, and determine the strengths and resources that the family brings to therapy. Assessment strategies are sensitive to gender, race, and cultural issues.

Hypothesizing   The trainee exhibits the ability to formulate multiple hypotheses about a case based on articulated principles of a theory of change. She or he can develop treatment plans which include a rationale for intervention based on hypotheses; set clear, reachable goals in consultation with the family; focus the treatment toward a therapeutic goal; and modify the existing case plan when appropriate.

Interventions   The trainee demonstrates an understanding of intervention techniques by structuring interventions that defuse violent or chaotic situations, deflect scapegoating and blaming, and interrupt negative patterns and destructive communication cycles. The ability to intervene also includes appropriately challenging clients on their position, explicitly structuring or directing interactions among family members, and helping families establish boundaries. The trainee is able to elicit family/client strengths and utilize them in both session discussions and homework assignments.

Other interventions that illustrate skill include normalizing the problem when appropriate, helping clients develop their own solutions to problems, giving credit for positive changes, reframing, and appropriately using self-disclosure. The trainee uses theory-specific interventions appropriately and is able to articulate a rationale for these interventions.

Communication Skills   Communication skills are demonstrated by active listening and reflecting; the use of open-ended questions; and short, specific, and clear oral forms of communication. The trainee's body language should convey a relaxed state and match the tone of the conversation. The trainee is also able to coach clients in learning communication skills rather than merely "lecturing" and instructing.

Personal Skills   Personal skills that are important for a successful therapy trainee to possess include a desire to be a family therapist, intelligence, curiosity, common sense, self-direction, commitment, patience, empathy, sensitivity, flexibility, the ability to manage his or her anxiety, authenticity, expression of a caring attitude, and acceptance of others. The trainee should also exhibit warmth, a sense of humor, a nondefensive attitude, congruency, the ability to take responsibility for his or her mistakes, the ability to apply his or her own personal mode of therapy, and possess no debilitating personal pathology. The trainee demonstrates emotional maturity and the ability to be self-reflexive. The trainee demonstrates an appropriate attitude of expertness toward clients, congruent with her or his theory of change.

Session Management   The trainee is able to manage the therapy process by effectively introducing clients to the therapy room, explaining equipment and setting, if necessary, and explaining the policies and procedures of the agency/clinic. The trainee is able to engage the family in therapeutic conversation, controlling the flow of communication as per her or his therapy plan. The trainee is able to manage intense interactions appropriately, demonstrating skill at both escalating and de-escalating intensity at appropriate times. The trainee is able to manage time, finishing sessions as scheduled, and is able to schedule further appointments, consultations, and referrals smoothly and effectively. The trainee is able to collect fees in an appropriate manner.

Professional Skills

Supervision   The trainee attends supervision meetings as scheduled and is prepared to discuss cases with colleagues, to formally present her or his own case, and to present audio or video material as requested. The trainee is respectful and positive about other trainees' cases and presentations, and is helpful and not demeaning about a fellow trainee's skills. The trainee makes use of supervision by accepting and utilizing supervisory feedback.

Recognition of Ethical Issues   A marriage and family therapy trainee knows and observes the code of ethics of AAMFT and is familiar with the laws of the state regarding privileged communication, mandatory reporting, and duty-to-warn issues. The trainee follows the supervisor's policies regarding reporting and consulting with the supervisor and/or other authorities; the trainee appropriately uses supervision and consultation regarding ethical issues. The trainee avoids potentially exploitative relationships with clients and other trainees. The trainee deals appropriately with his or her own issues as they affect therapy and is willing to take responsibility for her or his own actions.

Paperwork   The trainee maintains case files appropriately and follows clinic procedures for paperwork in a timely manner.

Professional Image   The trainee dresses appropriately according to the standards of the setting. The trainee is able to present an aura of confidence without arrogance and presents herself or himself to other professionals in an appropriate manner. The trainee is on time for sessions and supervision and treats staff with respect.

Professional Conduct   The trainee has the ability to initiate and maintain appropriate contact with other professionals along with maintaining a personal professional image. The trainee does not publicly denigrate or criticize colleagues. The trainee consults with professionals and others involved with cases appropriately, with appropriate signed releases, and in a professional manner, always keeping the client's welfare foremost. The trainee shows the ability to handle unexpected and crisis situations with poise and skill, using consultation when appropriate.

The trainee is punctual with therapy sessions and other professional meetings. The trainee follows clinic policies in setting and collecting fees.

Evaluation Skills

Therapy   A trainee skilled in evaluating therapy is able to verbalize the thoroughness of assessment; the link between theory, assessment, and hypotheses/interventions; the effectiveness of interventions; and how well the objectives of the therapy have been met in terms of both the clients' goals and the therapist's perspective and analysis. The trainee can articulate aspects of the clients' feedback in relation to assessment and intervention. The trainee is able to articulate links between conceptual, perceptual, interventive, and outcome data.

Self   The trainee therapist is skilled in evaluating himself or herself in terms of skills: conceptual, perceptual, executive, professional, and evaluative. The trainee is able to recognize signs in himself or herself that contribute to the ongoing understanding and analysis of the case and is able to articulate personal issues that may be interacting in therapy. The trainee is not unduly defensive about feedback, but is able to integrate multiple perspectives and incorporate them into a plan for enhancing his or her development as a family therapist. The trainee works with the supervisor in an ongoing evaluation of therapy skills and strives to improve areas that require it and, at the same time, clearly articulate strengths in behavioral terms.

Theory of Choice   The previous skill areas were generic; i.e., they apply across theoretical models of intervention. This section is for the trainee therapist and supervisor to use to evaluate the trainee's growing knowledge and expertise in a model or theory that is identified by the supervisor and trainee together. The trainee is able to identify assumptions and concepts of the theory, the primary techniques used in the theory, the role of the therapist, and evaluation strategies. The trainee is able to use the concepts and interventions in practice, identifying data to the supervisor that illustrate the concepts. The trainee is able to recognize and identify the strengths and weaknesses of the theory as used in practice.

BASIC SKILLS EVALUATION DEVICE©

Therapist _____   Date _____

Supervisor _____   Experience Level _____

Conceptual Skills	Inadequate Information	Deficient	Below Expectation	Meets Expectation	Exceeds Expectation	Exceptional Skills
1. Knowledge Base						
2. Systems Perspective						
3. Familiarity with Therapy Model						
4. Self as Therapist						

Comments:

Perceptual Skills	Inadequate Information	Deficient	Below Expectation	Meets Expectation	Exceeds Expectation	Exceptional Skills
1. Recognition Skills						
2. Hypothesizing						
3. Integration of theory practice						

Comments:

Executive Skills	Inadequate Information	Deficient	Below Expectation	Meets Expectation	Exceeds Expectation	Exceptional Skills
1. Joining						
2. Assessment						
3. Hypothesizing						
4. Interventions						
5. Communication Skills						
6. Personal Skills						
7. Session Management						

Comments:

Professional Skills	Inadequate Information	Deficient	Below Expectation	Meets Expectation	Exceeds Expectation	Exceptional Skills
1. Supervision						
2. Recognition of Ethical Issues						
3. Paperwork						
4. Professional Image						
5. Professional Conduct						

Comments:

Evaluation Skills	Inadequate Information	Deficient	Below Expectation	Meets Expectation	Exceeds Expectation	Exceptional Skills
1. Evaluation of Therapy						
2. Evaluation of Self						

Comments:

Theory Skills (Use Preferred Model)	Inadequate Information	Deficient	Below Expectation	Meets Expectation	Exceeds Expectation	Exceptional Skills
Knowledge of Theory						
Utilizes Theory in Practice						
Recognizes Strengths and Weaknesses of Theory						

Comments:

References

Ackerman, N. W. (1958). *The psychodynamics of family life.* New York: Basic Books.

Ackerman, N. (1981). The functions of the family therapist. In R. J. Green & J. L. Framo (Eds.), *Family therapy: Major contributions.* New York: International Universities Press.

Amatea, E., & Sherrard, P. (1989). Reversing the school's response: A new approach to resolving persistent problems. *American Journal of Family Therapy, 17,* 15–26.

Amatea, E., & Sherrard, P. (1991). Systematic practice in schools provides a new frontier. *Family Therapy News,* 5–6.

American Art Therapy Association. (2001). URL www.aata.org.

American Psychiatric Association. (1994). *Diagnostic and statistical manual of mental disorders* (4th ed.). Washington, DC: American Psychiatric Association.

Anderson, C., Reiss, D., & Hogarty, G. (1986). *Schizophrenia and the family: A practitioner's guide to psycho-education and management.* New York: Guilford Press.

Anderson, H. (1991). Opening the door for change through continuous conversations. In T. C. Todd & M. D. Selekman (Eds.), *Family therapy approaches with adolescent substance abuse* (pp. 176–189). Needham Heights, MA: Allyn & Bacon.

Anderson, H. (1999). Reimagining family therapy: Reflections on Minuchin's invisible family. *Journal of Marital and Family Therapy, 25*(1), 1–8.

Anderson, S., & Bagarozzi, D. (1989). *Family myths: Psychotherapy implications.* New York: Haworth Press.

Aponte, H. (1976a). The family-school interview. *Family Process, 15*(4), 464–477.

Aponte, H. (1976b). Underorganization in the poor family. In P. J. Guerin Jr. (Ed.), *Family therapy: Theory and practice* (pp. 432–448). New York: Guilford Press.

Aponte, H., & Van Deusen, J. (1981). Structural family therapy. In A. S. Gurman & D. P. Kniskern (Eds.), *Handbook of family therapy* (pp. 310–360). New York: Brunner/Mazel.

Aponte, H. J. (1994). *Bread & spirit: Therapy with the new poor: Diversity of race, culture and values.* New York: Norton.

Barker, P. (1981). *Basic family therapy.* Baltimore: University Park Press.

Barlow, P. H., Hayes, S. C., & Nelson, R. O. (1984). *The scientist practitioner. Research and accountability in clerical and educational settings.* New York: Pergamon Press.

Barton, C., & Alexander, J. F. (1981). Functional family therapy. In A. S. Gurman & D. P. Kniskern (Eds.), *Handbook of family therapy* (Vol. 1, pp. 403–443). New York: Brunner/Mazel.

Bateson, G. (1972). *Steps to an ecology of mind.* New York: Dutton.

Bateson, G. (1979). *Mind in nature: A necessary unity.* New York: Dutton.

Bateson, G., Jackson, D., Haley J., & Weakland, J. (1956). Toward a theory of schizophrenia. *Behavioral Science, 1*(4), 251–264.

Baucom, D. H., Epstein, N. R., & Rankin, L. A. (1989). The role of cognitions in marital relationsips: Definitional, methodological, and conceptual issues. *Journal of Consulting and Clinical Psychology, 57,* 31–38.

Baucom, D. H., Epstein, N. R., & Rankin, L. A. (1995). Cognitive aspects of cognitive-behavioral marital therapy. *Clincial handbook of couple therapy.* New York: Guilford Press.

Baucom, D. H., Sayers, S., & Sher, T. G. (1990). Supplementing behavioral marital therapy with cognitive restructuring and emotional expressiveness training: An outcome investigation. *Journal of Consulting and Clinical Psychology, 58,* 636–645.

Berg, I. K., & Gallagher, D. (1991). Solution focused brief treatment with adolescent substance abusers. In T. C. Todd & M. D. Selekman (Eds.), *Family therapy approaches with adolescent substance abusers* (pp. 93–111). Boston: Allyn & Bacon.

Bergin, A. E., & Garfield, S. L. (1978). Overview, trends and future issues. In A. E. Bergin & S. L. Garfield (Eds.), *Handbook of psychotherapy and behavior change: An empirical analysis.* New York: Wiley.

Bergin, A. E., & Garfield, S. L. (1994). *Handbook of psychotherapy and behavior change* (4th ed.). New York: Wiley.

Bernal, G., & Flores-Ortiz, Y. (1991). Contextual family therapy with adolescent drug abusers. In T. Todd & M. Selekman (Eds.), *Family therapy approaches with adolescent substance abusers* (pp. 70–92). Needham Heights, MA: Allyn & Bacon.

Bernal, G., & Ysern, E. (1986). Family therapy and ideology. *Journal of Marital and Family Therapy, 12*(2), 129–136.

Bertram, D. (2001). Walking the MFT walk while talking the DSM-IVTR talk. Louisville, KY: Presentation to the University of Louisville MFT Program.

Bodin, A. (1981). The interactional view: Family therapy approaches of the Mental Research Institute. In A. S. Gurman & D. P. Kniskern (Eds.), *Handbook of family therapy* (pp. 267–309). New York: Brunner/Mazel.

Boscolo, L., Cecchin, G., Hoffman, L., & Penn, P. (1987). *Milan systemic family therapy: Conversations in theory and practice.* New York: Basic Books.

Boss, P. (1999). *Ambiguous loss.* Cambridge, MA: Harvard University Press.

Boszormenyi-Nagy, I. (1966). From family therapy to a psychology of relationships: fictions of the individual and fictions of the family. *Comprehensive Psychiatry, 7,* 408–423.

Boszormenyi-Nagy, I. (1973). *Invisible loyalties: Reciprocity in intergenerational family therapy.* New York: Harper & Row.

Boszormenyi-Nagy, I. (1987). *Foundations of contextual therapy: Collected papers.* New York: Brunner/Mazel.

Boszormenyi-Nagy, I., & Framo, J. L. (1965). *Intensive family therapy.* New York: Harper & Row.

Boszormenyi-Nagy, I., & Krasner, B. (1986). *Between give and take: A clinical guide to contextual therapy.* New York: Brunner/Mazel.

Boszormenyi-Nagy, I., & Spark, G. M. (1973). *Invisible loyalties: Reciprocity in intergenerational family therapy.* New York: Harper & Row.

Boszormenyi-Nagy, I., & Ulrich, D. N. (1981). Contextual family therapy. In A. S. Gurman & D. P. Kniskern (Eds.), *Handbook of family therapy* (pp. 159–188). New York: Brunner/Mazel.

Bowen, M. (1978). *Family therapy in clinical practice.* New York: Aronson.

Bowlby, J. (1969). *Attachment and loss: Vol. 1. Attachment.* New York: Basic Books.

Boyd-Franklin, N. (1989). *Black families in therapy: A multisystem approach.* New York: Guilford Press.

Boyd-Franklin, N., & Bry, B. H. (2000). *Reaching out in family therapy: Home-based, school, and community interventions.* New York: Guilford Press.

Breunlin, D. (1985). Expanding the concept of stages in family therapy. *States: Patterns of change over time* (pp. 95–120). Rockville, MD: Aspen.

Breunlin, D., Schwartz, R. C., & MacKune-Karrer, B. M. (1992). *Metaframeworks: Transcending the models of family therapy.* San Francisco: Jossey-Bass.

Brock, G., & Barnard, C. (1988). *Procedures in family therapy.* Needham Heights, MA: Allyn & Bacon.

Brock, G. W. (1997). Reducing vulnerability to ethics code violations: An at-risk test for marriage and family therapists. *Journal of marital and family therapy, 23*(1), 87–90.

Broderick, C. B., & Schrader, S. S. (1981). The history of professional marriage and family therapy. In A. S. Gurman & D. P. Kniskern (Eds.), *Handbook of family therapy* (pp. 3–40). New York: Brunner/Mazel.

Bronfenbrenner, U. (1979). *The ecology of human development: Experiments by nature and design.* Cambridge, MA: Harvard University Press.

Brown, J., Brown, C., & Portes, P. (1991). *The families in transition program.* Louisville, KY: University of Louisville Press.

Brown, J. H., Eichenberger, S. A., Portes, P., & Christensen, D. N. (1991). Family functioning factors associated with the adjustment level of children of divorce. *Journal of Divorce and Remarriage, 17,* 81–95.

Brown, J. H., & Vaccaro, A. (1991). *A manual for resource and youth services coordinators.* Louisville, KY: University of Louisville and Cities in Schools.

Butler, R. (1963). The life review: An interpretation of reminiscence in the aged. *Psychiatry, 26,* 65–76.

Campbell, D., Draper, R., & Crutchley, E. (1991). The Milan systemic approach to family therapy. In A. S. Gurman & D. P. Kniskern, *Handbook of family therapy* (Vol. 2, pp. 324–362). New York: Brunner/Mazel.

Campbell, J., Liebman, M., Brooks, F., Jones, J., & Ward, C. (1990). *Art therapy, race and culture.* London: Jessica Kingsley Publishers, Ltd.

Carter, B., & McGoldrick, M. (1989a). *The changing family life cycle: Framework for family therapy* (2nd ed.). Needham Heights, MA: Allyn & Bacon.

Carter, B., & McGoldrick, M. (1989b). Forming a remarried family. In B. Carter & M. McGoldrick (Eds.), *The changing family life cycle: Framework for family therapy* (2nd ed., pp. 399–432). Needham Heights, MA: Allyn & Bacon.

Carter, E. A., & McGoldrick, M. (1980). *The family life cycle: A framework for family therapy.* New York: Gardner Press.

Coatsworth, J. D., Santisteban, D. A., McBride, C. K., & Szapocznik, J. (2001). Brief strategic family therapy versus community control: Engagement, retention, and an exploration of the moderating role of adolescent symptom severity. *Family Process, 40*(3), 313–332.

Cocoran, J. (2000). *Evidence-based social work practice with families.* New York: Springer Publishing.

Colapinto, J. (1991). Structural family therapy. In A. S. Gurman & D. P. Kniskern (Eds.), *Handbook of family therapy* (Vol. 2, pp. 417–443). New York: Brunner/Mazel.

Coleman, S. (1985). *Failures in family therapy.* New York: Guilford Press.

Commission on Accreditation for Marriage and Family Therapy Education. (1997). Manual on Accreditation. Washington, DC: Author.

Cordova, J. V., Jacobson, N. S., & Christensen, A. (1998). Acceptance versus change interventions in behavioral couple therapy: Impact on couple's in-session communication. *Journal of Marital and Family Therapy, 24*(4), 437–456.

Cordova, J. V., Warren, L. Z. & Gee, C. B. (2001). Motivational interviewing as an intervention for at-risk couples. *Journal of Marital and Family Therapy, 27*(3), 315–326.

Cormier, W. H., & Cormier, L. S. (1991). *Interviewing strategies for helpers: Fundamental skills and cognitive behavioral interventions* (3rd ed.). Pacific Grove, CA: Brooks/Cole.

Crando, R., & Ginsberg, B. G. (1976). Communication in the father-son relationship: The parent-adolescent relationship development program. *The Family Coordinator, 4,* 465–473.

Cross, T. L. (1995). Understanding family resiliency from a relational worldview. In H. I. McCubbin, E. A. Thompson, A. I. Thompson, & J. E. Fromer (Eds.), *Resiliency in ethnic minority families: Native and immigrant American families* (Vol. 1, pp. 143–157). Madison, WI: University of Wisconsin–Madison Center for Family Studies.

Cunningham, P. B., & Henggeler, S. (1999). Engaging multiproblem families in treatment: Lessons learned throughout the development of multisystemic therapy. *Family Process, 38*(3), 265–281.

De Shazer, S. (1985). *Keys to solution in brief therapy.* New York: Norton.

Diller, J. V. (1999). *Cultural diversity: A primer for the human services.* Belmont, CA: Brooks/Cole/Wadsworth.

Dinkmeyer, D., McKay, G., Dinkmeyer, J. S., Dinkmeyer, D., & McKay, J. (1997). *Parenting young children.* Circle Pines, MN: American Guidance Service.

Duncan, B., & Parks, M. B. (1988). Integrating individual and systems approaches: Strategic-behavioral therapy. *Journal of Marital and Family Therapy, 14,* 151–161.

Duncan, B. L., & Miller, S. D. (2000). *The heroic client.* San Francisco: Jossey-Bass.

Dunst, C., Trivette, C., & Deal, A. (1988). *Enabling and empowering families: Principles and guidelines for practice.* Cambridge, MA: Brookline Books.

Durrant, M. (1988). Gwynne: A new recipe for life. *Case Studies, [Special Edition].* 25–28.

Duvall, E. (1977). *Marriage and family development* (5th ed.). Philadelphia: Lippincott.

Efran, J., Lukens, M., & Lukens, R. (1990). *Language, structure and change.* New York: Norton.

Epston, D., & White, M. (1992). *Experience, contradiction, narrative and imagination: Selected papers of David Epston and Michael White, 1989–1991.* Adelaide, Australia: Dulwich Centre Publications.

Erickson, M., & Rossi, E. (1979). *Hypnotherapy: An exploratory casework.* New York: Irvington.

Ericson, P., & Rogers, L. E. (1973). New procedures for analyzing relational communication. *Family Process, 12*(3), 245–268.

Falicov, C. (1988). *Family transitions: Continuity and change over the life cycle.* New York: Guilford Press.

Falloon, I. R. (1991). Behavioral family therapy. In A. S. Gurman & D. P. Kniskern (Eds.), *Handbook of family therapy* (Vol. 2, pp. 65–95). New York: Brunner/Mazel.

Feixas, G. (1990). Personal construct theory and systemic therapies: Parallel or convergent trends? *Journal of Marital and Family Therapy, 16*(1), 1–20.

Ferreira, A. (1963). Family myth and homeostasis. *Archives of General Psychiatry, 9,* 457–463.

Figley, C., & Nelson, T. (1989). Basic family therapy skills. I: Conceptualization and findings. *Journal of Marital and Family Therapy, 4*(14), 349–366.

Fleuridas, C., Nelson, T., & Rosenthal, D. M. (1986). The evolution of circular questions: Training family therapists. *Journal of Marital and Family Therapy, 12*(27), 113–128.

Fleuridas, C., Rosenthal, D. M., Leigh, G. K., & Leigh, T. E. (1990). Family goal recording: An adaptation of goal attainment scaling for enchancing family therapy assessment. *Journal of Marital and Family Therapy, 16,* 389–406.

Framo, J. (1976). Family of origin as a therapeutic resource for adults in marital and family therapy: You can and should go home again. *Family Process, 15,* 193–210.

Framo, J. (1981). The integration of marital therapy with sessions with family of origin. In A. S. Gurman & D. P. Kniskern (Eds.), *Handbook of family therapy* (pp. 133–158). New York: Brunner/Mazel.

Gambino, R. (1974). *Blood of my blood: The dilemma of Italian-Americans.* New York: Doubleday.

Garcia-Preto, N. (1982). Family therapy with Puerto Rican families. In J. McGoldrick, J. K. Pearce, & J. Giordano (Eds.), *Ethnicity and family therapy* (pp. 164–186). New York: Guilford Press.

Garfield, R. (1981). Mourning and its resolution for spouses in marital separation. In J. C. Hansen & L. Messinger (Eds.), *Therapy with remarriage and families* (pp. 1–15). Rockville, MD: Aspen.

Garfield, S., & Bergin, A. (1978). *Handbook of psychotherapy and behavior change* (2nd ed.). New York: Wiley.

Garfield, S. L. (1994). *Research on client variables in psychotherapy* (4th ed.). New York: Wiley.

Garrett, J., Landau-Stanton, J., Stanton, M. D., Stellato-Kobat, J., & Stellato-Kobat, D. (1997). ARISE: A method for engaging reluctant alcohol- and drug-dependent individuals in treatment. *Journal of Substance Abuse Treatment, 14,* 235–248.

Gehart, D. R., & Tuttle, A. R. (2003). *Theory-based treatment planning: Integrating theory and practice.* Pacific Grove, CA: Brooks/Cole.

Gergen, K. J. (1985). The social constructionist in modern psychology. *American Psychologist, 40,* 266–275.

Gergen, K. J. (1994). *Realities and relationships.* Cambridge, MA: Harvard University Press.

Goldner, V. (1988). Generation and gender: Normative and covert hierarchies. *Family Process, 27,* 17–31.

Goldstein, A. (1973). *Structured learning therapy.* New York: Academic Press.

Gonzales, N. A., Hiraga, Y., & Cauce, A. M. (1995). Observing mother-daughter interaction in African-American and Asian-American families. In H. I. McCubbins, E. A. Thompson, A. I. Thompson, & J. A. Futrell (Eds.), *Resiliency in ethnic minority families: African-American families* (Vol. 2, pp. 259–286). Madison, WI: University of Wisconsin–Madison Center for Family Studies.

Goolishian, H. A., & Anderson, H. (1992). Strategy and intervention versus nonintervention: A matter of theory? *Journal of Marital and Family Therapy, 18*(1), 5–15.

Gottman, J. (1979). *Marital interaction: Experimental investigations.* New York: Academic Press.

Green, R. J., & Framo, J. L. (1983). *Family therapy: Major contributions.* New York: International Universities Press.

Greenberg, L. S., & Johnson, S. M. (1988). *Emotionally focused therapy for couples.* New York: Guilford Press.

Griffith, J. L., & Griffith, M. E. (1994). *The body speaks: Therapeutic dialogues for mind-body problems.* New York: Basic Books.

Group for the Advancement of Psychiatry Committee on the Family. (1995). Beyond DSM-IV: A model for the classification and diagnosis of relational disorders. *Psychiatric Services, 46,* 926–931.

Gurman, A. S., & Kniskern, D. P. (Eds.). (1981). *Handbook of family therapy.* New York: Brunner/Mazel.

Gurman, A. S., & Kniskern, D. P. (Eds.). (1991). *Handbook of family therapy* (2nd ed.). New York: Brunner/Mazel.

Guttman, H. A., Feldman, R. B., Engelsmann, F., Spector, L., & Buonvino, M. (1999). The relationships between psychiatrists' couple and family therapy training experience and their subsequent practice profile. *Journal of Marital and Family Therapy, 25*(1), 31–42.

Haley, J. (1967). Toward a theory of pathological systems. In G. H. Zuk & I. Boszormenyi-Nagy (Eds.), *Family theory and disturbed families* (pp. 11–27). Palo Alto, CA: Science and Behavior Books.

Haley, J. (1976). *Problem-solving therapy.* San Francisco: Jossey-Bass.

Haley, J. (1980). *Leaving home: The therapy of disturbed young people.* New York: McGraw-Hill.

Hanna, S. M. (1995). On paradox: Empathy before strategy. *Journal of Family Psychotherapy, 6*(1), 85–88.

Hanna, S. M. (1997). A developmental-interactional model. In T. D. Hargrave & S. M. Hanna (Eds.), *The aging family: New visions in theory, practice and reality* (pp. 101–130). New York: Brunner/Mazel.

Hanna, S. M., & Hargrave, T. D. (1997). Integrating the process of aging and family therapy. In T. D. Hargrave & S. M. Hanna (Eds.), *The aging family: New visions in theory, practice and reality* (pp. 19–38, 122). New York: Brunner/Mazel.

Hansen, J., & Keeney, B. (1983). *Diagnosis and assessment in family therapy.* Rockville, MD: Aspen.

Hansen, J., Pound, R., & Warner, R. (1976). Use of modeling procedures. *Personnel and Guidance Journal, 54,* 242–245.

Hardy, K. V., & Laszloffy, T. A. (1995). The cultural genogram: Key to training culturally competent family therapists. *Journal of Marital and Family Therapy, 21*(3), 227–237.

Hare-Mustin, R. (1978). A feminist approach to family therapy. *Family Process, 17,* 181–194.

Hargrave, T. D., & Anderson, W. (1992). *Finishing well: Aging and reparation in the intergenerational family.* New York: Brunner/Mazel.

Hargrave, T. D., & Hanna, S. M. (1997). *The aging family: New visions in theory, practice and reality.* New York: Brunner/Mazel.

Hayes, J., & Wall, T. (1998). What influences clinicians' responsibility attributions? The role of problem type, theoretical orientation, and client attribution. *Journal of Social and Clinical Psychology, 17,* 69–74.

Henggeler, S. W., Schoenwald, S. K., Borduin, C. M., Rowland, M. D., & Cunningham, P. B. (1998). *Multisystemic treatment of antisocial behavior in children and adolescents.* New York: Guilford Press.

Hiebert, W., Gillespie, J., & Stahmann, R. (1993). *Dynamic assessment in couples therapy.* New York: Lexington Books.

Hirschmann, M. J., & Sprenkle, D. H. (1989). The use of therapeutic paradox among members of the American Association for Marriage and Family Therapy. *American Journal of Family Therapy, 17*(4), 348–358.

Hoffman, L. (1981). *Foundations of family therapy.* New York: Basic Books.

Hoffman, L. (1983). A co-evolutionary framework for systemic family therapy. In J. Hansen & B. Keeney (Eds.), *Diagnosis and assessment of family therapy* (pp. 35–62). Rockville, MD: Aspen.

Hoffman, L. (1998). Setting aside the model in family therapy. *Journal of Marital and Family Therapy, 24*(2), 145–156.

Holtzworth-Munroe, A., & Jacobson, N. S. (1991). Behavioral marital therapy. *Handbook of family therapy* (Vol. 2, pp. 96–133). New York: Brunner/Mazel.

Hosford, R., & de Visser, C. (1974). *Behavioral counseling: An introduction*. Washington, DC: American Personnel and Guidance Press.

Howard, J. (1978). *Families*. New York: Simon & Schuster.

Hubble, M., Duncan, B., & Miller, S. (1999). *The heart and soul of change*. Washington, DC: APA Press.

Imber-Black, E. (1993). *Secrets in families and family therapy*. New York: Norton.

Imber-Black, E., Roberts, J., & Whiting, R. (1988). *Rituals in families and family therapy*. New York: Norton.

Jacobson, N. S. (1984). A component analysis of behavioral marital therapy: The relative effectiveness of behavior exchange and problem solving training. *Journal of Consulting and Clinical Psychology, 52*, 295–305.

Jacobson, N. S. (1991). Toward enhancing the efficacy of marital therapy and marital therapy research. *Journal of Family Psychology, 4*(4), 373–393.

Jacobson, N. S., & Christensen, A. (1996). *Integrative couple therapy*. New York: Norton.

Jacobson, N. S., Holtzworth-Monroe, A., & Schmaling, K. B. (1989). Marital therapy and spouse involvement in the treatment of depression, agoraphobia, and alcoholism. *Journal of Consulting and Clinical Psychology, 57*, 5–10.

Jacobson, N. S., & Margolin, B. (1979). *Marital therapy: Strategies based on social learning and behavior exchange principles*. New York: Brunner/Mazel.

Jenkins, A. (1991). *Invitations to responsibility: The therapeutic engagement of men who are violent and abusive*. Adelaide, Australia: Dulwich Centre Publications.

Johnson, L., Bruhn, R., Winek, J., Kreps, J., & Wiley, K. (1999). The use of child-encountered play therapy and filial therapy with Head Start families: A brief report. *Journal of Marital and Family Therapy, 25*(2), pp. 169–176.

Johnson, S. M. (1998). Listening to the music: Emotion as a natural part of systems theory. *Journal of Systemic Therapies, 17*, 1–18.

Johnson, S. M., Makinen, J. A., & Millikin, J. W. (2001). Attachment injuries in couple relationships: A new perspective on impasses in couples therapy. *Journal of Marital and Family Therapy, 27*(2), 145–156.

Karpel, M. (1986). Questions, obstacles, and contributions. In M. A. Karpel (Ed.), *Family resources: The hidden partner in family therapy* (pp. 3–64). New York: Guilford Press.

Kaslow, F. W. (1996). *Handbook of relational diagnosis and dysfunctional family patterns*. New York: Wiley.

Keith, D., & Whitaker, C. (1985). Failure: Our bold companion. In S. Coleman (Ed.), *Failures in family therapy* (pp. 8–26). New York: Guilford Press.

Kelly, G. A. (1963). *A theory of personality: The psychology of personal constructs*. New York: Norton.

Kendall, P. C., & Braswell, L. (1993). *Cognitive-behavioral therapy for impulsive children*. New York: Guilford Press.

Kerr, M. (1981). Family systems theory and therapy. In A. S. Gurman & D. P. Kniskern (Eds.), *Hankbook of family therapy* (pp. 226–266). New York: Brunner/Mazel.

Kinney, J., Haopala, P., & Booth, C. (1991). *Keeping families together: The home builders model*. New York: Aldine De Gruyter.

Kiresuk, T. J., & Sherman, R. E. (1979). Goal attainment scaling: A general method for evaluating community mental health programs. *Community Mental Health, 4*, 443–453.

Kiser, D., Piercy, F., & Lipchik, E. (1993). The integration of emotion in solution-focused therapy. *Journal of Marital and Family Therapy, 19,* 233–242.

Knudson-Martin, C. (2000). Gender, family competence and psychological symptoms. *Journal of Marital and Family Therapy, 26*(3), 317–328.

Koplewicz, H. S., & Goodman, R. F. (1999). *Childhood revealed: Art expressing pain, discovery, hope.* New York: Abrams.

Koppitz, E. M. (1968). *Psychological evaluation of children's human figure drawings.* New York: Grune & Stratton.

Kramer, J. (1985). *Family interfaces: Transgenerational patterns.* New York: Brunner/Mazel.

Krumboltz, J., Varenhorst, B., & Thoresen, C. (1967). Nonverbal factors in effectiveness of models in counseling. *Journal of Couseling Psychology, 14,* 412–418.

Kuehl, B. P. (1995). The solution-oriented genogram: A collaborative approach. *Journal of Marital and Family Therapy, 21*(3), 239–250.

Kwiatkowska, H. Y. (1967). Family art therapy. *Family Process, 6*(1), 37–55.

Kwiatkowska, H. Y. (1978). *Family therapy and evaluation through art.* Springfield, IL: Charles C Thomas.

Lambert, M. J., & Bergin, A. E. (1994). The effectiveness of psychotherapy. In A. E. Bergin & S. L. Garfield (Eds.), *Handbook of psychotherapy and behavior change* (4th ed., pp. 143–189). New York: Wiley.

Landau-Stanton, J. (1986). Competence, impermanence, and transitional mapping: A model for systems consultation. In L. C. Wynne, S. H. McDaniel, & T. T. Weber (Eds.), *Systems consultation: A new perspective for family therapy* (pp. 253–269). New York: Gardner Press.

Landau-Stanton, J., & Stanton, M. D. (1985). Treating suicidal adolescents and their families. In M. Pravder Mirkin & S. Koman (Eds.), *Handbook of adolescents and family therapy* (pp. 309–328). New York: Gardner Press.

Lankton, S. (1988). *Ericksonian hypnosis application, preparation and research.* New York: Brunner/Mazel.

Lankton, S., & Lankton, C. (1983). *The answer within: A clinical framework of Ericksonian hypnotherapy.* New York: Brunner/Mazel.

Lankton, S., Lankton, C., & Matthews, W. (1991). Ericksonian family therapy. In A. S. Gurman & D. P. Kniskern (Eds.), *Handbook of family therapy* (Vol. 2, pp. 239–283). New York: Brunner/Mazel.

LaVoie, J. (1985). Health in the family life cycle. In J. Springer & R. Woody (Eds.), *Health promotion in family therapy* (pp. 46–70). Rockville, MD: Aspen.

Lebow, J. L. (1987). Training psychologists in family therapy in family institute settings. *Journal of Family Psychology, 1,* 219–231.

Leitch, M. L., & Thomas, V. (1999). The AAMFT-Head Start training partnership project: Enhancing MFT capacities beyond the family system. *Journal of Marital and Family Therapy, 25*(2), 141–154.

Lewis, R., Piercy, F., Sprenkle, D., & Trepper, T. (1991). Family based interventions for helping drug abusing adolescents. *Journal of Adolescent Research, 5,* 82–95.

Lindblad-Goldberg, M., Dore, M. M., & Stern, L. (1998). *Creating competence from chaos: A comprehensive guide to home-based services.* New York: Norton.

Lipchik, E. (1987). Purposeful sequence for beginning the solution-focused interview. In E. Lipchik (Ed.), *Interviewing.* Rockville, MD: Aspen.

Locke, H., & Wallace, K. (1959). Short marital-adjustment and prediction tests: The reliability and validity. *Marriage and Family Living, 21,* 251–255.

Long, J. (1997). Alzheimer's disease and the family: Working with new realities. In T. D. Hargrave & S. M. Hanna (Eds.), *The aging family: New visions in theory, practice and reality* (pp. 209–234). New York: Brunner/Mazel.

Lusebrink, V. B. (1992). A systems oriented approach to the expressive therapies: The expressive therapies continuum. *The arts in psychotherapy, 18*(4), 395–403.

Madanes, C. (1981). *Strategic family therapy.* San Francisco: Jossey-Bass.

Madsen, W. C. (1999). *Collaborative therapy with multi-stressed families: From old problems to new futures.* New York: Guilford Press.

Mahoney, M. J. (1991). *Human change process.* New York: Basic Books.

McCubbin, H. I. (1980). Family stress and coping: A decade review. *Journal of Marriage and the Family, 42,* 855–871.

McCubbin, H. I., Dahl, B., & Hunter, E. (1976). *Families in the military system.* Beverly Hills, CA: Sage.

McCubbin, H. I., Thompson, E. A., Thompson, A. I., & Fromer, J. E. (1995). *Resiliency in ethnic minority families: Native and immigrant American families.* Madison, WI: University of Wisconsin–Madison Center for Family Studies.

McDaniel, S. H., Hepworth, J., & Doherty, W. (1992). *Medical family therapy: A biopsychosocial approach to families with health problems.* New York: Basic Books.

McDowell, T. (1999). Systems consultation and Head Start: An alternative to traditional family therapy. *Journal of Marital & Family Therapy, 25*(2), 155–168.

McFarlane, W. (2002). *Multifamily groups in the treatment of severe psychiatric disorders.* New York: Guilford Press.

McGoldrick, J., Pearce, J. K., & Giordano, J. (Eds.), (1982). *Ethnicity and family therapy.* New York: Guilford Press.

McGoldrick, M. (1982). Ethnicity and family therapy: An overview. In J. McGoldrick, J. K. Pearce, & J. Giordano (Eds.), *Ethnicity and family therapy* (pp. 3–30). New York: Guilford Press.

McGoldrick, M., & Gerson, R. (1985). *Genograms in family assessment.* New York: Norton.

McGoldrick, M., & Giordano, J. (1996). Overview: Ethnicity and family therapy. In J. McGoldrick, J. K. Pearce, & J. Giordano (Eds.), *Ethnicity and family therapy* (2nd ed., pp. 1–27). New York: Guilford Press.

Medalie, J. H. (1979). The family life cycle and its implications for family practice. *Journal of Family Practice, 9,* 47–56.

Menses, G., & Durrant, M. (1987). Contextual residential care: The application of the principles of cybernetic therapy to the residential treatment of irresponsible adolescents and their families. *Journal of Strategic and Systemic Therapies, 6,* 3–15.

Metcalf, L., Thomas, F., Duncan B. L., Miller, S. D., & Hubble, M. A. (1996). What works in solution-focused brief therapy: A qualitative analysis of client and therapist perceptions. In S. D. Miller, B. L. Duncan, & M. A. Hubble (Eds.), *Handbook of solution-focused brief therapy.* San Francisco: Jossey-Bass.

Miklowitz, D. J., & Goldstein, M. J. (1997). *Bipolar disorder: A family-focused treatment approach.* New York: Guilford Press.

Miller, S., Nunnally, E., Wackman, D., & Miller, P. (1988). *Connecting with self and others.* Littleton, CO: Interpersonal Communication Programs.

Miller, S. D., Duncan, B. L., & Hubble, M. A. (1997). *Escape from Babel: Toward a unifying language for psychotherapy practice.* New York: Norton.

Minuchin, S. (1974). *Families and family therapy.* Cambridge, MA: Harvard University Press.

Minuchin, S. (1984). *Family kaleidoscope.* Cambridge, MA: Harvard University Press.

Minuchin, S. (1987). My many voices. In J. K. Zeig (Ed.), *The evolution of psychotherapy* (pp. 5–28). New York: Brunner/Mazel.

Minuchin, S., & Fishman, H. C. (1981). *Family therapy techniques.* Cambridge, MA: Harvard University Press.

Minuchin, S., Montalvo, B., Guerney, B., Rosman, B., & Schumer, F. (1967). *Families of the slums: An exploration of their structure and treatment.* New York: Basic Books.

Napier, A., & Whitaker, C. (1978). *The family crucible: The intense experience of family therapy.* New York: Harper & Row.

Nelson, T. S. & Johnson, L. N. (1999). The basic skills evaluation device. *Journal of Marital and Family Therapy. 25*(1), 15–30.

Newfield, N. A., Kuehl, B. P., Joanning, H., & Quinn, W. H. (1991). We can tell you about "psychos and shrinks": An ethnography of the family therapy of adolescent drug abusers. In T. Todd & M. D. Selekman (Eds.), *Family therapy approaches with adolescent substance abusers* (pp. 277–316). Needham Heights, MA: Allyn & Bacon.

Nichols, M. P., & Schwartz, R. C. (2001). *Family therapy: Concepts and methods* (5th ed.). Boston, MA: Allyn & Bacon.

Nichols, W., & Everett, C. (1988). *Systemic family therapy: An integrative approach.* New York: Guilford Press.

O'Callaghan, J. B. (1988). Family school consultation, state of the art analysis and blueprint. *46th annual conference of the American Association for Marriage and Family Therapy.* New Orleans.

O' Hanlon, B. (1999). *Evolving Possibilities: Selected Papers of Bill O'Hanlon.* Philadelphia: Brunner/Mazel.

O'Hanlon, W. H. (1982). Two generic patterns in Ericksonian therapy. *Journal of Strategic and Systemic Therapies, 1*(4), 21–25.

O'Hanlon, W. H. (1987). *Taproots.* New York: Norton.

O'Hanlon, W. H. (1991). Acknowledgement and possibility. A workshop at Family and Children's Agency. Louisville, KY.

O'Hanlon, W. H., & Weiner-Davis, M. (1989). *In search of solutions: A new direction in psychotherapy.* New York: Norton.

Olson, D. H., Porter, J., & Ravee, Y. (1985). *FACES I.* St. Paul: Family Social Science, University of Minnesota.

Papp, P. (1980). The use of fantasy in a couples group. In M. Andolfi & I. Zwerling (Eds.), *Dimensions of family therapy* (pp. 73–90). New York: Guilford Press.

Papp, P. (1983). *The process of change.* New York: Guilford Press.

Patterson, G. R. (1971). *Families: Applications of social learning to family life.* Champaign, IL: Research Press Co.

Patterson, G. R., Reid, J. B., Jones, R. R., & Conger, R. E. (1975). *A social learning approach to family intervention,* vol. 1–4. Eugene, OR: Castalia Publishing Company.

Paul, G. L. (1967). Strategy of outcome research in psychotherapy. *Journal of Consulting Psychology, 31,* 109–118.

Paul, N., & Paul, B. B. (1975). *A marital puzzle.* New York: Norton.

Penn, P. (1982). Circular questioning. *Family Process, 19,* 267–280.

Petker, S. (1982). The domino effect in a system with two or more generations of unresolved mourning. *The Family, 9*(2), 75–79.

Piaget, J. (1952). *The origins of intelligence in children.* New York: Norton.

Piercy, F., Laird, R., & Mohammed, Z. (1983). A family therapist rating scale. *Journal of Marital and Family Therapy, 9*(1), 49–59.

Piercy, F., & Sprenkle, D. (1986). *Family therapy sourcebook.* New York: Guilford Press.

Pinsof, W. M., & Catherall, D. (1986). The integrative psychotherapy alliance. *Journal of Marital and Family Therapy, 12,* 137–152.

Pittman, F. (1991). The secret passions of men. *Journal of Marital and Family Therapy, 177*(17), 17–23.

Pittman, F., DeYoung, C., Flomenhaft, K., Kaplan, D., & Langsley, D. (1966). Crisis family therapy. In J. H. Masserman (Ed.), *Current psychiatric therapies* (Vol. 6, pp. 187–196). New York: Grune & Stratton.

Prochaska, J. O., DiClemente, S. C., & Norcross, J. C. (1992). In search of how people change. *American Pschologist, 47,* 1102–1114.

Quinn, W., & Davidson, B. (1984). Prevalence of family therapy models: A research note. *Journal of Marital and Family Therapy, 10*(4), 393–398.

Rainsford, G. L., & Schulman, S. H. (1981). The family in crisis: A case study of overwhelming illness and stress. *Journal of the American Medical Association , 246,* 60–63.

Rappaport, A. F. (1976). Conjugal relationship enhancement program. In D. H. L. Olson (Ed.), *Treating relationships* (pp. 41–66). Lake Mills, IA: Graphic Publishing.

Robbins, T. D. (1994). *Family builders: A collaborative family/school initiative.* Louisville, KY: Archdiocese of Louisville.

Rogers, C. (1961). *On becoming a person.* Boston: Houghton Mifflin.

Rolland, J. (1994). *Families, illness and disability: An integrated treatment model.* New York: Basic Books.

Ronaldson, C. A., & Hanna, S. M. (2001). *Opening Borders Between Art Therapy, Family Therapy and Other Mental Health Professions.* American Art Therapy Association 32nd Annual Conference. Albuquerque, NM.

Ronaldson, C. A., & Peacock, M. (2001). Guiding principles for art therapy. *Unpublished Manuscript.*

Rosen, S. (1988). What makes Ericksonian therapy so effective? In J. K. Zeig & S. R. Lankton (Eds.), *Developing Ericksonian therapy* (pp. 5–29). New York: Brunner/Mazel.

Rubin, J. (1999). *Art therapy: An introduction.* Philadelphia: Brunner/Mazel.

Ruesch, J., & Bateson, G. (1951). *Communication: The social matrix of psychiatry.* New York: Norton.

Sager, C. (1981). Couples therapy and marriage contracts. In A. S. Gurman & D. P. Kniskern (Eds.), *Handbook of family therapy* (pp. 85–132). New York: Brunner/Mazel.

Satir, V. (1972). *People making.* Palo Alto, CA: Science and Behavior Books.

Scalise, J. (1992). Life or death: A family suicide watch. *GrassRoutes: Stories from Family and Systemic Therapists, 1*(1), 22.

Schoenwald, S. K., Henggeler, S. W., Brondino, M. J., & Rowland, M. D. (2000). Multisystemic therapy: Monitoring treatment fidelity. *Family Process, 29*(1), 83–103.

Schwenk, T. L., & Hughes, C. C. (1983). The family as a patient in family medicine: Rhetoric or reality? *Social Science and Medicine, 17,* 1–16.

Segal, L., & Bavelas, J. B. (1983). Human systems and communications theory. In B. B. Wolman & G. Strickler (Eds.), *Handbook of family and marital therapy* (pp. 11–27). New York: Plenum.

Selekman, M. D., & Todd, T. (1991). Major issues from family therapy research and theory: Implications for the future. In T. Todd & M. D. Selekman (Eds.), *Family therapy approaches with adolescent substance abusers* (pp. 311–325). Needham Heights, MA: Allyn & Bacon.

Selvini Palazzoli, M. (1978). *Self starvation.* New York: Aronson.

Selvini Palazzoli, M. (1985). The problem of the sibling as the referring person. *Journal of Marital and Family Therapy, 11*(1), 21–34.

Selvini Palazzoli, M. (1986). Towards a general model of psychotic family games. *Journal of Marital and Family Therapy, 12,* 339–349.

Selvini Palazzoli, M., Boscolo, L., Checchin, G., & Prata, G. (1978). *Paradox and counterparadox.* New York: Aronson.

Selvini Palazzoli, M., Boscolo, L., Cecchin, G., & Prata, G. (1980a). Hypothesizing, circularity, neutrality: Three guidelines for the conduct of the session. *Family Process, 19*(1), 7–19.

Selvini Palazzoli, M., Boscolo, L., Cecchin, G., & Prata, G. (1980b). Why a long interval between sessions? The therapeutic control of the family-therapist supersystem. In M. Z. I. Andolfi (Ed.), *Dimensions of family therapy* (pp. 161–169). New York: Guilford Press.

Selvini Palazzoli, M., Cirillo, S., Selvini, M., & Sorrentino, A. M. (1989). *Family games: General models of psychotic processes in the family.* New York: Norton.

Selvini Palazzoli, M., & Prata, G. (1982). Snares in family therapy. *Journal of Marital and Family Therapy, 8*(4), 443–450.

Sheinberg, M. (1992). Navigating treatment impasses at the disclosure of incest: Combining ideas from feminism and social constructionism. *Family Process, 31*(3), 201–216.

Sheinberg, M., & Penn, P. (1991). Gender dilemmas, gender questions and the gender mantra. *Journal of Marital and Family Therapy, 17*(1), 33–44.

Siegel, D. (1999). *The developing mind: Toward a neurobiology of interpersonal experience.* New York: Guilford Press.

Simon, R. (1992). *One on one: Conversations with the shapers of family therapy.* Washington, DC: The Family Therapy Networker.

Sluzki, C. (1992). Transformations: A blueprint for narrative changes in therapy. *Family Process, 31*(3), 217–230.

Snider, M. (1992). *Process family therapy.* Needham Heights, MA: Allyn & Bacon.

Spanier, G. B. (1976). Measuring dyadic adjustment: New scales for assessing the quality of marriage and similar dyads. *Journal of Marital and Family Therapy, 38*, 15–28.

Spiegel, J. (1982). An ecological model of ethnic families. In J. McGoldrick, J. K. Pearce, & J. Giordano (Eds.), *Ethnicity and family therapy* (pp. 31–51). New York: Guilford Press.

Stanton, M. D. (1981). Strategic approaches to family therapy. In A. S. Gurman & D. P. Kniskern (Eds.), *Handbook of family therapy* (pp. 361–402). New York: Brunner/Mazel.

Stanton, M. D. (1992). The time line and the "why now?" question: A technique and rationale for therapy, training, organizational consultation and research. *Journal of Marital and Family Therapy, 18*(4), 331–344.

Stanton, M. D., & Todd, T. C. (1982). *The family therapy of drug abuse and addiction.* New York: Guilford Press.

Steinglass, P., Bennett, L., Wolin, S., & Reiss, D. (1987). *The alcoholic family.* New York: Basic Books.

Stuart, R. B. (1976). An operant interpersonal program for couples. In D. H. L. Olson (Ed.), *Treating relationships* (pp. 119–132). Lake Mills, IA: Graphic Publishing.

Stuart, R. B. (1980). *Helping couples change: A social learning approach to marital therapy.* Champaign, IL: Research Press.

Stuart, R. B., & Stuart, F. (1972). *Marital pre-counseling inventory.* Champaign, IL: Research Press.

Suddaby, K., & Landau, J. (1998). Positive and negative timelines: A technique for restoring. *Family Process, 37*(3), 287–298.

Sue, S., & Zane, N. (1987). The role of culture and cultural techniques in psychotherapy: A critique and reformulation. *American Psychologist, 42*, 37–45.

Thomas, V., McCollum, E. E., & Snyder, W. (1999). Beyond the clinic: In-home therapy with Head Start families. *Journal of Marital and Family Therapy, 25*(2), 177–190.

Todd, T. C. (1986). Structural-strategic marital therapy. In N. S. Jacobson & A. S. Gurman (Eds.), *Clinical handbook of marital therapy* (pp. 71–106). New York: Guilford Press.

Todd, T. C., & Selekman, M. D. (1991a). Beyond structural-strategic family therapy: Integrating other brief systemic therapies. In T. C. Todd & M. D. Selekman (Eds.), *Family therapy approaches with adolescent substance abusers* (pp. 241–274). Boston: Allyn and Bacon.

Todd, T. C., & Selekman, M. D. (Eds.), (1991b). *Family therapy approaches with adolescent substance abusers.* Needham Heights, MA: Allyn & Bacon.

Tomm, K. M. (1984). One perspective on the Milan systemic approach: 1. Overview of development, theory and practice. *Journal of Marital and Family Therapy, 10,* 113–125.

Tomm, K. M., & Wright, L. M. (1979). Training in family therapy: Perceptual, conceptual and executive skills. *Family Process, 18,* 227–250.

Treadway, D. (1989). *Before it's too late.* New York: Norton.

Van Deusen, J., Stanton, M. D., Scott, S., Todd T., & Mowatt, D. (1982). Getting the addict to agree to involve his family of origin: The initial contact. In M. D. Stanton & T. C. Todd (Eds.), *The family therapy of drug abuse and addiction* (pp. 39–59). New York: Guilford Press.

Wadeson, H., Durkin, J., & Perach, D. (1989). *Advances in art therapy.* New York: Wiley.

Waldegrave, C. (1990). Social justice and family therapy. *Dulwich Centre Newsletter, 1,* 6–45.

Walsh, F., & Rolland, J. (2003). Strengthening family resilience: Mastering the challenges of illness, disability and loss. Workshop presented at Loma Linda University Department of Counseling and Family Sciences, Loma Linda, CA.

Wamboldt, F., & Wolin, S. (1989). Reality and myth in family life: Changes across generations. In S. Anderson & D. Bagarozzi (Eds.), *Family myths: Psychotherapy implications* (pp. 141–166). New York: Haworth Press.

Warner, R., & Hansen, J. (1970). Verbal-reinforcement and model-reinforcement group counseling with alienated students. *Journal of Couseling Psychology, 14,* 168–172.

Warner, R., Swisher, J., & Horan, J. (1973). Drug abuse prevention: A behavioral approach. *NAASP Bulletin, 372,* 49–54.

Watzlawick, P., Beavin, J., & Jackson, D. (1967). *Pragmatics of human communication.* New York: Norton.

Watzlawick, P., Weakland, J. H., & Fisch, R. (1974). *Change: Principles of problem formation and problem resolution.* New York: Norton.

Weakland, J., Fisch, R., Watzlawick, P., & Bodin, A. (1974). Brief therapy: Focused problem resolution. *Family Process, 13,* 141–168.

Weber, T., McKeever, J., & McDaniel, S. (1985). The beginning guide to the problem-oriented first family interview. *Family Process, 24*(3), 356–364.

Weeks, G. R. (1991). *Promoting change through paradoxical therapy.* New York: Brunner/Mazel.

Weeks, G. R., & Abate, L. (1982). *Paradoxical psychotherapy: Theory and technique.* New York: Brunner/Mazel.

Weiss, R. L., & Perry, B. A. (1979). *Assessment and treatment of marital dysfunction.* Eugene, OR: Marital Studies Program.

Weltner, J. S. (1985). Matchmaking: Choosing the appropriate therapy for families at various levels of pathology. In M. Pravder Mirkin & S. L. Koman (Eds.), *Handbook of adolescents and family therapy* (pp. 39–49). New York: Gardner Press.

Whitaker, C. A. (1976). Comment: Live supervision in psychotherapy. *Voices, 12,* 24–25.

Whitaker, C. A. (1982). The ongoing training of the psychotherapist. In J. R. Neill & D. P. Kniskern (Eds.), *From psyche to system: The evolving therapy of Carl Whitaker* (pp. 121–138). New York: Guilford Press.

Whitaker, C. A. (1986). Personal Communication.

Whitaker, C. A., & Keith, D. V. (1981). Symbolic-experiential family therapy. In A. S. Gurman & D. P. Kniskern (Eds.), *Handbook of family therapy* (pp. 187–225). New York: Brunner/Mazel.

White, M. (1983). Anorexia nervosa: A transgenerational system perspective. *Family Process, 22*(3), 255–273.

White, M. (1986). Negative explanation, restraint, and double description: A template for family therapy. *Family Process, 25*(2), 169–184.

White, M. (1990). Couple therapy and deconstruction. Annual conference of *American Association for Marriage and Family Therapy,* Washington, DC.

White, M. (1995). *Re-authoring lives: Interviews & essays.* Adelaide, Australia: Dulwich Centre Publications.

White, M., & Epston, D. (1991). *Narrative means to therapeutic ends.* New York: Norton.

Williamson, D. (1981). Personal authority via termination of the intergenerational hierarchical boundary: A "new" stage in the family life cycle. *Journal of Marital and Family Therapy, 7,* 441–452.

Wright, L., & Leahey, M. (1984). *Nurses and families: A guide to family assessment and intervention.* Philadelphia: Davis.

Wynne, L. C. (1987). A preliminary proposal for strengthening the multiaxial approach of DSM-III: Possible family-oriented revisions. In G. Tischler (Ed.), *Diagnosis and classification in psychiatry: A critical appraisal of DSM-III* (pp. 477–488). Cambridge, England: Cambridge University Press.

Wynne, L. C., Shields, C. G., & Sirkin, M. I. (1992). Illness, family theory, and family therapy: I. Conceptual issues. *Family Process, 31*(1), 3–18.

Yingling, L., Miller, W., McDonald, A., & Galewater, S. (1998). *GARF assessment sourcebook: Using the DSM-IV Global Assessment of Relational Functioning.* New York: Brunner/Mazel.

Zeig, J. K., & Lankton, S. (1988). *Developing Ericksonian therapy.* New York: Brunner/Mazel.

Name Index

Subject Index

TO THE OWNER OF THIS BOOK:

I hope that you have found *The Practice of Family Therapy: Key Elements Across Models*, Third Edition, useful. So that this book can be improved in a future edition, would you take the time to complete this sheet and return it? Thank you.

School and address: _____

_____

Department: _____

Instructor's name: _____

1. What I like most about this book is: _____

_____

_____

2. What I like least about this book is: _____

_____

_____

3. My general reaction to this book is: _____

_____

_____

4. The name of the course in which I used this book is: _____

_____

5. Were all of the chapters of the book assigned for you to read? _____

   If not, which ones weren't? _____

6. In the space below, or on a separate sheet of paper, please write specific suggestions for improving this book and anything else you'd care to share about your experience in using this book.

_____

_____

_____

OPTIONAL:

Your name: _____ Date: _____

May we quote you, either in promotion for *The Practice of Family Therapy: Key Elements Across Models*, Third Edition, or in future publishing ventures?

Yes: _____ No: _____

Sincerely yours,

Suzanne Midori Hanna and Joseph H. Brown